THE LABOUR PARTY IN OPPOSITION 1970–1974

1970–1974 was a pivotal period in the history of the Labour Party. This book shows how the Labour Party responded to electoral defeat in 1970 and to what extent its political and policy activity in opposition was directed to the recovery of power at the following general election. At a point in Labour's history when social democracy had apparently failed, this book considers what the party came up with in its place.

The story of the Labour Party in opposition, 1970–1974, is shown to be one of a major political party sustaining policy activity of limited relevance to its electoral requirements. Not only that, but Labour regained office in 1974 with policies on wages and industrial relations whose unworkability led to the failure of the Labour government 1974–1979, and the Labour Party's irrelevance to so many voters after 1979.

Using primary sources, the author documents and explains how this happened, focusing on the party's response to defeat in 1970 and the behaviour of key individuals in the parliamentary leadership in response to pressure for a review of policy.

The Labour Party in Opposition 1970–1974 will be essential reading for students and researchers of political history and the Labour Party.

Patrick Bell lectures in British Politics at the University of Durham. He was previously Lecturer in History at the University of Leeds.

BRITISH POLITICS AND SOCIETY
Series Editor: Peter Catterall

Social change impacts not just upon voting behaviour and party identity but also the formulation of policy. But how do social changes and political developments interact? Which shapes which? Reflecting a belief that social and political structures cannot be understood either in isolation from each other or from the historical processes which form them, this series will examine the forces that have shaped British society. Cross-disciplinary approaches will be encouraged. In the process, the series will aim to make a contribution to existing fields, such as politics, sociology and media studies, as well as opening out new and hitherto-neglected fields.

THE MAKING OF CHANNEL 4
Edited by Peter Catterall

MANAGING DOMESTIC DISSENT IN FIRST WORLD WAR BRITAIN
Brock Millman

REFORMING THE CONSTITUTION
Debates in twenty-first century Britain
Edited by Peter Catterall, Wolfram Kaiser and Ulrike Walton-Jordan

PESSIMISM AND BRITISH WAR POLICY, 1916–1918
Brock Millman

AMATEURS AND PROFESSIONALS IN POST-WAR BRITISH SPORT
Edited by Adrian Smith and Dilwyn Porter

A LIFE OF SIR JOHN ELDON GORST
Disraeli's awkward disciple
Archie Hunter

CONSERVATIVE PARTY ATTITUDES TO JEWS, 1900–1950
Harry Defries

POOR HEALTH
Social inequality before and after the Black Report
Edited by Virginia Berridge and Stuart Blume

(Continued)

THE LABOUR PARTY IN OPPOSITION 1970–1974

Patrick Bell

Routledge
Taylor & Francis Group

LONDON AND NEW YORK

First Published in 2004 in Great Britain
by Routledge
11 New Fetter Lane, London EC4P 4EE

Simultaneously published in the USA and Canada
by Routledge
270 Madison Avenue, New York, NY 10016

Routledge is an imprint of the Taylor & Francis Group

© 2004 P. Bell

Typeset in Baskerville by
Integra Software Services Pvt. Ltd, Pondicherry, India
Printed in Great Britain by
Antony Rowe Ltd, Chippenham, Wiltshire

All rights reserved. No part of this publication may be reproduced,
stored in or introduced into a retrieval system or transmitted
in any form or by any means, electronic, mechanical,
photocopying, recording or otherwise, without the prior
written permission of the publisher of this book.

British Library Cataloguing in Publication Data
A catalogue record for this book is available
from the British Library

Library of Congress Cataloging in Publication Data
A catalog record for this book has been requested

ISBN 0–7146–5456–6 (cloth)
ISSN 1467–1441

SHORT LOAN COLLECTION
WITHDRAWN

To my father and to Lesley

CONTENTS

FOREWORD

Labour's defeat in the general election of June 1970 and its hard-won
return to government in March 1974 were both unexpected events. The
years of opposition between those dates were a period of transition and of
trauma. They saw intense re-examination of the party's social and economic
policies, especially on the NEC's Home Policy Committee, after what was
generally agreed to be the failure of Labour's attempts to revive the economy
through a strategy of planning during the Wilson years of 1964–70. Ben
Pimlott once wrote that the failure of planning in promoting sustained
economic growth in those years left a fundamental void at the heart of
Labour's philosophy thereafter. No longer could it be taken for granted as
obviously superior to a Tory free-market free-for-all. Tony Crosland
observed that Labour might talk of three and a half per cent growth but
no-one 'had the foggiest idea' of how it might be achieved. But beyond
detailed policy disputes, Labour was caught up in a wider torment, the
increasingly bitter debates between those who felt that old socialist dogmas
on industry, unemployment or social justice needed basic revision, and
those who advocated a new injection of socialist remedies, including more
nationalization, taxation of wealth, and creating what critics called a siege
economy. The latter was pressed with especial fervour within the trade
unions, growing fast and newly galvanized after the failure of the Wilson
government to reform industrial relations after *In Place of Strife* in 1969.
Passionate arguments on these fundamental issues showed signs of tearing
the party apart in these opposition years. The tension between revisionist
right and fundamentalist left, the latter much swayed by the charismatic
lead of Tony Benn, plagued Labour throughout the Wilson and Callaghan
governments in 1974–79. The outcome was the breakaway of the SDP and
Labour's catastrophic election defeat in 1983, its worst electoral performance
since the first world war.

It is the record of these debates on economic policy, a 'social contract'
with the unions, and membership of Europe, within policy committees,
the parliamentary party, Shadow Cabinet, and the Liaison Committee
with the TUC, that provides the major themes of Patrick Bell's study,

which I first encountered when acting as external examiner of his doctoral thesis. He examines these matters in all the main power bases of the party – the NEC, PLP, party conference and the unions. He also considers the key personalities involved – the intellectual friends of Roy Jenkins whose role became, as Dr. Bell shows, increasingly marginalized; Tony Crosland, trying to rescue the old social democratic programmes from the debris of the sixties; Michael Foot, tribune of the Old Left, appearing in the Shadow Cabinet for the first time; and, most powerful of all as events turned out, Jim Callaghan, giving direction to rank-and-file discontents on industrial relations and Europe as chairman of the Home Policy Committee, and, despite serious illness, emerging as the party's strong man and Wilson's probable successor. Harold Wilson himself remains here, as ever, enigmatic. Beyond party manoeuvres was a background of dramatic turmoil, a huge inflationary explosion which shook the global economy, war in the Middle East, entry into the Common Market, crises in Ireland and Rhodesia, and mounting union and other conflict at home over housing finance, industrial relations policy and two nationwide strikes in the coal industry, the first since 1926. These were the years of Clay Cross and the Saltley flying pickets, of 'Bloody Sunday' and the three-day week. In the end they overwhelmed Edward Heath's experiment in corporate government and brought a surprised Harold Wilson almost unwillingly back to office if not power. It is a critical phase of Labour history and Patrick Bell provides a pioneering account of it. Some may see these years as a dark abyss when Labour's ideological divisions became incurable, and led to the eventual retribution of Thatcherism. Others may see them more positively as a time when themes such as democratic participation or feminism, hitherto neglected by the post-war social democratic consensus, came to the fore. There can, however, be no dispute on the immense importance and interest of these opposition years. Patrick Bell has done us all good service in recounting them with such scholarship and lucidity.

Oxford, June 2004   KENNETH O. MORGAN

SERIES EDITOR'S PREFACE

The world of political opposition, and the role opposition plays, is not one which has been heavily studied in Britain. Governments arrive in opposition ill-equipped for the frustrations, and the hard graft of occasionally winning the argument but always losing the vote or indeed the taunts, as Wilson's Labour faced in 1971, that they are *Yesterday's Men*. They lose the initiative and are reduced either simply to reacting to policies they do not make with as much intellectual and ideological coherence as they can muster, or to preparing – with greatly reduced resources – alternatives against some future return to power. In the power vacuum of opposition, however, policy options are frequently the only bones to chew over. A period of opposition can therefore exacerbate intra-party tensions, not least when governments lose office, as Wilson's did in 1970, already internally divided over key issues.

To be in government in the early 1970s, of course, was not particularly comfortable either. The economy may have recovered reasonably well by 1970 from the shock of the 1967 devaluation under Roy Jenkins's rather austere management, conflicts about which Labour took with them into opposition. Heath's incoming Conservative government, however, faced a number of inflationary shocks which were to make a mockery of his rhetoric in the 1970 general election, and forced him to adopt a more thoroughgoing prices and incomes policy than that under Labour he had so criticised in the late 1960s. The Tories had prepared carefully for their return to government, but were frequently blown off course in this way by exogenous pressures.

While no elections are good to lose, it could be argued that some elections, and 1970 might count among these, are not particularly good to win. Opposition might have afforded a relatively sheltered haven from which to think out strategies to address the problems which buffeted the Heath government. In the fevered world of Labour policy making, which Patrick Bell evokes so well here, this, however, is not quite what happened. The autarkic prescriptions of the left's Alternative Economic Strategy were as much a reaction to Jenkins's stewardship of the British economy 1967–70, and complaints about the framing of the 1970 manifesto, as they were a reflection of subsequent events. Insofar as the latter impinged on the process, it was the travails of Upper Clyde Shipbuilders (UCS), and how to insulate British labour from similar shocks in future, rather than the oil price hikes of 1973 that drove thinking. Such attempts to manage what might be referred to, albeit anachronistically, as 'globalisation' seemed, however, to many of the party's leaders as being as likely to succeed as the abortive attempt to rescue UCS. Yet, as Bell shows, they were not particularly successful at offering other alternatives themselves. The social democratic right, in particular, failed to mobilise to control the policy process. Jenkins's failure to make more impact is one of the key themes of the book. The benefits he hoped would accrue to the British economy from joining a much larger market which would expose British industry to greater competition could have been presented, at least in the longer term, as an alternative means of controlling inflation without recourse to the suggested solutions, successively offered from the 1960s to the 1980s, of prices and incomes policy, autarky, monetarism or unemployment. However, although some on the Left, like Stuart Holland, were already on the road to some kind of pre-Delors vision of socialism in Europe, many in the party remained more concerned about the constraints Europe might impose upon them. As a result, Europe proved less of a panacea than a means of depriving the party leadership of Jenkins's services.

Instead, the circumstances of opposition in 1970–74, as Bell demonstrates, conspired to make the trade unions more central to Labour's policy processes. This was partly because the Heath government's failed efforts to reform industrial relations placed the unions at centre stage, and partly because, without other options, Labour had no choice but to default to prices and incomes policy, by and large on union terms, in 1974 when they returned to government. In the meantime, however, few if any of the intra-party debates provoked by the experience of government in the 1960s had yet been resolved.

On one level, of course, Labour's period of opposition in 1970–74 was nevertheless successful. At the first test they won back power, albeit barely. But this owed little to Labour's achievements in opposition. Unlike Blair in 1994–97 they did not find a new language with which to describe themselves – and also their Tory opponents – and position themselves in the electoral marketplace. Unlike Thatcher in 1975–79 or Heath ten years earlier, there was no detailed policy programme heralding a new departure. Unlike Wilson himself in 1963–64, they did not even have much to offer on governmental reorganisation, such changes as occurred in 1974 being driven more by the exigencies of cabinet making in a divided party. Bell's eloquent account of Labour's four years in the wilderness in 1970–74 takes us on a long journey, casting light on many of the issues and conflicts of the day, but one in which the Labour tribe seemed to end up more or less where they started. Not only that, but the seeds of the conflicts and splits of ten years later were already being shown.

Peter Catterall
21 November 2003

ACKNOWLEDGEMENTS

This book is based primarily on documents held by the institutions listed below and I am indebted to a number of archivists, librarians and individuals who placed valuable material at my disposal: Stephen Bird, Andrew Flinn and Nicholas Mansfield at the National Museum of Labour History in Manchester, without whose expert assistance and formidable knowledge of the Labour Party Archive I could not have progressed; Sue Donnelly at the British Library of Political and Economic Science; Susan Crosland, for permission to quote from the Anthony Crosland Papers; Richard Temple of the Modern Records Centre at the University of Warwick; and Alan Haworth and Catherine Jackson of the Labour Party at the House of Commons, for permission to quote from Parliamentary Labour Party Regional and Subject Group Minutes. Catherine Jackson, in particular, has been a constant and valuable source of expertise and friendship. Neil Plummer, Lynne Thompson and the staff of the Brotherton Library at the University of Leeds were unendingly resourceful and helpful. Several current and former Members of Parliament and Labour Party/TUC personnel were generous with their time: the late Frank Allaun, Geoff Bish, Lord Callaghan of Cardiff, Richard Clements, Michael Foot, the late Lord Jenkins of Hillhead, Professor David Marquand, the late Lord Murray of Epping Forest, Lord Orme, Lord Owen, Lord Rodgers of Quarry Bank, Dennis Skinner MP, Lord Taverne and Lord Thomson of Monifieth.

I am equally indebted to current and former colleagues: Steven Allen, Dr William A. Callahan, Dr John Gatehouse, Bill Kirkpatrick, Julie Kirkpatrick, Corinna Matthews, Wendy Redhead, Professor Philip Williamson and Paul Zealand (University of Durham); Dr Stephen Brumwell, Professor Geoffrey K. Fry, John Morison, Professor Kevin Theakston and Dr Ellis Tinios (University of Leeds); Beverley Eaton, Professor Ian Kershaw, Dr David Martin and Cheryl Plant (University of Sheffield). Above all, I am grateful to Dr Owen A. Hartley and Dr Richard C. Whiting of the University of Leeds, for their guidance and rigorous examination of my ideas over a number of years. I have benefited from their experience, judgement and friendship and could never thank them enough. I am grateful also to Dr Peter Stirk and Professor Robert Williams of the Department of Politics at the University of Durham, for granting me the time to complete the book, and to Professor Caroline Kennedy-Pipe of the University of Sheffield, for her invaluable support and encouragement. Dr Stephen Welch, at Durham, very kindly read the completed manuscript and made a number of useful comments. I record my thanks also to Dr Peter Catterall, Andrew Humphrys, Professor Kenneth O. Morgan, Allison Summers and all at Taylor & Francis for their part in seeing the book into print.

Finally, I extend warm thanks to a number of friends and individuals who provided practical help and support at various stages in the writing of the book: the late Carolyn Ainscough, Sally Bailey, Sue Bailey, Margaret Balls, the late Joyce Bell, Michael Bell, Paul Bell, Mike Brough, Helen Butters (née Dargan), Chris Calnan, Steve Clark, Kath Coussement (née Barley), Jack Craven, John Cushion, Steve Doherty, Sister Nora Dowd, Arlene Flexman, Wendy Fox (née Barker), Baljit Gandhi, the late Ken Goddard, John Hardiman, Suzie Harrison, Steve Hollingsworth, Joanna Lack, Andrew Lister, William F. Lyon, John McDonough, Dr Paul Priest, Kevin Swift, Alicca Vyse-Peacock, Father James Walsh and Carol Wise. Two people merit special recognition. My father, Gerard Bell, has been a source of inspiration and support. Lesley Raine has been central to the enterprise from the outset and made countless suggestions that improved the text.

Responsibility for any shortcomings or errors in the book is mine alone.

PRINCIPAL LABOUR SHADOW CABINET AND CONSERVATIVE GOVERNMENT PERSONNEL 1970–74

Labour Party	Shadow Portfolio
Harold Wilson	Leader of the Opposition 1970–74
Tony Benn	Trade and Industry 1970–74
James Callaghan	Home Office 1970–71
	Employment 1971–72
	Foreign and Commonwealth Office 1972–74
Barbara Castle	Employment 1970–71
	Social Security 1971–72
Anthony Crosland	Environment 1970–74
Michael Foot	Power 1970–71
	Leader of the House of Commons and European Common Market 1971–72
	European Common Market 1972–74
Denis Healey	Foreign and Commonwealth Office 1970–72
	Treasury 1972–74
Douglas Houghton	Chairman, Parliamentary Labour Party 1970–74
Roy Jenkins	Deputy Leader and Treasury 1970–72
	Home Office 1973–74
Harold Lever	European Affairs 1970–72
	Trade and Industry 1972–74
Bob Mellish	Chief Whip 1970–74
Fred Peart	Parliamentary Affairs 1970–71
	Agriculture 1971–72
	Defence 1972–74
Reg Prentice	Employment 1971–74
Merlyn Rees	Northern Ireland 1972–74
William Ross	Scotland 1970–74
Peter Shore	European Common Market 1971–74

Edward Short	Education and Science 1970–71
	Deputy Leader and Leader of the House of Commons 1972–74
George Thomson	Defence 1970–72
Shirley Williams	Health and Social Security 1970–71
	Home Office 1971–73
	Prices and Consumer Protection 1973–74

Conservative Party	**Ministerial Portfolio**
Edward Heath	Prime Minister 1970–74
Anthony Barber	Chancellor of the Duchy of Lancaster 1970
	Chancellor of the Exchequer 1970–74
Robert Carr	Secretary of State for Employment 1970–72
	Lord President of the Council and Leader of the House of Commons 1972
	Home Secretary 1972–74
John Davies	Minister of Technology 1970
	Secretary of State for Trade and Industry 1970–72
	Chancellor of the Duchy of Lancaster 1972–74
Sir Alec Douglas-Home	Foreign Secretary 1970–74
Iain Macleod	Chancellor of the Exchequer 1970
Reginald Maudling	Home Secretary 1970–72
Geoffrey Rippon	Minister of Technology 1970
	Chancellor of the Duchy of Lancaster 1970–72
	Secretary of State for the Environment 1972–72
Peter Walker	Minister of Housing and Local Government 1970
	Secretary of State for the Environment 1970–72
	Secretary of State for Trade and Industry 1972–74
William Whitelaw	Lord President of the Council and Leader of the House of Commons 1970–72
	Secretary of State for Northern Ireland 1972–73
	Secretary of State for Employment 1973–74

ABBREVIATIONS

ACAS   Advisory Conciliation and Arbitration Service
ACP   Anthony Crosland Papers
ACTT   Association of Cinematograph, Television and Allied Technicians
AEU   Amalgamated Engineering Union
ASTMS   Association of Scientific, Technical and Managerial Staffs
AUEW   Amalgamated Union of Engineering Workers
BLPES   British Library of Political and Economic Science
CAP   Common Agricultural Policy
CAS   Conciliation and Arbitration Service
CBI   Confederation of British Industry
CDS   Campaign for Democratic Socialism
CIR   Commission on Industrial Relations
CLP   Constituency Labour Party
CLV   Campaign for Labour Victory
CP   Cabinet Papers
CPSA   Civil and Public Services Association
DATA   Draughtsman's and Allied Technical Association
DEA   Department of Economic Affairs
DTI   Department of Trade and Industry
GMC   General Management Committee
HC   House of Commons
HPC   Home Policy Committee
IMF   International Monetary Fund
IMP   Ian Mikardo Papers
IRC   Industrial Reorganisation Corporation
IRI   Industrial Reconstruction Institute
JRP   Jo Richardson Papers
LCE   Labour Committee for Europe
LPA   Labour Party Archive
LPAR   Labour Party Annual Report
MFC   Michael Foot Collection
NCL   National Council of Labour

NEB	National Enterprise Board
NEC	National Executive Committee
NEDC	National Economic Development Council
NIRC	National Industrial Relations Court
NUGMW	National Union of General and Municipal Workers
NUM	National Union of Mineworkers
NUPE	National Union of Public Employees
NUR	National Union of Railwaymen
NUS	National Union of Seamen
PC	Parliamentary Committee
PLP	Parliamentary Labour Party
SDP	Social Democratic Party
TGM	Tribune Group Minutes
TGWU	Transport and General Workers' Union
TPP	Terry Pitt Papers
TUC	Trades Union Congress
UCATT	Union of Construction, Allied Trades and Technicians
UCS	Upper Clyde Shipbuilders
USDAW	Union of Shop, Distributive and Allied Workers

INTRODUCTION

In June 1970, the Labour Party lost an election the opinion polls had indicated it would win and which party leaders believed they were winning. The way the party responded to and explained its defeat, and the extent to which it used opposition to prepare to storm back to power with a fresh set of answers to the problems which had destabilised the Labour government 1964–70, forms the basis of this book. Labour spent only three years and eight months in opposition, which did not allow the party sufficient time for an objective assessment of future policy requirements. Instead, Labour acquired a radically socialist party programme because of a breach between the parliamentary leadership and the trade unions over the Wilson government's attempted industrial relations reform in 1969[1] – which emboldened the National Executive Committee (NEC) and Labour Party Conference in opposition – and because the Conservative government took fright when unemployment began to rise and switched to a highly interventionist industrial strategy. As a consequence, the future was handed to Margaret Thatcher.

The breach between the parliamentary leadership and the trade unions was exacerbated by the rise of Jack Jones and Hugh Scanlon to leadership of the Transport and General Workers' Union (TGWU) and the Amalgamated Union of Engineering Workers (AEUW) in 1969 and 1968 respectively. Jones and Scanlon provided 'an axis with different instincts and responses from those of their early post-war predecessors, who had ruled their organisations with an iron rod, and had felt protective towards Attlee'.[2] They felt no loyalty towards Wilson who, along with Barbara Castle, had in their view sought to emasculate free trade unionism. Aside from ruling out an agreement on wages and industrial relations reform, Jones and Scanlon also declared their opposition to British membership of the Common Market, isolating Roy Jenkins (Labour's senior pro-Marketeer) at a stroke and leaving Harold Wilson in no doubt about the price of a reconciliation.

The Labour Party in opposition is not simply a story of the Wilson government in exile. For just over two years, from April 1971 to June 1973,

1

the party's discussion of policy was organised through the NEC research programme. This method of policy-making was intended to reduce the influence of the parliamentary leadership on party policy. The research programme gave a voice to those sections of the party that attached greater importance to the performance of the Labour government than to the loss of power. Because of the way the Labour Party made policy at the time, the Research Department was indispensable to the process. So, from the outset, policy-making was influenced by individuals at Transport House who believed the Labour government had abandoned the manifesto in office and that the party had fought the 1970 general election with the wrong policies. For this reason the Research Department (through the research programme) and the Labour Party Conference are best understood as a power base in their own right and a rival source of authority to the parliamentary leadership.

The second power base in this story is the trade unions, who operate separately from the party structure precisely because they are so powerful. The non-participation of the most influential trade union leaders in Labour's research programme process in opposition was the single most important factor in determining how significant the research programme would prove. The most powerful voice in the labour movement at this time belonged collectively to the trade unions and individually to Jack Jones, whose position as general secretary of the largest trade union in Britain removed the need for him to take a formal role in the party's official research programme process. Indeed, such was the strength of organised labour that the Labour Party's formal structures had to be supplemented by the establishment, on the trade unions' terms, of a TUC–Labour Party Liaison Committee in 1972 to facilitate a dialogue between the Trades Union Congress (TUC) and the Labour Party.

On its own, the NEC research programme held insufficient attraction for Jones and the TUC, despite the fact that it offered the prospect of a final policy document which would address the concerns of trade unionists. Jones preferred instead to deal with the parliamentary leadership of the party directly, seeing it as the best way of securing a commitment on a range of policies that would be honoured in government. Unlike the NEC and the party conference, the trade unions could neither be ignored nor marginalised by a future Labour government once an agreement had been reached. This development in the relationship between the elites of the industrial and political wings of the labour movement eventually gave the parliamentary leadership the advantage in its relationships with the NEC and the party conference. In the short term, the establishment of the TUC–Labour Party Liaison Committee was beneficial to the parliamentary leadership. However, because the Liaison Committee produced an agreement on prices but not on wages, this relationship had the effect of storing up problems for the Labour government 1974–79.

The NEC, party conference and trade unions had their own power bases, but what of Labour's parliamentarians, the third power base in this story? Prominent in the Parliamentary Labour Party (PLP) in this period were a group of centre-right MPs who regarded Roy Jenkins as their natural leader (since referred to as the 'Jenkinsites', but not by the individuals themselves at the time). The Jenkinsites had a growing awareness of what Labour required to extend its electoral appeal (less socialism, more capitalism), but their hero lacked the taste for open battle with the party to force the issue. For Jenkins, the best hope of resuscitating social democracy in the Labour Party (by achieving high economic growth) lay in British membership of the Common Market, which by 1971 was overwhelmingly opposed by the party conference and the TUC. Without the leader and a formal organisation in the constituencies, they were unable to fend off anti-Market sentiment and a left-wing drift on wider policy. Jenkins was no Hugh Gaitskell, and no Gaitskell meant no Campaign for Democratic Socialism (CDS), the centre-right pressure group that reversed left-wing gains on defence policy at the party conference a decade earlier. The Jenkinsites could have made a valuable contribution to Labour's policy debate in opposition, but only by challenging for the leadership on a distinctive radical right manifesto. They had the policies;[3] they did not have, in Jenkins, the candidate.

Beyond this faction was James Callaghan, whose appreciation of where power lay in the labour movement was so astute that he was effectively a faction in his own right. The PLP enjoyed a high level of representation on the subcommittees, study groups and working parties of the Home Policy Committee (which oversaw the research programme) because the former Home Secretary exploited his position as its chairman to involve the PLP at every level of the process. At the heart of the NEC research programme therefore sat the arch-fixer of the PLP, actively compensating for the bias shown by the research secretary and his assistant (Terry Pitt and Geoff Bish respectively) towards the party's left wing. The structure of the research programme and the way the Labour Party discussed policy in opposition were both significantly influenced by Callaghan, who straddled the PLP–NEC divide more effectively than any of his colleagues in the Shadow Cabinet. Such was Callaghan's power base that Harold Wilson was unable to move against him when he broke ranks in 1971 to declare his opposition to British membership of the Common Market, leaving Wilson little choice but to follow suit to the detriment of the Jenkinsites and social democracy in the Labour Party. Wilson had little room to manoeuvre. Jenkins was no Gaitskell. The pike in the river was Callaghan.[4]

The dynamics of these competing power bases were animated by a number of policy issues. The NEC research programme took place against the backdrop of a highly divisive Conservative government whose economic and industrial policies constituted the biggest challenge to Keynesian orthodoxy since the adoption of the 1944 White Paper on employment policy. 'Government has been attempting too much' was the recurring theme of a neo-liberal agenda. 'For a brief moment in 1970–71', writes Samuel Beer, 'the new Conservative government appeared determined to resist the forces which had transformed the subsidy system from an investment programme into a welfare programme for business'.[5] This attempted 'mental leap away from the total Keynesian tradition' sparked a seismic eruption of radical socialism in the Labour Party.[6] In Parliament, the PLP fought protracted (albeit unsuccessful) battles to prevent Conservative policies on industrial relations reform, housing reform and British membership of the Common Market from reaching the statute book. The fact that the Labour government had itself sought to reform industrial relations, introduced its own housing reforms and applied for British membership of the Common Market was an embarrassment, but opposition to the Conservative government was no less determined for that.

Many in Labour's ranks were, of course, opposed to a policy on trade union reform wherever it came from. At the Labour Party Conference in 1970, left-wing MPs led the stampede to condemn the Wilson government's folly over *In Place of Strife*. For some members of the Shadow Cabinet, opposing the Conservative government was a redemptive process: for others in the party, a release. Part of Labour's problem in this period (and beyond) was that the party remained temperamentally suited to opposition rather than to the responsibilities of government. In this respect Labour had not moved on from 1931. Contrary to Wilson's claim, the Labour Party had not become the natural party of government. If it had, *In Place of Strife* would have become law.

Disillusionment with the Wilson government set in well before the publication of *In Place of Strife*. Both the unions and the party conference had good reason to feel aggrieved by a Labour government that had restricted free collective bargaining, drastically reduced public expenditure, reintroduced prescription charges, presided over rising unemployment, supported the American war in Vietnam, retained Polaris and restricted immigration, notoriously so in the case of the Kenyan Asians in 1968. The government's achievements, among them the Housing Act and Redundancy Payments Act (1965), the Docks and Harbours Act (1966), the expansion of higher education in 1967 and creation of the Open University in 1969, the Equal Pay Act (1970) and keeping Britain out of the Vietnam War were too easily overlooked. With Jones's and Scanlon's conference votes detached from the parliamentary leadership, a more even distribution of power between the PLP, NEC and party conference seemed likely. From the chair at conference, Tony Benn encouraged calls for increased party democracy and more radical policies, cleverly exploiting the Conservatives' ideological approach to government to proclaim that 'the era of so-called "consensus politics" is over'.[7]

The NEC research programme facilitated a break with consensus politics. At the Research Department, Terry Pitt oversaw the establishment of working groups on economic planning and the public sector, which brought to prominence Stuart Holland (former economic assistant to the Labour government) who would be the source of much of the industrial policy content of Labour's major statement of policy in opposition, *Labour's Programme 1973*. In the 18 months up to the party's adoption of *Labour's Programme 1973*, Holland submitted over two dozen papers to the Industrial Policy Subcommittee and its related working groups.[8] The industrial policy content of *Labour's Programme 1973* potentially provided for a hugely damaging split between the PLP and the party. Holland's proposal that Labour should nationalise Britain's 20 leading manufacturers, one of the three big banks and the leading insurance companies (the 'twenty-five companies' proposal) alarmed the parliamentary leadership and alienated the electorate.[9]

The socialism of the NEC research programme challenged a parliamentary leadership still heavily dependent upon Anthony Crosland's *The Future of Socialism* (1956) for its intellectual authority. Crosland's notion of the existence of a democratic economy to facilitate social justice and reform, on which revisionist ideology hinged, was questioned by Holland's identification of a meso-economic sector, 'the handful of giant corporations, many of them multi-national, which dominated manufacturing industry and which government was becoming less and less able to control'.[10] Yet Crosland saw 'no reason to alter the revisionist thesis that government can generally impose its will (provided it has one) on the private corporation'.[11] Crosland himself confused many of his admirers (including several displaced Croslandites among the Jenkinsites) by aping the language of Clause IV in calling for the public ownership of all land, 'except for owner-occupied houses and small farms'[12] and embracing *Labour's Programme 1973* as the most radical plank in the party's thinking. He could live with left-wing ideology at this time more comfortably than Jenkins, being of the opinion that a move to the left was required, 'not in the traditional sense of a move toward old fashioned Clause IV Marxism but in the sense of a sharper delineation of fundamental objectives, a greater clarity about egalitarian priorities, and a stronger determination to achieve them'.[13]

The real crisis for the parliamentary leadership in opposition was intellectual: Crosland no longer had the answer. Deprived of their intellectual guru, the parliamentary leadership had little to fall back on. The Jenkinsites, rather than compete with Holland policy paper for policy paper, championed the Common Market as a way to secure the consistent high growth that had eluded the Wilson government and undermined Crosland's thesis, in the process achieving little other than their own marginalisation. Instead, the parliamentary leadership had to rely upon a return to office to solve an intellectual crisis, a high-risk strategy that effectively guaranteed the failure of the 1974–79 government.

A return to government was not the answer. The trade union response to the performance of the Wilson government 1964–70 was entirely negative: free collective bargaining, no industrial relations reform and no Common Market. Boxed in on policy by the NEC research programme, the parliamentary leadership had little choice but to seek an accommodation with the unions on the unions' terms, namely the TUC–Labour Party Liaison Committee policy document *Economic Policy and the Cost of Living* (1973) which committed a future Labour government to price control, food subsidies, increased pensions and benefits, yet excluded industrial relations reform and an agreement on wages. Bizarrely, this agreement between the Labour Party and the TUC acquired the epithet the Social Contract.

Labour's period in opposition 1970–74 was one of decline. *Labour's Programme 1973* and *Economic Policy and the Cost of Living* were consequences of Labour's failure in government 1964–70 to secure high levels of economic growth and reform industrial relations. At the same time, Edward Heath's disastrous premiership (coming after Wilson's defeat over *In Place of Strife*) further weakened the authority of the executive in British politics. His unsuccessful attempt to revise the Keynesian post-war settlement strengthened the trade unions' hand in their negotiations with the Labour Party over the terms of the Social Contract, with long-term consequences for the Labour Party as an electoral force.

Notes

1 In 1969, Barbara Castle, the Secretary of State for Employment, published a White Paper on industrial relations, *In Place of Strife*, the fourth clause of which authorised the Employment Secretary to order a conciliation pause in unconstitutional stoppages, and if necessary to order a return to the status quo. TUC Report, 1969, p. 211.
2 B. Pimlott, *Harold Wilson* (London, HarperCollins, 1992), p. 574.
3 See J. P. Mackintosh, D. Marquand and D. Owen, *A Change of Gear* (London, *Socialist Commentary*, 1968); R. Jenkins, *What Matters Now* (London, Fontana, 1972).
4 For an account of Callaghan in opposition 1970–74, see K. O. Morgan, *Callaghan: A Life* (Oxford, Oxford University Press, 1997), pp. 359–407.
5 S. Beer, *Britain Against Itself* (London, Faber & Faber, 1982), pp. 214, 68.
6 Symposium, 'Conservative Party Policy Making 1965–70', *Contemporary Record*, 3, 3(1990), p. 38 (Brendon Sewill).
7 Labour Party Annual Report (LPAR), 1972, p. 103. Benn was similarly omnipresent in the Labour Party in this period but lacked Callaghan's seniority and widespread support.
8 M. Hartley Brewer, 'Scaled-down version', *The Guardian*, 3 November 1975, p. 14.

9 Increased public ownership, a feature of *Labour's Programme 1973*, enjoyed the support of only 20 per cent of all voters, and only 37 per cent of those who identified themselves as Labour voters. S. E. Finer, *The Changing British Party System* (Washington, DC, American Enterprise Institute for Public Policy Research, 1980), p. 124.

10 Hartley Brewer, 'Scaled-down version'.

11 G. Foote, *The Labour Party's Political Thought*, 2nd edn (London, Croom Helm, 1986), p. 241.

12 LPAR, 1973, p. 212.

13 Foote, *The Labour Party's Political Thought*, p. 242.

1

LABOUR'S RESPONSE TO DEFEAT (I): BLACKPOOL 1970, THE LABOUR PARTY CONFERENCE

Prologue: the pre-conference debate

Writing in *The Guardian* two days after Labour's defeat in the general election of June 1970, Peter Jenkins concluded that 'Mr Wilson's Government has been turned out because Labour failed to deliver enough of the goods to enough of the people enough of the time'.[1] Jenkins, considered by Barbara Castle at least to be 'normally a Roy Jenkins fan',[2] displayed little sympathy towards his namesake in a second article five days later when, under the heading 'Roy muffed it', he criticised the former Chancellor for his overly cautious pre-election Budget, and blamed Wilson for his decision to call a June election. Jenkins's second article followed the publication by the Central Statistical Office of the expenditure figures for the first quarter of 1970, in his opinion 'the best explanation of the election result so far'. Because the economy had not expanded between January and March, he argued, the April Budget had been a missed opportunity to reflate the economy for electoral gain. 'In other words there was not much of a jingle in the housewives' handbag when Mr Wilson went to the country.'[3]

In a 20 June editorial, *The Guardian* warned that 'the idealism and crusading spirit which Labour somehow lost after 1964 will have to be recreated – and convincingly if the Conservatives are not to have another 13-year term':

> Just possibly, with a favourable trade balance and debts nearly paid, Labour would have proved more radical. Mr Roy Jenkins or his successor might have been ready at last to take risks in achieving growth and ready to use taxation to redistribute wealth. Social services might have been expanded and the housing problem restored.[4]

The paper's editorial line and the tone of Jenkins's articles were essentially only mildly reproachful. The paper did not question the substance of the Labour government's policies, merely the commitment to them.

In *New Statesman* Alan Watkins asked 'Why were we all so wrong?' On prices, taxation and inflation Heath had been 'no more specific than Mr Wilson. Indeed on rising prices and inflation he was less so'. Having predicted a Labour victory, Watkins could find no better explanation for the party's defeat other than to attribute it to the vagaries of the election campaign itself. Readers were encouraged to believe that five years and eight months of Labour government had come to an end on the strength of the remarks made by Lord Cromer, the retired Governor of the Bank of England, about the decline in the economy since 1964, Tony Benn's attack on Enoch Powell's allegedly racist views on immigration, the doctors' pay dispute and the national newspaper strike in June.[5] This analysis confirmed at least Harold Wilson's belief that the Conservative Party had won an undeserved victory. Paul Johnson, writing in the same issue, more soberly echoed the analysis of Peter Jenkins in *The Guardian*. The April Budget had been 'misjudged'; Wilson 'should never have allowed himself to be conned into an early election'.[6]

Newly installed as the editor of *New Statesman*, Richard Crossman opined that 'the only relevant lesson of the election is that three months was too brief a period of convalescence from the self-inflicted wounds of nearly six years'. What Labour needed to be able to confront the new government was not 'the smack of firm shadow government', but 'an immediate militancy in day to day opposition combined with a bout of radical rethinking out of which there can emerge a programme of action that will restore the confidence of the constituencies and Trade Unions in the political leadership'.[7] By contrast, *Socialist Commentary* (the publication of Labour's centre-right), edited by Rita Hinden, looked forward to 'an opposition led by a brilliant team of ex-Ministers with a wealth of experience behind them'. In Hinden's estimation the immediate reason for the party's defeat was to be found at Transport House. Labour's organisation, she claimed, had been 'faulty'. 'The leadership of the Party showed no interest in remedying this fatal weakness, and the National Executive seemed adamantly resistant to organisational reform.'[8]

In July 1970 Crossman invited Roy Hattersley and Eric Heffer to explain Labour's defeat under the heading 'Could Labour have won?' Hattersley, having served as a minister in the Labour government, found little fault with its record by 1970 and excused the defeat in terms of the timing of the decision to go to the polls:

> ...the political recovery was real but fragile. There was belief in our economic success, but no deep conviction. Proof had not appeared in the family pay packet and voters remained confused

about the evidence and sceptical about the arguments. Old wounds were too easily reopened. The scar tissue had not been given time to grow. It is possible to argue that a week earlier the wounds had not begun to bleed or that four months later they would have healed completely.[9]

Heffer, offering a perspective from the back benches, argued that the Labour government had lacked a coherent theory and had forgotten its power base. 'The only time it appeared to get really bold was when it tackled the trade unions, and this false boldness almost wrecked the Labour movement.' The reality of 1964–70, he wrote, revealing the extent of the left's disenchantment with Wilson, was that Labour had 'a sort of Gaitskellism' without the Crown Prince. 'I say a sort of Gaitskellism, because to say it was outright Gaitskellism would be doing Hugh Gaitskell an injustice. He never blurred the political edges, and too many edges have been blurred on too many issues.'[10]

Throughout the summer *New Statesman* carried letters from readers questioning the extent to which Labour had ever posed an alternative society. For six years, wrote Vaughan James, 'we tinkered with the economy in the best Tory traditions'. Michael Pickering ridiculed 'the Stanley Baldwin act which didn't come off and the failure to present a firm socialist policy'. James Mitchell attacked the paper itself, for its 'special vendetta against Mr Wilson', and hoped 'you, and all those Hampstead-cum-campus types who write letters to you are satisfied'. Barton Dodd blamed the parliamentary leadership for failing to 'deliver the goods': 'The man in the street is not interested in homosexual law reform, in easier abortions, in easier divorce, in liberation of women, in the ending of capital punishment – mere sops to the intellectuals. What we want is an improvement in the lot of the poor, the sick and the underprivileged. And it is here that the Labour Party have lost the confidence of the British people.'[11]

The range of explanations for Labour's defeat was indicative of the fragmentary nature of the party's support. When Frank Allaun MP – hugely influential in *Tribune* (the newpaper of Labour's left wing) – wrote that 'for the future, for Labour's leaders the lesson must surely be to carry out the policies urged by the annual delegate conference', his was no more the authentic voice of Labour than any of the above.[12]

Tribune responded to Labour's defeat with a front-page editorial 'Why it happened – and what we are going to do', and by launching 'The Great Debate' in its letters column. 'The major factor in the defeat,' wrote Richard Clements, the paper's editor, 'was the policy which the Government had pursued in office. This, above all else, characterised the future prospects of future Labour Governments as bleak indeed.'[13] Foremost among these was Roy Jenkins's April Budget which the paper had condemned at the time for giving only 'a small hint of the strength of the argument against the

Treasury view inside the Labour movement'.[14] Mesmerised by the reactions of the press, the Labour leadership had failed to listen to its own supporters: 'It does not give much feeling of success to those who believed that what this country now needed was not a continuation of the squeeze, but a growth rate which would alleviate the hardships which have been imposed on the working people of this country during the period of the squeeze.'[15]

Labour could have avoided defeat, the paper believed, had it adopted the policies advocated by the TUC and the left wing of the party (which included a target growth rate of 6 per cent), but having declined to do so could have at least indicated 'what it was going to do about those policies which had created so much dissension and hardship and ill-feeling'. During the election campaign there had been no word about solving the unemployment problem or refurbishing the National Health Service 'and the other Welfare schemes which had been damaged by the Treasury's insistence on appeasing the bankers'. Clements's editorial concluded with an outline for opposition which greatly influenced the substance of the debates on party policy and the sovereignty of conference decisions at Blackpool. Party members, he argued,

> must start to argue about how we get the policy of the Labour Party back on the road to Socialism. We must get an acceptance of the policies which the whole of the TUC and a large number of the Labour Party activists have put forward over the past two years. That means being very sure that this year's Labour Party conference will have on its agenda resolutions which elaborate that policy. And we must make sure that the leadership of the party is going to campaign on this policy.[16]

Declaring its passionate belief in democracy, *Tribune* launched 'The Great Debate' 'to start the argument about the general election result'. The response was predictable. What was needed, wrote Walter J. Wolfgang, was 'a final programmatic – and not merely rhetorical – breach with consensus politics', a view echoed by A. A. Bryant, who wrote that the labour movement must 'get back on the road to true socialism, not just to try and manage capitalism'. James Fishwick thought such an upheaval unlikely; the rebuilding of the Labour Party 'as a socialist party, dedicated to revolutionary reform, is entirely beyond the second-rate men and women who form this moribund group of time-serving, chicken-hearted social democrats'.[17] The notion of an 'argument' about the general election result in *Tribune* of all publications was ironic, as contributors to the letters column were essentially loyal to the paper's editorial line. The real argument was with the parliamentary leadership of the party and 'The Great Debate' took place to facilitate the rehearsal of the polemical speeches which were a feature of the Blackpool conference.

Readers were encouraged to demonstrate their dissatisfaction with the Labour government by submitting conference resolutions to the NEC. Frank Allaun, in a letter prominently displayed in the paper on 26 June, informed readers that the final date for the submission of resolutions was 3 July, only 15 days after the general election, a date to which the party was constitutionally bound, despite his protests. This he regarded as an attempt to stifle debate and he appealed to both Constituency Labour Parties (CLPs) and national trade unions to call special meetings 'to consider their resolutions for the Blackpool conference'.[18] Two weeks later he was able to announce 'there is to be a REAL Labour Party Conference after all'. Due, in part, to his vigilance the number of resolutions received by the NEC in the intervening period had risen from ten to 250. Allaun was fulsome in his praise for *Tribune* 'for having drawn attention to the need to submit resolutions',[19] and there can be little doubt that the existence of a weekly newspaper attuned to the thinking of left-wing activists in the constituencies played a significant role in determining the conference agenda.[20]

In the weeks leading up to conference, *Tribune* attempted to put pressure on former ministers by publishing a series of critical articles written by members of the parliamentary Tribune Group (a left-wing successor group to the Bevanites). On 4 September, Norman Atkinson called on Harold Wilson to 're-establish his credentials as a socialist', and asked whether it was the gnomes, the Treasury, the City or a member of the Cabinet 'who kicked the legs from under our high wage-fast growth-full employment policies which literally oozed from Transport House prior to 1964'.[21] On 18 September, Stan Orme dismissed as futile the Labour government's attempts to *persuade* the private sector of industry: 'In a situation where more and more public money is being poured into the private sector (something like £800m a year) where mergers are becoming an everyday occurrence, where the international company is playing an ever-increasing part in our employment and our economy, it is time for a basic shift in control and ownership.'[22]

Tribune's summer campaign for a change of policy culminated in an eve-of-conference rally on 27 September at which Atkinson pilloried the Wilson government's economic record of devaluation and repeated deflationary packages: 'From an £800m deficit, we created a £500m surplus, but at what cost! We have absolutely murdered the Labour movement.'[23] The previous day Shirley Williams had written in *The Times* that 'the tone of conference resolutions on the performance [of the Labour government] is one of sorrow rather than anger'.[24] She was wrong. The anger of activists at Blackpool was genuine.

Blackpool 1970: the Labour Party Conference

At Blackpool activists responded to Labour's defeat, and to the failure of the Labour government to implement policy agreed at conference, by

reopening the decade-old debate on the sovereignty of conference decisions, and by calling for Clause IV socialism. Two debates, on the party
programme and on conference decisions, revealed the extent to which
trade union leaders were prepared to endorse this response. At the heart
of the debate on the party programme were two competing motions:
Composite Resolution 28, moved by Ken Lomas MP on behalf of the
National Union of Public Employees (NUPE) and accepted by the NEC,
and Composite Resolution 29, moved by Don Hughes of Liverpool, Walton
CLP (the constituency of the Tribunite MP Eric Heffer) which the NEC
recommended conference reject. Composite Resolution 28 called on the
Labour Party 'to re-establish a clearly defined sense of socialist purpose',
and instructed the NEC to present to the following year's conference
'a programme designed to: a) secure greater equality in the distribution of
wealth and income; b) extend social ownership and control of industry
and land by Socialist planning; c) develop industrial democracy and the
role of the Trade Union Movement in industrial, political and economic
affairs'. Lomas praised 'the tremendous achievements of six years of Labour
Government', but condemned its failings: 'We even sank to the depths of
what Harold Wilson once called "the last refuge of the bankrupt Tory
Chancellor", and re-introduced prescription charges, in direct violation of
every single party conference decision.' The labour movement, he believed,
'is a Party of planners or it is nothing, and we have got to plan our growth
rate; we have got to plan our incomes; we have got to plan our prices
policy, and we have to make sure that we have an effective policy that can
be put into effect. Therefore, I hope that together with the Trade Union
Movement we can get down to the job of trying to find a policy that will do
just that.'[25] Seconding the motion, Jim Mowat (West Renfrewshire CLP)
attributed Labour's defeat to either too much socialism or, as he believed,
too little. That voters had found it difficult to distinguish between the two
main parties, was a dreadful indictment. 'I feel it is vital that they be left in
no doubt next time, because the gulf between us is enormous, and if it is
not, then it damn well should be.'[26]

Composite Resolution 29 similarly instructed the NEC and the PLP to
're-orientate the policy of the party towards the general Socialist perspective
of the Labour Movement', before diverging from this common ground to
advocate a programme 'to take real economic power by bringing into public
ownership the 280 monopolies, private banks, finance houses and insurance
companies, thus eliminating the power of the large private financial interests
represented by the Tories'. Don Hughes (Walton CLP) did not question
the sincerity of the parliamentary leadership upon taking office in 1964,
'but, you know, with 86 per cent of the economy in private hands and the
rest in public hands the 86 per cent of the economy will dominate. So far
from us controlling the economy, our leaders in 1964 and onwards were
controlled by the economy.' There was no practical alternative, he told

delegates, but for Labour to 'learn, re-learn and learn again the . . . need to stand on Clause IV of our Constitution'.[27]

Gay Walton (Coventry North CLP), seconding, criticised the parliamentary leadership for failing to keep the promises they had made before Labour won power:

> When in opposition the leadership of the Party said, 'When faced with an economic crisis we shall nationalise the banks and building societies,' but when in power and faced by an economic crisis they adopted orthodox and capitalistic methods to combat the crisis, and once again the ordinary people of this country were called upon to make the sacrifice, while the rich people suffered no hardship.[28]

The next Labour government, she warned, must avoid the fateful error of ignoring 'the wishes and voices of the constituencies and affiliated organisation from whom springs the support and strength of the Labour Party Movement'.[29]

Given the opportunity the parliamentary leadership would no doubt have dispatched both motions. The language of Composite Resolution 28 was moderate in tone but its reference to the Labour government's defiance of conference decisions did Wilson and his colleagues no favours. On its own the motion would have been considered hostile. Set against the extreme fantasy of Composite Resolution 29, however, it was a motion parliamentary leaders on the NEC could live with and eventually hope to contain.

Composite Resolution 29 was the product of co-ordinated factional activity at constituency level. Hughes admitted as much when he revealed that it had been composed by 12 CLPs. It was, quite unmistakably, *Tribune*'s motion, and the complement to Composite Resolution 16 in the debate on conference decisions moved by Chris Muir of Manchester, Exchange CLP, the constituency of the Tribunite MP Will Griffiths. It called on the parliamentary leadership, whether in government or opposition, 'to reflect the views and aspirations of the Labour and Trade Union Movement, by framing their policies on Annual Conference Decisions'. Significantly, no trade unionist spoke in support of Composite Resolution 29 in the debate. Hughes and his seconder aside, the motion drew the support only of Eric Brierley (Pudsey CLP) who contrived to support both motions on the grounds that 'a radical social policy, a fair and humane social policy, is not, will not and never has been a substitute for a Socialist policy'.[30]

For the PLP, Jack Ashley called for the party to stick to its principles and convert the public not by platitudes but by reasoned arguments, while Robert Sheldon counselled that 'Socialism in Britain is an expensive business . . . all the promises we make can never ring true until we explain how we are going to get the money to provide for it.' For the trade unions, Lord Cooper (general secretary of the National Union of General and Municipal Workers – NUGMW) told delegates that 'had there been unity between the Trade Union Movement and the Government on a wages policy I am certain we would not have been worried today about the Conservative Government'. Alf Allen (general secretary of the Union of Shop, Distributive and Allied Workers – USDAW), ignoring both motions, called upon the parliamentary leadership and trade union leaders 'to get together quickly…now – not in moments of crisis when we are in government but now – to deal with some of the problems which we believe we ought to be looking at'.[31] In Allen's words lay the seeds of the TUC–Labour Party Liaison Committee, a concept which would strengthen the position of the parliamentary leadership in its dealings with conference, if not with trade union leaders, by taking the formulation of economic policy away from the party.[32]

The NEC's acceptance of Composite Resolution 28, which received the unanimous support of conference, guaranteed only that the party would actively *discuss* policy in opposition, albeit on a grand scale. The NEC's own statement to conference, *Building a Socialist Britain*, equally said only that the party 'must work towards an extension of common ownership, and a better balance between the public and private sector of the economy',[33] a form of words which no one would dispute but which, given that the statement had passed across James Callaghan's desk at the Home Policy Committee before reaching delegates, unsurprisingly committed the NEC, or those members of the parliamentary leadership who were also members of the NEC, to very little.

Conference's rejection of Composite Resolution 29 by a margin of nearly three to one, suggests that *Tribune*'s vociferous summer campaign for a change of policy met with only limited success.[34] Despite conference's support for Composite Resolution 28, there is little evidence to suggest that the general election defeat directly empowered the Tribunite faction in the constituencies, at conference or at Westminster. At Blackpool the parliamentary leadership preserved its position by adopting a non-confrontational policy, hence the acceptance by the NEC of Composite Resolution 28, backward looking as it was. Composite Resolution 29, by contrast, was rejected by conference because the Labour Party in 1970 was simply less extreme than its compositors would have it be, and because no matter how many activists got up and made speeches at Blackpool, or wrote letters to *Tribune* demanding Clause IV socialism, trade union leaders on this occasion were unwilling to support them.

The sovereignty of conference decisions

With the TGWU and the AUEW having become detached from the parliamentary leadership, Jack Jones and Hugh Scanlon, with nearly 2 million conference votes between them, potentially held the balance of power at Blackpool. Yet both stopped short of blanket support for the activist left. As Minkin writes, 'in this period no more than in the past were the trade unions, including the one led by Hugh Scanlon, prepared to accept outside imposition of their own industrial policy. What they would not accept from the TUC they would certainly not accept from the Party Conference.'[35] Instead they used their combined vote selectively to defeat the platform on three card votes, the first of which came at the end of the debate on conference decisions,[36] and also came within 94,000 votes of reversing the party's support for British membership of the Common Market.[37]

In the debate on conference decisions, conference voted by a majority of 284,000 votes (out of the 5,886,000 cast) in favour of Composite Resolution 16,[38] which deplored 'the Parliamentary Labour Party's refusal to act on Conference decisions'. Moving the resolution, Chris Muir (Manchester Exchange CLP) gave 'four examples where the Labour Government injured our feelings by not sticking to Conference decisions'. These included 'the tragic reintroduction of prescription charges'; the deflationary economic measures and the 600,000 unemployed; the failure to dissociate the party 'with the fruitless, cruel American policy in Vietnam'; and the wage freeze policy and interference in the negotiating rights of the trade unions. 'If our leaders regard themselves as a privileged elite indulging in platform platitudes, flaunting our decisions', said Muir, 'they will lead us to destruction'.[39]

Seconding the motion, Ted Kelly (Portsmouth West CLP) told delegates that the Labour Party 'should have a meaning to the party activists . . . who, year in year out, are on the streets canvassing and touting for shillings and sixpences in order that their Constituency Party may function properly'. Apathy and frustration in the constituencies, he continued, was the product of 'the policies of the past government which were, in many cases, directly opposed to those democratically expressed by Party members through Conference'. Margaret McCarthy (Oxfordshire Federation), making the sole contribution from the floor in a short debate, stated that unless party members were given a greater say in the decision-making process of the party's policy 'we . . . might as well give up and invite all the pressure groups to come along and say what they want to say, because all we have become is one more pressure group'.[40] Asking no more than that the 'broad outlines' of policy be determined at conference, she questioned whether it was really so unreasonable for party members to ask why the Labour government had felt unable to implement conference decisions:

> I think that what we all resent most is, not that decisions have not been carried out, but that we have been treated with a cynicism in the rejection of conference decisions – which has illustrated to us

with the utmost clarity that all we are useful for is that, if a Trade Union we can cough up the money and, if a Constituency Party, we should get out on the doorsteps and canvass in order to put into power honest, sincere but elitist Members of Parliament who then demonstrate that they are not particularly interested in what we have to say to them.[41]

Commenting on speculation that the NEC intended to request that Composite Resolution 16 be remitted, McCarthy warned that this would be a mistake: 'if they ask this, we should politely say "we are sorry. This time we want it passed" and that we shall pass it'.[42]

The debate on conference decisions, short as it was, had taken place, said Harold Wilson replying for the National Executive, because the NEC had asked the Standing Orders Committee to provide the time for 'discussing the issues raised in this Resolution'.[43] This was a debate the parliamentary leadership, had it so chosen, could have avoided. The NEC received only eight resolutions on the subject of conference decisions and, when the Conference Arrangements Committee met on 26 August 1970 to determine the agenda for Blackpool, it was listed only as a second-priority subject for debate.[44] Wilson, however, believed the motion raised important constitutional issues, and took it upon himself to restate the constitutional position. The objectives of the parliamentary party, he reminded delegates, were 'to give effect, as may be practicable, to the principles from time to time approved by the Party Conference'. These words, he added, could be found in Clause IV of the party's constitution. A Prime Minister was 'responsible to the House of Commons, and acts on the basis of the Cabinet judgement of what is necessary in the public interest in so far and as long as he commands the confidence of the House of Commons, and he cannot be from day to day instructed by any authority from day to day other than by Parliament'.[45]

The constitutional position thus clarified, Wilson proceeded to describe as unimaginable, circumstances in which a Labour Prime Minister or a Labour government with a majority would not 'seek to act in accordance with the general policy, and indeed wishes, of this Movement'. He inevitably qualified these remarks by stating that 'timing and priorities must be a matter for the Government'. The NEC, he added, did not associate itself with 'the somewhat condemnatory tone . . . in which conference is asked to deplore the PLP's refusal to act on Conference decisions'.[46]

To applause and cheers, Composite Resolution 16 was carried by conference in defiance of the NEC by 3,085,000 votes to 2,801,000.[47] 'Mr Wilson fails to smother vote', wrote David Wood in The Times the following morning. 'The conference would not heed his appeal or his argument. In a petty way many delegates wanted to take vengeance on Mr Wilson, Labour ministers and the parliamentary party for a variety of sins that had to do with statutory incomes policy, prescription charges, and deflationary packages of 1966 and 1968.' Significantly, Wood added that Wilson and the PLP 'evidently did not take their defeat today seriously'.[48] That the debate and therefore the defeat could have been avoided indicates that Wilson accepted that losing the vote was the price of restating the constitutional position of a Labour Prime Minister. To have done so in the course of his leader's speech would have been to challenge conference head on, which was neither his political style, nor what the occasion called for. Instead, he simply reminded delegates of what the party's constitution actually said, a tactic he was to repeat at conference in 1973.

Wood interpreted the vote as a personal defeat for Wilson, but the Labour leader had made no concession to conference and had stood his ground without recourse to the confrontational tactics of his predecessor. However, as Wood wrote, the debate was rich in ironies. Wilson's defence of the constitutional rights of the parliamentary leadership raised eyebrows among the former Gaitskellites, who recalled his failure to support Hugh Gaitskell on the same issue a decade earlier. The constituency activists who had previously condemned the impact of the right-wing trade union block vote on the card vote at conference as an 'undemocratic sham and an abomination', now that they were bolstered by the 2 million votes at the disposal of Jones and Scanlon, declared the card vote a 'perfect instrument of democracy'.[49]

For Wood, the parallels with Gaitskell's defeat in 1960 were irresistible, but after nearly six years of Labour government the prospect of an emasculated parliamentary leadership was remote. The experience of the Labour government had further assimilated the party to the norms of parliamentary democracy whether party members admitted to it or not. The NEC's defeat in the card vote demonstrated the negative impact of an unaligned trade union vote at conference, and of this the Labour leader took note. It was a shot across the bows from Jones and Scanlon over incomes policy and trade union reform, but at this stage signified little more. Of far greater significance was the outcome of the vote on the party programme, which indicated that the two union leaders remained fully aware of with whom, eventually, a deal on economic policy would need to be agreed.

Building a Socialist Britain

Building a Socialist Britain, presented to conference by James Callaghan, was Labour's first policy statement since the general election. Its genesis lay in the 8 July 1970 decision of the Home Policy Committee that Terry Pitt should draft a statement 'outlining the tasks which the party should now undertake'.[50] The final text, agreed by the NEC on 25 September, apart from restating basic Labour beliefs such as 'society's problems must be solved by co-operation for the common good rather than an appeal to self-interest', offered little evidence of revised thinking as a result of the general election defeat. The sentence, 'There are some major issues to which we have still not found the solution', was not the coded admission of failure it appeared to be. Four years of enforced deflationary economic measures after 1966 led only to the statement that 'full employment, steady prices, a satisfactory balance of payments *and* substantial growth' remained 'the greatest challenge'. As these objectives were exactly those of the Conservative government, indeed of every post-war government, *Building a Socialist Britain* said nothing to suggest Labour would be more successful in office in future, or in what way policy would differ substantially from the period 1964–70. In this respect the NEC statement was a victory for the parliamentary leadership.

The reasons for the Labour government's defeat were given as, first, 'the tremendous difficulties we found in focusing public attention on the real issues in the campaign; second, the vastly superior financial backing which the Tory Party enjoyed; third, the widespread lack of under-standing of Labour's programme of achievement'. The unpopularity 'of some measures taken by the Labour Government', was listed fourth and last.[51]

In the context of the relationship between the parliamentary leadership and the wider party membership, the most significant section of *Building a Socialist Britain* was the last, 'The Party as an Instrument of the People'. When the Home Policy Committee met on 16 September to complete the final draft of the statement, the wording of this section was subject to an amendment – not accepted – couched in the language of *Tribune*, calling upon the parliamentary leadership to 'honour decisions by the annual del-egate conference, the supreme policy-making body of our party. This should apply whether Labour is in Government or opposition.'[52] Labour leaders were of course highly effective when it came to fending off amendments they regarded as hostile, and in doing so on this occasion they defended the autonomy of future Labour ministers. Yet at Blackpool they actively courted trade union leaders in hope of an agreement on economic policy.

The rejected amendment included a strategy for revitalising the party from the grass roots up, a strategy the Labour government had sought to discourage. 'In the commendable desire to educate the Labour party to the realities of power,' *The Economist* wrote, 'and to prove that Labour was a party of responsibility, Wilson and his colleagues crushed out protest rather than encouraged it'.[53] While the final text of the statement acknowledged the need to find 'ways of keeping open for the next Labour Government those necessary two-way lines of communication with our Party and our supporters, that are essential if our programme is to be evolved, accepted, understood and carried through', it did so only as the minimum cost of preserving the status quo.[54]

The Economist responded to the publication of *Building a Socialist Britain* by suggesting an alternative title: 'We don't know why Labour lost'.[55] As the NEC was promising to co-operate with the trade unions in seeking a solution to unemployment and rising prices, *The Economist* had a point. A more appropriate title might have been 'We won't admit why we lost'. Wilson, after all, was fully aware of the nature of Labour's problem. Prior to 1964 he and his colleagues had adhered to the interpretation of the party and the trade unions as an alliance confronting the imbalance in society and the economy. By 1969 he accepted that the most damaging imbalance in society was in fact that between the government and trade unions.[56] Having tried and failed to reform industrial relations in 1969, and having driven union leaders towards the camp of the Labour government's critics within the party as a consequence, there was little he could do in September 1970 but sign up to the NEC statement.

It was fortunate for the parliamentary leadership that it fell to Callaghan, as chairman of the Home Policy Committee, to present the NEC statement to conference. As the minister who had risked his parliamentary career to resist the Labour government's White Paper on industrial relations in 1969, he addressed delegates as a confirmed ally of the trade unions. None was more skilled than the former Home Secretary when it came to convincing delegates that they had heard what they wanted to hear, and accordingly *Building a Socialist Britain*, which contained no word of criticism of the Labour government, was commended to conference as a document which looked 'critically at the last six years'.[57]

The debate on legislation on trade unions: Barbara Castle in the stocks

Moving Composite Resolution 22 on behalf of the Transport and General Workers' Union, Jack Jones opened the debate on legislation on trade unions by inviting conference to express 'its total opposition to restrictions on collective bargaining and the policy the Conservative Government proposes for the reform of industrial relations which is designed to interfere with the internal affairs of trade unions'.[58] This was by way of a response not only to Edward Heath's declared intention to reform the trade unions, but also to Barbara Castle's eve-of-conference call for a new agreement on incomes policy. Writing in *New Statesman* on 25 September, Castle had argued that 'the greatest act of folly which the Labour movement could commit would be to sweep the whole question under the carpet and coast back to victory on the inadequacies of the Tory Government having failed to argue out and resolve this central contradiction in our own ranks'.[59] Castle's timing could not have been worse. The debate on legislation on trade unions, which served no apparent purpose other than to facilitate 'an orgy of trade union oratory'[60] consequently became also a debate on incomes policy, pre-empting the debate on economic policy due to take place three days later.

In her article Castle stated that she had no intention of proclaiming *mea non culpa* about any of the policies for which she had been ministerially responsible, adding that she did not intend to enter this plea about prices and incomes policy. She knew, she wrote, 'none better – the imperfections of the policy as we operated it. But that does not condemn the policy.' Its abandonment had not brought much comfort to the underprivileged: 'The gap between him and his more powerful brethren is widening steadily.'[61] In a cogently argued analysis she anticipated the hostility she would encounter at Blackpool:

> I have always been a supporter of a prices and incomes policy because I believe it leads us to the heart of a socialist society. Its opponents argue that the socialist society must come first. But then they are left with the dilemma of showing what they *mean* by a socialist society and a catch-as-catch-can scramble for wage increases, in which the biggest share goes to the most powerful, is hardly the best demonstration of the principle. No doubt we have to turn a Labour government into a socialist one. But we can't do that unless the trade union movement is socialist too.[62]

Castle highlighted both the conservatism of the trade unions and the consequences of their refusal to co-operate with the Labour government. 'All that the destruction of a prices and incomes policy has achieved is that price increases now overtake wage increases with a new rapidity. Industrial militancy will become self-defeating unless we make it into a power-house of political change.'[63]

Castle's article followed the publication of Thomas Balogh's Fabian Tract *Labour and Inflation*, which in similar fashion advocated a return to incomes policy, and likewise succeeded in alienating Jack Jones. Balogh, who served as economic adviser to the Cabinet 1964–68, had long argued that a planned economy must entail the planning of incomes,[64] and in an earlier Fabian Tract had written that what was required from both unions and employers was 'a due regard for the requirements of the general economic position'.[65] But in the aftermath of Labour's defeat it was the unions he accused of smashing 'the most helpful social experiment of our time' through their refusal to co-operate with the Labour government after 1968:

> The consistently far higher level of employment that has been achieved since the war in *all* countries has wrought a similar change in the power balance between employers and trade unions in favour of the latter. The achievement has been by far the most outstanding social gain made since before the war. It completely

changed the relationship between the 'bosses' and the workers banded in unions.[66]

Jones, needless to say, arrived at the rostrum ready to rebut both Balogh and Castle, and no doubt Anthony Crosland too, who had written in *The Times*, the day after Castle's *New Statesman* article had appeared, that the corollary of increased growth was an incomes policy.[67] The trade union movement, Jones told conference, was being 'assailed and attacked . . . by pampered, academic people . . . the whole lot of whom, for the most part, have never been covered by a wage claim because, frankly, they have never worked for a living: Let them go down and work in the mines, or work in the racket and tension of a machine shop or try to keep pace with a fast-moving assembly line. Let them work in a dank, dirty hold of a ship, sweating one minute and shivering the next, with rats and insects lurking about, and then say their wage claims are irresponsible.'[68]

Jones appealed to conference to support the TGWU motion[69] and 'fight to keep the unions free as the shield and defenders of workers everywhere'.[70] What Tony Benn in his diary described as a tremendous speech about the class war,[71] was equally an attack by the labour movement's industrial elite upon the political elite, Benn included, a point reinforced by Dick Seabrook's (president, USDAW) loaded remark in support of the motion doubting 'if anybody in this conference could possibly oppose it'.[72]

'To the visible delight of the acting chairman, Mr Ian Mikardo,' *The Economist* reported, 'a succession of heated left-wingers followed Mr Jones to declare they would have nothing to do with an incomes policy or a Tory Government, in that order.'[73] John Forrester of the Draughtsmen's and Allied Technical Association (DATA) seconded the motion, informing the parliamentary leadership that they could expect no co-operation on incomes policy 'until such a time as it has the power to exercise control over all other facets of economic activity', an indication of the extent to which former ministers were expected to redefine their concept of socialism in opposition. Hugh Scanlon, for his part, would talk about a socialist incomes policy 'when we own the means of production, distribution and exchange',[74] an attitude which found an echo in the constituencies. 'If we want an incomes policy,' said Keith Morrell (Labour's candidate for the St Marylebone by-election caused by Quentin Hogg's elevation to the peerage)[75] 'it has to be a truly Socialist policy and not a policy to afflict the working people in this country'.[76] Morrell's politics proved more popular with delegates at Blackpool than with voters in St Marylebone.[77]

Taking his cue from Jack Jones, Sam McCluskie directed his words at 'individuals within this party, and if the cap fits let them wear it, and I would head it, "To those whom it may concern", that the National Union of Seamen will have no part of penal sanctions from any section of the working class movement'.[78] Castle, of course, had made no mention of

In Place of Strife in her *New Statesman* article, or of resurrecting the penal sanctions included in that particular White Paper, but her crime in 1970 was to have mentioned it at all in 1969, a date trade unionists were evidently in no hurry to progress beyond. Castle, *The Economist* observed, sat 'philosophically on the platform, as if in the stocks' as first Stan Orme, on this occasion the harshest of her parliamentary colleagues, and then Danny McGarvey, 'the stentorian boilermaker', condemned her to purgatory.[79]

Parliament during the previous four or five years, said Orme, had resembled an industrial seminar: 'Everybody, of course, that took part in it had not necessarily worked in industry, but they had a lot to say about it.' If Castle was to be credible in the House of Commons, 'it will be farewell to past policies'. There could be no resurrection of the Labour Industrial Relations Bill Mark I or incomes policy, 'as the Movement will have none of it'. McGarvey, coming 'to what Stan Orme says', warned Castle she would be stabbing the unions in the back if she did not admit she had been wrong in the past: 'By making one dramatic statement as shadow minister in the House all the struggles that lie ahead and some of the bad blood created during the arguments on *In Place of Strife* will disappear, and the trade unions will find they have a converted friend in whom they can put their trust.'[80] 'The Labour party without the discipline of office is no place for the squeamish or politically sensitive', noted *The Economist*.[81]

Castle replied to the debate unbowed by the criticism. Orme's instruction to her to forget all her former policies was greeted with disbelief: 'All of them Stan? The 90 per cent of the Industrial Relations Bill, which was the biggest charter for trade unionism in this country's history, do you want me to forget that?' To applause, she told him she would not. Quoting from the NEC statement *Building a Socialist Britain*, she committed the parliamentary leadership to working out 'in co-operation with the Trade Union Movement...the conditions within which...conflicting aims can be reconciled'. Admitting that the Labour government carried 'the lion's share of the responsibility for the political revulsion we all experienced against the very concept of a prices and incomes policy', she stressed that if such a policy were to be acceptable in the future, the co-operation of the shop-floor worker would have to be earned.[82]

Had Castle spoken prior to Jack Jones, the debate might have found its appropriate focus, the Conservative government's intended Industrial Relations Bill, the purpose of which, Castle and McGarvey agreed, was 'to blame the responsibility for the inflation which the Government has no idea how to cure on what it calls the irresponsibility of the trade unions'. It had always been her intention to widen the debate beyond incomes policy and her *New Statesman* article was a component of that strategy. She too wished to see the transformation of society, but by somewhat less uncompromising means than those demanded by Hugh Scanlon. Trade unions, she believed, were obliged to accept responsibilities towards society, 'but only if other people accept them, too',[83] as Balogh had written in 1963.

In place of an incomes policy

Such was the depth of trade union hostility to incomes policy that, even before Roy Jenkins had uttered a word on the subject for the NEC, Jack Jones had expressed the hope that during the debate on economic policy 'the platform will not find it necessary to waste the time of conference, leaving the debate entirely to the floor'. When Penny Corfield (Battersea North CLP) moved Composite Resolution 19, which acknowledged 'the lead of the Labour Government in emphasising the need for an incomes policy', and actually proposed no more than that conference consider 'the efficacy of a legally-fixed minimum wage as the basis of an incomes policy', she confessed to finding it 'a bit intimidating to come to the rostrum to move a Resolution which has already been condemned out of hand...by a leading trade unionist in another debate'.[84] It came as no surprise that the trade unions had used the debate on legislation on trade unions to run through their own agenda irrespective of the timetable finalised by the Conference Arrangements Committee. To have expected them to speak on trade union issues on the Monday of conference without mentioning incomes policy until Thursday was simply unrealistic.

Because he had made his views on incomes policy clear earlier in the week, Hugh Scanlon could not understand why the platform had accepted Composite Resolution 19, or why it had not been withdrawn. 'It is incomprehensible to us that after all the blood-letting, after all the confrontation of 1968 and 1969, after Monday's debate, this issue is going to be reopened.' Corfield, moving the resolution, pointed out that she and her co-compositors were 'not just constituency members, but we are trade unionists, too', and that 'we must go forward together or not at all'. Repeatedly she attempted to allay trade union suspicions that the resolution was intended 'to give the kiss of life to the corpse of wage restraint'.[85] There was nothing in the resolution, she told conference, to suggest this:

> We believe that the only basis for an effective policy on incomes is through co-operation with the unions and the TUC. The Trade Union Movement have themselves already recognised the need for such a policy in their economic reviews of 1969 and 1970. This must surely be the starting point for a dialogue between the unions and the Party. Such an approach in no way implies Government intervention – either direct or indirect – in the process of collective bargaining. Nor is there anything in the Resolution to imply this.[86]

However, Jones and Scanlon were determined to resist any discussion of the policy and it was therefore simply a matter of how the votes added up. 'Whatever else is in this Motion,' said Harry Urwin (deputy general secretary, TGWU) 'it quite clearly postulates the desirability of an incomes policy. If the Motion is carried it will create such deep divisions in our Movement that the possibility of Labour forming another Government will be seriously prejudiced.'[87]

Rejection of Composite Resolution 19, albeit by a narrow margin,[88] left the Labour Party without a credible economic policy. As a result, the debate on economic policy was simply an extension of the debate on the party programme, with yet further calls for Clause IV socialism. Seconding Resolution 74, which called for the planned growth of wages, Bernard Donaghy (Widnes CLP) echoed the sentiments expressed by Don Hughes in the earlier debate, in instructing the party 'to learn once and for all, the lesson that previous Labour Governments have failed to learn, that political power without full economic control dooms every Labour Government to failure'. Delegates responded to Donaghy's rhetoric, and to John Forrester's provocative assertion that 'for the past 22 years this Party has run away from Clause IV',[89] by defying the platform for a third time to support Composite Resolution 11, stating conference's 'fundamental opposition to mergers motivated by maximisation of profits'.[90]

Replying to the debate, Roy Jenkins defended the NEC's acceptance of Composite Resolution 19 in a powerful speech which sought to shame those opposed to it. 'It is, of course, unusual for a Constituency Party Resolution which the Executive is willing to accept and which asks it to work out a Socialist policy involving the consideration of such radical measures as a minimum wage and the redistribution of wealth to be opposed from the floor in Conference.' Support for the resolution, he pointed out, 'would involve no commitment other than to talk together and try to work out better solutions for the future'.[91] Jenkins was repeatedly applauded as he spoke, but acknowledged the likelihood of defeat:

> ...this may not be the year when some unions feel able to give their full attention to a new deal for the relationship of incomes to our economic problems. Okay. We can take a little longer. But, whether this year or next, we shall have to come back to this, because, you know, there is no real future for this Movement in a complete free-for-all. This is not the way to get the more rapid and sustained growth we all want. It is not the way to keep our exports competitive. I very much doubt if it is the best way to increase real wages, and it is certainly not the way to deal with the problems of the lower paid.[92]

'The uneasy unity between the political and industrial wings of the Labour movement is a sham and a charade,' wrote Alan Watkins in *New Statesman* upon his return from Blackpool, 'and there is not the slightest point in pretending otherwise. The sham can be presented, the sham kept up, because three questions are involved which can easily be confused. There is, first, government resistance to pay claims outside the context of an incomes policy; second, an incomes policy; and, third, trade union reform. The first two questions, though separate, have a close affinity. The third raises different principles and has to be taken separately. Yet resistance to pay claims and union reforms were, in typical conference style, lumped together. As a meaningful contribution to party policy, the debate was killed before it started.'[93]

Prior to conference Norman Atkinson had called on Harold Wilson to re-establish his credentials as a socialist,[94] and at Blackpool the former Prime Minister duly obliged. Wilson never appeared more happy to be a socialist than when the Labour Party was in opposition. In contrast to the general election campaign, during which the word socialist had appeared in his speeches only once,[95] at Blackpool, as Alan Watkins observed, it made 'a reappearance in the Wilsonian vocabulary', featuring ten times in the course of his leader's speech, 'for what that may be worth'.[96] The answer, of course, was not much.

Notes

1 P. Jenkins, 'The wizard of was', *The Guardian*, 20 June 1970, p. 15.
2 B. Castle, *The Castle Diaries 1964–1976* (London, Papermac, 1990), p. 407.
3 P. Jenkins, 'Roy muffed it', *The Guardian*, 25 June 1970, p. 13.
4 Editorial, 'What future for Labour?', *The Guardian*, 20 June 1970, p. 10.
5 A. Watkins, 'Why were we all so wrong?', *New Statesman*, 26 June 1970, p. 3.
6 P. Johnson, 'London Diary', *New Statesman*, 26 June 1970, p. 7.
7 Editorial, 'Labour after defeat', *New Statesman*, 10 July 1970, p. 2.
8 Editorial, 'Not without comfort', *Socialist Commentary*, July 1970, p. 1.
9 R. Hattersley, 'Could Labour have won?', *New Statesman*, 31 July 1970, pp. 10–11.
10 E. Heffer, 'Could Labour have won?', *New Statesman*, 31 July 1970, pp. 10–11.
11 'Letters to the Editor', *New Statesman*, 26 June 1970, p. 7
12 'Letters to the Editor', *New Statesman*, 26 June 1970, p. 7
13 *Tribune*, 26 June 1970, p. 1.
14 *Tribune*, 17 April 1970, p. 1.
15 *Tribune*, 26 June 1970, p. 1.
16 *Tribune*, 26 June 1970, p. 1.
17 *Tribune*, 26 June 1970, p. 7.
18 *Tribune*, 26 June 1970, p. 7.
19 F. Allaun, 'NOW A REAL LABOUR PARTY CONFERENCE', *Tribune*, 10 July 1970, p. 1.
20 The NEC received 40 resolutions on the party programme and eight on conference decisions. Manchester, Labour Party Archive (LPA), Third Meeting of

the Conference Arrangements Committee, 26 August 1970; National Executive Committee (NEC), Minutes, 25 September 1970.

21 'Wilson challenged by left-wing MP', *The Times*, 3 September 1970, p. 2.

22 'New Labour policy urged', *The Times*, 18 September 1970, p. 2.

23 G. Clark, 'Left-wing MPs accuse Mr Wilson of betraying Socialism', *The Times*, 28 September 1970, p. 2.

24 S. Williams, 'Politics is about people', *The Times*, 26 September 1970, p. 18.

25 LPAR, 1970, pp. 167–8.

26 LPAR, 1970, p. 169.

27 LPAR, 1970, pp. 170–1.

28 LPAR, 1970, p. 171.

29 LPAR, 1970, p. 171.

30 LPAR, 1970, pp. 171–80.

31 LPAR, 1970, pp. 172–5.

32 The TUC–Labour Party Liaison Committee met for the first time on 21 February 1972.

33 NEC, *Building a Socialist Britain*, LPAR, 1970, p. 326.

34 Composite Resolution 29. For the resolution, 1,693,000; against, 4,269,000. LPAR, 1970, p. 180.

35 L. Minkin, *The Labour Party Conference* (Manchester, Manchester University Press, 1980), p. 331.

36 In addition to the defeat on conference decisions, the platform was defeated on the issues of incomes policy (Composite Resolution 16: for, 2,851,000; against, 3,139,000) and company mergers (Composite Resolution 11: for, 3,688,000; against, 2,316,000). LPAR, 1970, p. 229.

37 LPAR, 1970, p. 174.

38 For the resolution, 3,085,000; against, 2,801,000. LPAR, 1970, p. 185.

39 LPAR, 1970, p. 180.

40 LPAR, 1970, p. 182.

41 LPAR, 1970, p. 183.

42 LPAR, 1970, p. 183.

43 LPAR, 1970, p. 183.

44 LPA, Conference Arrangements Committee, Minutes, 26 August 1970; NEC, Minutes, 25 September 1970.

45 LPAR, 1970, pp. 183–4.

46 LPAR, 1970, p. 184.

47 LPAR, 1970, p. 185.

48 D. Wood, 'Mr Wilson fails to smother vote', *The Times*, 1 October 1970, p. 1.

49 Wood, 'Mr Wilson fails'.

50 LPA, Home Policy Committee (HPC), Minutes, 8 July 1970; NEC, Minutes, 22 July 1970.

51 NEC, *Building a Socialist Britain*, LPAR, 1970, pp. 324–6.

52 RD.10/September 1970, 'Addition Note to RD.6 (Revised)', LPA, HPC, Minutes, 16 September 1970; NEC, Minutes, 25 September 1970.

53 *The Economist*, 'Protest and respectability', 26 September 1970, pp. 13–14.

54 NEC, *Building a Socialist Britain*, LPAR, 1970, p. 326.

55 *The Economist*, 'We don't know why Labour lost: part 1', 5 September 1970, p. 21.

56 W. Beckerman (ed.), *The Labour Government's Economic Record 1964–70* (London, Duckworth, 1972), p. 74.

57 LPAR, 1970, p. 163.

58 LPAR, 1970, p. 112.

59 B. Castle, 'A socialist incomes policy', *New Statesman*, 25 September 1970, pp. 4–5.

60 A. Watkins, 'Spotlight on politics: fissures on the rock', *New Statesman*, 2 October 1970, p. 3.
61 Castle, 'A socialist incomes policy'.
62 Castle, 'A socialist incomes policy'.
63 Castle, 'A socialist incomes policy'.
64 Foote, *The Labour Party's Political Thought*, p. 238.
65 T. Balogh, *Planning for Progress*, Fabian Tract 346 (London, 1963), p. 15, in Foote, *The Labour Party's Political Thought*, p. 238.
66 T. Balogh, 'Consensus: the alternative to deflation', *New Statesman*, 11 December 1970, p. 5.
67 A. Crosland, 'Social objectives for the 1970s', *The Times*, 26 September 1970, p. 10.
68 LPAR, 1970, p. 113.
69 Composite Resolution 22 had in fact been accepted by the NEC.
70 LPAR, 1970, p. 114.
71 T. Benn, *Office Without Power: Diaries 1968–72* (London, Hutchinson, 1988), 28 September 1970, p. 306.
72 LPAR, 1970, p. 118.
73 *The Economist*, 'Lord Balogh mentions the unmentionable – and Jack Jones erupts', 3 October 1970, p. 21.
74 LPAR, 1970, pp. 114–21.
75 Quentin Hogg, Conservative MP, St Marylebone 1963–70.
76 LPAR, 1970, p. 116.
77 The St Marylebone by-election was held on 22 October 1970. Morrell received 4,542 votes out of a total of 16,828 votes cast. The Conservative Party held the seat, its candidate securing 10,684 votes. LPAR, 1971, p. 21.
78 LPAR, 1970, p. 115.
79 *The Economist*, 'Lord Balogh mentions the unmentionable'.
80 LPAR, 1970, pp. 119–23.
81 *The Economist*, 'Her Majesty's Opposition', 3 October 1970, pp. 15–16.
82 LPAR, 1970, p. 126.
83 LPAR, 1970, pp. 124–6.
84 LPAR, 1970, pp. 176, 214–15.
85 LPAR, 1970, pp. 215–22.
86 LPAR, 1970, p. 215.
87 LPAR, 1970, p. 224.
88 For the resolution, 2,851,000; against, 3,139,000. LPAR, 1970, p. 229.
89 LPAR, 1970, pp. 213–21.
90 For the resolution, 3,688,000; against, 2,316,000. LPAR, 1970, p. 229.
91 LPAR, 1970, p. 226.
92 LPAR, 1970, p. 226.
93 Watkins, 'Spotlight on politics'.
94 *The Times*, 'Wilson challenged by left-wing MP', 3 September 1970, p. 2.
95 D. Butler and M. Pinto-Duschinsky, *The British General Election of 1970* (London, Macmillan, 1971), p. 2, n. 1.
96 Watkins, 'Spotlight on politics'.

2

LABOUR'S RESPONSE
TO DEFEAT (II): THE
PARLIAMENTARY LEADERSHIP
IN OPPOSITION,
JUNE 1970–JUNE 1971

On 19 June 1971, *The Times* marked the first anniversary of Labour's defeat with a profile of Harold Wilson, 'One year after'. Christopher Walker, having spent 'seven days in the footsteps of the Leader of the Opposition', found Wilson 'facing what is probably the most tricky issue of party management to have confronted him since he took over from Gaitskell in 1963: the Common Market', yet content to have 'proved wrong' those commentators who had predicted he would retire from the political fray and return to academia. One year after the loss of office he had recovered 'the bounce and panache' that had momentarily eluded him in the shock of defeat. Walker witnessed a rejuvenated former Prime Minister fulfilling his new role with ease, performing an array of duties including opening a toll bridge in Doncaster and watching a display of traditional dancing by the Britannia Coconutters at a Labour Gala in Rawtenstall.[1]

On 29 June 1970, 11 days after the general election, Harold Wilson was unanimously re-elected Leader of the Labour Party. Nine days later Roy Jenkins defeated Fred Peart and Michael Foot in the ballot for the deputy leadership. In between, Bob Mellish, the Chief Whip, was re-elected unopposed. 'No more disparate triumvirate has ever formally headed any British political party', *The Economist* commented.[2] In the ballot for the Parliamentary Committee (Shadow Cabinet) on 16 July 1970, nine of the 12 MPs elected were members of the previous Cabinet.[3] Thus, within four weeks of the party's defeat, the key positions in the Parliamentary Labour Party (PLP) hierarchy were filled. The Queen's Speech of 2 July 1970 dictated that the party leader be in place to reply to the address in the House of Commons on that day, but there was no provision for Wilson's re-election which occurred before the PLP had the opportunity to discuss either the general election result or a strategy for opposition.[4]

Within 24 hours of Roy Jenkins's election as deputy leader, Will Griffiths, chairman of the Tribune Group, requested an on-the-record statement from Wilson on which would be the ultimate authority in opposition at Westminster, the Shadow Cabinet or the PLP meeting. Wilson replied that 'as always the Party meeting was the ultimate authority'. However, when pressed by Norman Atkinson over what procedures had been adopted to appoint frontbench spokesmen, he was less accommodating: 'this was for the Parliamentary Committee to consider. By tradition, once that Committee was elected it was the duty of the Leader of the Party in consultation with the Officers, to nominate spokesmen.'[5] As the standing orders of the PLP made no provision for an interim Management Committee to carry on until the new Parliamentary Committee was elected, an Interim Steering Committee was selected by Wilson.[6]

These exchanges took place on the eve of publication of an interview with the Labour leader in *The People* on 10 July. Opposition, Wilson told Terence Lancaster, would allow 'time for reflection and thinking and democratic discussion within the Party', adding there would be 'no lurches of policy from what we did in Government'.[7] This gave rise to suspicion among backbench MPs, notably those associated with the Tribune Group, that the parliamentary leadership intended to restrict debate in the PLP. The Tribune Group contested both the deputy leadership and the Shadow Cabinet elections without success,[8] and it fell to Richard Clements, in a *Tribune* editorial of 10 July, to warn the leadership that events since the general election defeat had endangered rather than cemented the unity of the party: 'No one should be in any doubt that Mr Jenkins's narrow majority over the total votes cast for Michael Foot and Fred Peart do not give him, or the party leadership, a mandate to carry on the same old policies which led to electoral defeat.'[9]

To suggest the newly elected parliamentary leadership lacked a mandate was nonsense. Wilson and Jenkins were popular choices, the latter having comfortably outdistanced Foot and Peart on the first and only ballot necessary to determine who was to succeed George Brown.[10] Clements, on this occasion a non-parliamentary spokesman for the parliamentary left, effectively challenged the right of the parliamentary leadership to influence the policies of the party on the grounds that Jenkins was unrepresentative of his newspaper's readership: 'Because of his election as deputy leader, Roy Jenkins, will now be a member of a body to which he has never before gained election from annual party conference; ... his political and economic philosophy has been consistently rejected by the rank and file party members in their voting for the NEC'.[11] Jenkins, however, owed his position in the party in 1970 to his effectiveness as a minister since 1965, and was highly regarded by many of his fellow MPs. His emphatic victory in the ballot for the deputy leadership followed 24 hours after his demolition of Iain Macleod during the debate on the economic section of the Queen's Speech on 7 July 1970.[12] To deny the legitimacy of his political philosophy simply exposed the concern of a relatively small number of backbench MPs who, because of the overwhelmingly moderate composition of the PLP, doubted the suitability of the party meeting at Westminster as a forum in which to impress upon the parliamentary leadership the need for greater accountability when the party next formed a government. Michael Foot's election to the Shadow Cabinet was one way of ensuring this concern was not ignored, but not all of Foot's new colleagues were inclined to take him seriously: '... a few of the old lags from the previous Cabinet greeted me with leers on their faces or a lick round the lips, both gestures suggesting that I was in for some trouble'.[13]

The ex-Cabinet in opposition

The Shadow Cabinet met for the first time in opposition on 16 July 1970, and the experience was a huge culture shock for Foot: 'The whole discussion proceeded in a most disorderly manner, much less formal... than meetings of the Tribune Group. One had to elbow one's way into the discussion.' As an outsider he was appalled to observe the frivolity of the occasion, with the discussion 'at moments slightly raucous or comic'. Wilson 'seemed to carry little authority'. Callaghan was 'obdurate and not very forthcoming' and 'reminded me of nothing so much as the Herbert Morrison I had seen in the old days of the National Executive, who would never admit defeat. Voted down on one proposition, he would always come back with an alternative which was designed to restore the original claim he wanted.' Jenkins 'seemed dour and not very versatile'; Barbara Castle, 'to her credit, was chirpy and provocative'. Denis Healey was 'blunt and common-sensical'; Crosland, 'superciliously amused', viewing 'the whole scene with a more agreeably satirical air than the others'. Membership of the Shadow Cabinet, he concluded, 'will take years off my life and theirs'.[14]

One reason Foot was in the Shadow Cabinet was to challenge the ex-Cabinet over the increase in the level of unemployment under the Labour government. This was not so easily achieved given that Wilson was convinced he had been denied a third consecutive election victory because of Conservative 'trickery' and was not inclined to consider alternative explanations unnecessarily. His interpretation of the reason for Labour's defeat sustained as the agreed position of the Shadow Cabinet well into opposition.[15] Nor was the newly elected deputy leader interested in an inquest. Jenkins regarded the outcome of the election as 'good both for the political health of the country and for the balance of politicians' lives'.[16] Yet by the time the Labour government devalued the pound in November 1967, there were already nearly 600,000 unemployed.[17] The 1970 general election was the first occasion in the party's history when it had fought an election without a commitment to full employment. Foot wanted to know how soon the parliamentary leadership would restore the commitment. There was, he observed, 'some resentment about this question being raised at all'.[18]

When confronted by Foot over the fact that they had overseen a massive rise in the number of unemployed, and had left office not knowing 'whether the figure was going up further', Shadow Cabinet members responded by agreeing it would be better to deal with the matter on another occasion, subject to the Shadow Chancellor preparing a full report. Discussion was initially thus stifled. 'Much the best remark of the whole meeting', Foot wrote, 'was made by Douglas Houghton, who said that the assembled reminded him of a Government in Exile. The ex-Ministers seemed to be chiefly concerned about how their Departments were proceeding – or getting on without them. He thought this was an inadequate basis for a future policy.'[19]

The future policies of the party

The PLP met to discuss the future policies of the party on 15 July 1970. The tone of this meeting, one month on from the general election defeat, contrasted sharply with the 29 June meeting which saw Wilson re-elected leader. On that occasion, according to Leo Abse, MPs had 'huddled together like a pack of hypnotized rabbits, silent, utterly immobilized and submissive... unable to adjust to the fact that the listening opposition leader no longer could bind them by patronage and magic'.[20] The 15 July meeting was held in response to a letter sent to Wilson by John Mendelson, vice-chairman of the Tribune Group, requesting that the PLP be given the opportunity to 'consider the policies of the Party'.[21] While some MPs chose to explain the election defeat in terms of the need to overhaul the party's organisation in the belief that this alone 'could win back 30 or 40 seats',[22] others pointed to the need to settle the conflicting interpretations of the party's ideology. This latter group of MPs did not share a common analysis, but accepted that the Labour government's way of running the country had been rejected.

Mendelson believed that economic policy was the issue before the meeting. Incomes policy had failed and the Labour government had been unable to finance the party's social objectives by means other than wage restraint, which alienated its trade union partners, or penal rates of direct taxation, which alienated voters. Robert Sheldon followed Mendelson and insisted growth must take priority over both sterling and the balance of payments. He was supported by Douglas Jay, who advocated the adoption of a system of flexible exchange rates.[23] Labour had arrived at a similar conclusion when it had last been in opposition, and Sheldon did no more than echo the bravado of both Jenkins and Callaghan prior to taking office in 1964.

In 1961 Jenkins had declared that Labour 'should be prepared to go through a period of weak balance of payments...a period of losing reserves if necessary, in order to get over the hump of stepping up our rate of growth'.[24] Callaghan, one year later, had stated that if faced with a choice between 'stagnation here and a firm balance of payments', or 'growth and...the difficulties that would arise in the balance of payments... I would choose the second'.[25] That Labour was discussing this again in 1970 illustrates how little economic theory the party had to fall back on, a decade on from Jenkins's remarks, and after six years in government.

Only John Mackintosh appeared willing to consider a post-socialist economic solution for Labour. A thoroughly realistic scrutiny of policy, he warned, would be 'a harsh, unpleasant task', but there was, he believed, little choice but to take a decision on incomes policy, on a Tory Industrial Relations Bill and on the provision of social services in a low-growth society: 'We must think out the kind of society we want, and how we were to achieve it; there were no easy answers, and we should be prepared to tell our people this.' Callaghan replied to the debate on behalf of the leadership without any reference to ideology or economic policy. It was not that the former Home Secretary had not heard what had been said, simply that the party 'had now to apply ourselves to the task of winning the General election'.[26] This was the occasion, write Kellner and Hitchens, when Callaghan 'struck his unity note for the first time'.[27] He lost no time in describing the discussion as 'extremely valuable' and indicated that it would continue, which it did not.[28] Opposition, he informed his colleagues, presented the party with an organisational challenge. Excellent policies would of course be needed, but 'a revitalising and modernisation of organisation could ensure against defeat in 1975'. This interpretation of the party's requirements when voiced by William Price earlier in the meeting was challenged by Foot, who stated that organisation was 'a question of morale', and that 'criticisms must be voiced'. His comments were perhaps unconsciously valedictory: within 24 hours of this meeting he was in the Shadow Cabinet. Labour, he continued, had been defeated at a time 'when [the] Tory leadership had never been more ineffectual and weak. In spite of this weakness we had had a lower poll than in 1950 or 1951. Unemployment had been disgracefully high under the last Administration – would we fight the next Election on a commitment to full employment? How was it to be done credibly? Not on the policies of the last six years.'[29]

Callaghan avoided responding to these or any other comments which risked widening the debate. His inclusive approach to opposition was intended to soothe grievances in all sections of the party. Transport House – snubbed during the general election[30] – would be 'the power house' behind Labour's campaign to regain power. The NEC (ignored by the Labour government), taking instruction from conference (also ignored), would rightfully determine party policy, and might – Callaghan helpfully suggested – even wish to draw on the expertise of MPs in doing so. As early as one month after the general election defeat, Callaghan had a clear strategy for the Labour Party in opposition. He was determined that each section of the party would be equally responsible for the policies of a future Labour government: 'There had not been sufficient communication in the past between those doing the job and those who criticised. We should try to overcome this.'[31]

'No hard words as Labour face election lessons', wrote the political editor of *The Times* the following day. 'Mr Callaghan fulfilled expectation by taking the role of the link man between the disconnected centres of party power: the late Cabinet, the Parliamentary Committee (or Shadow Cabinet), the National Executive Committee, and the trade unions.' Callaghan, the report continued, found it gratifying 'that in more than two hours of PLP discussion there had been no criticism either of the leadership or of the timing of the election.'[32] Foot's contribution to the discussion was omitted from the report.

In an article for *New Statesman* in August 1970, Callaghan wrote that the two vital lessons to be learnt from the election defeat were, first, the need for a much better organisation in the constituencies and a much bigger yearly income at Transport House and, second, that a way had to be found 'to stir Labour voters into action by "engaging their beliefs, enthusiasm and interest"'.[33] How the latter was to be achieved was left unsaid. Wilson, however, in an interview for the BBC's 'World Tonight' programme broadcast on 27 August, once again firmly ruled out any discussion of the reasons for the election defeat, stating 'there is no post-mortem when there is no body'. Plainly, the only explanation of events he would accept was his own: 'Against the Labour Party at election time were the scars of things we did to get the economy right. So much was made of rising prices and it is inevitable that the Government in power gets the blame.'[34]

Crosland: objectives for the 1970s

In September, on the eve of conference, Anthony Crosland published his early thoughts on Labour's objectives for the decade ahead. In the first of two articles for *The Times* which appeared consecutively on 25 and 26 September 1970, entitled 'Social objectives for the 1970s', he called on the party to stand on its principles in opposition. His starting point was a tentative one, 'since it is too soon fully to appraise the lessons of the last six years', but he identified four basic objectives for which Labour stood and which distinguished it from the Conservatives. First, Labour's traditional social welfare goal – the relief of poverty, distress and social squalor – would continue to be 'an exceptionally high priority, when considering the claims on our resources'. Second, there would be a more equal distribution of wealth, 'to help create a more just and humane society'. Third, this would ensure the less well-off had access 'to housing, health and education of a standard comparable, at least in basic decencies, to that which the better off can buy for themselves out of their private means'. And fourth, in what was 'not of course an exhaustive list', there would be strict social control over the environment, 'to lessen the growing divergence between private and social costs in such fields as noise, fumes, water pollution and the rest', from which the rich could buy protection. He argued that what the party needed at conference was 'not some great shift of direction, but a reaffirmation of these agreed social democratic ideals'.[35]

Crosland admitted there was little that was painful about this prescription for the party and added 'it would be nice to end this article here'. He acknowledged the central difficulty facing Labour in the second half of 1970 was that the pursuit of these agreed ideals had policy implications 'which are not merely an anathema to all active Conservatives, but go counter to the current majority mood of the country'. This included the role of the state, levels of public expenditure and the degree of social control and collective responsibility. But it would be a mistake, he concluded, 'to think that public attitudes cannot be influenced by democratic leadership. The party must take a stand on principle and propagate that stand vigorously and incessantly over the next four years. For were we to accept these attitudes and defer to them, our statement of objectives would be so much pious froth.' He ended with a robust defence of the record of the Labour government: 'The problem with financing high public expenditure is one of the most complex facing civilised societies; and the gap between myth and reality makes it worse. In these circumstances it is to the lasting credit of Mr Wilson's Government that it significantly increased the share of public expenditure in gross national product, thus enabling major social advances to be made.'[36]

In his second article, 'The price and prize of sustained growth', Crosland focused on the cause of Britain's low rate of growth, which at 2.2 per cent over the previous five years had been lower than in the previous decade. Among the causes, he claimed, were the fact that British productivity was low by European standards (even when at its maximum) and that successive governments since 1945 had kept growth artificially low by manipulating the level of home demand – 'crudely, stop-go and deflation' – to control both the balance of payments and inflation. Alternative instruments of economic policy such as devaluation and incomes policy were 'fraught with difficulties: the pound's role as a world currency, the existence of the sterling balances, the pressure of the United States and other financial authorities, traditions of free collective bargaining and so on'. The 1967 devaluation measures had failed to change the situation because in the first instance it had been necessary to restrain home demand in the interests of exports.[37] This eventually produced the huge balance of payments surplus, but also contributed to the increase in unemployment.[38]

Crosland's analysis offered little that was new, and much that had already been expressed at the PLP meeting of 15 July, which had effectively returned the party to where it was before taking office in 1964. 'I am clear,' he wrote, 'that we must now consciously and explicitly give priority to growth.' This would require a *political* decision: 'Economists and Treasury officials can easily list the various objectives of economic policy; growth, full employment, stable prices and a healthy foreign balance. But when the objectives conflict, as they almost always do, it is for the politicians to decide which shall have priority.'[39]

Senior Labour leaders had been saying this for over a decade and now Crosland was repeating it, even though the Labour government had discovered it to be politically impossible in office. In July 1971 Callaghan too would return to this theme, the irony of which was not lost on Peter Jenkins, writing in *The Guardian* and recalling Callaghan's record as Chancellor:

> He put parity before country and before party. He personally saw to it that the growth ticket on which Labour had been elected in 1964 was torn up before an invited audience of the Governor of the Bank of England, Treasury mandarins, the US Secretary of Treasury, and members of the international banking community …When devaluation came, after three wasted years, Mr Callaghan stood head and shoulders above all others in the last ditch.[40]

In September 1970 Crosland's solution was 'a much greater flexibility of interest rates' and a willingness to make 'timely adjustments to the parity whenever the alternative would be squeeze and deflation'.[41] This was welcomed by members of the NEC Industrial Policy Subcommittee which began to meet in April 1971, of which Crosland was a (largely inactive) member. The NEC statement *Economic Strategy, Growth and Unemployment*, prepared by the subcommittee and presented to the 1971 conference where it was unanimously approved by delegates, stated that a Labour government 'must be prepared, whenever necessary to make an orderly realignment to our exchange rate – at least whenever the alternative is a policy of massive deflation and stagnation'.[42] *Economic Strategy, Growth and Unemployment* was obviously read with interest by the government: on 23 June 1972 Anthony Barber, the Chancellor of the Exchequer, allowed the pound to float (down by 9 per cent) a decision made inevitable, writes John Campbell, 'by the Nixon administration's suspension of the convertibility of the dollar in August 1971, which put intolerable pressure on the pound'.[43] Crosland foresaw the risk of inflationary pressures, but concluded on balance that the benefits of growth and full employment would outweigh the cost at least in the short term. No government, however, he conceded, could endure indefinitely a 7 per cent rate of inflation, 'so whichever direction we start to look our eyes swivel back inexorably towards prices and incomes policy if we want sustained growth'. The search for an acceptable policy, he acknowledged, would be formidable but the party had little choice: 'For without sustained growth, we cannot achieve any of our objectives; and without exchange-rate flexibility and a prices and incomes policy, we cannot achieve sustained growth.'[44]

Crosland's adherence to a redistributive economic policy was immediately challenged by Ronald Butt in a review of the articles in the *Sunday Times*:

> Suppose the Conservatives can prove that a 'more just and humane society' (Mr Crosland's own words) can be better achieved by resisting the further redistribution he wants? Mr Crosland has conceded quite frankly that his social policies demand the growth that Labour failed to obtain. He does not, however, allow for the possibility that the failure of growth may be partly due to the redistributive and interventionist policies which he also advocates. If the Conservatives can create a society in which individuals have more responsibility for the big things in their own lives, and one which is also humane, Mr Crosland's radical but moderate case will be difficult to sustain.[45]

Significantly, Butt's analysis echoed the thinking of three of Crosland's senior colleagues in the Labour government. In 1969 Denis Healey had spoken of the negative impact of the comparative increase in affluence among Labour voters. In the Labour clubs in his constituency he discovered 'four out of five complaints are that income tax is too high and that we should not pay out so much in family allowances'.[46] This was a theme Jenkins, as Chancellor, had also developed. He warned colleagues of 'a taxation revolt' among the electorate if Labour devoted ever higher levels of the national income to public expenditure.[47] But perhaps the most telling remarks were made by George Brown, whose memoirs were serialised in the *Sunday Times* in the autumn of 1970: 'In a real sense, the Labour Party is suffering now from its own achievement. The outstanding achievement is to have brought about a degree of prosperity reflected in the standard of living of the bulk of the people in Britain far beyond what we thought possible in 1945, and infinitely far beyond anything we ever dreamed of in the 1930s.'[48]

Crosland was looking backwards. In 1974 or 1975, he expected Labour would have another opportunity to realise its pre-1964 objectives. He did not accept Brown's analysis that even though Labour had raised people's standards and earning capacity, enabling them to enjoy 'a vast new range of life, ... somehow we haven't persuaded people that all this has to be paid for'. Brown was convinced this was an inevitable phase: 'first you make people physically and financially better off, and then you have to wait for human understanding and compassion to catch up', adding ruefully that 'you can only afford to be a Conservative after Labour has been in power for a few years!'[49]

Post-mortem: Crosland, Healey and Jenkins, autumn 1970

In the autumn of 1970 Crosland, Healey and Jenkins met privately to discuss the experience of the Labour government. They concluded that the most important failures of the government were, first, inadequate arrangements for the forming of major policy decisions; second, the failure of economic management to achieve sustained growth (partly a consequence of the first failure); and third, a growing isolation of the government from backbenchers and from Labour opinion outside Parliament. On the first point they felt ministers had had 'too little time and opportunity to think about basic policy matters'. There had been too many meetings of the Cabinet and its committees, and ministers had had to spend 'too much time learning to run their Departments...because of lack of previous Ministerial experience,...made worse by too frequent changes of Ministers'. What discussion there had been about long-term policies had been 'ill-prepared'. The Strategic Economic Policy Committee, set up after 1966, had 'rarely discussed genuinely strategic questions'.[50] There was unanimous agreement between the three that in future more attention would need to be given to the machinery for top decision-taking: 'The need to be on top of the Department requires time and attention by the Minister, and also requires him to have authority over his Department, so that, though possible, it should be rare for a Minister to be overruled in Cabinet on a Departmental matter.'[51]

This led to a discussion on voting in Cabinet. It was agreed that this was undesirable and had been too common in the Labour government; Labour Cabinets were too large, with too many ministers of no real political weight, whose votes nevertheless sometimes decided important issues.[52] In future, policy should be determined *before* the Cabinet met.[53]

By its very nature this discussion was an exercise in elitism: three of Labour's noted intellectuals meeting privately to discuss how, in retrospect, they might have run the Labour government more effectively. The irony is that they were probably right to believe they could have done so, but their prescription for decision-making by a Labour Cabinet – greater centralisation of power at the top of the PLP – had it become common knowledge, could only have alienated almost all sections of the Labour Party membership.[54] It was widely suspected by MPs on the left of the party that the parliamentary leadership secretly desired such an arrangement. When the NEC Home Policy Committee met on 16 September 1970 to finalise the wording of the NEC statement to conference later that month, it was (unsuccessfully) proposed that it should state that the Labour Party 'welcomes not only the services of the rank and file, but also their views'.[55]

The establishment of an inner Cabinet in the last two years of the Labour government, in some respects reflected the three's preference for a 'more continuous discussion of problems amongst the top people', and had enabled a select group of senior ministers 'to discuss issues *before* people's ideas were too precisely formulated'.[56] But this did not resolve the problem of determining its composition without embarrassing those who were excluded.[57] The Labour government, they felt, had only got near to co-ordinating its economic policy effectively when a small group had been involved with contingency planning for an economic crisis between summer 1968 and autumn 1969, when it had been 'usual for the Chancellor's view to prevail in this group'. Otherwise, Cabinet committees had suffered from having 'too many Departments represented, so that marginal interests clogged decision-making'. Conversely, the Department of Economic Affairs (DEA) versus the Treasury relationship had not worked because the Prime Minister had frequently had to act as an arbiter between the two, and had 'neither the time nor the machinery to ensure consistent policies'. In the course of the discussion there was disagreement only about the role of the Cabinet Office. 'One view was that the Office helped Ministers' policy thinking only when there was no impinging on the Office's dominant loyalty to the prime minister, but this was countered by the comment that the prime minister had felt that the Cabinet Office saw their role as serving the Cabinet rather than serving him.'[58]

On the second point, economic policy, the three agreed that the failure to achieve sustained economic growth had been a disaster for all concerned 'as this was the policy area where the Party had made most promises and aroused highest expectations'. Too little thought had been given 'to simple, cheap measures that could produce political benefit'. Further, devaluation had been discussed too much in terms of such a measure *or* cuts, 'when it should have been a question of "devaluation *and* cuts" as an effective package'. Prior to devaluation, public expenditure had grown 'lumpily': 'more coherent policies would have spread the load more evenly over the period and therefore more acceptably'.[59]

On the final point, relations with the party – the last two points being dealt with briefly by comparison to the discussion on decision-taking – they agreed the government had lost control of the PLP 'when things were going badly'. This in turn had created difficulties in the constituencies. The large government 'payroll' failed to smother the discontent as it simply 'increased the resentment felt by those *not* offered jobs'. Fewer jobs would therefore 'reduce the extent to which the question came into back-benchers' minds'. Predictably, given the elitist nature of both the exercise and the analysis, 'the discussion produced no general conclusions on how to ensure better relations between the PLP leadership and the CLPs and trade unions'.[60] Crosland, Healey and Jenkins had spent nearly six years at the heart of the Labour government and by their own admission had failed their supporters. In the autumn of 1970, the Labour Party was in no mood to trust to its establishment elite. Alone among former ministers to recognise this was Anthony Wedgwood Benn, as much a member of Labour's establishment as the above mentioned, but who, as 'Tony Benn', swam with the tide of popular opinion favouring participation by the wider membership in the daily functioning of the party.

The voice of *Tribune* in the Shadow Cabinet

Crosland, Healey and Jenkins were contemporaries who shared basically the same beliefs. None favoured a radical departure in opposition from the policies of the Labour government. When the Shadow Cabinet met to discuss the Conservative government's industrial relations proposals in October 1970, Healey and Jenkins led the argument against the party adopting too condemnatory a stance in opposition to proposals which appeared to find favour with the public. Opposition, they argued, should be moderate in tone. Barbara Castle's description of the proposals as 'a Black Leg's Charter' did not quite meet this requirement. 'It was hard to avoid the conclusion', wrote Foot taking the opposite view to the deputy leader, 'that if Roy Jenkins had been the Leader of the Party, we would have been heading [for] a row with the Trade Unions on this issue, for a start'.[61]

The lethargy of senior members of the parliamentary leadership infuriated Foot, who as an outsider struggled to inject a sense of urgency into the discussion of policy. When economic policy was eventually discussed at Foot's request on 13 October 1970, Jenkins began by pointing out that as nearly all the measures so far proposed or hinted at by the new government would only begin to take effect two or three years hence, it proved there was little wrong with his own policies as Chancellor. Possibly, in the future, greater effort should be made to increase growth, he added, but in 1968 and 1969 it had been essential to restore the balance of payments to avoid the very real threat of further devaluation. With the exception of Foot, no member of the Shadow Cabinet demurred. Harold Lever, of whom Foot clearly expected more, went so far as to describe the former Chancellor's analysis as 'impeccable', and made 'no criticisms whatsoever'. When Foot drew attention to the fact that at least 600,000 were without work and challenged Jenkins over what level of unemployment he considered acceptable, Jenkins described the question as unfair, a sort of 'Have you stopped beating your wife?' question, and declined to be more specific.[62]

Discussion of possible future levels of growth under a Labour government prompted Crosland to admit, seemingly without the slightest concern, that 'everybody wants to see a three and a half per cent rate of growth if possible and it is quite easy to say it in opposition, but no-one knows how we are going to get it'. He personally had not 'the foggiest idea how it was going to be achieved. But that doesn't mean we shouldn't be able to say it.' This, Foot wrote, was said with a jovial cynicism 'which was not properly appreciated in some quarters – notably Lord Beswick, who thought that Crosland had uttered some scandalous obscenities'. Foot, by contrast, welcomed these remarks as the most valid statement he had heard from any politician for a very long time,[63] which indicates he took them more seriously than Crosland, who believed that Labour's policies were basically sound and opposition was not something to get too worked up about.

After three months as a member of the Shadow Cabinet, Foot concluded that 'several of them, including even, Crosland are merely waiting to attack the Tories on their policy. They think they are going to have so much offered to them on a plate that they won't have to worry about defining the indefinable in Labour's policies.'[64] With Crosland and Callaghan already calling for some sort of incomes policy, it was apparent that former ministers had little new to add to the policies they had pursued over the previous six years. 'We had a long, boring discussion on the economic situation and everybody hummed and hawed and gave their view', wrote Benn, commenting on the exchange between Jenkins and Foot in his own account of the same Shadow Cabinet meeting. 'I have no confidence at the moment in Labour economists or the capability of a Labour Government to handle the economy any better than anybody else and I don't believe that this is what politics is about any more. But economic management is so deeply entrenched in the thinking of Harold Wilson and others that it is difficult to get away from it.'[65]

The bankruptcy of the Labour Party and the Shadow Cabinet

At the 11 November meeting of the Shadow Cabinet, Crosland, injecting a new note of seriousness into the proceedings, raised the matter of research and secretarial support for ex-ministers. How, he asked, could former ministers be expected to absorb and reflect upon the lessons of office, challenge the government, and also serve their constituents without a level of support in some way comparable to that they had enjoyed in government. He suggested three ways in which the burden might be eased: by assistance from party headquarters 'which he thought unlikely', by creating a Department of the Opposition, or by raising private finance to fund the cost of secretarial and research assistance.[66] This deficiency in Labour's organisational structure was compounded by the announcement that month that the party was seriously in debt. *The Times* reported on 25 November that Callaghan, wearing his party treasurer's hat, had warned colleagues on the finance committee of the PLP that if the Conservative government ran its full term of office, Labour might have a deficit of £500,000 when the general election came.[67] Wilson's subsequent announcement that, thanks to an offer of financial assistance from a sympathiser, the party was in a position to employ two shorthand typists, simply highlighted the deficiencies in Labour's organisational structure.[68] Wilson's determination to staff a political office on a scale in accordance with his status as a former Prime Minister but beyond what the party could provide led him to accept financial support from business people sympathetic to the party, most of whom in Ziegler's words were respectable, but some of whom, unfortunately, were 'raffish figures who flirted on the fringes of illegality and, in one or two cases, were later decisively to overstep the mark'.[69]

Because of the state of its finances the Labour Party was unable to redress the weaknesses in its organisational structure. There was eventually to be some relief courtesy of the Rowntree Trust which, after a series of meetings in early 1971 between its secretary, Pratap Chitnis and Callaghan, Jenkins and Douglas Houghton, offered to fund two political fellowships to provide research assistance for members of the opposition frontbench. It was not until March 1972, however, almost two years into opposition, that the appointments were made. Matthew Oakeshott of Nuffield College was appointed to assist Roy Jenkins, then deputy leader,[70] and David Lipsey, Research Officer of the National Union of General and Municipal Workers (NUGMW), to assist Crosland. The second fellowship was originally intended for Callaghan as Shadow Home Secretary, but it went instead to Crosland 'in view of the enormous load of work... thrown on the Shadow Minister for the Environment by the Housing Finance Bill and the reform of local Government'.[71] Rowntree Trust support was strictly limited and the terms of it equally so defined. Beyond this, shadow ministers had to make do with whatever level of support Transport House could provide.

It was fitting that the matter of research and secretarial support for former ministers was raised by Crosland. He, after all, had famously exploited Labour's period in opposition after the party lost power in 1951 to revise British socialist theory. The lack of opportunity to repeat this service after 1971, at a time when elements in the party were pressing for the elimination of social democratic influence over policy, was interpreted by some as a dereliction of duty. As Hatfield writes, 'moderates in the party never found another influential theorist around whom they could rally in the dialectics of the left'.[72] In all probability, dissatisfaction stemmed from his refusal to take a lead in the party's debate over the Common Market despite his pro-Market sympathies, an issue which for some in the party became a litmus test of social democratic credentials.[73]

It was not that Crosland did not comprehend the need for 'a major new work of political economy' for the 1970s, but that he personally could

'offer only the practical thoughts of a practising and fully-occupied politician'.[74] Douglas Eden, writing in *Encounter* in June 1979, confirmed that,
as early as 1971, Crosland had decided there would be 'no more original
works', and that it was for 'others, for a younger generation to develop
new ideas from the Social Democratic tradition'.[75] Accordingly, the Fabian
Tract he published in January 1971, *A Social-Democratic Britain*, summarised
his thinking since June 1970 and developed the ideas of his two September
articles for *The Times*. Returning once more to the question of growth,
he admitted that when writing *The Future of Socialism* he had been too
complacent, readily accepting official projections forecasting a nearly
stationary population: 'hence, like others at the time, I did not foresee
the huge demands on our resources for housing, education and health,
which a rising population brings in its train'. That the Labour government
had increased the share of public expenditure in GNP even when growth
had been slow, he considered an achievement in itself.[76]

New thought in *A Social-Democratic Britain* was directed against the
anti-growth thesis championed at this time by Professors Misham and
Galbraith. Misham's argument that growth could increase (and affluence
spread) only at the expense of the environment, had led him to propose
a ban on all international air travel, and the creation of towns where the
only form of transport permitted would be horses and horse-drawn carriages.
Affluence in Misham's opinion, Crosland concluded, was 'obviously more
agreeable when it is a minority condition'. As for Galbraith's suggestion that
the working class desired washing-machines, cars and overseas package
holidays only because they had been brainwashed and their tastes contrived
by advertising, Crosland responded indignantly that his constituents
desired such things 'because the things are desirable in themselves'.[77]

Crosland thrived on the intellectual stimulation provided by Misham
and Galbraith but it amounted to little more than a contest of wits. No
matter how eloquently he presented the case for increased growth and the
need to afford it priority over minority interests, it remained essentially
wishful thinking. There was little in *A Social-Democratic Britain* to suggest
that Crosland or the Labour Party had – in Crosland's own words – the
foggiest idea how to secure lasting growth. As Ronald Butt had hinted in
his review of Crosland's September articles, the problem for Labour was
that his working-class constituents were just as likely, if not more so, to
get their washing-machines, cars and overseas package holidays under
a Conservative government.[78]

The case for Mr Wilson

Throughout the first year of opposition, writes Pimlott, Wilson was
'uncharacteristically silent'.[79] This view is shared by Butler and Kavanagh
who, in their study of the February 1974 general election, record that

'in the aftermath of defeat Mr Wilson retreated into his shell for a year, writing his self-exculpatory memoirs'.[80] The idea of Wilson hidden away in his study and neglectful of his responsibilities as party leader is one that has gained currency, but which is open to question. When the PLP and the NEC met jointly to consider the Queen's Speech on 2 July 1970, Wilson told the meeting that, with the exception of housing, South Africa and education, it would be difficult 'at this stage to launch specific attacks'.[81] Initially at least, there was little for the Labour leader to do except let the new government settle in and gradually break its election promises. Controversial as Conservative policies on housing, South Africa and education were, they were not unexpected and, Wilson aside, there were several Labour politicians fully capable of responding on these issues. This said, his was the first name on Labour motions in the House of Commons attacking both the sale of arms to South Africa[82] and the government's Expenditure Statement, the latter condemned as being 'mean and unfair between different sections of the community, particularly in the social services and housing'.[83] On the most controversial issue of the early months of opposition, the government's consultative document on industrial relations, the first name on Labour's amendment to Heath's Proposed Motion (Industrial Relations) was, once again, that of the party leader.[84] What Wilson therefore failed to do as Leader of the Opposition can only be a matter of opinion.

From the ex-Cabinet there was little complaint. Along with Wilson they were more than satisfied to see first Iain Macleod, then Anthony Barber humbled by Jenkins in the House of Commons and forced to concede that the economy they had inherited from Labour was not in crisis and was therefore, by implication, healthy as a result of Labour's policies. Inevitably this sense of vindication provoked anger among those in the party who did not subscribe to this interpretation of what constituted a political triumph. These, predictably, included Foot who argued it was 'dangerous for the leadership of the Party to insist that, because they had made no substantial major financial changes, the present Tory Government was in effect carrying out the financial judgement laid down in the Labour Chancellor's budget'.[85] If this were the case, he warned, there could be no doubt as to which of the two parties was responsible for the level of unemployment.

'To an outsider', wrote David Wood in *The Times* in January 1971, 'none of the criticisms aimed at Mr Wilson seems to be very substantial and some look downright petty.' Wood's article, 'The political future of Mr Wilson', aired publicly mutterings at Westminster 'about the apathy and misjudgements of Wilson as Opposition leader'.[86] Some Labour MPs, Wood suggested, were dissatisfied with Wilson's seeming lack of appetite for political battle. True, he had not called for a one-day general strike in protest at the government's industrial relations proposals as had some left-wing members of the PLP,[87] but as shown above he made clear his opposition to the proposals in Robert Carr's consultative document. Indeed, criticism of his response to Carr's document puts dissatisfaction with his leadership style clearly into perspective. The charge against Wilson was that he had 'stultified the Opposition by retaining Barbara Castle, who was compromised up to the hilt, as the Shadow Secretary of State for Employment to fight the Industrial Relations Bill'.[88] The irony of Castle's appointment was lost on no one but in reality she was no less compromised than Wilson, and the real issue was why the Labour leader was opposed to legislation which, in the words of Roy Jenkins, was 'about 80 per cent the same as what Barbara had proposed two years before'.[89] Labour MPs opposed to interference by the courts in industrial relations were naturally inclined to adopt a more combative response to the government's plans. Such an approach was consistent with the polarised view of politics articulated by the Tribune Group. However, once it is understood that dissatisfaction with Wilson's leadership was rooted in that particular section of the PLP, the attendant criticism is set in its proper context and better understood.

Accusations of disinterest and tactical misjudgements – for example, Wilson's decision to let Jenkins preside over meetings of the Shadow Cabinet in his absence, or the refusal to submit Labour names for the political honours list – are difficult, in retrospect, to take seriously. Yet Wilson did take them seriously, and one week later Wood published a second article, 'Mr Wilson's answer to party critics', the source of which was undoubtedly the Labour leader.[90] This directed the focus of attention away from industrial relations and concentrated instead on rebutting the charge that he was giving precedence to writing the history of the Labour government[91] over his duties as Leader of the Opposition. 'The memoirs have undoubtedly fascinated him and he has been determined that they shall be a contribution to contemporary politics of the first importance', wrote Wood, who proceeded to point out how since leaving office Wilson had made more than 30 speeches, 'far more than any other member of the Shadow Cabinet', and also that he had regularly taken his place at Question Time in the House of Commons. For each criticism reported in Wood's first article there appeared a rebuttal in the second. Thus, Jenkins had chaired meetings of the Shadow Cabinet only twice, on the first occasion due to Wilson's attendance of a memorial service for de Gaulle, on the second because he was fulfilling a speaking engagement to which he had committed himself prior to the general election. Regarding the honours list, he could 'scarcely be held solely responsible for any tactical misjudgements', as daily meetings were held with the deputy leader, the chairman of the PLP and Chief Whip to 'consult on the events of the day, and settle operational orders'.[92] This use of Wood's column to set the record straight points to a degree of insecurity in Wilson over his position as leader. This, perhaps, was the legacy of the election defeat. To have been rejected by the electorate in favour of Heath was bad enough, but to be criticised – unfairly, he felt – by his colleagues can only have added to his sense of injustice.

Criticism of Wilson's leadership style stemmed in part from activist disillusionment with the record of the Labour government, the general election manifesto and campaign, and this attached to the leader in particular, when news of his intention to write the history of the Labour government and the details of his publishing agreement emerged in the summer of 1970. 'For five months, he was a full-time author, part-time Leader of the Opposition', writes Pimlott.[93] Even if this is so he had, as Wood wrote, 'no guilty sense of having left undone those things he ought to have done'.[94] If, at Westminster, Wilson was a shadow of the politician he had been as Leader of the Opposition 1963–64, he failed only by his own high standards. Undoubtedly, he was criticised because of the subject matter of his book rather than because the actual task of writing it impacted unfavourably upon his effectiveness as Leader of the Opposition. Jenkins, for example, at the same time wrote a series of biographical essays for *The Times* for a handsome reward with impunity.[95] The resolution submitted to conference demanding that 'members of the previous Labour Government who publish their memoirs dealing with the Labour administration . . . give 10 per cent of their earnings from these memoirs to the Labour Party funds', a resolution subject to an amendment insisting 50 per cent be substituted for 10,[96] was no doubt aimed as much at George Brown as at Wilson, the former deputy leader having committed his own thoughts on the Labour government to paper for serialisation in the *Sunday Times* ahead of the publication of his memoirs.[97] In these circumstances it was difficult for Wilson to dispel the impression that he was lining his pockets any less enthusiastically than Brown. His assertion to his Shadow Cabinet colleagues that 'he was not writing his memoirs at all, but a factual account of the administration' was, Foot records, 'greeted with polite laughter'.[98]

Wilson was discredited by the project from beginning to end and his motives were rightly questioned. He received little praise when the book was published in 1971. 'It is ironic', wrote David Watt in a review for the *Financial Times*, 'that a work which was obviously conceived as an exercise in self-vindication should be so self-incriminating'.[99] Crosland, more generously, privately acknowledged the 'monumental labour that must have entailed', and admitted to a 'horrible fascination' upon reading it. Wilson, he noted, had 'learned nothing and forgotten nothing'.[100]

One year after

From the outset of opposition, Wilson maintained it would simply be a matter of time before Labour would be presented with opportunities to attack the Conservative government. As it became apparent that Heath had a different set of priorities in respect of the balance of payments surplus, the Labour leader began to spell out what the Labour government would have done in similar circumstances. He told BBC Radio's 'The World This Weekend' in February 1971, it would have used the surplus on Britain's overseas trade account, 'so that, while no longer vulnerable to speculators for a long period ahead, they got more rapid growth in the economy. Such action would help reduce costs, restrain increases in prices and give workers more confidence about full employment.'[101] These remarks echoed those of Roy Jenkins in a speech in Glasgow seven days earlier, in which the former Chancellor had warned it would 'be tragic for the development areas above all, but for the country as a whole, if the present balance of payments strength, greater even than we believed it to be in June, is frittered away without being used as a platform for sustained economic growth and a return to full employment'.[102] Fortuitously for both Jenkins and Wilson, defeat in 1970 ensured that the true extent of the economic recovery under Labour of which they boasted – symbolised by the balance of payments surplus – could neither be tested nor easily disproved.

In a speech in New York in May 1971, Wilson conceded that a statutory incomes policy was no longer viable as an instrument of economic policy. Had prices and wage settlements continued to rise under the Labour government, or if such a scenario were to occur in the future, the only solution would have been a voluntary freeze on wages and prices: 'I set out not as an assumption, but as a fact, that – to the extent that a voluntary policy of restraint can be accepted – economic society as a whole can permit a degree of higher production, leading to higher productivity, with all that means for fuller employment and for higher wages in the future.'[103] This was an admission that Labour had no workable economic policy independent of the trade unions. It was evident that the parliamentary leadership possessed few alternatives to an incomes policy from the frequency with which it was discussed. While Wilson was feeling his way towards a policy the trade unions would not categorically reject, his colleagues in the parliamentary leadership continued to press for a more binding version of the voluntary agreement he envisaged. Crosland, Castle and Callaghan each saw the need for Labour and the trade unions to resolve the issue swiftly as a prelude to a concerted attack on the Conservative government's industrial relations strategy. Wilson, by contrast, preferred to allow an agreement to *emerge* in politically favourable circumstances.[104]

Discussion of an incomes policy was part of a process which enabled Callaghan to establish his 'position' on the major issues facing the Labour Party in opposition. Of his decision to campaign for the principle of an incomes policy in 'the heart of the enemy camp', David Wood observed that he was deliberately making his party reputation out of bridge building between politicians and trade union leaders. His objective was to 'reassure the trade union movement of the Labour leadership's opposition to the Industrial Relations Bill and to coax them to change their attitudes so that political Labour and its industrial supporters can co-exist in the old partnership'.[105]

By May 1971 it was clear Callaghan was placing himself firmly at the head of mainstream opinion in the party. In an address to the May Day Festival of Labour in London, he spoke about the Common Market in terms of it being a choice between entry or helping the '800,000 unemployed or more'.[106] Four months earlier, at a meeting of the Shadow Cabinet on 18 January 1971, he had spoken of his desire not to wreck the party over the issue, having prefaced this remark by admitting to being 'genuinely puzzled and confused' about entry.[107] Callaghan, wrote Wood in response to the former Home Secretary's decision to oppose entry, 'has earned a reputation inside the party for fence-sitting until a well-chosen moment occurs; that is to say, until he knows where the Labour majority lies'. But, like Wilson, Callaghan's sole aim was to preserve party unity.[108] As chairman of the NEC Home Policy Committee he had positioned himself at the heart of the policy review to act as a brake on the party's tendency to self-destruct. Opposition to the Common Market was a way of signalling to the party that a split which would harm its chances of re-election could not be countenanced.

'With a sympathetic audience before him,' wrote Christopher Walker in his profile of Wilson, 'One year after', 'he took the opportunity to indulge in some politically effective "Tory bashing". As his text he took a speech which Mr Heath had made to the housewives of Leicester before the last election, in which he had promised to act on prices if he became Prime Minister. "I assume he was trying to woo them," he remarked, to a loud burst of derisive laughter.' Twelve months on from the general election defeat, Wilson was in confident form as he addressed the Post Office Engineering Union at Blackpool. The Conservative government, as he had predicted it would, had broken its election promise on prices and was the architect of its own unpopularity. The next Labour government, he told them, would offer accelerated industrial expansion 'in return for clear commitments to restrain prices and various types of incomes, including profits and rents'.[109]

Wilson faced the prospect of an uncomfortable start to the second year of opposition due to the party's divisions over the Common Market, but the first had been an unlikely success.[110] The parliamentary leadership remained firmly in control of policy. The review of the party programme was to take place under the watchful eye of Callaghan, and the former Cabinet remained, almost en masse, in place at the head of the PLP. This owed much to Wilson's management of the party in the first weeks of opposition.

Notes

1 C. Walker, 'One year after', *The Times*, 19 June 1971, p. 15.
2 *The Economist*, 'Everyone will be pleased to see them on their hols', 25 July 1970, p. 19.
3 The newcomers were Michael Foot, Douglas Houghton and Shirley Williams.
4 LPA, Michael Foot Collection (MFC), Cabinet Papers (CP), C1, *Notes on Shadow Cabinet Meetings, 16 July–13 October 1970*, 15 September 1970.
5 LPA, Parliamentary Labour Party (PLP), Minutes, 9 July 1970.
6 LPA, PLP, Minutes, 29 June 1970. The Interim Steering Committee comprised Wilson, Castle, Stewart, Callaghan, Houghton, Mellish, Peart, Crosland, Benn, Healey, Shore, Crossman, Lord Shackleton, Lord Beswick, and Frank Barlow (secretary).
7 *Tribune*, 17 July 1970, p. 3.
8 Michael Foot's election to the Shadow Cabinet was an obvious exception. He received 124 votes and came sixth in the ballot. The next best placed MP associated with the Tribune Group was Eric Heffer, who received 78 votes. LPA, PLP, Minutes, Session 1970–71.
9 *Tribune*, 10 July 1970, p. 6.
10 Brown was defeated in the 1970 general election by the Conservative Party candidate Dudley Stewart-Smith, who received 35,757 votes to Brown's 33,633. Times Newspapers Limited, *The Times Guide to the House of Commons 1970* (London, 1970), p. 50.
11 *Tribune*, 10 July 1970, p. 6.
12 Tony Benn's diary account states that 'Roy Jenkins destroyed Iain Macleod on the question of whether or not there had been an economic crisis at the point when the Tories came into power. Macleod had to admit there hadn't.' Benn, *Office Without Power*, 7 July 1970, p. 300.
13 LPA, MFC, CP, C1, 16 July 1970. Foot had been a vocal critic of the Wilson government from the backbenches 1964–70.
14 LPA, MFC, CP, C1, 16 July 1970.
15 LPA, Parliamentary Committee (PC), Minutes, 16 June 1971.
16 R. Jenkins, *A Life at the Centre* (London, Macmillan, 1991), p. 312.
17 Butler and Pinto-Duschinsky, *The British General Election of 1970*, p. 25.
18 LPA, MFC, CP, C1, 15 September 1970.
19 LPA, MFC, CP, C1, 15 September 1970.
20 P. Ziegler, *Wilson: The Authorised Life* (London, Weidenfeld & Nicolson, 1993), p. 371.
21 LPA, PLP, Minutes, 8 July 1970.
22 LPA, PLP, Minutes, 15 July 1970 (William Price MP).
23 LPA, PLP, Minutes, 15 July 1970.
24 *House of Commons Debates, 5th series*, 1960–61, vol. 638, cols 1038, 1040. Quoted in W. Beckerman (ed.), *The Labour Government's Economic Record 1964–1970* (London, Duckworth, 1972), p. 52, n. 2.
25 *HC Debs, 5th ser.*, 1961–62, vol. 656, col. 51. Quoted in Beckerman, *The Labour Government's Economic Record 1964–1970*, p. 59, n. 3.
26 LPA, PLP, Minutes, 15 July 1970.
27 P. Kellner and C. Hitchens, *Callaghan: The Road to Number Ten* (London, Cassell, 1976), p. 111.
28 The Parliamentary Committee Minutes for 16 July 1970 record that the meeting planned for 22 July, at which the discussion of 15 July was to continue, was cancelled as the NEC was meeting that day. No date was arranged for the specific purpose of continuing the discussion.

29 LPA, PLP, Minutes, 15 July 1970.
30 See Butler and Pinto-Duschinsky, *The British General Election of 1970*, pp. 47–61.
31 LPA, PLP, Minutes, 15 July 1970.
32 *The Times*, 'No hard words as Labour face election lessons', 16 July 1970, p. 2.
33 Quoted in H. Noyes, 'Labour left gives Wilson warning of poll inquest', *The Times*, 29 August 1970, p. 2.
34 *The Times*, 'Wilson rules out post-mortem on election', 28 August 1970, p. 1.
35 A. Crosland, 'Social objectives for the 1970s', *The Times*, 25 September 1970, p. 10.
36 Crosland, 'Social objectives'.
37 A. Crosland, 'The price and prize of sustained growth', *The Times*, 26 September 1970, p. 12.
38 The increase in unemployment between 1966 and 1970 must be seen in perspective. As Alec Cairncross writes: 'From the spring of 1967 until the end of 1970 unemployment remained broadly between 2.0 and 2.6 per cent – limits which many in the early 1960s would have identified with full employment.' A. Cairncross, *The British Economy since 1945* (Oxford, Blackwell, 1992), p. 167.
39 Crosland, 'The price and prize'.
40 P. Jenkins, 'Jim's newthink', *The Guardian*, 5 July 1971, p. 11.
41 Crosland, 'The price and prize'.
42 LPAR, 1971, p. 373. The work of the Industrial Policy Subcommittee in this period is discussed below.
43 J. Campbell, *Edward Heath* (London, Jonathan Cape, 1993), p. 454.
44 Crosland, 'The price and prize'.
45 R. Butt, 'Labour: the ominous lull', *Sunday Times*, 27 September 1970, p. 12.
46 D. Healey, 'Britain in a Changing World', *Socialist Commentary*, (December 1969), pp. 5–8, in Butler and Pinto-Duschinsky, *The British General Election of 1970*, p. 123.
47 A. Howard, 'The professional', *New Statesman*, 17 July 1971, pp. 10–12.
48 G. Brown, *In My Way* (London, Gollancz, 1971), pp. 269–71.
49 Brown, *In My Way*, pp. 269–71.
50 Anthony Crosland Papers (ACP), London, British Library of Political and Economic Science (BLPES), Part II, Member of Parliament, c. 1950–77, 4/13.
51 BLPES, ACP, 4/13.
52 BLPES, ACP, 4/13.
53 An approach adopted by Tony Blair after 1997.
54 It was of course a disaster for the Labour government when *In Place of Strife* was introduced by Barbara Castle, supported by Harold Wilson, without consultation.
55 LPA, RD.10/September 1970, 'Addition Note to RD.6 (Revised)', HPC, Minutes, 16 September 1970; NEC, Minutes, 25 September 1970. This proposal was not accepted. See Chapter 4 below.
56 BLPES, ACP, 4/13.
57 See for example A. Howard (ed.), *The Crossman Diaries* (London, Methuen, 1979), pp. 606, 608–9.
58 BLPES, ACP, 4/13.
59 BLPES, ACP, 4/13.
60 BLPES, ACP, 4/13.
61 LPA, MFC, CP, C1, 8 October 1970.
62 LPA, MFC, CP, C1, 13 October 1970.
63 LPA, MFC, CP, C1, 13 October 1970.
64 LPA, MFC, CP, C1, 13 October 1970.
65 Benn, *Office Without Power*, 13 October 1970, p. 308.

66 LPA, PC, Minutes, 11 November 1970.
67 J. Groser, 'Deficit of £250,000 for Labour by 1973', *The Times*, 25 November 1970, p. 5.
68 LPA, PC, Minutes, 27 January 1971.
69 Ziegler, *Wilson*, p. 366.
70 Oakeshott remained as personal assistant to Jenkins after his resignation as deputy leader on 10 April 1972.
71 Douglas Houghton to Pratap Chitnis, 9 November 1971. LPA, PC, Minutes, Session 1971–72.
72 M. Hatfield, *The House the Left Built: Inside Labour Policy-making 1970–75* (London, Gollancz, 1978), p. 45.
73 Jenkins writes in his memoirs: 'Crosland understood all the implications and had voted right, but then absolutely declined to take the matter seriously. When I endeavoured to enlist his support . . . he shrugged his shoulders and he was off to Japan to study urban planning, which was more important.' Jenkins, *A Life at the Centre*, p. 352.
74 A. Crosland, *Socialism Now* (London, Jonathan Cape, 1974), p. 15.
75 D. Eden, 'Colin Welch's Crosland', *Encounter*, 52, 6 (June 1979), pp. 91–3.
76 A. Crosland, *A Social-Democratic Britain*, Fabian Tract 404 (London, 1971), as it appears in Crosland, *Socialism Now*, pp. 73–5.
77 Crosland, *A Social-Democratic Britain*, in Crosland, *Socialism Now*, pp. 78–9.
78 See Butt, 'Labour: the ominous lull'.
79 Pimlott, *Harold Wilson*, p. 571.
80 D. Butler and D. Kavanagh, *The British General Election of February 1974* (London, Macmillan, 1974), p. 19.
81 LPA, PLP, Minutes, 2 July 1970.
82 LPA, PC, Minutes, 20 July 1970.
83 LPA, PC, Minutes, 27 October 1970.
84 LPA, PC, Minutes, 26 November 1970.
85 LPA, MFC, CP, C1, 15 September 1970.
86 D. Wood, 'The political future of Mr Wilson', *The Times*, 11 January 1971, p. 13.
87 At a Tribune Group–trade union leaders' dinner held on 14 December 1970, the MPs Syd Bidwell and Neil Kinnock voiced their support for Clive Jenkins's call for a one-day general strike. LPA, Ian Mikardo Papers (IMP), 14 December 1970.
88 Wood, 'The political future'.
89 Witness Seminar (WS), 'The Labour Committee for Europe', *Contemporary Record*, 7, 2 (Autumn 1993), p. 390 (Lord Jenkins).
90 D. Wood, 'Mr Wilson's answer to party critics', *The Times*, 18 January 1971, p. 1.
91 H. Wilson, *The Labour Government 1964–1970: A Personal Record* (London, Weidenfeld & Nicolson, 1971).
92 Wood, 'Mr Wilson's answer'.
93 Pimlott, *Harold Wilson*, p. 571.
94 Wood, 'Mr Wilson's answer'.
95 'I was able that July to assemble from my publishers, for whom I envisaged a series of "back-to-back" studies of American Presidents and British Prime Ministers, and from *The Times*, for which William Rees-Mogg commissioned a series of long biographical essays which subsequently grew into a book entitled *Nine Men of Power*, a package which gave the prospect of a writing income of about £20,000.' Jenkins, *A Life at the Centre*, p. 308.
96 LPA, Document F17/70, Finance and General Purposes Committee, Minutes, 22 September 1970; NEC, Minutes, 25 September 1970.

97 Brown, *In My Way*.
98 LPA, MFC, CP, C1, 13 October 1970.
99 Ziegler, *Wilson*, p. 362.
100 BLPES, ACP, 16/7.
101 *The Times*, 'Mr Wilson predicts serious recession in Britain with worsening unemployment', 22 February 1971, p. 2.
102 F. Roberts, 'Mr Crosland lists growing cash burdens for families in lower income range', *The Times*, 15 February 1971, p. 11.
103 *The Times*, 'Mr Wilson foresees voluntary freeze', 5 May 1971, p. 1.
104 Wood, 'Mr Wilson's answer'.
105 D. Wood, 'Mr Callaghan leads move to get trade union acceptance of a Labour incomes policy', *The Times*, 11 January 1971, p. 2.
106 *The Times*, 'Ministers have debased business morality, Mr Callaghan says', 3 May 1971, p. 1.
107 Benn, *Office Without Power*, 18 January 1971, p. 326.
108 D. Wood, 'Labour leaders move towards opposition to EEC entry', *The Times*, 26 May 1971, p. 1.
109 Walker, 'One year after'.
110 By the end of 1970 Labour was ahead of the Conservatives in the opinion polls and remained so, aside from the occasional blip, through to January 1974. Campbell, *Edward Heath*, pp. 332–3.

3

LABOUR IN PARLIAMENT: THE HEATH GOVERNMENT AND THE POLITICS OF OPPOSITION 1970–74

Edward Heath's premiership undermined Labour's unity and electoral prospects. Initially, his government picked up where Wilson's left off. Reform of industrial relations and housing went further than Wilson had felt able or desired to go, but it was Heath's pursuit of British membership of the Common Market that did greatest harm to Labour's internal cohesion. What had been the policy of the Wilson government after 1966 became a fundamentally divisive issue in opposition. The problems that flowed from this were exacerbated by the Heath government's economic and industrial policies, which led to the adoption by Labour of radical and unpopular policies, damaging the party's long-term electoral prospects.

In the three years and eight months that it lasted, Heath's Conservative government introduced a range of measures that the Labour Party vigorously opposed in Parliament, but failed to block. Chief among these were the Industrial Relations Bill, the Housing Finance Bill and Britain's entry into the Common Market. Yet the story of the Labour Party in Parliament 1970–74 is one of effective opposition. Heath had an overall majority of 30, sufficient to secure the government's business but not large enough to subdue Labour. In fact, Labour was galvanised by Heath. His government's attempt to modernise British economic and industrial performance gave succour to those in the Labour Party (primarily, but not exclusively, left wingers) who believed that radicalism in government was a matter of political will.[1] Consequently, the Heath government had an impact on Labour's own consideration of economic and industrial policy through the NEC research programme: first, by pursuing a policy of disengagement from industry 1970–72 that Labour rejected and, second, by pursuing an industrial strategy after 1972 that

54

was more socialist than anything Labour had managed between 1964 and 1970.

Heath entered 10 Downing Street on 19 June 1970 buttressed by a personal mandate for change. Yet his government's policies on housing, the trade unions, taxation, prices, industry, employment and the Common Market were so provocative that the recently defeated Labour Party was revived by a perceived partisan threat to their allies and supporters in the country. There followed a bitter and closely contested Parliament. Rejected by the electorate, Harold Wilson and his colleagues found their purpose in resisting a range of measures which, as they were to repeatedly claim, risked returning Britain to the misery of the 1930s. Labour did not win many votes in the 1970–74 Parliament but, with the exception of the Common Market, the PLP presented a united front. Away from Westminster, the party was absorbed in the NEC research programme. Up until 1973, determined resistance to the Heath government in Parliament went hand in hand with the formulation of Labour's most radical policy programme since 1935.

Heath proved an unlucky Prime Minister. There was little his government could do about the energy crisis that resulted from the Arab–Israeli War in 1973, which had a disastrous effect on world oil and commodity prices, sending the balance of payments deficit spiralling. Equally, there was little his government could do to prevent the miners from imposing an overtime ban in pursuit of a 40 per cent wage claim at the height of the oil crisis. (Heath's refusal to discard the government's anti-inflationary policy at the miners' behest necessitated the introduction of a three-day working week in an effort to conserve energy supplies.) But his government was responsible for the policy of disengagement from industry that saw unemployment rise to 1 million, and for the subsequent U-turn on domestic policy that damaged the Conservative Party. And, if the 1970 general election was Heath's personal triumph, the February 1974 general election was his failure. His legacy was a minority Labour government saddled with a trade-union-approved programme for government that proved a disaster for the Labour Party and Britain.

Waking up Britain

'The Heath Government', writes Ian Gilmour, 'tried to do too much. Entry into Europe, the reform of industrial relations, the transformation of local government, the thoroughgoing reform of the taxation system, the rationalisation of housing subsidies and, during the last eighteen months, the imposition of comprehensive control of prices and incomes.'[2] This hugely ambitious programme appeared highly partisan to Labour. Further, it posed a direct challenge to the line that Wilson had taken during the general election campaign and to which he would return for cover in opposition, that by the time of its defeat the Labour government had at last got the economy right, as evidenced by the large balance of payments surplus that Roy Jenkins had bequeathed to his successor at the Treasury, Iain MacLeod. Britain, Wilson argued, did not require the shock therapy that the new government proposed. The sheer scale of Heath's ambition was an insult to former Labour ministers, who lost no opportunity in pointing out that they had sacrificed their own policy programme in the national interest to overcome the crippling economic inheritance of 1964, a balance of payments deficit of approximately £800 million. Of course, if the measures Heath proposed really were necessary then perhaps the Labour government's achievement had not been so remarkable after all. However, as Wilson was about to write his own 800-page account of the Labour government's record,[3] it was inevitable that he would condemn the new government's programme.

Having exhorted the country to 'Wake up!' in the course of the general election campaign, Heath, once elected, immediately sent his ministers on holiday, despite the urgency of the problems the country apparently faced. The new Prime Minister, writes John Campbell, 'was determined not to miss his summer's sailing'.[4] Not for him the first 100 hundred days of frantic activity favoured by his predecessor. Government by gimmickry was not his style. In fact, the return of the Conservative Party to office proved something of an anti-climax. Iain MacLeod (in his only statement to the House of Commons as Chancellor of the Exchequer before his premature death less than five weeks into the new administration) was forced to concede that, actually, the economy was not quite in the state of crisis that the Conservative Party, abetted by Lord Cromer, had encouraged the electorate to believe.[5] This concession fuelled Labour suspicions that far from intending to act in the national interest, as the Labour government had done at a cost of great pain to its own supporters, the newly elected Conservative government was instead spoiling for a fight.

The Industrial Relations Bill: a 'pernicious and vicious piece of class legislation'

The reform of industrial relations, long promised by the Conservative Party and abandoned by the Labour government in the face of trade union (and PLP) hostility as recently as 1969, was one Heath's first priorities upon taking office. A consultative document was published in the summer of 1970 setting out the government's proposals. Prominent among these were the right to join or, more importantly, not to join a trade union (threatening the end of the closed shop); legally binding collective agreements to tackle the problem of unofficial strikes; a compulsory 60-day cooling-off period where strike action was imminent, and the forfeiture of legal immunity for unions involved in 'unfair industrial practices'. Additionally, unions would be invited to register with the National Industrial Relations Court (NIRC) newly established 'to deal with offences under the Bill'.[6] On the plus side, registered unions would be recognised and afforded greater protection against unfair dismissal. According to Robert Taylor, 'Heath and his colleagues regarded their detailed industrial relations proposals as rational, sensible and essentially modest'[7] but, at the TUC Congress in September, Hugh Scanlon denounced the proposals as 'the most serious threat to the liberties of organised labour for well over half a century'. W. L. Kendall of the Civil and Public Services Association (CPSA) called upon the general council 'to mobilise the entire trade union movement for action in the coming confrontation'.[8] When Robert Carr, the Secretary of State for Employment, informed TUC leaders on 13 October that the central pillars of the government's proposed Bill were non-negotiable, the battle lines were drawn.

The fight against the Industrial Relations Bill on the floor of the House of Commons began on 26 November 1970. Dismissing the consultative document as 'a document written by lawyers for lawyers',[9] Barbara Castle, on vulnerable ground after *In Place of Strife* but in full war paint on this occasion, savaged Carr over the proposed assault on the closed shop: 'The right to belong to a union, followed by the equal and unqualified right not to belong to a union, written for the first time into the law of this land, is a blackleg's charter.' Any legislation brought forward based on the proposals outlined in the document, she told him, would be fought line by line and destroyed. These words were echoed by Eric Heffer, a dissident in the 1964–70 Parliament, but in 1970 seated firmly on Labour's front bench for the precise purpose of fighting this particular measure. 'The right to work laws mean the very opposite of the right to work', he told the House. 'What they mean is the right to be a non-unionist, the right to be a blackleg, the right to undermine the organised trade union movement.'[10] Castle and Heffer shared a common vocabulary. The significance of this for Labour was that whereas Heffer, as a member of the Tribune Group of Labour MPs, had been a vocal critic of the Wilson government's economic, industrial and foreign policies, Castle had been a member of the Cabinet that had formulated and implemented them. But the radicalism of the Heath government was contagious, and Labour began its period in opposition using the language of the party's left wing.

For Heffer, the Industrial Relations Bill and, subsequently, the Housing Finance Bill, were acts of class war; for Castle, Carr's Bill offered the prospect of political rehabilitation. What should have made her squirm – Wilson's invitation to her to shadow Carr at Employment – in fact emboldened her to take the fight to her opponents, not all of whom, initially, were to be found on the government benches. Castle was on her mettle from the outset and Conservative taunts of 'scuttle, scuttle, scuttle' had no impact. On the eve of the Bill's second reading on 14 December, she lambasted Carr for his apparent belief 'that one can cure the problem in 1970 by turning the clock back to the 1870s'. Heffer drew attention to the Bill's debt to the Conservative Lawyers' Association's 1958 document, 'A Giant Strength', a debt which proved that 'their whole ideas are based upon political dogma built up since 1958 and not upon a real understanding of industrial relations'.[11]

The following day Douglas Houghton, the chairman of the PLP, and whose own links with the trade union movement stretched back to 1921, spoke powerfully against the Bill. Sceptical of any Conservative whose stated aim was the strengthening of the trade unions, Houghton recalled the words of the late Arthur Deakin, Ernest Bevin's successor as general secretary of the TGWU: 'It is not the wording of the motion that matters so much as who is moving it.' Houghton's intervention demonstrated where the body of opinion in the party lay. In the circumstances, it was unsurprising that Labour MPs who only 18 months earlier had accepted the need for industrial relations reform chose to keep their own counsel. One exception was Christopher Mayhew, who had inherited Bevin's seat but not his dedication to the cause of organised labour. Regretting that his rt hon. friends had failed to table a reasoned amendment to the Bill, with a view to improving it in committee, Mayhew distanced himself from the language of Castle and Heffer: 'I cannot understand or support the violent, unre-strained and partisan attacks made on the Bill...To describe it as a monstrous tyranny which takes us back over half a century,...or as a blackleg's charter does not seem to me appropriate.' This rebuke was swiftly followed by the warning that it was 'not good enough to declare one year that the national interest imperatively demands all-out support for *In Place of Strife* and the next year that the national interest imperatively demands the destruction of the very similar Industrial Relations Bill'. What the national interest required, he concluded, was a reasoned amendment and a constructive attempt to improve the Bill. All of this may have been perfectly true and there were no doubt some on the frontbench who privately concurred with everything he said but, with outright opposition to the Bill having swiftly become a litmus test for socialism, this was not the time to admit it. It certainly wasn't the occasion to suggest, as Mayhew did, that it was no longer true 'that those whom we represent are necessarily served by the demands of the trade unions'.[12]

Mayhew's speech had little impact. By the time Harold Wilson closed for Labour, the spotlight was firmly back on the government and, particu-larly, the Prime Minister, whom Wilson, displaying great prescience, accused of showing 'as much understanding in the revolutionary situation as the court of Louis XVI or Nicholas II'. Wilson, of course, was without equal in the House for sheer cheek: 'for its basic and irrelevant approach, no less than for its provocation and unworkability', he rejected the Bill.[13]

Outside Parliament, the TUC took to the streets. A 'day of protest' was held on 12 January 1971, which concluded with an address by Harold Wilson and Victor Feather at the Albert Hall. The following month, between 120,000 and 140,000 trade unionists marched through London to demonstrate their determination to 'Kill the Bill'. In March, a special Trades Union Congress held in Croydon 'strongly advised' affiliated unions to deregister and ignore the government's newly created statutory bodies. On this occasion, a call by Jones and Scanlon to have the special congress 'instruct' affiliated unions to deregister or face expulsion from the TUC was narrowly rejected, but at the annual congress in September Scanlon got his way and 30 affiliated unions were expelled. Eventually, organised labour's outright hostility to the measure would paralyse the government's attempt to reform industrial relations in Britain. Certainly Heath and his ministers never anticipated that the trade unions would resort to a policy of deregistration, which became the policy of the TUC despite the fact that it left unions vulnerable 'to crippling financial damages from the Industrial Court in the event of their involvement in unlawful disputes'. Carr, for one, was completely wrong-footed: 'I never expected the trade unions would oppose the Bill on the question of registration. And from their narrow short-term point of view it was a damnably effective tactic.'[14] But in 1971, with the Conservatives willing to use the guillotine to drive the measure through, there was never any doubt that the Industrial Relations Bill would become law. However, for the trade unions the real significance of the fight in Parliament was that it saw the PLP commit itself to repeal of the measure. In this respect, the TUC, steered by Jones and Scanlon, was fighting on two fronts. The immediate battle was with the Conservatives, but their long-term strategy was to box a future Labour government into a voluntary policy on industrial relations.

Dogged by Labour's detailed and immensely time-consuming examination of the Bill in the House of Commons, the government used the guillotine to limit consideration of the amendments to the Bill recommended by the House of Lords.[15] On 28 July, William Whitelaw, the Leader of the House, citing the London Government Bill 1963 and the Transport Bill 1953 as precedents justifying the government's decision, announced the allocation of five days for final consideration of the Bill, after which all outstanding amendments would be taken in a single vote. Barbara Castle, pointing out that the precedents cited by Whitelaw were both Conservative (as Heffer put it, 'One of yours' and 'Another one of yours') quoted damningly from Erskine May: 'such procedure is clearly inapplicable beyond the end of war'. Ably supported by Heffer, who challenged Whitelaw over a timetable that would require the examination of 60 amendments a day for five days, Castle accused the government of using 'this apparently generous allocation of five days . . . to cloak the surreptitious introduction of an undemocratic principle...of preventing this House from voting on Amendments individually'. This was enough to draw Robert Carr to his feet. To describe 56 days of parliamentary debate, taking up 481 hours of parliamentary time, as a denial of democracy was, he suggested, 'claptrap'.[16]

'The battle in Parliament', writes Campbell, 'was long and bitter':

> ... such was Labour's obstruction, marked by several demonstrations and more than one suspended sitting, that there was no debate at all on more than half the Bill's 150 clauses – including the whole section setting up the NIRC – before the guillotine came down. At the end of the Report Stage Members had to vote continuously for eleven and a half hours on sixty-three successive divisions before the Government thwarted the Opposition's attempt to block the Third Reading by scrapping its last forty-two amendments.[17]

The Industrial Relations Bill became law on 5 August 1971 and, ironically, potentially strengthened the position of Harold Wilson and his senior colleagues in their attempt to overcome the glaring weakness in the party's economic strategy – the absence of an agreement on wages with the trade unions – that had so damaged the Labour government after 1964. In his speech to the Labour Party Conference in October 1971, Wilson told delegates that the party was pledged to repeal the Act, but tantalisingly appeared to link repeal to an agreement on wages:

> At an industrial relations conference in New York last May, I tried to lay down the conditions of a solution, namely 'a voluntary compact between Government and industry – both sides of industry – in which Government can go forward boldly with economic policies necessary to increase production, knowing that this need not lead to inflation so long as it could count on industrial co-operation and restraint'.
>
> This is a reality we all recognise as fundamental to the future. When we, as we are pledged, assert the repeal of the Conservative Government's legalistic, inhuman and fundamentally unworkable Industrial Relations Act, we are pledged equally to discussion between the political and industrial wings of our Movement on the voluntary means of strengthening industrial relations and eliminating the causes of industrial tension.[18]

Wilson was fully aware that Labour's electoral fortunes were tied to an agreement with the unions on wages. This superseded the party's discussion of ideology through the NEC research programme because the problem of the trade unions, as Heath was finding out, went beyond ideology. Labour's immediate concern was not socialism but a 'voluntary compact' with the unions. By a coincidence of scheduling, the next speaker to address conference was Jack Jones. Aside from a modest request to the party 'to draw a line against any future attempts at legislative restrictions on independent trade unionism', the general secretary of the TGWU was at his most conciliatory: 'let us go on, on the foundations of the pledge to repeal and create a new approach'. The practical outcome of these two speeches was the creation of a TUC–Labour Party Liaison Committee to improve communication between the two wings of the labour movement. Delegates were reminded that such an improvement was necessary by Heffer, who found time not only to dismiss the Industrial Relations Act as 'the most pernicious and vicious piece of class legislation that has come before this country since before the Second World War', but also to remind conference that the reason the party in Parliament had at times experienced difficulty in fighting the Act was because 'we had, to some extent, our hands tied behind our back, because it was our party who unfortunately, for a short period of time, got led up a byway and opened the door to some extent in relation to this Industrial Relations Act'.[19]

The fight against the Industrial Relations Bill in Parliament ended when the Bill received the royal assent. Elsewhere, the TUC continued to oppose the Act by refusing to acknowledge its legitimacy until it was effectively put into abeyance by Heath.[20] The PLP in the meantime could do no more than wait upon a return to office for the chance to make good its pledge to repeal.[21] But it had done its duty by fighting the Bill to the last and in doing so had finally won back the trust of the trade unions that had been lost in 1969. As Don Concannon MP told conference: 'I think most of us will look back with pride at the last session of the House of Commons which broke a lot of records and found that the Tory Party were having to use wartime measures to get this legislation onto the statute book.'[22]

The Housing Finance Bill: 'an obvious antagonism towards those who pay rent'

No sooner had the Industrial Relations Act reached the statute book than the Conservative government pressed on with its next major and equally inflammatory measure, the Housing Finance Bill. Introduced by Peter Walker, Secretary of State for the Environment, the aim of the Bill was to establish 'fair rents', thereby redirecting housing subsidies 'from all council tenants to those, whether public or private tenants, in greatest need'.[23] Walker himself claimed that the measure would make Britain 'the first capitalist country in the world where no one could be evicted simply because they had not the money', and claimed that one of his predecessors at Housing – Labour's Dick Crossman, no less – agreed 'it would be the most Socialist measure to be introduced in housing'.[24] But what Walker and Heath intended as 'a major and progressive social reform aimed at tackling the problems of bad housing and homelessness', the Labour Party interpreted as yet another piece of class-inspired, partisan legislation, aimed at introducing market forces into the provision of public housing. As Campbell writes, the downside of Walker's apparent benevolence, and the aspect that Labour emphasised, 'was that council house rents for those tenants deemed to be able to afford them should rise to something nearer an economic level'.[25]

Labour's opening salvo against the measure was launched by Anthony Crosland, when the Bill was given its second reading on 15 November 1971. Decrying it as the product of 'the social philosophy of the 1930s rather than the 1970s', he attacked the Bill as 'the most reactionary and socially divisive measure that is likely to be introduced in the lifetime of this Parliament – and that is saying a good deal'.[26] The Housing Finance Bill was never likely to be taken on merit. On the Labour benches it was regarded as the continuation of a broader battle of which the Industrial Relations Bill had been the main clash so far. Indeed, such was the confrontational tone of the Heath government that any measure introduced by it simply could not be supported by Labour on the grounds of its provenance.[27] The implication of this approach to opposition was ominous for those Labour MPs sympathetic to British membership of the Common Market. For the Conservatives, Nicholas Scott wryly observed 'how quickly this measure has replaced the Industrial Relations Bill as the most divisive measure in the eyes of hon. Gentlemen opposite'.[28]

Crosland led by example in opposing the Bill's passage through the House of Commons. Assisted by a dedicated group of primarily left-wing Labour MPs, unusual bedfellows with whom he found common ground on this issue, he was invigorated by a fight that, for the most part, took place in standing committee. As Kevin Jefferys writes, 'During one of the longest committee stages in post-war politics, Crosland was frequently found leading a small band of Labour MPs through gruelling all-night sessions at the House.'[29] He regarded the Bill as stupid and illogical. 'One cannot transfer a market concept to a non-market situation', he told the House. He was supported by Ron Brown, who suggested that 'The principle feature of this Bill is an obvious antagonism towards those who pay rent.'[30]

The battle over the Housing Finance Bill was fought out in Standing Committee E, from 25 November 1971 to 29 March 1972. The committee met 57 times over a five-month period for a total of 248 hours. House of Commons stenographers transcribed 1.5 million words. Crosland himself could find 'no trace of any Committee stage of a Bill lasting anything like this length of time since the First World War'.[31] Meeting thrice weekly, the committee worked its way through the Bill's 103 clauses and 11 schedules line by line. It was a marathon effort. Crosland remained vigorously engaged throughout, attending 51 of the 57 meetings, but he was critical of Walker, who was not present to lead on the Bill for the government: 'It was he who said ... that it was "the most important reform in housing to take place this century".' Walker, as it happened, was otherwise engaged launching another measure of huge ambition, the Local Government Bill, which proposed no less than to redesign local government in England and Wales.[32] Frank Allaun cared little whether Walker was present or not, telling the committee that it was there to deal with 'the most vicious part of an altogether evil Bill, notably, the removal of £200 million a year housing subsidy compared with what it would have been by 1975'.[33]

While Crosland and his team embarked upon a war of attrition at Westminster, the wider party's deliberations over how to deal with the measure (specifically whether or not to endorse a policy of non-implementation by Labour-held councils across the country) threatened to displace Parliament as the main focus of the party's activity. As it stood, councils would be obliged to increase weekly rents by 50p in April 1972 or, if delayed, by £1 in October. Labour swiftly promised to repeal the measure, but the main difficulty Wilson and his Shadow Cabinet colleagues faced was reining in those in the party set upon defying the law. It was under the direction of the NEC rather than the PLP that this issue would be resolved. In a draft statement on housing policy discussed in December 1971, the NEC Housing Finance Working Group, anticipating Labour gains from the Conservatives in the local elections scheduled for May the following year and with them the responsibility for implementing the Tory legislation, stressed that it was essential 'that the reason for these rent increases is laid firmly at the Government's door'. When the working group (chaired by Allaun) met again in January 1972, a revised version of the draft statement was approved. Treading a fine line between legitimate obstruction and illegality, the statement suggested to Labour groups on local housing authorities 'that they do not impose the 50p rent increase on their weekly council rents at the beginning of April as suggested in the Conservative Housing Finance Bill, since this would be imposing hardship on people unnecessarily. The Bill is unlikely to have become law by April and we suggest that Local Authorities should not do the Government's dirty work for them.'[34] This became official party policy when the NEC issued a statement on the Bill on 20 January 1972; however the threat of non-implementation did not go away. Crosland, speaking in the House of Commons on 13 March 1972, distanced himself from any unconstitutional action, but argued that government had only itself to blame: 'if one practices the politics of confrontation as the Government have done, one finds that two can play at confrontation'.[35] In standing committee, he reiterated that 'it is no part of my duty as a democrat, a socialist and still less as an elected Member of my party's parliamentary committee, to condone, let alone encourage, defiance of the law', but Allaun warned Conservative members of the committee that they were 'crying for the moon' if they thought that they could increase rents by £1 a week 'and expect to get away with it without trouble'.[36]

The government brought the committee's consideration of the Bill to a swift end on 29 March 1972, by once again resorting to use of the guillotine on a major measure to curb Labour's endless opposition. Attending his fifty-first and final meeting, Crosland tellingly observed 'that in all our discussions there has been no suggestion...that people in this country are paying too little for housing...There has been no justification or explanation of why this step had to be taken.' Frank Allaun demanded that the Bill be called what it really was, 'The Rent Increase Bill'.[37] Labour members of Standing Committee E did not cause the Bill to be rewritten, nor did the PLP defeat the government in the House of Commons on the third reading. However, in running the Conservatives close time and again during the divisions on amendments to the Bill (even inflicting the occasional defeat) they subjected a government with a modest majority to a severe examination of its proposals by means of orthodox parliamentary opposition.

The People's Republic of Clay Cross[38]

The Conservative government got its measure but for the Labour Party there remained the problem of non-implementation. On 11 April 1972, Harry Nicholas, the general secretary of the Labour Party, wrote to the secretaries of all the Labour groups, central and CLPs reminding them that the NEC had decided 'after great consideration not to recommend a national policy of total non-implementation by Labour Councils'. This interpretation of the NEC's position was disputed by Allaun, who drew the general secretary's attention to the paragraph in the NEC statement 'Opposition to the Housing Finance Bill' issued on 10 March, which stated that 'the NEC has decided that it is not possible to give advice to local authorities on a national basis. This does *not* mean that this legislation should be accepted without resistance. Each Labour group must decide in the interests of its tenants and in the light of local circumstances, its own method of fighting this iniquitous legislation.'[39] In the House of Commons, Allaun accused the government of betraying council tenants: 'Never before in the history of this House and in the history of housing have councils been forced to make a profit out of their tenants. This is absolutely obnoxious and it is equally obnoxious to the local authorities.' The likely consequences of the measure were spelt out even more clearly by Eric Heffer. The government's measure was 'leading people...to argue about the whole question of whether it is any longer possible to accept the type of laws that Government are introducing'.[40]

The significance of Allaun's and, particularly, Heffer's remarks is that they highlighted the divide in the party between those who believed that the marathon fight against the Bill in committee plus the pledge to repeal signalled the limits of acceptable and constitutional opposition, and those, essentially to be found in the Tribune Group, who believed that Heath's break with consensus necessitated a rewriting of the rules. Heffer cited the example of a previous leader of the party, George Lansbury, who 'rather than put extra burdens on the people in his Borough, Poplar, he said "no, I will go to prison first" '.[41] Allaun, at least, chose to temper his words at the Labour Party Conference that October, telling delegates that 'my instinct is completely against implementation, but I cannot instruct or tell councillors to put their heads on the block; it is they who would suffer the consequences, not I'.[42] The previous month, 43 Labour-controlled local authorities had publicly opted for non-implementation. However, faced with the prospect of automatic disqualification from office and a £6,000 surcharge on each individual involved, all but one of them reversed their position. This left Clay Cross Council in North Derbyshire, which proceeded to put up 'the most sustained challenge to central government from a recalcitrant local authority since Poplar', and in the process became a huge embarrassment for the parliamentary leadership. 'Heath is going to fail in Clay Cross the same as Nixon failed in Vietnam', Councillor Graham Skinner confidently predicted.[43]

Clay Cross proved a bigger headache for Labour than for the government because it made martyrs of the Labour group in the eyes of party activists. When the NEC recommended to conference in 1972 withholding support for councils opting for a policy of non-implementation, delegates rejected the recommendation. In the meantime, rents did not go up in Clay Cross. The issue came to a head at conference the following year. Resolution 191, moved by Leicester East CLP, not only deplored the lack of initiative shown by the NEC in failing to defend Clay Cross Council, but also committed a future Labour government to remove retrospectively all penalties incurred by the Clay Cross councillors in their fight against the Act. Supporting the resolution, Judith Chegwidden (Putney CLP) told delegates that 'In indemnifying these councillors we merely recognise that these councillors were right yesterday, they are right today, and tomorrow they will still be right.' Replying for the NEC, Edward Short, Labour's deputy leader, stated that 'the NEC cannot possibly advise Labour councillors to act unlawfully', adding that a future Labour government would pass Acts of Parliament which some, no doubt, would bitterly resent, 'But we will expect them to carry them out.'[44] Short might wisely have left the matter there, having firmly emphasised the party's commitment to the rule of law. But he chose instead, 'To the general astonishment of the Shadow Cabinet and parliamentary colleagues',[45] to describe Clay Cross as 'something rather special' and pledge that the next Labour government would remove the disqualification from office from them. Before that, the NEC would 'consider ways and means of assisting councillors in their financial difficulties arising out of their refusal to implement the Housing Finance Act'.[46]

Short had risen to the deputy leadership in 1972, following the resignation of Roy Jenkins. Crosland had been a far more interesting option, but his candidature was sabotaged by supporters of Jenkins who, piqued by his refusal to join the fight for membership of the Common Market and determined to prevent their hero from being supplanted in the party hierarchy by a credible rival, had orchestrated a winning level of support for Short. For reasons best known to himself, Short, by singling out Clay Cross, had given encouragement to those bent upon making the party more overtly socialist. 'You made him Deputy Leader to stand up to the Left, I seem to recall', Crosland chided Jenkins; 'I trust you are giving your hero full support.'[47]

Ironically, it fell to Crosland to make good Short's promise. As Secretary of State for the Environment in 1974, he took no pleasure in partly extending to the Clay Cross councillors the amnesty introduced by the Conservative government for those late in implementing the Act. The disqualification from office was lifted; the £6,000 surcharge was not. It was an ignoble end to Crosland's noble efforts to defeat the Housing Finance Bill in Parliament. But, in November 1974, he had the satisfaction of introducing the Bill repealing Walker's Act.[48]

Economic and industrial policy: 'a soft, sodden morass of subsidised incompetence'

The parliamentary battles over the Industrial Relations Bill and Housing Finance Bill were predictably bitter, but they proved excessively divisive because the tone of government policy in the first half of the 1970–74 Parliament was so deeply antagonistic. Before the House of Commons reassembled after the 1970 summer recess, and before Heath and his colleagues got down to the serious business of implementing their manifesto promises, Harold Wilson used his annual speech to the Labour Party Conference to warn the country to prepare for a return to the misery of the 1930s: 'in the social services back to pre-Beveridge; back in housing to pre-Wheatley; back in health to pre-Bevan'.[49] When Anthony Barber, Iain Macleod's successor as Chancellor, rose to his feet in the Commons on 27 October 1970, to announce a £330 million reduction in public expenditure for 1971–72, tax cuts, the abolition of Labour's cherished Industrial Reorganisation Corporation (IRC), the discontinuation of the Regional Employment Premium (from September 1974), plus an increase in prescription charges, the introduction of museum and gallery charges and the discontinuation of free school milk for the over-sevens, Labour's resentment knew no bounds. 'Stupid as well as vicious', was Eric Heffer's immediate verdict.[50]

But no one antagonised Labour quite so much as John Davies, who had crossed swords with the Wilson government when Director-General of the Confederation of British Industry (CBI) 1965–69. Elected to Parliament for the first time in 1970, Davies had been installed by Heath at the Ministry of Technology after just one month in the House. Before the year was out he had been elevated to head the Department of Trade and Industry (DTI) where, in Gilmour's words, he 'demonstrated the disadvantage of inexperience'.[51] Davies's choice of language at the dispatch box appeared deliberately tailored to cause maximum offence. Announcing on 5 November the government's determination to make industry stand on its own feet or go to the wall, he declared that the consequence of treating the whole country as lame ducks was 'national decadence'. The vast majority, he told the House, 'lives and thrives in a bracing climate and not in a soft, sodden morass of subsidised incompetence'.[52] No rejection of the Labour government's industrial policy could have been more pointed. But, by his choice of words and the discourtesy he showed to the House by reading a prepared speech (rather than replying to the debate on Barber's mini-Budget from which he had been almost wholly absent), Davies designated himself as Labour's Aunt Sally for the duration of his time at the DTI.

Replying for Labour, James Callaghan condemned Davies for making 'no serious reply to the debate' and for instead making 'a brutal and insensitive speech'. A new minister had a special obligation to come to the House 'and learn what it is all about'. To laughter from the benches behind him, Callaghan added, only slightly menacingly, that 'no-one wants to hound a new Member'. More seriously, the former Chancellor recommended that in view of the balance of payments surplus, the government 'could afford to take a somewhat greater risk in order to put more men back at work'. But for the present, Labour's priority was 'to ensure that these policies are destroyed and rejected as soon as possible ... we shall do our best to make certain that we fight their policies as hard as we can'.[53]

It took six days for Davies's words to rebound on the government. On 11 November 1970, Frederick Corfield, the Minister for Aviation Supply, informed the House that the government would provide a loan of £42 million to Rolls-Royce aero-engines to forestall bankruptcy and enable the company to honour its contract to build the RB211-22 engine for the Lockheed TriStar aircraft. Corfield was an easy target. Did not his statement, inquired Tony Benn, make an absolute nonsense of everything that Davies had said about the IRC (which had been monitoring the work of Rolls-Royce) and lame ducks, 'since what the Government have done in giving this £42 million today is to brand one of our great companies world wide as a lame duck in a subsidised soft morass of competition'. 'The duck was not exactly sound when the right hon. Gentleman left it', Corfield gamely retorted.

But the momentum was with Labour. 'Is the Minister aware', asked Benn, 'that what annoys the House is the hypocrisy of making speeches of the kind that have been made and then coming forward to ask for the enormous sums which everybody recognised might be necessary?' Government embarrassment over the loan (which put a dent in the professed policy of disengagement from industry) turned into humiliation when, only two months later, on 4 February 1971, Corfield announced to the House that the government had taken the decision to 'acquire such assets of the aero-engine and marine and industrial gas turbine engine divisions of the company as may be essential... To ensure continuity of those activities of Rolls-Royce which are important to our national defence.'[54]

Corfield avoided using the word nationalisation, but the significance of his announcement was not lost on those in Labour's ranks seeking, through the NEC research programme, to point the party in this direction. One such was Heffer who, while undoubtedly delighted to have a Conservative government making the case for state ownership, still found time to offer the minister some career advice: 'You are not credible anymore: pack it in.' Benn delivered his own withering assessment of the decision four days later. 'It is not only Rolls-Royce which went bankrupt, but the Government's whole industrial policy.' Equally damning, and perhaps of greater concern to Heath and his ministers, was Enoch Powell's verdict from the back benches, charging the government with having 'cast doubt and discredit in the principles of capitalism and private enterprise for which the Conservative Party stands'. On 11 February, a two-line Bill nationalising parts of Rolls-Royce passed through the Commons in a single day and received the royal assent six days later. Heath's effort to wake up Britain was rapidly becoming a calamity.[55]

UCS, unemployment, U-turn

By April 1971, the consequences of the government's reduction in public expenditure and efforts to control inflation were becoming ever more apparent in the shape of 814,149 unemployed. As lame ducks went to the wall, the length of the dole queue grew to 1930s proportions. This did not deter Davies from announcing in June that government support for Upper Clyde Shipbuilders (UCS), a consortium of shipyards established by the Labour government in 1968, was to end. The following month he announced the liquidation of the loss-making consortium, by then £28 million in debt: 'The government has decided that nobody's interest will be served by making an injection of funds into the firm as it now stands.'[56] The UCS workforce hit back, brilliantly wrong-footing the government by declaring a 'work in'. At Westminster, Harold Wilson told Benn that he would 'neither condemn nor condone the occupation' but, being of a mind to mock the Prime Minister, he was considering 'sailing up the Clyde in a boat, visiting the doomed shipyards while Heath was yachting in the Admiral's Cup'. He even 'suggested he might wear his outfit as an Elder Brother of Trinity House, which is the honorary title all Prime Ministers have'. Benn, who as Minister of Technology had created UCS, was deeply offended, having attached himself very publicly to the cause of UCS employees by lunching with them in the Clydebank yard canteen within 24 hours of Davies's statement to the House, a gesture which some interpreted as 'full support for illegality'. Davies, rather than brand his Labour predecessor a lawbreaker, settled instead for the epithet 'evil genius'.[57] In Glasgow, the 'work in' was extensively covered by the media and quickly garnered massive indigenous support which sustained until the government, rattled by a warning from the chief constable of the city that closure of the yards would provoke civil disorder of an intensity unseen outside Northern Ireland, backed down and injected a further £35 million in February 1972, preserving 4,000 jobs.[58]

'The truth is that the Heath government lost its nerve in 1971–72 because of rising unemployment', writes Martin Holmes.[59] Throughout 1971, the number of jobless crept inexorably towards the 1 million mark. Labour devoted more of their allocated Supply Day debates to this subject in 1970–72, than to any other. From the outset of opposition, shadow ministers set out to tarnish the Heath government by recalling the 1930s; these were the 'Guilty Men' of the 1970s. In October 1971, Wilson told conference that unemployment was 'far above any figure which has been accepted at any time, by any political party, since the war, since the nation resolved never again to return to the dismal and divided 30's'. Roy Jenkins likewise described the government's record as 'the most abject and deliberate betrayal of election promises in modern British history. It makes Stanley Baldwin's 1935 about-turn on Abyssinia look like an outstanding act of honest statesmanship.'[60] In Parliament, Benn accused the Chancellor of using unemployment to get a grip on inflation 'a brutal remedy', adding that 'After the war, following the experience of the pre-war years, there was a general understanding that we would never go back to the situation of major unemployment which we had during the 1930s.' Jenkins focused on 'the fundamental issue of whether the Government are receding from the basic principles in the 1943 White Paper and taking refuge in the view that if there is severe inflation in the economy it absolves them from their central employment responsibility...do the Government accept this responsibility or are they retreating from the position which every British Government until them since the end of the war have accepted?'[61] No opportunity was missed to emphasise the incivility of the Conservatives and the alien nature of Heath's government. When the jobless figures for November were published on 16 December 1971, the number stood at 966,802.

Heath had a hinterland that included music and yachting which made him an especially easy target as the political temperature rose. At the 1971 Labour Party Conference, Michael Scarborough (Keighley CLP) had mocked the Prime Minister for taking 'time off from sailing to get back to the serious business of playing the organ', while the jobless tally grew.[62] When the figure of 1 million unemployed was announced in January 1972, against the backdrop of a miners' strike that would last into the middle of February and plunge the country into a series of power cuts, Wilson was unsparing in his condemnation of Heath in the Commons:

> Last Friday he left these shores, the first dole queue millionaire to cross the Channel since Neville Chamberlain. I was thinking of him as he went, and I was pleased to read that he conducted a madrigal. I wish he could have been with me meeting the shop stewards of Fisher-Bendix, attempting to avert a further 750 redundancies and the total closure of that factory...I wish the right hon. Gentleman could have heard the madrigal that my constituents were singing about him.
>
> They are a Government who have been proud to tear up even the mild prospectus of full employment of Sir Winston Churchill's coalition Government, and have destroyed the consensus by which post-war Governments have governed. But, above all, they are a Government who, by a combination of negligence, arrogance and wrongly directed policies, by an obsession with the balance sheet and not human beings, have produced a level of unemployment on which the whole country had thought we'd turned our backs for ever.[63]

In a mammoth speech that lasted one hour and eight minutes, Wilson demonstrated that, irrespective of Heath's contempt for his style of leadership, he was still a class act at the dispatch box, able to dominate a Prime Minister presiding over unprecedented levels of chaos.[64] The government was being assailed on all fronts: over the Industrial Relations Act; the Housing Finance Bill; unemployment; and now by the miners, defeat at whose hands, writes Robert Taylor, brought 'the beginning of a change in the whole direction of...economic policy'.[65] The 'better tomorrow' promised by the Conservatives during the 1970 general election campaign had failed to materialise.

'A more sensible way to settle our differences'[66]

Heath ran up the white flag. The government's strategy to transform British economic and industrial performance had failed. Humiliated by the miners, and under intense pressure over unemployment ('the most dreadful short period of concentrated stress ever endured by a British Government in peacetime', writes Campbell),[67] he went on television to announce his willingness to involve the trade unions in the government's effort to curb inflation. Talks between the government and the TUC followed in Downing Street on 9 March 1972. These, in Heath's words, would be 'wide-ranging without any limitations on the subjects concerned'.[68] Twelve days later, Barber presented a reflationary budget to Parliament that cut taxes by £1.2 billion and increased public expenditure by virtually trebling the Public Sector Borrowing Requirement for 1972–73. Pensions and benefits were also raised.[69] The stated aim of these measures was a growth rate of 5 per cent per year. It was a U-turn of unimaginable proportions. Heath had personally written in the 1970 manifesto that 'once a policy is established, the Prime Minister and his colleagues should have the courage to stick to it'.[70] The Conservative Party became unrecognisable under his leadership.

Barber's budget was supplemented by the publication the next day of a White Paper, *Industrial and Regional Development*, which, in announcing the appointment of a Minister for Industrial Development and the establishment of an Industrial Development Executive to oversee the investment of £315 million for 1973–75, effectively revived the Ministry of Technology and the function of the IRC.[71] Wilson could afford to be generous in his response. Barber had vindicated the economic and industrial policies of the Labour government: 'In a panic the right hon. Gentleman has done some good things and we congratulate him on that.' Roy Jenkins, wasting no opportunity to embellish his own achievements at the Treasury, was less benign, berating Barber for his past profligacy: 'twenty-one months of the strongest balance of payments in our history frittered away'.[72]

But, above all, Labour MPs reserved their ridicule for Davies. In the course of defending his previous utterances, to a predictable response from the benches opposite, he personified the humourless and po-faced nature of the Heath government. Insisting to the end that there was still no case for government 'bailing out failure caused by ineptitude and incompetence', he declared that he had never been 'an advocate of abandoning to their fate major sectors of British industry'. But it was when he uttered the words 'In a new and rapidly changing world...Government cannot afford to stand aside', that Labour Members, recalling his earlier evangelism for disengagement from industry, were reduced to helpless laughter:

> Hon. Members opposite may find that extraordinarily humorous...
> In a new and rapidly changing world industrial and commercial
> environment, Government cannot afford to stand aside...We
> have therefore decided to take powers to help industry to

modernise, adapt and rationalise . . . This matter is not humorous; far from it. Hon. Members opposite, with grave faces, have consistently spoken to me, day after day, about the problems of regional policy. Here I am determinedly seeking to make an impact on the problem and there is an extraordinary and quite outward degree of hilarity among hon. Members opposite.[73]

Labour MPs queued up to tease and condemn Davies, but the first to pass comment was the leader of the Liberal Party, Jeremy Thorpe, who commented that no one could accuse the Secretary of State of being doctrinaire: 'Indeed, some would regard him as the poor man's Wedgwood Benn.' The authentic Benn, Brian Walden informed Davies, was away loading his gun 'in the sure and certain knowledge that wherever he points it he will score a bulls-eye'. Turning first to the Budget, Walden likened Anthony Barber to Columbus on his return to the Court of Spain, having set out to get to India: 'If one turns up in a different place, there must be some modicum of restraint about how far one takes credit for what one has done.' Warning the Chancellor that he risked suffering from indigestion 'from too much eating of words', his thoughts turned to Davies, 'upon whose heroic speech I must now make a few comments':

> The Secretary of State appeared a bit annoyed, and also rather surprised, at the reception that it was getting. The right hon. Gentleman seemed to be worried that his own side of the House appeared to be treating his speech with a certain stoic gloom and that we were treating it with a certain hilarity. He thought we did not grasp the fact that we live in a changing world, a phrase he kept reiterating. It was not the changing world which amused us so much as the changing minds. We did not think that there was sufficient acknowledgement of where some of these ideas had come from. [74]

By the time Benn closed for Labour the following evening, Davies had thought better of exposing himself to further mockery. Lamenting the Secretary of State's absence, which possibly had something to do with his having been 'rather put out by the reception accorded his speech yesterday afternoon', Benn hoped he had understood that 'the laughter was directed not against the measures, which we shall study with great care, but, I am afraid, against the right hon. Gentleman himself, who consistently throughout his period in office has denounced measures very similar to the ones that he has now introduced.' This was a sweet moment for Benn, whose ministerial legacy had been rejected and now resurrected by Heath and Davies. 'Indeed, there were moments yesterday', he told the House, 'when I thought that we should hear from him about the white heat of the technological revolution'. But sarcasm gave way to a searing indictment of his opponent's record: 'As Director-General of the Confederation of British Industry, as a member of the National Economic Development Council before the change of Government, he, better than any other member on the Government Front Bench, knew the reality of the problems facing this country, Government and the regions.'[75]

It did not get any better for Davies. On 22 May, he endured an ominous silence from the Tory benches and cheers from the Labour side when the Industry Bill foreshadowed by Barber's Budget was given its second reading. Announcing, among other measures, the restoration of regional investment grants and the allocation of £45 million to the successor to UCS, he told the House that 'Both on the regional, and on the national score there is a need for the means of action. I mean to provide the means.' Thus, the Industry Bill would permit the Secretary of State to provide financial assistance (with the consent of the Treasury) where in his opinion it would benefit the economy of the UK or any part of the UK.[76] Welcoming the Bill, Benn drew attention to the similarities to Labour's own Industrial Expansion Act 1968:

> The instruments of intervention which the right hon. Gentleman invites the House to grant him are virtually unlimited in their impact. The criteria are left deliberately wide to permit the Government to assess the economic prospects of the companies they wish to support. Clause 7, laying down the purpose for which these powers may be used, has a familiar ring about it. Those purposes are 'to promote the development . . . of an industry . . . to promote the efficiency of an industry . . . to create, expand or sustain productive capacity in an industry . . . to promote the reconstruction, reorganisation or conversion of an industry . . . to encourage the growth of, or the proper distribution of undertakings, in an industry.' These purposes have a familiar ring because they come from another measure to which the right hon. Gentleman made no reference – the Industrial Expansion Act, 1968.
>
> The right hon. Gentleman had every one of those powers he now requires of us when he assumed his present office. He had those powers, including the power, to which he attaches such importance, to take equity with the consent of the company involved – a phrase again taken word for word from the Industrial Expansion Act. Yet he forced through Parliament as recently as last year a repeal of that Act, and he made no reference today to the fact that this is not his first Industry Bill as Secretary of State but his second.[77]

Davies was a defeated man. Pilloried from his own side by Sir Harry Legge-Bourke for introducing 'a Socialist Bill by ethic and philosophy', he was dispatched by Benn with the promise that Labour would use the measures 'more radically than the right hon. Gentleman himself will use them'. But Edmund Dell was keen to lay the blame where it ultimately lay: 'Our pragmatic Prime Minister, having marched his troops up the hill to laissez-faire and disengagement, is marching them down to selective intervention on a massive scale.'[78]

In place of free collective bargaining

Heath's talks with the TUC, ongoing since March, broke down on 2 November 1972.[79] Four days later, a 90-day freeze on wages, prices, rents and dividends (with the provision for a further 60-day extension) was announced.[80] 'We have come to the conclusion that we have no alternative but to bring in statutory measures', Heath told the House of Commons.[81] Wilson taunted him over 'the biggest reversal of positions he has taken on any subject'. Enoch Powell wondered if Heath had taken leave of his senses: 'Does he not know that it is fatal for any government, party or person to seek to govern in direct opposition to the principles on which they were entrusted with the right to govern?'[82] It was the worst of U-turns. 'Labour's compulsory wage control was a failure and we will not repeat it', the Conservative Party's 1970 general election manifesto had promised.[83] This had been written in the expectation that industrial relations reform, successfully implemented, 'would restore rationality to pay bargaining and thus halt the inflationary push of excessive wage settlements'.[84] Instead, the trade unions had the government on the run.

Heath executed this fundamental U-turn without a blush, welcoming the breathing space it would allow to reach a voluntary agreement with the TUC. Quite why the Conservative Party was impersonating the Labour Party by this stage was never convincingly explained. Anthony Barber subsequently argued that 'a good government will always do what it believes to be best in the national interest, even if it's highly embarrassing'.[85] But it was much more serious than that. Reversion to a statutory incomes policy signalled the defeat of the Conservative Party two and a half years before a general election was due.

At the same time, Peter Walker, newly installed at the DTI (Heath having finally put Davies out of his misery by moving him to become Britain's chief representative to the Common Market) was providing for the biggest expansion in the history of British Steel and halting the contraction of the coal industry at a combined cost to the taxpayer of £4 billion.[86] Far from ushering in a 'better tomorrow', Heath's government, in Benn's words, was providing the 'spadework for socialism'. In these circumstances, it was inevitable that Labour's own policy debate would be coloured by the abrupt change of course in economic and industrial policy. Davies, after all, had taken powers of intervention that were 'virtually unlimited in impact' and government subsidies to industry exceeded the amount brought forward by any previous government.[87] At the 1973 Labour Party Conference, Benn told delegates that the party's proposed industrial policy 'occupies a central place in meeting our central objective of bringing about the fundamental and irreversible shift in the balance of wealth and power in favour of working people and their families'.[88] Denis Healey's use of near identical language in his own speech that year demonstrated just how difficult Heath's loss of nerve had made life for Labour's parliamentary leadership.

Heath, Barber and Davies, but above all Heath, bequeathed to Wilson and his colleagues an industrial strategy which, when refined by the NEC research programme, saddled Labour with a policy that earned the party a 38 per cent opinion poll rating in the run up to the February 1974 general election. Roy Jenkins, whose influence on policy diminished after his resignation as deputy leader in 1972, was a rare voice of candour. 'It is not much good talking about fundamental and irreversible changes in our society and being content with a thirty-eight per cent Labour voting intention. Democracy means that you need a substantially stronger position than this to govern effectively at all, let alone effect a peaceful social revolution.'[89] Jenkins, of course, reckoned without Heath rounding off an unlucky and at times calamitous premiership by inviting the National Union of Mineworkers (NUM) to administer a second drubbing to the government,[90] propelling Labour back into office on a 37.1 per cent share of the vote.

Jenkins was by this time considerably closer to Heath on the major policy issues of the day than to his own party. Labour's leading social democrat was metamorphosing into a conservative at the expense of social democracy in the Labour Party. Jenkins and Heath had clashed in the House of Commons over the government's original economic policy and it was the former Chancellor who landed the heaviest blow following the announcement of the 90-day freeze when he asked the Prime Minister if he had 'now abandoned his constantly reiterated view that a statutory policy could only make inflation worse in the long run, or does he now regard the short-term situation as so disastrous that he cannot afford any longer to think about the long run?'[91] But the policy issue that united them above all else was that of proposed British membership of the Common Market, Jenkins's personal political objective in the 1970–74 Parliament, and the flagship policy of the Heath government.

The Labour Party and the Common Market: 'wading in *merde*'[92]

Edward Heath was determined to take the UK into the Common Market. Harold Wilson had also been determined in 1967 and had anticipated renewing the British application after the 1970 election, but here the similarity ended. Heath's dominance over his party was such that the Common Market did not become an internally divisive issue. There were enough Conservative MPs opposed to membership (upwards of 30) to threaten the government's majority if the Labour Party voted unanimously to oppose any terms Heath might secure but, as an issue in itself, the Common Market did not threaten the unity of the Conservative Party. For Labour MPs, the Common Market was a third major parliamentary battle to be fought. Already harrying the government over the Industrial Relations and Housing Finance Bills, many in the PLP looked forward to extending hostilities should the Conservative government succeed in its negotiations where the previous Labour government had failed. However, as a majority of the PLP had voted in favour of British membership of the Common Market in a vote in the House of Commons as recently as 10 May 1967, a fragmented response to Heath's policy was inevitable. Labour might have accommodated a difference of opinion in the PLP had the issue not become a litmus test for socialism for anti-Marketeers on the left, an article of faith for pro-Marketeers on the centre-right, and a threat to party unity for the leader. Therefore, in opposition 1970–74, a debate on proposed British membership of the Common Market became at the same time a debate on the future direction of the Labour Party.

From the outset of opposition Wilson struggled to defend the party's existing policy on the Common Market. Labour's 1970 general election manifesto had reaffirmed the intention to join an enlarged community 'provided that British and essential Commonwealth interests can be safeguarded'.[93] But, as early as September 1970, the forces of opposition to membership within the labour movement had begun to assert themselves. At the TUC Congress, a mildly worded composite motion calling for a programme of action 'to inform trade unionists ... of the full implications of this country's negotiations for entry to the Common Market' was rejected by 8,042,000 votes to 700,000, although the official TUC position remained that it was 'neither desirable nor necessary to take a decision either for or against British membership ... until the terms are known'.[94] A matter of weeks later, at the Labour Party Conference, Harry Urwin told delegates that Britain should reject any terms 'which would involve a threat to full employment', a contribution that appeared to ignore the 600,000 unemployed bequeathed by the Labour government. For the NEC, Joe Gormley did his best to defend the existing policy, suggesting that 'it is not good enough for us to say that we should change our policy on such important issues just because we do not happen to be in government', music no doubt to the ears of pro-Marketeers, but when the vote was taken conference came within 95,000 votes of supporting Urwin. Yet, once Jack Jones and Hugh Scanlon made it clear that they would oppose membership, the die was cast. Wilson had no intention of finding himself on the opposite side of the fence to the trade unions on a major issue for the second time in just over a year. He told conference that the party would not accept the argument 'that whatever the terms, we have to go in because we are too weak to stay out'.[95]

Wilson was conceding the need for unity, which for the time being at least would be on the trade unions' terms. Anxious to see Labour returned to power in 1974 or 1975, Wilson understood that this was less likely without trade union co-operation. Additionally, he was unhappy with the terms emerging from the negotiations with the French, although he was no doubt aware that a Labour government may not have fared any better. However, his immediate priority was the political cohesion of the Labour Party, which meant avoiding a split with the trade unions and beyond that reaching some sort of agreement on wages. If the price of such an agreement was to be damned by Roy Jenkins and other ardent pro-Marketeers in the party's ranks for his inconsistency (having as Prime Minister tabled the second British application) then so be it.

'Off-again, on-again, go-again Flanagan' and the language of Chaucer[96]

At Westminster, the central issue was how to accommodate those pro-Marketeers who, unlike Wilson and other pragmatists in the Shadow Cabinet, were determined to support entry irrespective of trade union and largely left-wing opposition. This placed Wilson in an unenviable position. In June 1970 he had looked forward to electoral success and to leading a renewed application for membership. Within months of Labour's defeat he found himself boxed in on the Common Market until trade union and public hostility to membership subsided. Had the PLP been united in favour of entry he would have been better placed to defend the manifesto. But the PLP was not united, and in 1971 it became emphatically disunited thanks to James Callaghan. Of all those who moved from being pro- to anti-Market in opposition, none was so important as the former Home Secretary. An Atlanticist by instinct and, crucially, in credit with the unions since leading the resistance to *In Place of Strife*, Callaghan declared his opposition to the Common Market (and the Common Agricultural Policy (CAP), which he suspected Heath would accept unreformed) in lurid terms. Speaking in Southampton on 25 May 1971, only four days after the Anglo-French summit that cleared the way for British entry, he warned not only of an end to the import of cheap food from the Commonwealth if Britain joined the Common Market, a fair and serious point, but also of a threat to the English language following remarks by President Pompidou that French should become the language of Europe because 'English was the language of the United States':[97] 'Millions of people in Britain have been surprised to hear that the language of Chaucer, Shakespeare and Milton must in future be regarded as an American import from which we must protect ourselves if we are to build a new Europe.' This was Callaghan at his worst, resorting to a level of criticism of the Common Market that risked portraying pro-Market Labour MPs as collaborators. If the price of membership was acceptance of French as the language of the Common Market (which it wasn't) he told his audience, 'then the answer is quite clear and I will say it in French to prevent any misunderstanding: "Non, merci beaucoup" '.[98]

Reviewing the speech, Anthony Howard observed of Callaghan that 'No one else in British public life can muster up quite those same plain man's tones with which to reduce a complex issue to a no-nonsense, down-to-earth matter. But, over and above that, he happens also to be in a position virtually to determine what Labour's eventual attitude to any Brussels terms will be', adding 'no one has ever questioned Mr Callaghan's capacity to sense the predominant mood of the party and then to respond to it'.[99] Essentially, Callaghan was being no more pragmatic than Wilson. Not unreasonably, he regarded the case for the Common Market as unproven.[100] If the unions were against entry, the party must follow suit in the interests of unity. In a letter to Jack Jones, he identified three common objectives: 'to beat Heath, to keep the party united, and to stop us going into the Common Market'.[101] There was nothing remarkable about these, except that the third dramatically reduced Wilson's scope for protecting the position of the pro-Marketeers.[102] An alliance between Callaghan and Jones was simply too powerful to challenge. If Wilson wavered on opposing entry, the unions had an alternative leader lined up to replace him. Not for Callaghan the deputy leadership of the party coveted by Jenkins's supporters for their hero; he was playing a longer game, the end point of which was the return of a Labour government he would be well placed to lead if Wilson stepped down. His 'language of Chaucer' speech, as it became known, kept most of the Labour Party united, but in demonising the Common Market, and by extension Labour's pro-Marketeers, it also contributed to the weakening of the PLP and subsequently the 1974–79 Labour government.

Although Wilson did not formally state his opposition to entry on the Heath terms until October 1971,[103] once Callaghan aligned himself with the unions the position of the pro-Marketeers was significantly weakened. It was no longer a question of whether Labour would reject entry, rather whether or not the PLP would be allowed a free vote when the time came for Parliament to vote on the matter. Inevitably, the pro-Marketeers became increasingly critical of Wilson as the ground beneath them began to shift. For those among them who regarded Roy Jenkins as their leader, there was much more at stake for the Labour Party than membership of the Common Market. If Wilson abandoned them over entry, he risked splitting the party in favour of the unions, conference and, crucially, a left-wing agenda for the party with which he did not agree and which would reduce his chances of recovering the premiership. Hounded themselves, they were insensitive to the difficulty of Wilson's position. Not surprisingly, he found their criticism difficult to take. Relations between the two were perhaps irrevocably damaged by the events of 17–20 July 1971, the weekend of a special Labour Party Conference on the Common Market and a hugely controversial meeting of the PLP.

A special conference to determine the party's official line on the Common Market had been called by the NEC (in May) in anticipation of a vote on the terms in the House of Commons in July. When the government subsequently scheduled the vote for October, the NEC decided against reaching a decision on the day of the conference, preferring to wait until its next meeting before recommending a particular line. Wilson's was the key speech, but it was by no means the most memorable, outshone by a number of outstanding contributions from both the pro- and anti-Market camps.[104] When he did speak he appealed for tolerance, but left no one in any doubt about what position he would adopt:

> ... the decision the NEC takes on 28 July, the decision Conference will be asked to take in October, will be fully consistent with what we have said over these four years and more. Never have we said – nor is a single word we, or I, have said capable of being construed as meaning – that we have to accept whatever terms emerged. We reserved the right to judge the terms of entry against the potential benefits, and on that test, and on no other, to decide for or against entry, and this we shall do.
>
> I reject the assertions, wherever they come from, that the terms this Conservative Government have obtained are the terms the Labour Government asked for – and we did not in fact get involved in the negotiations – the terms the Labour Government would have asked for, the terms the Labour Government would have been bound to accept. I reject these assertions.[105]

It was a risky strategy, appeasing the anti-Market left while at the same time trying to preserve the authority of a parliamentary leadership likely to be shorn of its pro-Marketeers over this issue. 'It was like watching someone being sold down the river into slavery, drifting away, depressed but unprotesting', writes Jenkins.[106]

In *The Times*, David Wood mourned 'An end to idealism on Europe', in an article highly condemnatory of the Labour leader's speech. 'He makes no attempt to balance the complex argument, or avoid prejudice or to spare the pride of the European socialists and trade unionists, much less the European politicians whose help and goodwill he was soliciting until the general election last year. He makes the Common Market sound like a Heath plot.'[107]

Wilson was notoriously sensitive to press criticism, and Wood's article, couched in the language of the pro-Jenkins Marketeers, could only alienate him at a time when the latter needed him most. It did not help matters that on the day Wood's article appeared, Jenkins made what Benn describes as a 'great speech' in favour of entry at a meeting of the PLP, which at the same time 'was of course a direct attack on Harold Wilson, and also on Healey and Crosland, who had climbed off the fence against the Market'.[108] It was not so much what Jenkins said but how his supporters responded to it that finally saw the pro-Marketeers cast adrift. Jenkins describes it as 'an uncompromising, even an inflammatory speech', that 'released some pent-up feelings against the sophistry of the Party's change of line'.[109] A majority of the Labour government would have accepted the Heath terms, he told the meeting. They 'were about as good as those with direct knowledge of the situation believed were realistically possible to get in 1967 and almost equally today'.[110] Talk of Britain betraying its kith and kin was nonsense. When, during his period as Chancellor, sterling had come under pressure, the Australians had proved 'without exception the toughest, roughest, most self-interested government with which I ever had to deal'. The suggestion by Callaghan that the economy should be run flat out for five years was not a policy, it was an aspiration: 'We were not lacking in aspirations in the early days of the last Government. What we were lacking was results.' And, as for left-wing calls for 'socialism in one country', 'That is always good for a cheer. Pull up the drawbridge and revolutionise the fortress. That's not a policy either: it's just a slogan, and it is one which becomes not merely unconvincing but hypocritical as well when it is dressed up as our best contribution to international socialism.' If Britain rejected the Common Market, he concluded, 'it would not be rugged independence which we would achieve. It would in practice be a greater degree of dependence upon suppliance towards the United States than anything we had known in the past.'[111]

It was a speech that demolished many of the arguments against entry and which made Jenkins's reluctance to confront the wider party all the more puzzling. At both the special conference and the Labour Party Conferences of 1971 and 1972, he declined to champion the Common Market cause, a point not lost on Benn who, from the chair at conference in 1972, humiliated him over his failure to take on his opponents in a less hospitable environment than a House of Commons committee room full of his own supporters.[112] But at the PLP meeting the speech was greeted, according to Jenkins, with 'more violent applause than any other speech which I have ever delivered. It came from about half the audience, punctuated every few sentences, and at the end continued for several minutes as a major demonstration'; according to Benn, the speech was greeted by a prearranged demonstration of support.[113] The effect of the speech, intended or otherwise, was described by Wood on the front page of

The Times the following morning as a fight to save Labour's unity in a crisis over the leadership.[114]

Jenkins's speech was an assault on the party's faint-hearts and not, typically, a challenge for the leadership.[115] But Wilson had had enough both of the sanctimonious pro-Marketeers and the out and out antis, the latter having briefed viciously against Jenkins in the wake of his speech. In a statement to the PLP the following day full of allusion to the Gaitskellites' successful prosecution of the Bevanites nearly 20 years earlier, he told the meeting that 'A Party within a Party is no less so because it meets outside the House, and in more socially agreeable surroundings', a dig at his deputy's taste for a comfortable life. He was reopening old wounds, interpreting the pro-Jenkins Marketeers' criticism of his handling of the Common Market issue as further evidence (eight years on from his election as party leader) of their questioning of the legitimacy of his leadership:[116]

> ...whoever is leader will have to deal with the forces and factions from wherever they may come. If I have to warn one faction about its unbecoming manoeuvring, I must also express my condemnation of those last night who reacted to it in a manner we have all been too familiar with in the past. Some were not outside the door last night before the knives were out, hatchets disinterred, the invocations to retaliation heard. There used to be a Keep Calm Group. I commend the idea to the Party.
>
> What I object to is when for purposes which may seem good for other less commendable reasons, aid and comfort is given to our political opponents, especially by careful and anonymous press briefing. Last night was not the first sortie. Last Saturday, before I spoke at Conference, some members of this Party had obtained by means of which they cannot be proud, a copy of the text of my speech and were denouncing it to Conservative newspapers in abusive terms. If this is what they feel, let them stand up and say it here, to me, to their colleagues. And in view of the choice of language used, far transcending any words used by any member of the Tory Party, I am surprised that any of those good colleagues can find it in their hearts to sully their purity by continuing to sit on the Front Bench at my invitation.[117]

This, Benn writes, 'was received with acute embarrassment by the Party'. Eight days later, the NEC agreed to oppose entry to the Common Market on the terms negotiated by the Heath government. It was a watershed for the Labour Party. Far from feeling sad about it, Callaghan informed his colleagues that he thought the Treaty of Rome an awful thing the more he knew about it.[118]

The Road to Brighton Pier revisited[119]

At the Labour Party Conference in October, the NEC resolution inviting the PLP 'to unite wholeheartedly in voting against the Government's policy' was moved by Denis Healey, who had somehow moved from being pro- to anti-Market without incurring the same level of odium as Wilson or, to a lesser extent, Crosland. Healey presented the resolution in terms of the Conservative government's domestic political agenda, which made opposition to entry seem both reasonable and sensible: 'And what about Mr Heath? What an extraordinary contrast between the rigid man of iron we see over here when he is dealing with the Clydeside workers, with Rolls Royce...and the way he crumples up in negotiation the moment he crosses the Channel... Unlike all the existing members, we have to give up cheap food from the Commonwealth in order to buy dear food from Europe.'[120]

The debate produced few surprises. George Brown managed a last hurrah, making sport of Callaghan's support for membership at the time of the 1967 application. Callaghan chided his former Cabinet colleague over his use of selective quotation but, recognising a spent force when he saw one, gently indulged him. 'George: well, George was George', he told delegates to much laughter.[121] But when the laughter subsided, Callaghan let slip a speech foreshadowing both Margaret Thatcher's 'No! No! No!' to Delors and European Monetary Union (EMU) in the House of Commons in 1990, and Norman Tebbit's infamous anti-EU speech to the 1992 Conservative Party Conference,[122] which was so bloodcurdlingly uncompromising as to seriously question the sanity of the pro-Marketeers if they imagined they could defy the party with impunity and still retain a position of influence:

> The extraordinary thing is – and I cannot understand why Heath accepted it, because George Brown did not accept it when he was negotiating – that the Tory Government have accepted the common agricultural policy in all its shapes and all its purposes...world prices are going down, and therefore one might reasonably expect the British consumer who, for over 100 years has been free to import food from any part of the world, might get the benefit of it, but this Government has the brass neck to put a levy of £5 a ton on every ton of Barley...and £4 a ton on every ton of wheat that is coming in...deliberately putting up the price of food against the housewife by 20 per cent as far as the price of cereals is concerned; a madness. Does anybody really believe that we would have accepted that sort of policy?...if everybody else is saying what a Labour Cabinet would have accepted, let me say I know damn well that there are many members of a Labour Cabinet who would

never have accepted that. Then somebody quibbles that the terms are as much as we ought to be willing to accept. No, no, no, no, no! It would never have been possible to have got us to have accepted this sort of crazy condition.

I hope there will be a demand for a card vote so that we can see quite clearly the real opinion of the Conference as it is expressed. And do not let anyone try to cloud the issue; the British people are entitled to know where we stand . . . it is our job on 28 October to get the Tories out of office. And, therefore, we need the maximum vote on that day irrespective of what Conservative Members do. The National Executive judges that the mood of the Party is that all members of the Party should join hands on this issue and accept the verdict of the Party.[123]

It was a speech every bit as powerful as Jenkins's to the PLP in July but, by emphasising the view of conference on this particular issue while having no intention of otherwise conceding ground on the sovereignty of conference decisions, he risked the autonomy of the PLP in government if it backfired.

Wilson, in his speech, looked ahead to the PLP meeting of 19 October, at which MPs would decide on how the party should vote in Parliament. 'Conference does not dictate that decision, but every Labour member before he votes in the Parliamentary Party meeting will give full weight to this Conference decision.'[124] This done, he turned up the heat on the pro-Marketeers:

There is not one Labour Member of Parliament who could have been elected by his own efforts. He is where he is because of the efforts and dedication of thousands upon thousands of those represented by delegates here today. And he is elected to be in his place and to do the job he was sent to do. Reading about this Conference you would think it's only about one thing. How X or Y or Z is going to vote on 28 October. Conference has declared its voice on that by 'inviting' members to follow its decision.[125]

Conference supported the NEC resolution overwhelmingly by a margin of five to one. The only outstanding issue was the suspected willingness of the pro-Marketeers to defy the party and vote with the government in Parliament.

The Shadow Cabinet motion opposing the government's proposal to enter the Common Market, 'on the terms negotiated', was moved by Wilson himself when the PLP met on 19 October.[126] The amendment proposing acceptance of the terms was moved by Michael Stewart. It was to this meeting that the Labour Party's debate over the Common Market had ultimately been heading all along. At issue was the wisdom of formalising a split over the Common Market by denying the PLP a free vote in Parliament, forcing pro-Marketeers to vote with a Conservative government it otherwise wished to see defeated and removed from office no less than any Labour MP opposed to entry. However, Wilson had reluctantly concluded that the price of unity was the demonisation of the pro-Marketeers even though, nine days later, speaking on the final day of the 'Great Debate'[127] in Parliament, he 'hedged so cleverly that it was clear that if a Labour Government was elected when he was Prime Minister, he would simply accept the Common Market'.[128]

Accordingly, he moved the motion opposing the terms without enthusiasm. The best he could manage as a justification for voting against the government was that 'if Mr Heath considered he had taken a democratic step by allowing his Party a free vote, it was our view that the only meaningful vote would be a free vote of the British people in a General Election'. Michael Stewart, moving his amendment, stated that a vote against the terms would be a missed opportunity for economic growth, but the argument had long been settled. So much so that Callaghan's thunderous warning that 'Taken to its logical conclusion, Mr Stewart's Amendment would have us in the Lobby with the Tories against thirty Tory rebels. Was this the path of good sense for the Party? To go against the TUC, Annual Conference, the people of this country?', was frankly overdone. The PLP voted in favour of Wilson's motion 159 to 89.[129]

Of greater importance was the motion moved by William Hamilton, which proposed a free vote and was the party's last chance to avoid a split. Appealing to MPs to 'tolerate one another on 28 October and thereafter give an undertaking to oppose by every means whatever the Government do', he added that the party could still get out of its present dilemma, 'but it required tolerance and compromise'. These words were echoed by Jack Ashley, seconding the motion, who warned that 'if a three line whip was imposed differences of opinion would be transformed into a split'. The anti-Marketeers had won a famous victory, he told the meeting. 'In time of victory there was room for compassion: the task was to keep the Party together and ensure the return of a Labour Government.' However, this was not the issue over which the PLP was going to declare UDI from the wider party and the unions. Hamilton's motion was defeated by 140 to 111 votes.[130]

The debate in the House of Commons from 21 to 28 October 1971, saw the best of the pro-Marketeers. Eloquent in his defiance, Bill Rodgers lamented that 'When opportunities are refused and vision withers, bitterness and cynicism take their place'. Charles Pannell declared uncompromisingly that 'I do not go into the Division Lobby behind any Tories; I go in by my own right. I am a free man, an International Socialist, and a member of the Labour Party, in that order, and on Thursday night my priorities will be right.' Recalling Michael Foot's assertion in 1967 that he would not be whipped into Europe, Pannell told the House that 'Frankly, I am not to be whipped out of it.' John Mackintosh accused the anti-Marketeers of having no overall philosophy, 'only a discrete group of fears. They are fearful people, fearful that they cannot adopt a brand of socialism involving a wide extension of public ownership and physical controls.' But from the front bench came a more earthy contribution: 'the only reason the French want us in the Common Market is that they wish to send their apples over here', Callaghan told the House.[131]

At the conclusion of the debate, Wilson did his best to draw a line under the party's and his own unhappy experience on the issue since losing office 16 months earlier: 'The condemnation of this Government is not that they failed to secure terms which would have ensured that the Labour Government's stated requirements were met. The condemnation of them is that they did not even try.' The last word, appropriately given his own role in influencing the party's position, belonged to Callaghan: 'Our conclusion in the Labour Party, having taken into account the costly terms of entry, is that we do not believe that the economic benefits of entry are sufficiently clear to justify the price that is asked.'[132]

Sixty-nine Labour MPs defied the party and voted with the government in favour of joining the Common Market. A further 20 abstained. A significant Conservative protest (39 against plus two abstentions) was easily cancelled out and little commented upon as Heath secured an overall majority of 112 (356 to 244). 'It was terribly tense', Benn wrote in his diary, 'there had been rumours of people fighting after the vote; in fact they were just shouting at Roy Jenkins as he went through the Lobby. It was awful.'[133] For high-profile pro-Marketeers this was as far as their rebellion could safely extend without plunging the party into civil war. Jenkins and most of the other 68 Labour MPs who voted for the terms, subsequently voted against the government (much to their dismay) as it attempted to pass the European Communities Bill into law.[134] The task of ensuring that the government was not defeated on the second and third readings of the Bill fell to lesser known figures on the Labour back benches such as George Russell Strauss, Freda Corbet, Michael Barnes and John Roper. Roper formed a close alliance with Kenneth Clarke in the Conservative Whips' office to co-ordinate Labour abstentions to offset the votes of die-hard anti-Market Conservatives on crucial divisions. Writes Edward Heath: 'Roper took utmost care to prevent havoc and ill-feeling in the Labour Party. To achieve this, he organised a rota among pro-European Labour MPs to ensure that there were different groups of people absenting themselves from the House for crucial amendments.'[135] It was not until 13 July 1972 that Roper and his dedicated band of abstainers could stand down. After more than 100 parliamentary votes, taking up over 300 hours of debate, the European Communities Bill received its third and final reading. The government's majority had at times fallen below ten, on one occasion as low as four. Had it not been for Roper and his colleagues the Bill might have fallen. As Jenkins writes:

> What we were desperately concerned about was avoiding a single defeat in any one of the ninety-two divisions on the bill which were to follow until, on 13 July, third reading was secured by a majority of seventeen. Had any single one of them gone wrong we would have been confronted with the most stark alternatives. Either we could have let the adverse vote stand, in which case we would have destroyed our vote of 28 October, for the legislation was so drafted that it had to be carried unamended for Britain to be able to enter the Community. Or some of us would have to switch our vote, in the most exposed position and under the most powerful searchlight, when the issue was brought back before the House and when there could be no doubt that we had the fate of the Government in our hands.[136]

Because of Roper, it never came to this, but the successful third reading of the Bill was not the end of the debate inside the Labour Party. For the anti-Marketeers the issue was never the Heath terms, it was 'never' to the Common Market full stop. In this regard the Bill's enactment made little difference. In March 1972, the Shadow Cabinet had voted in favour of a referendum on Britain's membership of the Common Market, and in October 1972 conference passed a motion calling upon a future Labour government to reverse the decision to join unless new terms were negotiated and the consent of the British people obtained. Michael Foot received a standing ovation when he told delegates 'do not let anyone imagine that the fight about the Common Market is over on January 1 [1973, the date on which British membership took effect]'.[137]

Wilson, speaking in support of the NEC statement advocating a referendum, called for the British people to be given the right to decide on the Heath terms (which he described as 'the most abject surrender of Britain's rights to France since Henry VI'). 'If this statement is rejected, you reject the right of the people to decide. No other resolution adequately provides for the British people having the last word, the right to self-determination which Norway has had, Denmark has had, Ireland has had, and we have said the British people must have.'[138] But, with Labour ahead in the opinion polls, a lead it held through to January 1974, and with the prospect of his becoming Prime Minister once again increasing, Wilson could look forward to a referendum on Britain's membership of the Common Market as a way of repairing the split of 28 October 1971. Given that he had applied to take Britain into the Common Market in 1967, it was unlikely that taking Britain out would be an objective of his next premiership. So he could afford to give the party and conference the policy it wanted, while relying on the British people to rescue the Labour Party from itself in due course by voting to stay in the Common Market on terms renegotiated by his government.

Until then the anti-Marketeers would have to be further appeased. Thus, the party declined the invitation to send delegates to the Strasbourg Assembly in 1973. 'From what I have seen of the nonsense at Strasbourg', said Stan Orme, 'it is taking Members of Parliament away from Westminster, where they ought to be doing their job to what is – and let us make no bones about it – a very cushy number.'[139] But the anti-Marketeers were in the ascendancy for the short term only. Senior members of the Shadow Cabinet were already busy at work designing the fig leaf that would be required when renegotiation of the terms eventually took place.

The Labour Party's internal debate over the Common Market was the single most important issue of consequence for the Labour Party in opposition. The Industrial Relations Bill deeply antagonised the whole labour movement, and the Housing Finance Bill prompted a parliamentary fight of epic proportions, but neither of these measures had quite the impact on Labour's cohesion and ideology that the Common Market did. Callaghan was the key figure in this. The champion of PLP participation in the NEC research programme, he was the villain (in the interests of party unity) on this occasion, adopting an anti-Market stance that turned the debate inside the PLP into a rerun of the battle over *In Place of Strife*. While it was never likely that Wilson would take a contrary line to the unions over entry, it remained at least a possibility (particularly in light of the contentiousness of the Heath government in virtually all other areas of policy) for as long as senior figures in the parliamentary leadership adhered to the 1970 manifesto. But, for the second time in two years, Callaghan sided firmly with the trade unions against his party leader on a major issue, leaving Wilson nowhere to go but in his footsteps.

The split of 28 October 1971 eventually resulted in the marginalisation of social democratic thought in the Labour Party, which exacerbated the problems encountered by the Labour government 1974–79, and undermined the party's electoral performance through to 1997. It also created an imbalance in the Labour Party–TUC relationship, which in turn dictated that the party would contest the February and October 1974 general elections on manifestos that gave priority to trade union demands ahead of an economic policy the party and the country could afford. In some respects, Wilson's handling of the Common Market issue in opposition was the true price of failure over *In Place of Strife*. His – and Castle's – inability to carry the Cabinet in 1969, leaving the trade unions unreformed and strengthened in their relationship with Labour, ultimately prevented the party from adopting the policy stances that were necessary in opposition after 1970 (including reform of industrial relations) and subsequently removed the party from serious competition for office after 1979.

The statecraft of Edward Heath

In some ways the Heath government continued the work of the previous Labour government. In addition to industrial relations, housing and the Common Market, the Conservatives picked up where Labour had left off on local government, the NHS and Northern Ireland. In the end, despite the tone of the Conservative Party's 1970 general election manifesto and John Davies's subsequent confrontational performances at the dispatch box, there proved little real difference between the Heath and Wilson governments. This left Labour's social democrats terribly exposed. By the time they worked out that they were actually conservatives (in the Heath mould) Margaret Thatcher had replaced Heath as leader and taken the Conservative Party beyond them.

Of course, the conduct of the Heath government in the early stages of the 1970–74 Parliament had a dramatic effect on Labour and altered the way the party thought about itself. The real legacy of Heath's premiership was not British membership of the Common Market, but rather the wrecking of the Labour Party by blurring the lines between conservatism and social democracy, and the theft of Labour's clothes in the process. He received no credit for this from the electorate in 1974, when he twice pushed the vote of both his own party and Labour below 40 per cent. The following year, he was displaced as leader by Conservative MPs for leading the party to defeat in the clothes of its opponent. In three years and eight months as Prime Minister, Heath came close to wrecking the Conservative Party as a party of government: he helped wreck the Labour Party without even being a member.

Notes

1 David Owen, for instance, writes about the frustration of Labour's radical right over the policies of the Wilson government 1964–70. See D. Owen, *Time to Declare* revised edn (London, Penguin, 1992), pp. 105–6.
2 I. Gilmour and M. Garnett, *Whatever Happened to the Tories: The Conservative Party since 1945* (London, Fourth Estate, 1997), p. 254.
3 Wilson, *The Labour Government 1964–1970*.
4 Campbell, *Edward Heath*, p. 305.
5 'Heath's dogged insistence that all was not . . . rosy in Labour's garden began to drip through. Valuable corroboration was provided by the former Governor of the Bank of England, Lord Cromer, who asserted on "Panorama" on 1 June that there was "no question that any government that comes into power is going to find a very much more difficult financial situation than the new government found in 1964".' Campbell, *Edward Heath*, p. 275.
6 P. Whitehead, *The Writing on the Wall* (London, Michael Joseph, 1985), p. 71. Campbell, *Edward Heath*, p. 365.
7 R. Taylor, *The Trade Union Question in British Politics: Government and Unions since 1945* (Oxford, Blackwell, 1993), p. 184.
8 TUC Report, 1970, pp. 582, 585.

9 Castle had a point. Carr himself subsequently admitted that when the Bill, which drew heavily upon the consultative document, was published he had 'had to have a brief in order to understand the purpose of the clause I was talking about. So it was complex to me, one of its main authors. What it seemed to other people I dread to think.' Whitehead, *The Writing on the Wall*, p. 71.

10 *HC Debs, 5th ser.*, 1970–71, vol. 807, cols 659, 666, 732.

11 *HC Debs, 5th ser.*, 1970–71, vol. 808, cols 1002, 1064. For Heffer's account of Labour's fight against the Industrial Relations Bill, see E. Heffer, *The Class Struggle in Parliament* (London, Gollancz, 1973).

12 *HC Debs, 5th ser.*, 1970–71, vol. 808, cols 1144, 1151, 1194–9.

13 *HC Debs, 5th ser.*, 1970–71, vol. 808, col. 1235.

14 Taylor, *The Trade Union Question*, p. 191.

15 Labour's opposition to the Bill stretched, without sanction by the leadership, to the disruption of parliamentary business. On 25 January 1971, up to 40 Labour MPs, mostly from the Tribune Group, staged a protest over the government's use of a guillotine motion in respect of the Bill, leading to a 10–15 minute suspension of the business of the House.

16 *HC Debs, 5th ser.*, 1970–71, vol. 822, cols 577–87, 614.

17 Campbell, *Edward Heath*, pp. 367–8.

18 LPAR, 1971, p. 165.

19 LPAR, 1971, pp. 169, 176.

20 For accounts of the TUC's resistance to the Industrial Relations Bill/Act, see Taylor, *The Trade Union Question*; Whitehead, *The Writing on the Wall*; and Campbell, *Edward Heath*.

21 The minority Labour government repealed the Industrial Relations Act in July 1974.

22 LPAR, 1971, p. 182.

23 Campbell, *Edward Heath*, p. 378.

24 P. Walker, *Staying Power* (London, Bloomsbury, 1991), p. 88.

25 Campbell, *Edward Heath*, p. 378. Writes Rodney Lowe: '... the aim of the policy was nothing less than the abolition of all existing housing subsidies and rent controls. Every local authority was instead required both to charge "fair rents" to all their tenants, in line with the practice in the private rented sector, and to participate in a national rent rebate scheme to help those in both the public and private sector who could not pay. Through a complex series of regulations, central government would make good any deficiency in a council's housing account (arising from rebate expenditure exceeding rent income) while recouping half of any surplus (to ensure some redistribution of income from rich to poor areas). The clear objective was to oblige council tenants to pay more economic rents for their housing while giving subsidies, for the first time, to tenants in the private rented sector – who were often far poorer.' R. Lowe, 'The social policy of the Heath government', in S. Ball and A. Seldon (eds), *The Heath Government 1970–74: A Reappraisal* (London, Longman, 1996), pp. 208–9.

26 *HC Debs, 5th ser.*, 1970–71, vol. 826, col. 48.

27 'If there are any reasonable parts of the measure –', wrote Frank Allaun MP, 'and it would be strange if in 103 clauses there were not some – then these can be re-enacted in a separate Bill.' LPA, Housing Finance Working Group, Minutes and Papers, 30 November 1971–27 March 1974, RD224/January 1972, 'Draft Statement on Housing Policy proposed by Frank Allaun MP'.

28 *HC Debs, 5th ser.*, 1970–71, vol. 826, col. 119.

29 K. Jefferys, *Anthony Crosland* (London, Richard Cohen Books, 1999), p. 162.

30 *HC Debs, 5th ser.*, 1970–71, vol. 826, cols 50, 88.
31 *HC*, 1971–72, Standing Committees, vol. VII, col. 4729.
32 'Walker's scheme...opted for a two-tier system of counties and districts designed to achieve a balance between the claims of efficiency and local sentiment. Education, social services, transport, fire services, police and some planning were allotted to the upper tier; housing, local planning, refuse collection and environmental services to the lower. In addition, six new metropolitan authorities were created in Birmingham, Manchester, Liverpool, Newcastle, Sheffield and Leeds. In the end a structure of 58 counties was reduced to 54, and a maze of some 1,300 lesser units reduced to around 400. (Scotland was recast into nine regions, with 49 local districts.)' Campbell, *Edward Heath*, p. 380. Labour opposed the measure, but not on anything like the scale of its opposition to the Industrial Relations Bill and the Housing Finance Bill.
33 *HC*, 1971–72, Standing Committees, vol. VI, cols 3–4, 16.
34 LPA, Housing Finance Working Group, Minutes and Papers, 10 January 1972.
35 *HC Debs, 5th ser.*, 1970–71, vol. 833, cols 54–5.
36 *HC*, 1971–72, Standing Committees, vol. VII, cols 4178, 4578.
37 Ibid., cols 4569, 4577.
38 Clay Cross 'not only declined to implement the Housing Finance Act but also doled out above the norm pay rises to its workers, free milk to its schoolchildren, free television licences to its pensioners, and municipalised some 300 houses'. A. Mitchell, 'Clay Cross', *Political Quarterly*, 45, 2 (1974), p. 165.
39 LPAR, 1972, Appendix 2, pp. 360, 356.
40 *HC Debs, 5th ser.*, 1970–71, vol. 835, col. 1159; vol. 836, cols 731–2.
41 *HC Debs, 5th ser.*, 1970–71, vol. 836, cols 731–2.
42 LPAR, 1972, p. 151.
43 Mitchell, 'Clay Cross', p. 165.
44 LPAR, 1973, pp. 209, 219.
45 S. Crosland, *Tony Crosland* (London, Jonathan Cape, 1982), pp. 281–2.
46 LPAR, 1973, p. 219.
47 Crosland, *Tony Crosland*, p. 282.
48 Crosland, *Tony Crosland*, pp. 281–2.
49 LPAR, 1970, p. 139.
50 *HC Debs, 5th ser.*, 1970–71, vol. 805, col. 59.
51 Gilmour and Garnett, *Whatever Happened to the Tories*, p. 248.
52 *HC Debs, 5th ser.*, 1970–71, vol. 805, cols 1211–13.
53 *HC Debs, 5th ser.*, 1970–71, vol. 805, cols 1378–9, 1382–3.
54 *HC Debs, 5th ser.*, 1970–71, vol. 806, cols 400, 407; vol. 810, col. 1922.
55 *HC Debs, 5th ser.*, 1970–71, vol. 810, col. 1925; vol. 811, cols 72, 82–3.
56 Whitehead, *The Writing on the Wall*, p. 80.
57 Benn, *Office Without Power*, 29 July 1971, pp. 363–4.
58 Three of the four yards were saved. The fourth was taken over by an American company and converted for the production of oil rigs.
59 M. Holmes, *The Failure of the Heath Government* (London, Macmillan, 1997), p. x.
60 LPAR, 1971, pp. 158, 227.
61 *HC Debs, 5th ser.*, 1970–71, vol. 825, cols 939, 944; vol. 826, cols 1251–2.
62 LPAR, 1971, p. 220. It fell to the Edinburgh Central CLP delegate to remind conference that there were already 600,000 unemployed 'when Labour went out of office'.
63 *HC Debs, 5th ser.*, 1970–71, vol. 829, cols 1023–4.
64 Labour's proposals for dealing with unemployment are discussed below, pp. 115–50.

65 Taylor, *The Trade Union Question*, p. 199. Having struck for a 47 per cent wage increase, the NUM won a settlement which included an increase of up to £6 per week, bonus shift payments and an extra week's holiday.

66 Heath in Whitehead, *The Writing on the Wall*, p. 86.

67 Campbell, *Edward Heath*, p. 406, in Gilmour, *Whatever Happened to the Tories*, p. 272.

68 R. Taylor, 'The Heath Government and industrial relations: myth and reality', in Ball and Seldon (eds), *The Heath Government 1970–74*, p. 178. The substance of the talks are discussed below, pp. 230–33.

69 Gilmour and Garnett, *Whatever Happened to the Tories*, p. 272.

70 F.W.S. Craig (ed.), *British General Election Manifestos 1900–1974* (London, Macmillan, 1975), p. 325.

71 S. Ball, 'A chronology of the Heath government', in Ball and Seldon (eds), *The Heath Government 1970–74*, p. 397; D. Wood, 'The Westminster Scene', *Political Quarterly*, 43, 3 (1972), p. 333.

72 *HC Debs*, 5th ser., 1970–71, vol. 833, cols 1397, 1525.

73 *HC Debs*, 5th ser., 1970–71, vol. 833, cols 1545–7.

74 *HC Debs*, 5th ser., 1970–71, vol. 833, cols 1555–6, 1623–6.

75 *HC Debs*, 5th ser., 1970–71, vol. 833, cols 1700–5.

76 A. W. Benn, 'Heath's spadework for socialism', *Sunday Times*, 25 March 1973, p. 61.

77 *HC Debs*, 5th ser., 1970–71, vol. 837, cols 1023–24.

78 *HC Debs*, 5th ser., 1970–71, vol. 841, col. 2402; vol. 837, cols 1023–37, 1095–6.

79 The talks are discussed below.

80 Further extended in April and November 1973. 'Labour's compulsory wage control was a failure and we will not repeat it', the Conservative Party's 1970 general election manifesto had promised. Craig, *British General Election Manifestos*, p. 331.

81 Campbell, *Edward Heath*, p. 479.

82 *HC Debs*, 5th ser., 1972–73, vol. 845, cols 628, 631.

83 Craig, *British General Election Manifestos*, p. 331.

84 Gilmour and Garnett, *Whatever Happened to the Tories*, p. 266.

85 Whitehead, *The Writing on the Wall*, p. 90.

86 On 11 December 1972, Walker announced a £1 billion investment in coal, nearly half of which would be used to write off the National Coal Board's accumulated deficit as at March 1973. A £3 billion investment in steel was announced ten days later.

87 *HC Debs*, 5th ser., 1970–71, vol. 837, col. 1023.

88 LPAR, 1973, p. 185.

89 LPAR, 1973, p. 183.

90 The NUM decided to call an all-out strike on 5 February 1974, which lasted throughout the general election campaign.

91 *HC Debs*, 5th ser., 1970–71, vol. 845, col. 636.

92 'I've been wading in shit for three months to allow others to indulge their conscience.' Harold Wilson in D. Healey, *The Time of My Life* (London, Michael Joseph, 1989), p. 360.

93 Craig, *British General Election Manifestos*, p. 366.

94 TUC Report, 1970, pp. 678, 688, 753.

95 LPAR, 1970, pp. 188, 197, 141.

96 'I recalled an engine-driver who became a folk legend for careless derailments in early American railroad history and who was known as "off-again, on-again, go-again Flanagan". My intention was to pause heavily at this stage, and then to

add: "I said *Flan*agan." John Harris vetoed it.' Jenkins on his speech to the PLP on 19 July 1971 and on Callaghan specifically. Jenkins, *A Life at the Centre*, pp. 322–3.

97 Campbell, *Edward Heath*, p. 358.

98 Morgan, *Callaghan: A Life*, p. 395.

99 Quoted in U. Kitzinger, *Diplomacy and Persuasion: How Britain Joined the Common Market* (London, Thames & Hudson, 1973), p. 300.

100 Morgan, *Callaghan: A Life*, p. 394.

101 Morgan, *Callaghan: A Life*, p. 395.

102 In his memoirs, Jenkins writes that Wilson hoped to get the party to vote in favour of entry, 'but at the worst, the very worst, we can fall back on a free vote'. Jenkins, *A Life at the Centre*, p. 316.

103 The main difference between the 'Heath terms' and those that presumably would have been acceptable to a Labour government, in Campbell's opinion 'never amounted to more than one per cent of GNP. The disproportionate emphasis on the terms was purely a political device to cover Labour's divisions.' Campbell, *Edward Heath*, p. 361. However, when Callaghan opened the renegotiations for the Labour government in April 1974, he identified the CAP, trade with the developing nations of the Commonwealth and the size of Britain's contribution to the Common Market budget as key issues. Morgan, *Callaghan: A Life*, p. 416. For a detailed account of the negotiations and the terms, see Kitzinger, *Diplomacy and Persuasion*.

104 'There were some brilliant speeches by Peter Shore, John Mackintosh, George Thompson, Michael Foot, Michael Stewart, Eric Heffer, Stan Orme, Jack Jones and Hugh Scanlon.' Benn, *Office Without Power*, 17 July 1971, p. 356.

105 LPAR, 1971, pp. 339–40, 355.

106 Benn, *Office Without Power*, 17 July 1971, p. 356; Jenkins, *A Life at the Centre*, p. 320.

107 D. Wood, 'An end to idealism on Europe', *The Times*, 19 July 1971, p. 13.

108 Benn, *Office Without Power*, 20 and 19 July 1971, p. 358.

109 Jenkins, *A Life at the Centre*, pp. 322–3.

110 LPA, PLP, Minutes, 19 July 1971.

111 Political Editor (D. Wood), 'Labour cabinet would have said yes to Six, Mr Jenkins says', *The Times*, 20 July 1971, p. 1; Political Editor (D. Wood), 'Jenkins attack on Australians staggers party meeting', *The Times*, 20 July 1971, p. 4.

112 I said at the beginning of the debate that I didn't intend to call many MPs but I knew that Conference would want to hear from Roy Jenkins and Michael Foot. I had not actually had a 'request to speak' card from Michael Foot but I had had a hand-written note and I had not had a card at all from Roy; indeed, I had heard rumours that Roy didn't wish to speak. So I asked Gwyn Morgan, who was sitting next to me, whether he'd send a message to Roy. He said he didn't know whether he wanted to speak, so I said, 'Well, that's entirely up to him, but would you send a message, to ask him when he would like to speak, and I will call him.' A message came back saying he didn't want to speak. I said to Conference, 'As Roy has indicated that he doesn't wish to speak, I will call Willie Hamilton to speak against the resolutions.'

Apparently at that moment people who were sitting near Roy shouted 'Chicken, coward,' and he was absolutely furious. This became quite an issue – had I done it deliberately or not? Well in fact, I did decide in the morning that I would do this because Roy had been attacking me all week for new levels of censorship, for trying to shut him up and for intolerance. So I decided I would put that to the test by making it clear that I had offered to call him to speak and let him face the consequences of not speaking. I knew his line – the 'low profile' which means you are afraid of the mass audience and you want to talk in private little groups about your principles and integrity. Also Roy has been attacking me for a total failure of leadership. I had failed, he argued, to give leadership to the Conference of the Party; he by contrast was always giving leadership. The plain truth is that he hasn't spoken at Conference about the Common Market for years, certainly not since he got anywhere near the top, and whatever people may say about me, I have certainly never lacked the guts to say what I thought. So, in fact, it was a prepared manoeuvre if you like; it's a crude way of putting it but it was a prepared decision – if he refused to be called – to expose the fact that he wouldn't speak. I wasn't absolutely sure that he didn't want to; that is the plain truth for the history books, in case anyone wants to know. And I am not at all sorry.

Benn, *Office Without Power*, 4 October 1972, pp. 454–5.

113 Jenkins, *A Life at the Centre*, p. 323; Benn, *Office Without Power*, 19 July 1971, p. 358.
114 D. Wood, 'Mr Wilson fights to save Labour Party's unity in crisis over leadership', *The Times*, 21 July 1971, p. 1.
115 Jenkins's inability to challenge Wilson for the leadership is discussed below.
116 See Benn, *Office Without Power*, 20 July 1971, p. 359.
117 LPA, PLP, Minutes, 20 July 1971.
118 Benn, *Office Without Power*, 20 July 1971, p. 359 and 28 July 1971, p. 362.
119 L. Hunter, *The Road to Brighton Pier* (London, Robert Barker, 1959). An account of the 1957 Labour Party Conference in Brighton, scene of Aneurin Bevan's somersault over the H-bomb (from anti- to qualified pro-). In 1971, scene of Harold Wilson's somersault over the Common Market.
120 LPAR, 1971, pp. 114–15.
121 LPAR, 1971, p. 138.
122 See R. Blake, *The Conservative Party from Peel to Major* (London, Heinemann, 1997), pp. 381–2.
123 LPAR, 1971, pp. 139–41.
124 LPAR, 1971, p. 162.
125 LPAR, 1971, pp. 166–7.
126 LPA, PLP, Minutes, 19 October 1971.
127 Nearly 200 MPs spoke in the debate.
128 Benn, *Office Without Power*, 28 October 1971, p. 382.
129 LPA, PLP, Minutes, 19 October 1971. In a separate vote, Stewart's amendment was supported by 87 Labour members, while 151 supported the Shadow Cabinet's recommendation that the terms be opposed.
130 LPA, PLP, Minutes, 19 October 1971.
131 *HC Debs*, 5th ser., 1970–71, vol. 823, cols 950, 1292, 1286, 2022, 994.
132 *HC Debs*, 5th ser., 1970–71, vol. 823, cols 2085, 2201–2.
133 Benn, *Office Without Power*, 28 October 1971, p. 382.
134 'I remember it as a day of misery. Shamefacedly slinking through the "no" lobby made a pathetic contrast with striding through the "aye" lobby on 28 October.' Jenkins, *A Life at the Centre*, p. 338.

135 E. Heath, *The Course of My Life* (London, Hodder & Stoughton, 1998), p. 385.
136 Jenkins, *A Life at the Centre*, p. 338.
137 LPAR, 1972, p. 208.
138 LPAR, 1972, pp. 210–15.
139 LPAR, 1973, p. 288.

4

JAMES CALLAGHAN AT THE HOME POLICY COMMITTEE 1970–71: ORGANISING THE NEC RESEARCH PROGRAMME

Prologue: the Research Department and the 1970 general election manifesto

From 1968 the Research Department at Transport House was active in preparing policies for inclusion in Labour's 1970 general election manifesto. The NEC statements *Progress and Change* in 1968, and *Agenda for a Generation*, *Labour's Economic Strategy* and *Labour's Social Strategy* in 1969, represented a 'major attempt by the Research department to lead the Party to a radical position' in anticipation of the campaign for re-election.[1] *Progress and Change* listed six points from the party's proposed agenda for Britain in the 1970s: overseas aid, race, the rights of the individual, nationalism, technology and the activity of modern industrial corporations. It named as a seventh priority the 'major redistribution of income and private wealth'. Stating that 'large accumulations of unearned wealth must make their contribution to a fair society', the NEC statement was unapologetic in justifying higher rates of personal taxation: 'The need to spend much more on social services has meant that none of us can have this money in our pockets *as well*. Restraint in this direction is the inevitable price we are paying for progress on this front.'[2]

The radical tone of *Progress and Change* was repeated over a range of proposals on the public and private sectors of industry the following year in *Agenda for a Generation*. Despite the disclaimer 'This is not a Manifesto',[3] *Agenda for a Generation* was clearly intended to provide the policies for a general election campaign expected within 12 months of its presentation to conference. 'In private, members of the Research Department were confident that the main proposals could not be omitted at this late stage.'[4]

Conference endorsed *Agenda for a Generation* by a majority of over 1 million votes in spite of the opposition of Jack Jones and Hugh Scanlon to the phraseology of the section dealing with productivity, prices and incomes, which called for an 'ordered and progressive growth of incomes, based on productivity and need'. Foreshadowing the debate on industrial policy to come, the statement proposed the establishment of a National Investment Board and a State Holding Company 'as the base for seizing new economic opportunities, including those in development areas'.[5] In the general election manifesto *Now Britain's Strong – Let's Make It Great to Live In*, this proposal was reduced to a single sentence which conceded only that the establishment of a Holding and Development Company 'with special regard to regional development needs, may well be necessary'.[6]

Agenda for a Generation identified the redistribution of income and wealth as one of the central issues facing Britain in the next generation:[7] 'Serious consideration must be given to an Annual Wealth Tax.'[8] Conference support for the statement encouraged the Research Department to believe the proposal would be included in the party's general election manifesto. The case for such a policy had been championed by no less a person than the deputy leader of the Labour Party. 'If people want better schools, more schools', George Brown, introducing the statement, told conference in 1969, 'better hospitals, more hospitals, better homes, more homes, better roads for their cars to travel on and more of them, if they want the expansion of all these social rights which we in the Labour party first brought to their attention and encouraged them to want, then they must be prepared to pay for them.'[9] However, Brown, no less than the Research Department, failed to anticipate Harold Wilson's opposition to the policy. 'What had been a Wealth Tax,' wrote Brown, 'became an unexceptional statement that those possessing greater wealth should contribute more than the poorer to national finances. Even this, however, was considered tactically dangerous, for the prime minister argued that the word "wealth" could be misconstrued, that it would be seized on by the Press and might cost us the election. So out went "wealth" and we ended with a pious exhortation that the richer should pay more than the poorer!'[10]

The Spectator perceived in Wilson's electoral strategy the substitution of specific commitments for the 'serviceable Baldwinesque props' of 'Safety First; responsibility; a breathing space; even, thanks to the gallant victory over the Springboks, Peace In Our Time'.[11] But his dismissal of the wealth tax proposal as 'wild Hampstead stuff...already refuted in the 1940s',[12] and the blurring of other contentious issues was grounded in conviction: he believed the policy was wrong. Wilson shared the concerns of his Chancellor, Roy Jenkins, who believed Labour had 'gone beyond the limits of taxation', and regarded as disastrous the impression given by *Agenda for a Generation* that Labour had 'old-fashioned ideas of restriction and heavy taxation, when it is taxation that is our difficulty'.[13]

The Research Department fell victim to 'the aura of power' attached to the parliamentary leadership in office. Writing in 1972 Tom McNally, the International Department Secretary, observed that in 1970 'the balance between Transport House, the Government and the NEC was balanced heavily in favour of the Government'. Research Department involvement in the election campaign was accordingly largely cosmetic, 'designed to calm fevered brows and mollify those who thought they should be in the inner councils but weren't'.[14] Inevitably the defeat of the wealth tax proposal 'by the weight of authority coming from the Chancellor and the Prime Minister' was a painful demonstration of where power was located in the party and gave rise to bitterness among staff at Transport House: Wilson 'thinks we are punks, and we know it'.[15]

McNally reasoned that in opposition and specifically in the build-up to the next election 'with the absence of "the aura of power" the relationship between the various bodies will be greatly changed'.[16] Certainly Wilson's aversion to policy initiatives emanating from Transport House had created the impression that the real mavericks in the Labour Party were to be found inside the parliamentary party. Despite its defeat over *Agenda for a Generation*, the Research Department was strongly placed to influence both the content of policy and the structure of the party's research programme. Ironically, Wilson's grip on the policy content of the election manifesto in 1970 ensured that Labour entered opposition with a raft of unused policies to hand – on the City, advertising, direct democracy, taxation, income and wealth, education, immigration, South African trade, women and so on – prepared by the Research Department between 1964 and 1970.[17] In theory Wilson's loss of the premiership removed the impediment to a radical restatement of the party's ideology. However, George Brown's loss of his parliamentary seat and consequently the chair of the Home Policy Committee was to prove equally significant.

James Callaghan and the Home Policy Committee

On 8 July 1970 James Callaghan 'got himself dug in'[18] as chairman of the NEC Home Policy Committee, the committee responsible for the formulation of domestic policy for inclusion in Labour's party programme. Callaghan was a member of the NEC in his capacity as party treasurer, a post he had held since 1967. Prior to July he had not been a member of the Home Policy Committee, yet within three weeks of the general election defeat he was elected chairman in succession to George Brown who, having lost his seat, was no longer deputy leader and therefore no longer a member of the National Executive. His capture of the chair was significant because he held firm views about what the Labour Party must do in opposition to regain power at the next election. Equally, his election signalled the intention of the parliamentary leadership to take a greater interest in the work of the Research Department in opposition. His election might have been blocked had the old Bevanite left been able to agree on a single candidate to oppose him. When Frank Allaun's proposal for an eliminating ballot was lost by five votes to three, neither Barbara Castle nor Ian Mikardo was prepared to step aside in favour of the other and both were subsequently defeated on a straight ballot. Their combined vote allocated to a single candidate would have been sufficient to have produced a tie.[19] Callaghan would most probably have secured victory on a second ballot, but his election was fortuitous as the outcome might have been reversed.

The ballot for the chair took place on the same day Roy Jenkins was elected deputy leader of the Labour Party, likewise in succession to George Brown.[20] Jenkins took the headlines the following morning, but it was Callaghan who, having chosen not to contest the deputy leadership, demonstrated a greater appreciation of where power was located in the Labour Party in opposition. 'If Labour had to elect a new leader within the next two to three years,' wrote James Margach in the *Sunday Times* on 12 July:

> Callaghan would be the most formidable challenger. Guided by his instinct for what makes Labour tick, he already has his hands on the real levers of power, as party treasurer and chairman of the home affairs committee of the National Executive, preserving the closest possible links with the unions and the party machine. He is likely to romp home at the top of the poll in this week's election for the Shadow Cabinet.[21]

Four days later the former Home Secretary duly topped the ballot for the Shadow Cabinet polling 178 votes, 13 clear of Denis Healey in second place.[22] Callaghan, Tony Benn observed, was 'building his power base absolutely everywhere'.[23]

The business of the election of the chairman completed, committee members turned their attention to the Research Department paper RD.5/July 1970 'The Research Programme', which suggested that 'defeat at the polls means a radical re-casting of the research programme now being undertaken by the Home Policy Committee and the Research Department'. The paper highlighted the omission of a party programme from the Research Department's list of policy documents: 'The Constitution makes a clear distinction between this and the election manifesto. The committee might wish to consider the preparation of such a document, to be used for educational purposes in the years of opposition.'[24]

RD.5/July 1970 'The Research Programme', listed three factors affecting 'the change of activity when the party goes into opposition'. First, 'in purely administrative terms, the office will find itself spending more time on briefing party spokesmen'; second, 'the research programme benefits from the availability of leaders who were previously too occupied with Government to spare their time'; and third, that 'after a period of adjustment, many outside advisers who were unwilling to devote their time to the party when we were in Government will now come back to work'. In addition the paper included an analysis of the impact of the Labour government's abandonment of the party in office. Fruitless consultations with ministers had taken place 'to the detriment of our concentration on future policy'. Opposition would release the Research Department 'from the time-consuming activities of monitoring tiny areas of Government policy, often with no political content whatsoever'.[25]

The aggrieved tone of the paper demonstrated the extent to which the competing agendas of the Research Department and the parliamentary leadership divided the party and weakened the organisation in 1970. One consequence of the Labour government's performance was that by the time of its defeat it had managed to alienate each of the non-parliamentary sections of the labour movement: the NEC, conference and the CLPs over the reintroduction of prescription charges, the trades unions over incomes policy and *In Place of Strife*, and the Research Department over the rejection of its proposals for the manifesto.

At the 8 July meeting it was agreed that a statement should be presented to conference in September and that it 'might be in the form of an "agenda", outlining the tasks which the party should now undertake'.[26] This statement became *Building a Socialist Britain*, described upon publication by James Margach as 'a cautious, soporific document which surprisingly satisfies Right, Left and Centre'[27] and which therefore satisfied the chairman of the Home Policy Committee. In the chair Callaghan, according to Benn, 'was very reasonable, asking everybody to comment and complimenting us all on what we said'. The newly elected chairman, he concluded, 'is a very skilful politician, there is no question about it; very skilful'.[28]

At the 15 July meeting of the PLP, Callaghan acknowledged that it was for neither the Shadow Cabinet nor the parliamentary party to make policy in opposition, but he nonetheless suggested that the NEC and the PLP be brought closer together 'than ever before', because the expertise of the PLP should not be neglected. The NEC (for which, in this instance, read the Home Policy Committee), he added was, as of 8 July, already considering a more formal arrangement for meetings between itself and the PLP to afford the latter 'greater access to the NEC Study Groups'. In this way, he told his parliamentary colleagues, the gap 'between those doing the job and those who criticised' would be bridged when the party returned to office.[29] Even at this early stage of opposition Callaghan was looking ahead to the next Labour government and to avoiding a repetition of the Labour Cabinet's problems with the NEC and conference after 1966.[30]

Callaghan pursued the formalisation of NEC–PLP relations on three fronts. At Shadow Cabinet on 15 September 'the view was expressed that the talents within the Parliamentary Party should be harnessed to work with the NEC's Study Groups on Party policy'.[31] The minutes do not reveal whose contribution this was but the wording echoes so closely Callaghan's speech at the PLP meeting of 15 July and anticipates his speech at conference introducing the NEC statement *Building a Socialist Britain* with such unerring accuracy, that one can conclude with a degree of certainty that the speaker is the former Home Secretary. Discussion of NEC–PLP relations continued at the Home Policy Committee meeting the following day, 16 September, where consideration was given to 'the need for co-ordinating policy studies, and for briefing'.[32]

Previously when the party had been in opposition, the services provided by the Research Department for the PLP had varied considerably 'according to the demands made on the Department by the National Executive Committee and its Subcommittees'. Members of the Research Department had been invited to attend the meetings of the committees and groups of the PLP, and briefing the front bench and providing assistance for opening and closing speeches in major debates had been a priority commitment. However, the quality of the service provided by the Research Department was secondary to the fact that what was described as a 'useful two-way channel of information' enabled the PLP to participate legitimately in the work of the NEC.[33] The NEC, of course, needed the support of the PLP. Upwards of 100 MPs contributed to the research programme through their membership of the committees, study groups and working parties of the NEC and it is doubtful that the research programme could have functioned effectively without them.[34]

Building a Socialist Britain: Callaghan's speech to conference 1970

Callaghan's presentation of *Building a Socialist Britain* to conference in 1970 was notable for his ability to retain the initiative on policy while appearing to offer concessions to the floor. Encouraging delegates to continue the discussion on policy beyond conference 'in constituency parties and in trade union branches', he immediately warned them that a debate inspired by idealism must be 'grounded in reality'. His own thinking on the priority to be given to consideration of policy was apparent: 'We cannot be overlong about it. We are looking to victory at the next General Election.' Three times in just over a minute he reiterated that the whole labour movement must use opposition to ensure the return of a Labour government.[35] He did not so much rewrite the record of the 1964–70 Labour government as divert the responsibility for the return of a future government onto those who blamed the parliamentary leadership for the failure of the Labour government. His speech boxed critics of the Labour government's record into a corner by implying that any action which threatened the return of a Labour government would be irresponsible and an act of disloyalty. Such sentiment was always going to be expressed at Blackpool but not necessarily from a common perspective. Callaghan's achievement on this occasion was beating Ian Mikardo to the platform microphone to say it first and from a parliamentary leadership perspective.

The NEC statement, he informed delegates, would repay careful study, but Bill Simpson for the NEC was candid about its deficiencies, admitting that it was 'very much an interim statement'.[36] However, it served a purpose in that it enabled Callaghan to deliver the most comprehensive exposition of his strategy for the party in opposition in the three months since the election defeat:

> ... in order to be effective we must strengthen the party machinery at all levels. We want to bring in the constituencies more, the regions of the party. We want to bring in those Members of Parliament who have considerable expertise, and many of whose abilities are, in my view, wasted because of the present way in which we organise our work. These too have much to contribute in opposition to helping us formulate an integrated policy. And I have another tactical reason in the back of my head why I said it is essential that the Parliamentary Party and the National Executive Committee, the constituencies and the trade unions should march together in opposition in devising our policy, we do not want any dichotomy when we are engaged in carrying it out. We want people to formulate it together, to agree on it together. To know what we can do, and then we shall not hear so much about the Parliamentary Labour Party doing one thing and the National Executive Committee wanting to do another.[37]

His final words addressed directly the report of the Research Department 1969–70, distributed to delegates earlier in the week, which recorded how on occasion it had been necessary 'to take up with Ministers those points of policy where a difference of emphasis occurred between the Government and the Party in the Country',[38] a point also addressed in *Building a Socialist Britain*: 'We shall now think out, as a first priority, ways of keeping open for the next Labour Government those necessary two-way lines of communication with our Party and our supporters, that are essential if our programme is to be evolved, accepted, understood and carried through.'[39]

The NEC statement came close to castigating the parliamentary leadership for its lack of communication with the party after 1966. At the 16 September meeting of the Home Policy Committee the above text was challenged and an additional critical paragraph proposed. The Home Policy document RD.10/September 1970 'Addition Note to RD.6 (Revised)' accused the Labour government of 'ignoring ... conference decisions (some of them embodied in the election programme) on legislation interfering with trade union rights, prescription charges, Vietnam and other issues in the last six years caus[ing] widespread disaffection', and demanded that the parliamentary leadership 'honour decisions by the annual delegate conference, the supreme policy making body of our party. This should apply whether Labour is in government or opposition.'[40] Although it was rejected by the Home Policy Committee, its wording captured accurately the mood of many of the speakers called to the rostrum by Ian Mikardo at Blackpool where, in the words of *The Economist*, 'the authentic voice of the *Tribune* reader was heard'.[41] However, the retention of the 'soporific' text (as described by James Margach)[42] testifies to Callaghan's success in controlling the official language of the party's consideration of the reason for electoral defeat.

The research programme and the Shadow Cabinet

Parallel to the Home Policy Committee's discussion of the structure of the research programme, the Shadow Cabinet began its own discussions of the organisational nature of party activity in opposition on 20 July 1970. It was agreed on this day that groups should be formed to shadow the various government departments, but a formal decision was postponed until 15 September, when the discussion was broadened to include the matter of liaison with party headquarters. Roy Jenkins, Shirley Williams, Douglas Houghton and Bob Mellish were requested to prepare a report on both matters.

This was completed by 10 October and was discussed by the Shadow Cabinet ten days later. The report recommended that the number of subject groups be kept to the minimum as the increasing demands on the time of MPs for the select committees and standing committees of the House of Commons 'affect adversely attendance in the Chamber and too many Party Committees will only add to the difficulty of keeping our benches well occupied'. However, it did not suggest what contribution the party's MPs were expected to make in the chamber without the necessary briefing, and instead concluded with an ill-disguised dig at the Tribune Group, the faction within the PLP most likely to dispute the priority given to Parliament by the leadership: 'We recognise that it is impossible to ban unofficial Committees within the Parliamentary Party, but we would appeal to our colleagues to work within the framework of the Party's Group organisation.'[43]

The report suggested in the first instance that the following groups be set up: Foreign and Commonwealth Affairs; European Affairs; Defence and Services; Agriculture, Fisheries and Food; Economic Affairs and Finance; Education and Science; Health and Social Security; Home Office (including Northern Ireland); Parliamentary Affairs; Power and Steel; Regional Planning; Housing; Local Government; Transport; Post Office and Communications. Subject groups on Employment and Productivity, and Industry, Technology and Board of Trade, it was recommended, should be delayed until, in respect of the former, the Industrial Relations Bill was 'out of the way', and in the latter case until the government's intentions on the future of the Departments of Technology and Trade became known. As to the chair of each group, Jenkins and his colleagues were 'of the opinion that it is desirable for Shadow Spokesmen to be Chairmen of the Groups, but it must be left to the Groups, as has been the practice over the past 25 years, to elect their Chairmen and Vice-Chairmen at the commencement of every new session'. Voting at group meetings 'ought *not* to be encouraged', they concluded.[44]

The report gave no consideration to liaison with party headquarters on this occasion, but the authors signalled their intention to continue their discussions at a future meeting with the treasurer of the party, Callaghan (wearing yet another of his official hats), and the general secretary, Sir Harry Nicholas.[45] These proposals were 'generally accepted' by the Shadow Cabinet (Overseas Aid was added to the list of suggested groups) and were carried forward to the PLP meeting of 4 November 1970.[46] At this meeting, concerns were raised about the omission of Consumer Affairs and Shipping from the list of groups, over the necessity of a separate group on Europe as recommended and on the position of the trade union group within the PLP. Doubts were also raised about the proposal that voting should not be encouraged at group meetings. This prompted Callaghan to intervene and address the meeting in his capacity as chairman of the Home Policy Committee. He wanted the views of the PLP on policy matters 'made known', and indicated 'there would be full representation of the Parliamentary Party on the Working Parties set up by the NEC'. The Research Department, he assured MPs, would give 'all the assistance it could to the Subject Groups and would continue to brief members on the big issues of the day', although he imagined the groups would concentrate primarily on 'tactical issues rather than on detailed studies'.[47]

Exactly what relevance this bore to the stated misgivings of Labour MPs over the status of the trade union group or on voting at subject group meetings is unclear, but Callaghan's intervention was sufficient to bring the discussion to a close, whereupon it was agreed that 16 subject groups be formed in six sections: a) Foreign and Commonwealth, Overseas Aid, Europe and Defence; b) Trade and Industry, Aviation, Power and Steel; c) Economic and Finance, Employment and Agriculture; d) Social Services, Education and Environment; e) Other Home Affairs;[48] and f) Parliamentary Affairs.[49] The overtly pro-PLP nature of his chairmanship of the Home Policy Committee appears to have caused him little difficulty. There is no evidence in the minutes of any hint of personal criticism of his management style, and on 9 November he defeated Barbara Castle by nine votes to six to retain the chair for the forthcoming year.[50]

The ownership of the research programme

The Home Policy Committee met for a second time prior to conference on 16 September, when Terry Pitt presented the paper RD.12/September 1970 'Programme of Work'. The proposed programme, he informed the meeting, 'would, of course, have to be revised in light of conference decisions'.[51] Pitt's unease with the irregularity of the process was apparent from the opening paragraph of the paper, in which he stated that it was 'more usual to consider the programme of work immediately after Annual Conference'.[52] Clearly he would have preferred the Home Policy Committee to have waited until after Blackpool before commencing its discussion of the research programme, but in opposition Home Policy activity acquired a new urgency and it was obviously the view of the new chairman that the committee could ill afford to wait three months before beginning its important work.

Pitt's paper provided the committee with an opportunity to consider its programme and the work of the Research Department 'in light of the main task we now face – that of winning the next election, with a policy programme clearly worked out'. This contrasted with the suggestion in RD.5/July 1970 'The Research Programme' of a party programme 'for educational purposes', which was obviously not viable given the climate of opinion in the party after defeat. Under the heading 'The Nature of Policy Preparation', the paper set out the organisational problem of finding the right balance between short-term and long-term requirements on policy: 'In particular it is very important *both* to devote maximum energy to future policy thinking *and* at the same time to give maximum support and service in the form of briefing to our spokesmen in the House of Commons and in the country.' Under a second heading, 'The Existing Research Programme', it was suggested that the existing NEC advisory committees be renamed subcommittees and that consideration be given to their membership, as the advisory committees, while considered to have been extremely valuable on specific policy matters, had found 'the development of any long term programme a complex proposition. This had been made more difficult by the fact that important co-opted members sometimes felt the work less than worthwhile, and of late have given less attention to meetings.' It was further suggested the parliamentary committee be given the right to appoint up to four members to the individual committees, each of which would then 'prepare immediately a fresh programme of work, covering at least a two year period for approval by the NEC'.[53]

This latter point predetermined party activity in opposition before conference had expressed a view on the matter, and suggests that Pitt's unease at the committee's discussion of the research programme prior to conference stemmed from a desire to preserve the autonomy of the

Research Department in opposition. While the parliamentary leadership had been concerned with government after 1964, the research programme had effectively become the property of the Research Department working with the Home Policy Committee. Yet, within weeks of the Labour government's defeat and without warning, Callaghan had parachuted in to take the chair of the Home Policy Committee and reclaim the research programme for the parliamentary leadership.

RD.12/September 1970 'Programme of Work' recommended that the committee's existing study groups[54] be allowed to continue their work and that 'the principle of appointing ad-hoc groups to report on specific terms of reference' should also continue.[55] These had served the NEC well between 1964 and 1970, the paper stated, 'and in many ways have been the main source of comprehensive policy preparation. The major documents on home policy since 1964 have all come from ad-hoc study teams.'[56] Under the heading 'Future Policy Issues', the paper described as barely believable

> that in the run-up to the 1964 General Election in spite of inviting a vast number of documents on a very wide range of policy issues, the Home Policy Committee never called for papers on the two central issues of the strength of the pound, and on the relationship between a radical Government and its Civil Service.
>
> In deciding the new research programme this problem is a crucial one – we shall be tempted to devote scarce resources to the study of 'easy' subjects, but a strong political will is the only guarantee of including the need to prepare ourselves again for the most difficult subjects of government.[57]

Consequently, there were 'crucial problems of political strategy' for the party to work out 'before the reins of government fall to us again'. These included 'Structure of Government – How do we guarantee a better dialogue between the next Labour Government and its own Party?' and 'Demand Management – How will a "voluntary" policy for prices and incomes be most effective?' The list of examples was described as being far from exhaustive, but 'added to our existing work, is a substantial programme'.[58]

Thus, even before conference voted in favour of a new party programme, the Home Policy Committee had begun to revise the structure of the party's research programme. Irrespective of the question of ownership of the research programme in opposition, the Home Policy Committee was responsible for its development. To this end it was resolved that the NEC 'be recommended to nominate two or three members to consider jointly with representatives of the PLP ways and means of linking the work of the two groups'.[59] As it stood, no formal link with the party in Parliament existed: 'backbench subject-groups of MPs are not coordinated in any way; and, on the other hand, the Parliamentary Party is not kept in touch with the NEC's policy work'.[60]

The research programme after Blackpool

Blackpool marked the transition from defeat to opposition. Thereafter the party began to organise for opposition in accordance with the prospect of five years out of power. However, the requirements of the PLP continued to be a priority. At Shadow Cabinet on 15 September the matter of the Research Department's ability to service the party in Parliament topped the agenda. While briefing the frontbench had been a priority prior to 1964 (and remained so after 1970) 'when matters arose in the House on which local, regional or highly specialised knowledge was required, these sometimes could not be dealt with at short notice or without disproportionate effort'. Provision of briefing for PLP subject groups had depended on the Research Department's 'other commitments and the subject dealt with'.[61]

The issue of Research Department support for the PLP was dealt with more effectively when the Home Policy Committee met for the first time after Blackpool, on 21 October 1970. Callaghan directed the committee to consider 'the job the Research Department was required to do in connection with the formation of policy for the next election, and the extent to which its resources could be committed to an extension of the role of briefing for the Parliamentary Labour Party'. After a 'full discussion' it was resolved that briefing be extended subject to the availability of resources, and that, as recommended in RD.12/September 1970 'Programme of Work', the PLP be invited to nominate members to the NEC's various subcommittees, subject to further consideration by the Joint Committee on Liaison. This caveat did not detract from the fact that Callaghan succeeded in securing an extension of support for the PLP without strife. Of added significance was the agreement at this meeting – in principle – that the PLP 'be invited to nominate members to the NEC's various SubCommittees', with the specifics to be considered at a later date by the Joint Committee on Liaison.[62]

The Home Policy Committee followed its own agenda, or at least that of the chairman, without reference to the conference debate on the party programme. Discussion instead focused on the structure of the research programme. The four NEC advisory committees, on Finance and Economic Affairs, Science and Industry, Social Policy, and Local and Regional Government, which since 1969 had 'only met to consider specific items referred to them',[63] were wound up, and a paper on the need for advisory groups was called for, for discussion at the next meeting. Of the seven existing study groups 'set up, with specific terms of reference, to produce reports', Regional Policy had completed its work and published a report, *Regional Planning Policy*, and along with Advertising and Taxation was also wound up.[64] The remaining four – Immigration, Higher and Further Education, Discrimination against Women and South African Trade – it was agreed, should continue their work.

When this meeting was continued on 27 October it became clear that in the intervening period the chairman had been busy impressing on the research secretary his ideas on the section in RD.12/September 1970 'Programme of Work' on 'Future Policy Issues' and the proposals on this subject detailed in RD.20/October 1970 'Supplementary Note' (also before the meeting). The latter dealt with the problem of developing a research programme 'which is flexible enough to take in new projects as and when the political climate changes'.[65] Callaghan proposed that a series of short papers of approximately 10,000 words in length be prepared by the Research Department 'on subjects to be decided, setting out the broad issues and the general approach'.[66] These would highlight the key issues in the NEC statements *Building a Socialist Britain* and *Agenda for a Generation*, a first and last indication that for the former there was life after conference. These would not be policy statements, 'but surveys of particular policy areas and would be designed to stimulate discussion throughout the Movement'.[67] Only then would the committee decide how best to deal with any particular subject, 'whether by the preparation of a discussion pamphlet by the office, by an individual or a study group or in some other way'. There is little reason to believe Callaghan favoured this way of making policy, but he certainly favoured keeping the party occupied and unified. A preliminary list of five subjects – Public Expenditure, International Companies, Future of the Aircraft Industry, Scale and Purpose of Military Spending, and Capital Sharing – was agreed with a view to the Research Department preparing outlines for a series of background pamphlets.[68]

The choice of these particular five subjects reflected the competing priorities of committee members. RD.20/October 1970 'Supplementary Note' had suggested 11 possible subject areas for consideration, from which only one – Public Expenditure – was selected for inclusion in the preliminary list. Callaghan, obviously, was unable to determine every aspect of the committee's agenda, but he was well placed to dictate the flow of activity. By the time outlines of the discussion pamphlets were presented to the committee on 9 November 1970, 'Scale and Purpose of Military Spending' had disappeared from the list of subjects to be considered by the committee, having been referred to the International Committee. On 'Public Expenditure and Taxation' no action was to be taken until both the Finance and Economic Affairs and Social Policy Subcommittees, neither of which were at this stage functioning, had been consulted as to how to proceed. A study group rather than a discussion pamphlet on 'Capital Sharing' was approved and a report to be co-authored by the TUC called for.[69] Consequently, consideration of the 'Future of the Aircraft Industry' was deferred until after the former had reported. Only on the subject of 'International Companies' was a discussion pamphlet immediately called for (as envisaged in RD.20/October 1970 'Supplementary Note') to be produced by the Research Department 'after consultation with TUC, the Social Democratic parties and other bodies in Europe'.[70]

'Participation '70'

Callaghan's proposal on background papers was countered at this meeting by the suggestion that constituency parties be enabled to participate in policy-making, facilitated 'by sending out questionnaires with a background paper on the problems involved in any particular subject. Reports could be prepared on the basis of the replies for presentation to annual conference.' It was duly resolved that the NEC 'be recommended to approve of the proposal for consulting constituency parties on policy-making by means of questionnaires'.[71] This was at best only a partial victory for advocates of a pluralist approach to policy-making. The list of subjects from which constituency parties would be invited to nominate their policy priorities was to be predetermined by the Research Department, subject to the committee's approval. A draft of the questionnaire, RD.28/November 1970 'Participation '70: Labour's New Policy Programme', was subsequently considered by the committee on 9 November, whereupon an amended draft was requested for submission to the full NEC.[72]

The 'Participation' scheme, instigated by Terry Pitt – who 'copied it from a scheme launched by the Swedish Labour Party'[73] – was one example of Research Department activity prior to the general election in 1970. Pitt's version of the scheme had been launched by the NEC shortly after the 1969 conference, when briefing material on 'Women and Social Security' had been circulated to constituency parties and affiliated organisations along with a questionnaire. A second consultation exercise on 'Economic Equality', planned for spring 1970, was postponed because of the decision to go to the polls early.[74] The stated intention of the scheme was to involve the CLPs and affiliated organisations 'more closely in the work of preparing Labour policy'. According to Sir Harry Nicholas, in 1969, 2,500 people had taken part in 200 separate discussion groups throughout the country.[75] For the purposes of the NEC report to conference in 1970 these figures were inflated to become 'almost 3,000 in 250 groups'.[76] Answers to the questionnaire indicated that 'Labour Party members at local level want a radical new social system, and that they overwhelmingly support one which acknowledges sexual equality'.[77] Yet this finding failed to merit more than the briefest mention in the 1970 general election manifesto: 'we believe that all people are entitled to be treated as equals: that women should have the same opportunities and rewards as men'. And the prospect of 'Participation '70' being anything other than a cosmetic exercise was remote.[78]

'Policy research', wrote Sir Harry Nicholas in his forward to RD.28/ November 1970 'Participation '70: Labour's New Policy Programme', 'is one of the most important tasks to be undertaken by the Party as we prepare ourselves for the next General Election. The NEC is anxious to give all Party members an opportunity to comment on the issues we should study. Only in this way will our new Policy Programme be comprehensive, relevant and forward-looking.'[79] Fifteen subjects ranging from 'Public Expenditure and Taxation' to the 'Commonwealth'[80] were listed for marking in order of priority, only for the exercise to be abandoned once again. On this occasion 'in view of local election activity this year, and particularly in view of boundary reorganisation of Constituencies and Local Parties, the publication of background material for the project has been delayed'.[81]

'Participation '70' said a great deal about the Research Department's approach to policy-making and its perception of how manifesto proposals should be formulated, but it was a scheme the party did not require in opposition and one which was doomed once the parliamentary leadership began to take an interest in policy. It is in this context that Callaghan's impact was most apparent. Under his chairmanship the Home Policy Committee did not shy away from pulling rank on the Research Department despite his assurance to the PLP on 15 July that Transport House would be the 'power-house' behind the party's effort to get elected.[82] The October meeting of the committee was only his third, yet the speed with which he exploited the authority of the chair testified to his acute political instincts. He worked remorselessly to limit the party's capacity for self-destructive debate by constantly seeking to narrow the focus of policy-making. He was not, as Kellner and Hitchens write, concerned so much with policy 'as with the activity of policy-making as a means of preserving party unity'.[83] Mindful of the correlation between policy and electoral liability, he secured agreement on this day that at future meetings an analysis of the findings of opinion polls would be on the agenda.[84]

'Participation' was attempted once more in 1972 when questionnaires listing 24 subjects were sent out eliciting 600 replies. At its launch the scheme was described by Tony Benn, party chairman that year, as a chance 'to prove that our policy is made in the local parties and trade unions, and is not handed down on tablets of stone, as in other parties'. Yet, despite this endorsement, as Michael Hatfield writes, 'nothing came of "Participation 1972". It received only cursory mention at the annual conference in October.'[85] It was plainly not the method by which policy would be made by the Labour Party in opposition.

The structure of the research programme

On 9 November the Home Policy Committee returned to discussion of the structure of the research programme whereupon it was decided to replace the NEC advisory committees of 1964–70 with six subcommittees to undertake 'the wide-ranging task of reviewing the party programme'.[86] Of these subcommittees, Finance and Economic Affairs, Social Policy, and Regional and Local Government retained broadly the brief of their predecessors. Industry and Science became separate committees, with the latter expanded to become Science and Education. The only wholly new committee was Agriculture. The paper before the Home Policy Committee members on this subject, RD.26/November 1970 'The Need for Standing Advisory or Subcommittees', listed four points in favour of subcommittees:

1. They offer an opportunity to set up a high level Committee important enough to attract outside advisers who are themselves national figures. For example, pre-1964, academics such as Professor Titmuss, Sir Charles Carter, Lord Bowden, Dr Kaldor, Lord Balogh and Mr Nield attended regularly. It is highly unlikely that figures of this eminence would be willing to involve themselves in the work of an ad hoc Study Group.

2. If properly organised such Committees offer the *only* mechanism at present for a serious regular dialogue between the Executive and other Frontbench PLP spokesmen. Again, prior to 1964 non-NEC members of the Parliamentary Committee regularly attended these Standing Committees (eg Douglas Jay, Patrick Gordon Walker, etc).

3. Such Groups offer an opportunity for the Home Policy Committee to ask advice on subjects which may be too urgent for, or too specific for, the setting up of an ad hoc Group.

4. The Groups themselves have an opportunity to range over a broader field than an ad hoc Study Group and generate advice to the NEC. For example, if such groups were appointed now their first task would be to advise on a programme of work in each field.[87]

It was intended that the six subcommittees would 'cover broadly' the PLP subject groups and that the membership of each would be made up of two or three members of the Home Policy Committee, members of the PLP 'and a number of outside experts'.[88] This decision provided for a direct role for the PLP in the NEC research programme, but it did not guarantee control of the process for the parliamentary leadership. Membership of the subcommittees, study groups and working parties of the Home Policy Committee was not subject to the patronage of the party leader and MPs were therefore freer to be open-minded in their deliberations on policy, a potentially damaging freedom to which Callaghan was alert. Additionally, the NEC had long harboured several of the PLP's dissident MPs and it was precisely these individuals, along with fellow Labour MPs of a similar ideological disposition, who were most likely to wish to participate in the process.

Callaghan exploited his position as chairman of the Home Policy Committee to empower the parliamentary leadership – himself included – but did so in a manner which avoided any contravention of his NEC remit and which emphasised the need, both politically and organisationally, for unity. He did this at a point in the government–opposition cycle when the NEC was at its most powerful. In this respect the strategic importance of his election cannot be overstated. The subcommittees, study groups and working parties of the Home Policy Committee, while free to devise and recommend policy, could not be certain it would be accepted either by the Home Policy Committee or the full NEC; or, in extremis, by the parliamentary leadership even if accepted by the NEC. But this is to run ahead of events.

Notes

1 Butler and Pinto-Duschinsky, *The British General Election of 1970*, p. 58.
2 NEC, *Progress and Change*, LPAR, 1968, pp. 340–1.
3 NEC, *Agenda for a Generation*, LPAR, 1969, p. 380.
4 Butler and Pinto-Duschinsky, *The British General Election of 1970*, p. 59.
5 NEC, *Agenda for a Generation*, pp. 383–4.
6 Labour Party, *Now Britain's Strong – Let's Make It Great to Live In*, in Craig, *British General Election Manifestos*, p. 348.
7 The other issues were as follows: 'the quality and quantity of economic growth; the democratisation of industrial power; a social strategy which recognises new needs; positive discrimination in favour of areas with special social needs; reform of institutions, and new methods of participation in decision-making; strong measures to close the gap between rich and poorer nations; continued commitment to human rights, and increasing support for international organisations.' NEC, *Agenda for a Generation*, p. 393.
8 NEC, *Agenda for a Generation*, p. 384.
9 LPAR, 1969, p. 233.
10 Brown, *In My Way*, p. 261.
11 *The Spectator*, 7406, 6 June 1970, p. 3.
12 Butler and Pinto-Duschinsky, *The British General Election of 1970*, p. 2, n. 1.
13 Howard, *The Crossman Diaries*, p. 648.
14 T. McNally, 'Transport House and the 1970 General Election', LPA, Terry Pitt Papers (TPP), D/PITT/C/59.
15 Butler and Pinto-Duschinsky, *The British General Election of 1970*, p. 48.
16 McNally, 'Transport House'.
17 LPA, HPC, Minutes, 8 July 1970; NEC Minutes, 22 July 1970.
18 Benn, *Office Without Power*, 8 July 1970, p. 300.

19 Callaghan received six votes, Castle four, Mikardo two. On the second ballot, Callaghan nine votes, Castle six. LPA, HPC, Minutes, 8 July 1970; NEC, Minutes, 22 July 1970.
20 Jenkins received 133 votes, Michael Foot 67, Fred Peart 48. Jenkins, *A Life at the Centre*, p. 311.
21 J. Margach, 'It's right to put your Left Foot in', *Sunday Times*, 12 July 1970, p. 2.
22 LPA, PLP, Minutes, 16 July 1970.
23 Benn, *Office Without Power*, 8 July 1970, p. 300.
24 LPA, RD.5/July 1970 'The Research Programme', HPC, Minutes, 8 July 1970; NEC, Minutes, 22 July 1970.
25 LPA, RD.5/July 1970 'The Research Programme'.
26 LPA, HPC, Minutes, 8 July 1970; NEC, Minutes, 22 July 1970.
27 J. Margach, 'How Tories will hurt – Callaghan,' *Sunday Times*, 27 September 1970, p. 2.
28 Benn, *Office Without Power*, 8 July 1970, p. 300.
29 LPA, PLP, Minutes, 15 July 1970.
30 The platform at conference was defeated three times in 1966, three times in 1967, six times in 1968 and once in 1969. See Minkin, *The Labour Party Conference*, p. 238.
31 LPA, PC, Minutes, 15 September 1970.
32 LPA, HPC, Minutes, 16 September 1970; NEC, Minutes, 25 September 1970.
33 'Note on the services provided by the Research Department when the Party was last in Opposition', LPA, PC, Minutes, 15 September 1970.
34 118 MPs served as members of the NEC subcommittees, study groups, working parties etc. LPAR, 1970–71.
35 LPAR, 1970, pp. 162–3.
36 LPAR, 1970, p. 177.
37 LPAR, 1970, p. 167.
38 LPAR, 1970, p. 36.
39 NEC, *Building a Socialist Britain*, p. 4, LPAR, 1970, pp. 323–6.
40 LPA, HPC, Minutes, 16 September 1970; NEC, Minutes, 25 September 1970.
41 *The Economist*, 'Lord Balogh mentions the unmentionable'.
42 Margach, 'How Tories will hurt'.
43 'Subcommittee's Report to the Parliamentary Committee on Organisation of the Groups of the Party in Opposition', LPA, PC, Minutes, 10 October 1970.
44 'Subcommittee's Report to the Parliamentary Committee on Organisation of the Groups of the Party in Opposition'.
45 'Subcommittee's Report to the Parliamentary Committee on Organisation of the Groups of the Party in Opposition'.
46 LPA, PC, Minutes, 20 October 1970.
47 LPA, PLP, Minutes, 4 November 1970.
48 This included: Home Office (including Northern Ireland) and Post Office and Communications (including Broadcasting).
49 LPA, PLP, Minutes, 4 November 1970.
50 A year later the situation was different. Callaghan and Mikardo each received seven votes when the ballot for the chair was held on 8 November 1971. LPA, HPC, Minutes, 8 November 1971; NEC, Minutes, 24 November 1971. A second ballot was held on 6 December 1971, in which Callaghan received nine votes to Mikardo's seven. LPA, HPC, Minutes, 6 December 1971; NEC, Minutes, 22 December 1971.
51 LPA, HPC, Minutes, 16 September 1970; NEC, Minutes, 25 September 1970.

52 RD.12/September 1970 'Programme of Work', LPA, HPC, Minutes, 16 December 1971; NEC, Minutes, 22 December 1971.
53 RD.12/September 1970 'Programme of Work'.
54 Advertising Committee; Study Group on Immigration; Higher and Further Education Study Group; Study Group on Regional Policy; Study Group on Discrimination against Women; Taxation Study Group; Study Group on South African Trade.
55 RD.12/September 1970 'Programme of Work'; NEC, Minutes, 25 September 1970.
56 Subjects covered included: the Docks; Industrial Democracy; North Sea Gas; New Towns; the Civil Service; Housing; Economic Strategy.
57 RD.12/September 1970 'Programme of Work'; NEC, Minutes, 25 September 1970. In an interview for BBC Radio 4 on 6 January 1973, Callaghan commented on the relationship between the Labour government and the Civil Service: 'People like Professor Kaldor, Robert Neild, Balogh, and there were others in Transport and other ministeries, they were able to argue with Civil Servants, as it were, on their own basis and at their own level and, indeed, perhaps rather better than some of the Civil Servants could put up, so I think that it did give a fair chance for the party's policies . . . they stood up to examination much better there.' LPA, TPP, D/PITT/C/44.
58 RD.12/September 1970 'Programme of Work'; NEC, Minutes, 25 September 1970.
59 LPA, HPC, Minutes, 16 September 1970; NEC, Minutes, 25 September 1970.
60 RD.12/September 1970 'Programme of Work'; NEC, Minutes, 25 September 1970.
61 'Note on the services provided by the Research Department when the Party was last in Opposition', LPA, PC, Minutes, 15 September 1970.
62 LPA, HPC, Minutes, 21 October 1970; NEC, Minutes, 28 October 1970.
63 LPAR, 1970, p. 36.
64 The study undertaken by the Advertising Committee was used as the basis of a document subsequently issued directly by the NEC; the work of the Study Group on Taxation was referred to the Finance and Economic Affairs Subcommittee. LPAR, 1971, p. 37.
65 RD.20/October 1970 'Supplementary Note', LPA, HPC, Minutes, 21 October 1970; NEC, Minutes, 28 October 1970.
66 LPA, HPC, Minutes, 27 October 1970; NEC, Minutes, 28 October 1970.
67 RD.20/October 1970 'Supplementary Note'.
68 LPA, HPC, Minutes, 27 October 1970; NEC, Minutes, 28 October 1970.
69 The terms of reference for the Study Group on Capital Sharing were as follows: 'To examine the process by which the growth of corporate wealth is financed mainly from retained profits, and the impact of this upon the distribution of income and wealth and upon consumer prices; to examine and report on methods of providing workers, consumers and the community as a whole, with a direct and increasing stake in this capital accumulation'. LPA, RD.61/February 1971 'Capital Sharing', HPC, Minutes, 8 February 1971; NEC, Minutes, 24 February 1971.
70 LPA, HPC, Minutes, 9 November 1970; NEC, Minutes, 25 November 1970.
71 LPA, HPC, Minutes, 27 October 1970; NEC, Minutes, 28 October 1970.
72 LPA, HPC, Minutes, 9 November 1970; NEC, Minutes, 25 October 1970.
73 Hatfield, *The House the Left Built*, p. 73.
74 Hatfield writes: 'It is not without interest that a second questionnaire was to be sent out in 1970 with the hidden intention of bringing further pressure

on Jenkins, as Chancellor of the Exchequer, to introduce a Wealth Tax, but it was overtaken by the general election in June.' Hatfield, *The House the Left Built*, p. 73.

75 LPAR, 1970, p. 37.
76 RD.28/November 1970 'Participation '70: Labour's New Policy Programme (revised)', LPA, HPC, Minutes, 9 November 1970; NEC, Minutes, 25 November 1970.
77 LPAR, 1970, p. 37.
78 Labour Party, *Now Britain's Strong – Let's Make It Great to Live In*, p. 345.
79 RD.28/November 1970 'Participation' 70: Labour's New Policy Programme (revised)'; NEC, Minutes, 25 November 1970.
80 The full list of subjects was as follows: Public Expenditure and Taxation; Welfare for Whom?; Radio, Press and Television; The New Environment; Public Enterprise; Private Industry and the Public; Planning and the Capital Market; Jobs and Industrial Change; Consumer Power; Participation in Democracy; Industrial Power; Overseas Development; Scale and Power of Military Spending; European Security; Commonwealth. RD.28/November 1970, 'Participation '70: Labour's New Policy Programme (revised)'; NEC, Minutes, 25 November 1970.
81 LPAR, 1971, p. 42.
82 LPA, PLP, Minutes, 15 July 1970.
83 Kellner and Hitchens, *Callaghan*, p. 114.
84 LPA, HPC, Minutes, 27 October 1970; NEC, Minutes, 28 October 1970.
85 Hatfield, *The House the Left Built*, pp. 74–6.
86 LPAR, 1971, p. 43.
87 RD.26/November 1970 'The Need for Standing Advisory or Subcommittees', LPA, HPC, Minutes, 9 November 1970; NEC, Minutes, 25 November 1970.
88 LPA, HPC, Minutes, 9 November 1970; NEC, Minutes, 25 November 1970.

5

THE NEC RESEARCH PROGRAMME: APRIL 1971–JULY 1972

Initially, the location of individuals within the research programme process was of greater importance than the division of ideas, which at this point was somewhat artificial. Those differences that did exist were masked by a common vocabulary (at least at the level of rhetoric) with both the Industrial Policy Subcommittee *and* Roy Jenkins stating, for example, that some form of intervention in the economy was desirable. This stage of the research programme is significant because it gave momentum to a view of economic and industrial policy which proved disastrous for the party. These first 16 months of policy-making activity culminated in the publication of an interim policy document, *Labour's Programme for Britain 1972*. The tension over ideas which subsequently emerged, and the implications of the final policy document – *Labour's Programme 1973* – for the parliamentary leadership, are considered in this chapter.

The NEC research programme was the method by which the Labour Party sought to accommodate two similar but conflicting views of the party's purpose. The first, to which government ministers had subscribed between 1964 and 1970, stressed the importance of domestic and international finance as the domain in which both the responsibility and radicalism of Labour's identity could be discharged. The second, championed by the NEC, the Research Department and the party conference, considered the reorganisation of capitalism around the interests of the worker and the producer to be the party's first priority. James Callaghan's achievement as chairman of the Home Policy Committee was to graft the PLP onto the research programme process. However, the participation of the PLP did not produce a policy document to the parliamentary leadership's liking (as might have been expected), nor did it guarantee an influential role for senior parliamentary leaders such as Jenkins. The formal structure of the research programme placed the former Chancellor at the heart of the process but, as the process itself was essentially the property of those sections of the party that had been opposed to government policy on a range of issues after 1966, his contribution was limited. Indeed, the way the Labour Party made policy in this period handed the initiative to the

Research Department, a body which was disillusioned with the parliamentary leadership and which had a clear idea of the policies it believed the party should adopt. In this latter respect, Research Department personnel resembled the academics who served the party in opposition.

The government–party division of 1966–70 was reflected in the composition and remit of the subcommittees, study groups and working parties of the Home Policy Committee. Jenkins chaired the Finance and Economic Affairs Subcommittee, whose membership included several Labour MPs who had either been with him at the Treasury, or who were recognised supporters of his. This subcommittee more than any other was associated with the economic policies of the Labour government, from which the research programme was supposed to distance the party. Their attempts to contribute to the research programme were obstructed by Terry Pitt who, having been overruled by the Prime Minister *and* the Chancellor over the contents of the general election manifesto in 1970, countered the unwanted involvement of Jenkins by limiting the remit of his subcommittee. Certainly, they were prevented from examining those areas of economic and industrial policy where the Research Department hoped to move the party's policy leftwards.

Pitt and his assistant, Geoff Bish, were antagonised by the involvement of Jenkins and his colleagues, whom they suspected of not taking policy-making seriously because they did not appear to have to work too hard at it. Yet, when David Marquand produced a paper of real substance, 'Problems of Economic Growth', which invited serious discussion of the party's view of economic policy, Pitt deliberately kept the Finance and Economic Affairs Subcommittee and the Industrial Policy Subcommittee apart, despite the degree of overlap between the work of the two groups. Thus, Labour's economic and industrial policy, which should have been discussed by the two subcommittees together, was instead looked at separately by the Industrial Policy Subcommittee, through which Pitt pushed the Research Department's policy initiatives. The 1971 NEC policy statement *Economic Strategy, Growth and Unemployment*, consequently drew upon only the ideas of the latter subcommittee and therefore included only half the argument.

The weakness of Jenkins's position within the research programme clearly derived from his past association with the Labour government, but also, and more significantly, from his lack of a power base beyond the Shadow Cabinet and the PLP. Tony Benn, for example, who was an influential member of the Industrial Policy Subcommittee, was a member of both the NEC *and* the Shadow Cabinet, and therefore straddled the PLP–non-PLP divide more effectively. Consequently, he had a greater influence on party policy than Jenkins in this period. When Jenkins resigned as deputy leader of the Labour Party in April 1972, his participation in the research programme, and that of Marquand, came to an end. He was succeeded by Denis Healey, who brought in his own team from the

PLP. Healey inherited a situation in which the parliamentary leadership–party division over the party's purpose had effectively been settled in favour of the NEC, the Research Department and the party conference. Marquand's ideas on redistribution out of growth had been challenged by those within the research programme who were inclined to see redistribution as an ethical problem. Healey's problem was how to manage the cost of this approach to policy-making.

The NEC research programme

Labour's research programme in opposition was technically a response to a specific conference resolution instructing the NEC to re-establish 'a clearly defined sense of Socialist purpose' for the party. When the subcommittees of the Home Policy Committee met for the first time in April 1971, seven months after the 1970 conference, PLP representation on any one of the six subcommittees was not less than 46 per cent of the total membership and in the case of the Finance and Economic Affairs Subcommittee was as high as 64 per cent. Although a high level of PLP involvement was necessary if the programme was to function effectively, this level of representation was disproportionately high given that the research programme was officially the property of the NEC. The reasons for this were twofold: first, James Callaghan (in his capacity as chairman of the Home Policy Committee) was determined to involve the PLP in the research programme to such an extent that responsibility for the policies included in the new party programme would be shared by all sections of the party, thus reducing the likelihood of a split between a future Labour government and the party as had occurred after 1966; second, without the involvement of the PLP, the research programme would have lacked credibility with the party's MPs, irrespective of the legitimacy of the NEC's remit. Furthermore, without the involvement of the PLP, the NEC would have lacked the people to mount such a wide-ranging research programme.

Between 1971 and 1973, 76 MPs (in addition to the 18 MPs who contributed to the programme in their capacity as members of the NEC) were co-opted to serve on the various subcommittees, study groups and working parties of the Home Policy Committee.[1] Yet for all Callaghan's influence, the research programme was an unwelcome exercise for the parliamentary leadership as, with the exception of Roy Jenkins and Anthony Crosland, it had no clear idea of the type of policies it wished to see included in the new party programme other than the sub-revisionist policies of the recent Labour government. And, because the leadership could not dominate the research programme intellectually, it slowed it down. It was not until two years after the party's election defeat that an interim statement of policy, *Labour's Programme for Britain 1972*, was published, and not before June 1973, with a general election imminent, that a final document, *Labour's Programme 1973*, was completed.

With the PLP so well represented, the research programme should in theory have produced a document acceptable to the parliamentary leadership. *Labour's Programme for Britain 1972* (the product of the first year of the research programme), when published in July that year, was given consultative status only by the NEC. However, it contained proposals which suggested that members of the PLP could not be relied upon to reach conclusions consistent with the political objectives of the parliamentary leadership and one can conclude, therefore, that Callaghan's insistence on a role for the PLP in the research programme failed to produce the intended result. How, then, did the first year of the programme produce a document which, when considered by the PLP on 13 July 1972, prompted Bill Rodgers to comment that the party 'would achieve a modest aim if our document did not reduce our chances of winning an election'?[2]

Economic Strategy, Growth and Unemployment

The first major statement of policy to emerge from the research programme was the NEC statement to the 1971 conference, *Economic Strategy, Growth and Unemployment*, written by the Industrial Policy Subcommittee between May and September that year. The subcommittee's authorship of the statement was hugely significant in terms of both the tone and content of Labour's subsequent policy statements in opposition, and was the first setback for the parliamentary leadership in respect of research-programme activity. Unlike the previous year's NEC statement, *Economic Strategy, Growth and Unemployment* was not overseen by the Home Policy Committee and for this reason was a hostile document for the parliamentary leadership.

Aside from stating 'The Labour Alternative' to the economic policies of the Conservative government (on this occasion 'an economic order in which industrial and financial decisions are dictated by the needs of the whole community'), the NEC statement set out the views of the Industrial Policy Subcommittee on four key aspects of policy: 'Unemployment and Growth', 'An Active Manpower Policy', 'An Active Regional Policy' and 'The Role of Public Ownership'. At the heart of the problem of unemployment, the document stated, was a lack of 'adequate demand' in the economy. It was therefore necessary for the party to reject deflation as a tool for dealing with the problem of inflation and the balance of payments, twin impediments to a policy of sustained economic growth and full employment. Rejecting the introduction of import controls to protect the balance of payments, the document recommended instead, whenever necessary, 'an orderly re-alignment to our exchange rate – at least whenever the alternative is a policy of massive deflation and stagnation'. As a means of containing inflation a series of measures to control prices was suggested, including the re-establishment of an Early Warning System on price increases and restraint at retail level.[3] A third impediment to growth – low productivity – could be overcome, it was anticipated, because the party's policies of expansion and full employment could be expected to provide 'a stimulus to investment and industrial change. And backed by our strategy of intervention at manpower, regional and industrial levels, this could well begin the so-called "virtuous cycle" of faster growth and higher productivity.' This section of the NEC statement concluded by stating that the aim of the party's industrial strategy was 'to recast industry into a more democratic and human mould ... our industrial policies are not intended to be judged solely against the crude criteria of human efficiency',[4] a statement consistent with Labour's discarded Marxist heritage.

Under the heading 'An Active Manpower Policy', the document stressed the need for an extensive programme of regional development as well as an active manpower policy and suggested that displaced workers should have 'the automatic right to training or retraining, and at all levels of occupational skill: redundancy should lead, therefore, not to unemployment, but to retraining and job changing'. Additionally, a new National Labour Board would be required, 'bringing under one organisation the present separate machinery for training, retraining and job placement'. The Board would be financed by the government and by the imposition of a training levy 'on the payrolls of all but the very smallest firms'. This would also require the introduction of statutory advance warning of redundancies and the compulsory notification of vacancies. Under the sub-heading 'Job Monotony and Job Enrichment', the document supported the principle of giving to workpeople, 'individually and collectively, powers and responsibilities which at present are jealously retained within the sphere of so-called "management prerogative"; the whole system of decision-taking in industry indeed, is brought into question'. The latter point fell under the umbrella of industrial democracy, an issue the party had been actively discussing since 1967. The Industrial Democracy Report, included in the NEC statement to conference in 1968, had argued that 'workers should be involved in an ever widening range of decisions within management, and should do so on the basis of a single channel of representation, one which did not hinge upon any distinction between subjects appropriate for bargaining and those appropriate for consultation'. In addition to considering the recommendations of the report, the document suggested that the party should also consider a role for workers 'in determining the composition of the management team, or in calling to account a Board or manager in which they have lost confidence'.[5]

'A further dimension of our policy of intervention', the document stated under the heading 'An Active Manpower Policy', 'must lie in seeking to end the persistent disparities in activity between different regions.' To this

119

end the NEC, drawing on the report of the Study Group on Regional Policy, *Regional Planning Policy*, published in June 1970, envisaged a number of initiatives. These included: public ownership; a series of incentives and disincentives to encourage firms to relocate in the poorer regions (including a 'congestion levy' to be imposed on firms choosing to operate in areas with an existing high rate of employment); Industrial Development Certificates; Office Development permits; and Regional Industry Boards (RIBs) 'with sufficient powers, expertise and finance to enable [them] to decide how best to promote development'. RIBs were to be given responsibility for all regional planning activity, including the development of 'Growth Complexes', the aim of which 'would be to establish a series of firms which were complementary or mutually dependent – thus avoiding the drawback of inadequate ancillary firms – and all of which would be backed by the necessary infrastructure of roads, water supplies, etc.' Grants to incoming firms would be freely available to the public sector, but to the private sector 'only in return for an equity stake in the company concerned'.[6]

The document conceded that the likelihood of Britain's entry into the Common Market 'may make certain aspects of it (the above strategy) impractical . . . And it now seems likely that the most effective stimulus to regional development which *will* be permissible will be public owner-ship.' However, introducing the section of *Economic Strategy, Growth and Unemployment* dealing with 'The Role of Public Ownership', the document emphasised that the party's economic strategy was 'concerned with a much wider concept of economic welfare than bare industrial efficiency'.[7] Under the sub-heading 'Public Enterprise in the Regions', the statement advocated the creation of a State Holding Company 'backed by considerable capital funds':

> For what has been lacking in past regional policies is a nucleus of management and entrepreneurial skills, able not only to build up new production and service facilities, but to gear these to the markets that are available, and to seize new opportunities for expansion as they arise. With a State Holding Company these opportunities could be taken up, if necessary, by the acquisition of existing companies – and thus their skills, markets and facilities – or through joint ventures with existing firms in the private sector.[8]

This was one example of the methods of extending the frontiers of public ownership being considered by the NEC. Outright nationalisation of whole industries would continue to be an option where appropriate, 'but given our diverse objectives in extending public ownership, we will be much more ready wherever necessary in the future, to bring *individual* companies into the public sector, as the Tories did with Rolls Royce'.[9] The document concluded by reiterating the point that a new economic policy was required based on:

> full employment, steady growth in selected regions of the country and sectors of the economy, precise policies (announced and agreed, *in advance*) to deal with obstacles to growth, radical programmes for manpower, a massive extension of democracy in industry. And it must embrace a new set of values where production and capital are concerned. Industry must be the servant of the community. Once man becomes the servant of our industrial system, then the historical fight to democratise our political system will have foundered on the rock of a new economic aristocracy even more unaccountable than the old.[10]

Economic Strategy, Growth and Unemployment was the product of the political climate in which it was written and a reaction to the Conservative government's record in office since June 1970: 930,000 unemployed, an increase of 350,000; the abolition of the Early Warning System on prices, the Consumer Council and the National Board of Prices and Incomes; the loosening of Industrial Development Certificate controls; the abolition of investment grants; Regional Employment Premiums ended as from 1974; the repealing of the core of the 1968 Industrial Expansion Act providing for selective aid to industry; and the abolition of the Industrial Reorganisation Corporation. This policy of 'disengagement', which the NEC 'completely rejected', had 'deliberately destroyed and weakened the very machinery needed to promote regional development...Only the machinery of the Receiver has remained – and thousands of workers on the Clyde, in other depressed regions and elsewhere, now face redundancy and the dole queue.'[11] Reference to Upper Clyde Shipbuilders (UCS) illustrated the extent to which the NEC statement was influenced by the extra-parliamentary campaign of the workers on the Clyde, who had been staging a 'work in' since the government's announcement in June 1971 that the yards were no longer economically viable and were to close. The response of the workforce – led by Jimmy Reid (then of the Communist Party) and prominently supported by Tony Benn who, as Minister of Technology, had organised the four shipyards on the Clyde as a consortium in 1968[12] – to the threat of redundancy 'turned UCS into a potent symbol of working-class self-help in defiance of hard-faced capitalism, winning considerable sympathy and popular support'.[13] It was against this backdrop of industrial strife that *Economic Strategy, Growth and Unemployment* was written. However, even without the catalyst of Conservative economic policies and events on the Clyde, authorship of the NEC statement was a golden opportunity for the Industrial Policy Subcommittee to produce a statement of policy which would be the property of the *whole* party and so advance the claims of the party conference for a greater say in deciding the policy of the party in opposition *and* in government.

Economic Strategy, Growth and Unemployment accordingly provided an impression of what the economic section of Labour's 1970 general election manifesto might have looked like had responsibility for its authorship rested solely with the Research Department. Where, for example, the manifesto had observed that 'Britain's publicly owned industries are already experimenting in new worker/manager relationships and new ways of securing workers' representation on their boards of management' and promised to encourage similar experiments in private industry,[14] the NEC statement spoke of the need to overcome the problem of the inability of workers 'to play an effective part in determining the composition of the management team, or in calling to account a Board or manager in which they have lost confidence'. The manifesto had had little to say on extending 'The Frontiers of Public Ownership', certainly nothing so unambiguous as the proud affirmation in the NEC statement that 'Labour's commitment to public ownership remains as strong as ever'.[15] This must have come as a surprise to the parliamentary leadership, despite Callaghan's words to conference in 1970 that there were some industries 'that would do better in the public sector than in the private sector'; words which he immediately followed up by stating that it was not his object 'here today', to draw up a shopping list, suggesting that it would not be his object in the near future either.[16]

Several of the policy proposals included in *Economic Strategy, Growth and Unemployment*, for example those on industrial democracy and the establishment of a State Holding Company, had previously been aired in the NEC discussion pamphlet *Labour's Economic Strategy*, published in July 1969.[17] Just as the NEC statement to conference in 1971 emphasised Labour's commitment to nationalisation, so too had *Labour's Economic Strategy* emphasised that the party's commitment to public ownership had not changed: 'We still believe that more and more of Britain's industries must move inevitably into public hands.'[18] In between had come the general election manifesto, the content reflecting Harold Wilson's success in preventing the inclusion of policies which might alienate the floating voters he believed were crucial to the party's re-election and in which, basically, he did not believe.[19] *Economic Strategy, Growth and Unemployment* therefore continued where *Labour's Economic Strategy* had left off and returned the initiative on policy to the Research Department.

The Industrial Policy Subcommittee and authorship of the NEC statement

Exactly how, given Callaghan's position as chairman of the Home Policy Committee and his success in influencing the tone of *Building a Socialist*

Britain (the previous year's NEC statement) did the parliamentary leadership lose control of the research programme to the extent that *Economic Strategy, Growth and Unemployment* became an official party statement? The NEC's acceptance of the Industrial Policy Subcommittee document indicates that Callaghan's attempt to occupy the party through the research programme was at best a qualified success and also that Terry Pitt, whose influence up to this point had been neutralised by Callaghan at the Home Policy Committee, had in the Industrial Policy Subcommittee an alternative outlet for the economic and industrial policies favoured by the Research Department as included in *Labour's Economic Strategy*.

Economic Strategy, Growth and Unemployment grew out of a paper, 'Unemployment and Manpower Planning', called for by the Industrial Policy Subcommittee, along with a synopsis of the 1967 Working Party Report on Industrial Democracy, when it met for the first time on 28 April 1971.[20] Written by Terry Pitt and his assistant Geoff Bish (secretary to the Industrial Policy Subcommittee) this paper was duly submitted for consideration at the second meeting of the subcommittee on 18 May, when it was agreed that the programme of work for the year ahead should include 'a major paper on Unemployment and Manpower policy for possible presentation to the 1971 Annual Conference'.[21] Initially, the main focus of the paper was to be unemployment, and a paper on this subject was presented to the subcommittee when it met for the third time on 15 June.[22] This 'provoked a long and wide-ranging discussion and among the general points raised was the need for the paper to deal much more fully with regional policy, with the severe difficulties involved in manpower forecasting, and with the problems involved in an attempt to act directly on prices. It was agreed to incorporate these points together with other amendments, in the next draft.'[23] It was also agreed (at the prompting of the paper's authors)[24] that the subcommittee recommend to the Home Policy Committee 'that a background paper on unemployment and economic strategy be prepared for presentation to the 1971 Annual Conference...broadly based upon the paper on Unemployment (RD.129) then before the Committee and would incorporate proposals on regional policy, public ownership, the private sector etc'.[25] This was subsequently brought to the attention of the Home Policy Committee by John Chalmers, the chairman of the Industrial Policy Subcommittee, when the former met on 12 July when it was resolved 'that a draft document be prepared by the subcommittee for consideration at the September meetings of the Home Policy Committee and the National Executive Committee'.[26] The following day the Industrial Policy Subcommittee met for the fourth time and considered RD.142/July 1971 'Unemployment, Growth and Economic Strategy', the latest draft of what was to become *Economic Strategy, Growth and Unemployment*, again written by Pitt and Bish, and taking into account the comments of the meeting of 15 June on the paper RD.129/June 1971 'Unemployment'. In the course of the discussion the implication for Labour's policy of the Conservative government's decision to scrap several elements of the machinery for intervening in the economy created by the Labour government became apparent: the Industrial Policy Subcommittee had been provided with the opportunity of 'starting from scratch'.[27]

The September deadline for the submission of a final draft of the paper to the Home Policy Committee obliged the Industrial Policy Subcommittee to meet for a fifth time on 27 July, when a revised, 'more polemic' draft of RD.142/July 1971 'Unemployment, Growth and Economic Strategy' (now numbered RD.147 and the wording of the title reordered to become 'Economic Strategy, Growth and Unemployment') was presented to the meeting. The background briefing to the paper argued that a future Labour government 'would need to adopt a set of economic priorities which properly reflect the ideals and values of the Labour Movement. And this must mean . . . clear policies in such areas as manpower, the regions, public ownership and public expenditure.' Redrafted, the paper placed greater emphasis on both the Conservative government's failures and on Labour's development of 'a new overall economic strategy'.[28]

A completed draft of *Economic Strategy, Growth and Unemployment* (RD.165), was considered by the Home Policy Committee on 13 September 1971. Callaghan made clear his dissatisfaction with the document by informing his colleagues that it was intended only as an interim statement on the party's approach 'and was not intended to commit the party on details at this stage'. However, with conference only three weeks away, there was little he could do to radically alter the content of the draft document and in the course of the discussion which followed 'the view was expressed that the document as written did commit the party to far-reaching detailed proposals'. This observation, it would appear, was sufficient to galvanise those subcommittee members sympathetic to the chairman's view and it was resolved that 'the Research Secretary be asked to redraft the statement, making it shorter and less categoric in form'.[29] Pitt's subsequent redrafting of the document was a cosmetic exercise. When the Industrial Policy Subcommittee met for a sixth and last time prior to conference on 21 September, committee members reaffirmed 'that the suggested policy commitments in the paper should be retained'.[30] On 6 October 1971, Barbara Castle presented *Economic Strategy, Growth and Unemployment* to conference on behalf of the NEC.

The composition of the Industrial Policy Subcommittee

The Industrial Policy Subcommittee met six times between 28 April and 21 September 1971, during which time 27 subcommittee members attended at least one meeting.[31] In respect of authorship of *Economic Strategy,*

Growth and Unemployment, three of the six meetings were crucial to the statement's content: 15 June, at which meeting in light of the discussion of the paper RD.129/June 1971 'Unemployment', it was agreed to recommend to the Home Policy Committee that it (the Industrial Policy Subcommittee) prepare a background paper on unemployment *and* economic strategy for presentation to conference; 13 July, the meeting at which the paper RD.142/July 1971 'Unemployment, Growth and Economic Strategy' was the focus of the discussion; and 27 July, the last occasion on which the embryonic statement (which by this stage had become RD.147/July 1971 'Economic Strategy, Growth and Unemployment') was discussed by the subcommittee prior to its submission to the Home Policy Committee and the full NEC.

The meetings of 15 June, 13 July and 27 July were attended by 19, 17 and 15 Industrial Policy Subcommittee members respectively. However, only seven members of the subcommittee were present at all three meetings: Geoff Bish of the Research Department and secretary to the subcommittee; John Chalmers of the Amalgamated Society of Boilermakers and chairman of the subcommittee; Edmund Dell MP, frontbench spokesman with responsibility for private industry, government relations with industry, monopolies and restrictive practices; Margaret Jackson of the Research Department; Dr Bill McCarthy of Nuffield College and formerly a research secretary to the Donovan Commission on the Trade Unions and Employers' Organisations; Terry Pitt, the research secretary; and the economist Richard Pryke of Liverpool University.[32] These seven members – more accurately six plus Bish, the secretary – can therefore be regarded as having had the greatest opportunity to influence the content of *Economic Strategy, Growth and Unemployment* on the grounds that they were present on those occasions when the content of the statement was gradually determined. This is not to underestimate the input and influence of those subcommittee members who were present on 13 and 27 July, but not on 15 June, and indeed one can assume that given the involvement of economic specialists such as Derek Robinson (present on 13 and 27 July) that the final draft of the NEC statement was the work of all those who attended the July meetings. However, as only seven subcommittee members were present at each of the three key meetings identified, the faction within the Labour Party with which they were associated is significant.

Certainly the three Research Department representatives were considered at the time to be sympathetic to the left-wing Tribunite faction in the party. As Hatfield writes, Terry Pitt

> used his position as Research Secretary to influence the membership of the committees, the appointment of chairmen and the presentation of background papers. Legitimate advantage was taken of the procedure which allowed research staff to put before

a committee a programme of work before the chairman had been elected at the inaugural meeting. Outline proposals before a committee were rarely challenged, although pressure of time enforced modifications.[33]

Richard Pryke had been associated with the Tribune Group after 1965 and along with Henry Collins and Sean Gervasi had advised the group on economic policy,[34] while John Chalmers, the chairman, is described by Hatfield as 'a right winger with a leftish voting pattern because of his union's policies'.[35] Five of the seven, therefore, were likely to support the policies favoured by the Research Department and included in the three papers considered by the subcommittee between 15 June and 27 July 1971. Bill McCarthy's sympathies at the time can only be guessed at, but the fact that he was co-opted by Pitt suggests that he was considered a safe choice. Only Edmund Dell, the sole PLP member of the seven, was definitely not on the left of the party.

The first major statement of policy to emerge from the research programme was, therefore, the property of the Research Department. For Pitt and Bish this was particularly satisfying. Both men had been ever-present members of the 1969 Study Group on Economic Strategy, the group that wrote *Labour's Economic Strategy* for the NEC. Having been defeated by Wilson over that document in terms of its impact on Labour's general election manifesto[36] and subsequently stifled by Callaghan at the Home Policy Committee, the publication of *Economic Strategy, Growth and Unemployment* was a strategic triumph for the two men and for the Research Department generally.[37] Callaghan's hold on the research programme had been demonstrated to be weaker than it had seemed in the months following his election as chairman of the Home Policy Committee in July 1970, and an outlet for the economic and industrial policies favoured by the Research Department had been established.

The Finance and Economic Affairs Subcommittee and the NEC statement

How was it, given the existence of the Finance and Economic Affairs Subcommittee chaired by Roy Jenkins, a former Chancellor of the Exchequer and in 1971 the deputy leader of the party, that the Industrial Policy Subcommittee was able to steal the initiative on economic policy? It has been explained above how the Industrial Policy Subcommittee was given responsibility for authorship of the NEC statement by the Home Policy Committee, but how it got past Jenkins and his colleagues at Finance and Economic Affairs is another matter. However, the image of the subcommittee – dominated as it was by MPs sympathetic to its chairman – as lotus-eaters, equally pervasive elsewhere, is insufficient as an explanation for its failure to retain control of economic policy in opposition.[38]

The Finance and Economic Affairs Subcommittee met five times in 1971, on three occasions between April and the party conference in October and twice thereafter following the NEC elections and the reconstitution of the subcommittees of the Home Policy Committee.[39] Three meetings were held between April and July 1971: 29 April, 15 June[40] and 28 July, an almost identical schedule to that of the Industrial Policy Subcommittee, which met on 28 April, 15 June and 27 July, with one unscheduled meeting added on 13 July. It was due neither to lack of time nor to the timetabling of the initial meetings that Jenkins and his colleagues failed to influence the content of the NEC statement.[41] The activity of the subcommittee in relation to the statement must therefore be considered in the context of the research programme as set up after the 1970 conference and also by taking into consideration policy deliberation outside the research programme.

When the subcommittees of the Home Policy Committee were convened and began to meet in April 1971, it was not with a view to producing a statement of policy in time for the 1971 conference, despite the fact that Composite Resolution 28 at the Blackpool conference in 1970 had requested that the NEC do precisely that. Accordingly, Jenkins and his colleagues initially met with a frequency in keeping with the view that the formulation of a new party programme would be a carefully measured process, which would involve more than simply adopting previously rejected Research Department policy proposals.[42] So it was perfectly natural for them to break for the summer and to reconvene and reconstitute the subcommittee after the NEC elections at conference. If the subcommittee under Jenkins's chairmanship lacked the urgency of the Industrial Policy Subcommittee, it was because the research programme was not the sole vehicle for the consideration of economic policy for several of the MPs involved. Jenkins, Joel Barnett, Edmund Dell, David Marquand, Dick Taverne and John Roper were all members of the PLP Economic and Finance Subject Group who in April 1971 were actively engaged in dealing with the government's Finance Bill and the clauses thereof to be taken on the floor of the House of Commons.[43] All six were present at at least one of the three meetings of the Finance and Economic Affairs Subcommittee held between April and July 1971. Of the 17 subcommittee members who attended at least one of these meetings, ten were MPs easily identifiable as being on the centre-right of the PLP. Given the core membership of the Industrial Policy Subcommittee at this time, it is apparent that the two subcommittees were ideologically irreconcilable. If the Finance and Economic Affairs Subcommittee was at fault in its approach to the research programme, it was in not realising that the struggle for control of the party's economic policy, which had begun after the introduction of the July measures of 1966 and continued throughout the lifetime of the 1966–70 Parliament, was being continued by the left wing of the party in opposition, aided by the Research Department.

While the Industrial Policy Subcommittee was discussing the NEC statement in its embryonic form between April and July 1971, Jenkins and his colleagues discussed the subcommittee's programme of work (29 April), taxation and child allowances (15 June) and, finally, economic growth (28 July). This agenda, to some extent, was determined by the research secretary, Pitt, who provided an office paper outlining a possible programme of work for the subcommittee at the first meeting on 29 April. The introduction to RD.99/April 1971 'Programme of Work' stated that Finance and Economic Affairs was 'the major one of the six'[44] subcommittees and outlined the process by which policy was made:

> first, research papers from the office, from members of the group (especially the co-opted members) and any outside experts within the Party who may have a useful contribution to make; then discussion of the papers by the subcommittee; and, finally, a draft report from the office, to be processed through the subcommittee, the full Home Policy Committee and the NEC.[45]

The paper then proceeded to list taxation, financial institutions, the problems of sterling, public expenditure, monetary policy and prices and incomes as possible areas of study.[46] Discussion of this paper and the co-opting of additional members accounted for this first meeting of the subcommittee, although it was resolved that a study on taxation and public expenditure and also a joint study with the Industrial Policy Subcommittee (subject to agreement) of prices and incomes, be set in hand and that a short paper be prepared by the office on the relationship of income tax and social security benefit in the 'marginal rates' on the lower income groups.[47] The subcommittee did not meet again until 15 June, when much of the time was spent considering the papers of the Taxation Study Group originally submitted between January and March 1970.[48] Belatedly, it was resolved 'that a revised version of the office document on unemployment sent to the Industrial Policy Subcommittee, be circulated for the next meeting'.[49] By this stage, however, the Industrial Policy Subcommittee had agreed to recommend to the Home Policy Committee that RD.129 'Unemployment' serve as the basis for a paper to be presented to conference in October. Possibly at the prompting of Edmund Dell, who was a member of both subcommittees and was therefore alert to the political objectives which lay behind Industrial Policy Subcommittee activity, Jenkins and his colleagues asked David Marquand to prepare a paper on economic growth for the next meeting.[50] As the Finance and Economic Affairs Subcommittee did not meet again until 28 July, this initiative came too late to influence the content of the NEC statement. Marquand duly submitted his paper 'Problems of Economic Growth',[51] but as the Industrial Policy Subcommittee had met the previous day for the last time, specifically to discuss the statement, it had little impact. The minutes record merely that the Finance and Economic Affairs Subcommittee 'noted' the paper RD.147 'Economic Strategy, Growth and Unemployment' which was before the meeting.[52]

The question remains whether the Finance and Economic Affairs Subcommittee was deliberately diverted by Pitt and the Research Department from discussing economic policy within the context of the NEC statement. The fact that Jenkins and his colleagues were looking at 18-month-old papers on taxation when the Industrial Policy Subcommittee was seeking Home Policy Committee approval for a paper to be presented to conference, indicates that the former Chancellor was indeed excluded from a debate, the substance of which it was known he would oppose. In November 1971, Jenkins survived a challenge from Ian Mikardo for the chair of the subcommittee only with the aid of Callaghan,[53] who himself had been challenged by Mikardo for the chair of the Home Policy Committee one week earlier, as part of an attempt by left-wingers to wrest control of the research programme from the parliamentary leadership. Wickham-Jones describes Jenkins and his colleagues only as 'slow to get going',[54] but a comparison of the respective programmes of work placed before the Finance and Economic Affairs Subcommittee by the research secretary on 29 April 1971 and the Industrial Policy Subcommittee the previous day, again indicates that they were obstructed by Pitt. The list of possible topics for discussion by the Industrial Policy Subcommittee, such as the public sector, new candidates for public ownership, policies for the redistribution of incomes and wealth, planning and interventionism, the multinational corporation and a State Holding Company, all of which featured in the programme of work prepared by Pitt,[55] were of equal concern to the Finance and Economic Affairs Subcommittee, and it is no coincidence that, when they were mentioned in the party's 1970 general election manifesto, they were included under the heading 'A Strong Economy'.[56] The programme of work prepared for the Industrial Policy Subcommittee did state in its introductory paragraph that 'the work of the Committee must inevitably overlap the work of other committees, in particular the Finance and Economic Affairs Subcommittee',[57] but as a concession to those MPs who were members of that subcommittee and who were unsympathetic to the left, it was at best cosmetic.[58] Jenkins and his colleagues were aware of what was being discussed at Industrial Policy meetings. Both subcommittees were in receipt of the other's papers. If the Finance and Economic Affairs Subcommittee was denied the opportunity to contribute to the NEC statement, it was, says Bish, because the Research Department knew the subcommittee 'was not going to get down to serious business on economic policy', from which it can be inferred that the subcommittee rejected the Research Department's proposals on economic and industrial policy.[59] Jenkins and his colleagues, writes Wickham-Jones, quoting Dell, 'were not that interested in industrial politics because of its limited possibilities: it represented "boredom for the right and excitement for the left"'.[60]

To some extent, however, the Finance and Economic Affairs Subcommittee was responsible for its exclusion from the debate on economic policy between April and July 1971. Jenkins, anxious to avoid a repeat of the schism of 1951–52, shared Callaghan's view that the best way to control the party's discussion of policy was to stifle the debate by structuring the research programme in such a way as to make the discussion of policy an interminable process (a strategy which ultimately backfired as the left had long displayed both the stamina and the appetite for the minutiae of policy) and, in his own case, by discussing the specifics of policy with the party only as a last resort.[61] Also, those MPs who were members of the Finance and Economic Affairs Subcommittee and were members of the PLP Economic and Finance Subject Group as well, even though denied the opportunity to contribute to the NEC statement through the research programme (Dell excepted), were not discussing policy issues such as the public sector or new candidates for public ownership (when, for example, the latter group held its regular meetings at Westminster). The Industrial Policy Subcommittee, by contrast, *wanted* to discuss these topics and welcomed the opportunity to 'start from scratch' in response to Heath's rejection of the Labour government's interventionist economic strategy.

The Labour Party Conference and the NEC statement

Introducing *Economic Strategy, Growth and Unemployment* to conference, Barbara Castle paid tribute to the efforts of John Chalmers and his fellow members on the Industrial Policy Subcommittee. Chalmers, she told conference, 'had kept us at it meeting after meeting, so that we could produce this statement to conference'. There had also been unstinting effort from the Research Department, from the MPs, trade union members and the industrial policy experts 'who helped us to hack out some solutions'. She was less effusive when it came to the contribution of Jenkins and the Finance and Economic Affairs Subcommittee: 'those esoteric chaps in the finance and economic policy group came limping behind'. Castle's public display of antipathy towards Jenkins and his colleagues on this occasion left no doubt whose property the NEC statement was, and it was therefore ironic that it fell to Jenkins to wind up the debate on economic policy and unemployment which followed Castle's speech. Whereas Castle was 'so proud of having been given the task of introducing this National Executive document', Jenkins made no effort to identify with the statement. *Economic Strategy, Growth and Unemployment* was thus the document 'the NEC is presenting to you', a remark which despite Jenkins's own membership of that body conveyed his lack of enthusiasm for the document. Echoing Callaghan's words of 21 September to the Home Policy Committee, he told conference that it 'does not attempt to be a full-scale blueprint for action', adding that 'there is a great deal of detail and clarification to be filled in'.[62]

Reaction to *Economic Strategy, Growth and Unemployment* was mixed, ranging from Wilson's promise to reassert 'the principle of industrial intervention' and to establish a State Holding Agency 'on the lines of the IRC – but writ large this time, and with a clearer power to ensure that where society invests in private industry, society will stake a claim in the profits', to Ray Apps's (Brighton, Kemp Town CLP) who chided the platform with 'Does Barbara not know that to devalue is to cut the living standards of the working people of this country?',[63] a reference to the statement's advocacy of 'an orderly re-alignment' of the exchange rate 'whenever the alternative is a policy of massive deflation and stagnation'.[64] Wilson's rhetoric – 'every publicly owned asset the Conservatives sell off to their friends will be restored to the public and every speculator who enters the field, attracted by quick profits, will burn his fingers. They have been warned'[65] – allied to his reference to intervention in industry and a State Holding Agency, appeared to signal support for the NEC statement. This, no doubt, was his intention and such rhetoric was indeed more easily digested by conference than his actual comment on the statement, the true meaning of which was unfathomable:

> The National Executive Committee have placed before this Conference our first thoughts in the Conference Document on economic strategy, unemployment and growth, which we shall be debating tomorrow. It does not provide all the answers, but what it does do is to provide the questions to the answers, and clear guidance to Conference on how these questions will have to be answered.[66]

Another time *Economic Strategy, Growth and Unemployment* might have provoked a debate between right and left to rival the great confrontations of conferences past. Certainly the NEC statement represented an attempt by the left wing of the party to return Labour to a point in its history when Crosland's *The Future of Socialism* had not yet been written. It was therefore a direct refutation of the policies advocated and followed by the parliamentary leadership in one form or another since Gaitskell had succeeded Attlee as leader of the party in 1955. Yet at Brighton in 1971 Crosland remained silent when the statement was debated, while Jenkins (who had superseded Crosland as the recipient of the devotion of those MPs who as young, prospective Labour candidates had declared themselves to be Croslandites after the publication of *The Future of Socialism* in 1956) was found wanting and incapable of challenging the left head-on in the manner of his hero Gaitskell, being at this time preoccupied with the campaign to secure British entry into the Common Market, the issue which above all else dominated the 1971 conference.[67]

Crosland had been co-opted to sit on the Industrial Policy Subcommittee after the meeting of 15 June 1971, but did not attend his first meeting until 21 December that year and therefore made no contribution to the NEC statement.[68] Prior to its publication he spoke critically about the research programme, not of the way the exercise had been structured by Callaghan (whom he supported) but of what it was likely to produce; *Economic Strategy, Growth and Unemployment* no doubt being the example he had in mind. He proposed instead that no more than six members each from the Shadow Cabinet and the NEC be deputed as a policy-making and steering committee and given the task 'of surveying the whole field [of policy] and deciding what were the critical areas in which we need major policies and, above all, deciding the areas where we need new policies'. In the longer term 'a totally new solution was called for; a centre for Labour studies or research controlled by and responsible to the party, headed preferably by a younger Labour politician with a small staff but with continual access to both political and academic worlds'.[69] Policy, as he saw it, 'originated at the summit'.[70]

Crosland *did* comment on the NEC statement at Brighton, but away from the conference hall at the annual *Socialist Commentary* tea meeting, where he lamented the absence of any serious work on future policy since the election defeat in 1970:

> We have had at this year's Conference one single document from the NEC, which Harold Wilson rightly said posed questions rather than the answers. We have had a few Fabian pamphlets, some articles in left-wing journals, a trickle of individual efforts. But these do not add up to a systematic effort to survey the whole field of policy and to decide where we were reasonably successful last time, where we failed and where new answers have to be found.[71]

While welcoming the one part of the NEC statement which mirrored his own thinking – the suggestion that an orderly realignment to the exchange rate should, in certain circumstances, be considered – Crosland found little else to commend in what was the product of the first six months of the research programme in terms of economic and industrial policy. But he took comfort from Wilson's speech to conference, during which it had become clear that the 12 months to the 1972 conference would see, in Crosland's words, 'a sustained effort at future policy-making', adding that 'there now seems a determination on all sides to start serious talks on a future prices and incomes policy'.[72]

Crosland's view of the research programme and how policy should be made did not change the fact that the research programme had saddled the parliamentary leadership with the policies of the Research Department. Callaghan's inability to insist that the NEC statement be radically redrafted by the Home Policy Committee defined the boundaries of his influence, although by the time the committee received the statement in September 1971 it was too late to delay it, if there was to be a statement to conference by the NEC, as intended. The research programme was crucial to the parliamentary leadership's aim of preventing the party from splitting, and provided the means by which the discontent of those sections of the party which had felt disenfranchised under the Labour government could be absorbed and controlled, but it was established at the price of situating at the heart of the programme a Research Department biased towards the party's left wing. At the Home Policy Committee, Callaghan had been able to oversee the creation of a structure which would occupy the party through the discussion of policy, the only drawback being that the Research Department was in a position to finesse the policy agenda. In this respect the NEC statement to conference in 1971 was a defining moment, because the Research Department at last succeeded in having the party leader identify publicly with its policy agenda, despite the imprecise meaning of his words on the subject. Once *Economic Strategy, Growth and Unemployment* became an official party statement, the parliamentary leadership having failed to challenge it for the reasons set out above (some of which, it bears repeating, were beyond their control), the tone of the research programme was fixed and its likely outcome foreshadowed.

The NEC research programme, November 1971–July 1972

Research programme activity between November 1971 and July 1972 was directed towards the production of the NEC document *Labour's Programme for Britain 1972*, Labour's first comprehensive statement of policy after two years in opposition. The subcommittees, study groups and working parties of the Home Policy Committee had worked 'extremely hard', the NEC told the 1972 conference, 'in advising the Home Policy Committee on proposals suitable for inclusion in the draft policy statement. At the same time these groups have kept in hand their longer-term research work aimed at proposing detailed plans for the next Labour Government.'[73] *Labour's Programme for Britain 1972* ran to more than 50,000 words in accommodating the interim conclusions of the research programme to date. The NEC envisaged that the proposals in the document would be debated in the constituencies prior to conference, enabling the fullest discussion of the document when the party met at Brighton in October 1972: 'In light of the debate and decisions at Conference, it will be our intention to place before next year's Conference a shorter document which will recommend, for consideration by the Conference, the priorities for the next Labour Government. These priorities will in due course be reflected in our election manifesto.' In many respects *Labour's Programme for Britain 1972* was a less significant document than *Economic Strategy, Growth and Unemployment*, despite being more recognisably the product of the research programme as a whole rather than of just one – the Industrial Policy – subcommittee. As with the earlier document, in tone and content it reflected the Research Department's breakthrough on policy via the Industrial Policy Subcommittee the previous year. 'We are a democratic Socialist Party and proud of it', the document proclaimed in the first line of the opening paragraph. 'We put the principles of democracy and socialism above considerations of class and market economics.'[74]

Despite being dominated by the proposals on economic and industrial policy, *Labour's Programme for Britain 1972* demonstrated the breadth of research programme activity to the extent that the party appeared to have, or at least be in the process of formulating, a policy on virtually every subject. The Agriculture Subcommittee had policies on marketing, hill farming, fishing, forestry and rating and taxation of land. The Science and Education Subcommittee was 'considering the implications of proposals to end the system of independent schools and to remove all direct and indirect public subsidies to the schools prior to eventual abolition'. The Social Policy Subcommittee was considering pensions and the pensioners, means tests and charges, poverty and groups in need, finance of the National Health Service and democracy within it, care of the elderly and the disabled, the occupational health service and penal reform.[75] On the subject of housing the document was plainly influenced by the Conservative government's Housing Finance Act, which paved the way for socially necessary housing to become profit-making by removing the right of local authorities to determine the level of rent. Tenants unable to afford the new 'fair-rents', Labour argued, would be forced into the private housing market in all probability to face equally high levels of rent. The party's response was to pledge to repeal the 'pernicious' legislation in its entirety. The Housing Finance Working Group, chaired by Frank Allaun MP, framed its proposals in the context of class, attacking the disparity in the treatment of council tenants compared to owner-occupiers, the latter of whom received over £300 million a year tax relief, 'whilst council tenants receive in Government housing subsidies about £160 million'. Revisiting *Signposts for the Sixties*, the party's 1961 policy document, the working group proposed that land needed for development should be publicly owned 'since private speculation leads to massive costs to the community for ... socially necessary projects'.[76]

The research programme provided no role for the party leader. Harold Wilson neither sat on nor chaired any of the subcommittees, study groups or working parties which contributed to *Labour's Programme for Britain 1972*. The proposals on economic and industrial policy, on housing, on land, had each been discussed at length before Wilson saw them at the NEC in the weeks immediately prior to publication. He therefore had little opportunity to influence directly the content of the policy document, but he was better placed as party leader and as a member of the NEC to influence the context in which the proposals were presented to the public. Policy statements in the introductory paragraphs to the document were accordingly heavily qualified and, as with *Agenda for a Generation* in 1969, the document carried the disclaimer that it was not a manifesto, even 'though it contains proposals which will go into our manifesto. It makes proposals in some fields which could not be carried through in a single Parliament, and sets out objectives some of which would not be attained in five years through lack of resources.'[77]

Even more directly, the document warned that the next Labour government would have a vast list of commitments which would require lengthy legislation and in some cases substantial funding and resources. 'We therefore make it clear at the outset that Labour will have priorities, worked out in consultation with the whole movement.'[78] This, the document continued, might be a painful process but it was what politics was all about. This echoed closely Wilson's speech to conference at Blackpool in 1970 (replying to the debate on conference decisions) during which he explained that 'timing and priorities must be a matter for the Government. Priorities must above all be a matter for a Labour Government, because an interventionist government, a Socialist government, has to decide priorities every day of its life.'[79] Wilson was getting his excuses in first. As a great deal of the legislative programme of the next Labour government was already clear, it was unrealistic to expect that all of the proposals would be implemented in a single Parliament. Little of this envisaged legislative programme derived from the research programme. At Brighton in 1971 Wilson lamented the fact that 'so much of the legislation of the first two years of the next Labour Government will be of an anti-vandalistic character',[80] by which he referred to the party's existing commitments to repeal the Industrial Relations and Housing Finance Acts, and to reverse or change taxation and regional policy, the hiving off of public enterprises, school milk and museum charges. The next Labour government would also have detailed legislation on the nationalisation of the docks and a new pensions plan prepared by the previous Labour government.[81]

Ironically, the envisaged legislative programme as it stood (particularly in respect of the Industrial Relations Act and the Housing Finance Act) had been pushed for by a number of MPs, primarily from the left of the PLP but also from the centre. The implication of this was not lost on John

Mackintosh MP, who wrote in *Political Quarterly* that 'blanket rejection of the entire Industrial Relations Act, the entire policy of joining the EEC, the entire Housing Finance Bill and so on, ... would leave the next Labour Government committed only to a return to the 1968–70 status quo. The paradox is that the Left, who prided themselves on being the most persistent critics of the last Wilson Government, are now in practice working hard to ensure that the next Labour Government is as like its predecessor as possible.' Mackintosh accused the left of ducking the argument and proposing instead 'changes in the Labour Party's constitution whose practical effect would be to strengthen the power of those activist groups in the Party which in turn would vote for and bolster the position of the left inside the Parliamentary Labour Party'.[82] For the moment, however, the left had the initiative on policy and the introductory paragraphs to *Labour's Programme for Britain 1972*, when contrasted with the proposals which followed, merely emphasised the gap between the parliamentary leadership and the party and highlighted the importance of office to the parliamentary leadership as a means of controlling policy.

Labour's Programme for Britain 1972 repeated almost exactly the proposals included in the NEC statement to the 1971 conference. The level of unemployment, described in *Economic Strategy, Growth and Unemployment* as 'appalling', was now described as 'indefensible' and the words of Beveridge quoted in support of Labour's proposals for intervention: 'To ask for full employment whilst objecting to these extensions of State activity, is to will the end and refuse the means.' Similarly, as part of the party's strategy for containing inflation, the commitment to introduce an Early Warning System on prices, price controls and to restrain retail prices was restated. However, where the 1971 statement as part of its anti-inflationary strategy had proposed, when necessary, the orderly realignment of the exchange rate, *Labour's Programme for Britain 1972* took a step back, stating that 'Devaluation is never an easy way out. It puts up prices and hits the living standards of every family in the land.' It was no doubt said with the intention of exploiting the difficulties being experienced by the Conservative government, whose decision to float the pound on 23 June 1972 in the face of rapidly increasing inflation was presented by Labour as evidence of 'the complete collapse of their economic policies'.[83] This was not entirely opportunistic: the proposal had been attacked at the 1971 conference on the grounds that devaluation penalised working people.[84] Conversely, although entirely predictably given the context, *Labour's Programme for Britain 1972* defended the right of a future Labour government to make timely adjustments to the exchange rate if it saw fit. In the section of the document covering the Common Market, it was stated that Labour 'would reject any kind of international agreement which compelled us to accept increased unemployment for the sake of maintaining a fixed parity, as is required by current proposals for a European Economic and Monetary

Union'.[85] This was one issue where, for the party's anti-Marketeers, the living standards of working people took second place to hostility to the Common Market.

On regional policy the document proposed 'a coherent and comprehensive policy' based on the proposals in the 1971 statement and on the report of the Study Group on Regional Policy, *Regional Planning Policy*, published in 1970. It included 'A Manpower Subsidy' to encourage firms to move from congested areas and the development of 'Growth Complexes', 'self-sustaining industrial complexes seen as generating points for expansion in the regions'.[86] The commitment to introduce a State Holding Company 'as the instrument for integrating industries and firms into the public sector'[87] was also reaffirmed, as was the promised creation of a National Labour Board (renamed the National Manpower Board in 1972) through which 'displaced workers would have the automatic right to training or retraining, and at all levels of occupational skill'.[88] It was the third time in four years that proposals of this nature had been included in an official policy statement. However, repetition alone did not determine policy and at this stage none of the above had been adopted as party policy. Yet, set against the backdrop of Heath's industrial policies the impact of which, so it was felt, could be witnessed in the unemployment figures, the Industrial Policy Subcommittee's regional strategy appeared consistent with the policies of the previous Labour government. Further, there was a degree of consensus within the party that an interventionist regional policy was required, and in this respect the proposals were therefore a matter of interpretation. Wilson, speaking in the House of Commons in January 1972, listed 12 measures to combat unemployment, many of which bore a similarity to the proposals included in *Economic Strategy, Growth and Unemployment*. The third measure was a strengthened version of the Labour government's Industrial Reorganisation Corporation (established in 1966 to facilitate selective intervention and to encourage mergers) to be set up 'on the basis of an industrial partnership with a recognition that investment cannot be adequately expanded except on the basis of the assertion of public responsibility for an appropriate and expanding industrial programme'.[89] Three weeks later Bill Rodgers MP introduced a Private Member's Bill to set up a Regional Development Corporation which he envisaged 'going out for business seeking situations where, by means of loans, grants or equity – mainly, I would think loans – it keeps a factory in business, brings together firms which are complementary and can prosper in partnership when they would fail on their own, to identify a total situation for development in terms of types of industry and then of firms – a sort of executive search technique'.[90] At this stage regional policy was not the sole property of any one section of the party, despite the Industrial Policy Subcommittee's domination of the party's official consideration of the issue. Writing in *Socialist Commentary* in December 1971,

Edmund Dell appealed to the party to be 'less timorous about public ownership', describing the State Holding Company as 'likely to become increasingly important for the state to do directly what incentives have failed to encourage private enterprise to do sufficiently, for example to build up employment opportunities in the depressed regions'.[91]

By the time *Labour's Programme for Britain 1972* was published in July, the research programme had to some extent been superseded by the establishment of the TUC–Labour Party Liaison Committee, which met for the first time on 21 February 1972, and through which agreement was reached concerning the repeal of the Industrial Relations Act and the establishment of a Conciliation and Arbitration Service. This was only a beginning. At the 1972 conference the party was informed that the Liaison Committee would proceed to discuss 'the general economic and industrial policies of the next Labour government' and somewhat unconvincingly that *Labour's Programme for Britain 1972*, along with the TUC's *Economic Review*, would form the basis of the planned discussions.[92] Accordingly, the tone of *Labour's Programme for Britain 1972* reflected the quickening rapprochement in party–union relations effected since the publication of the 1971 NEC statement. The 1972 document dismissed the suggestion that the level of prices was determined exclusively by the level of wages and adopted the language of the unions in asking instead whose wage increases had led to scandalous land and house prices, to escalating rents and to the 17 per cent increase in food prices since the general election.[93] In return for repealing the Industrial Relations Act, Labour anticipated the full co-operation of the trade unions in the sphere of *voluntary* industrial relations reform.[94]

The fact that party leaders were discussing economic and industrial policy with trade union leaders outside the research process was hugely significant, demonstrating that the programme was a facade (at least in terms of economic and industrial policy) and that by early 1972 there were in fact two policy processes running simultaneously. While the subcommittees were developing new policy, party leaders were *agreeing* the content of actual policy with trade union leaders at the Labour Party–TUC Liaison Committee. This latter process, ironically, returned the initiative on policy to the parliamentary leadership by effectively removing discussion of economic and industrial policy from the research programme, a development which is discussed at greater length below.[95]

The NEC research programme and *Labour's Programme for Britain 1972*

The process by which research programme activity became focused on the production of a Green Paper, the status given by the NEC to *Labour's Programme for Britain 1972*, began at the September meeting of the Home

Policy Committee prior to the 1971 conference, when it was agreed 'there should be an overall long-term programme, setting out the aims of the party in all areas of policy, from which priorities could be extracted for the formation of a five-year programme for the next Labour Government'.[96] When the Home Policy Committee met for the first time after conference on 8 November 1971, the renewal of the research programme to this end was agreed. Before the meeting on this occasion was a programme of work for the year ahead prepared by the Research Department, which for the first time raised the question of whether the Home Policy Committee 'should aim to produce a single comprehensive statement of policy for the next Annual Conference'.[97]

The extent to which the research programme was by this time running away from the parliamentary leadership is evident from the way the recommendations included in the programme of work were designed to make research activity more purposeful and the objectives of the exercise more specific. If the Home Policy Committee decided in favour of a comprehensive statement of policy, the programme of work stated, 'for maximum impact ... we should consider the need to publish and circulate our document in July 1972 ... NEC statements at Annual Conference have a lessening impact if they are only unveiled at a time when the Conference is actually taking place.' The paper also suggested that the NEC could present the document as a party programme and by so doing 'could remove a lot of the difficulties which have dogged us in the past concerning the status of Conference decisions, and the role of the Leadership in selecting what is possible in a five-year Parliament, etc., etc.... It would also, of course, have the invaluable contribution of being the single greatest contribution possible to political education.'[98] This was suggested with the intention of tying the parliamentary leadership to policies produced by a research programme over which it had been unable to retain control and which, if accepted, would have shifted the balance of power within the party in favour of the wider membership at conference, thereby restricting the role of the parliamentary leadership in determining policy in government. By the end of the meeting it was decided that the document to be prepared in time for the 1972 conference would be 'a wide-ranging statement of policy, along the lines of a green paper', enjoying consultative status only, which in the circumstances was a triumph of sorts for the parliamentary leadership in that it further postponed the adoption of the Research Department agenda as official party policy.[99]

The transparency of the Research Department's strategy notwithstanding, the programme of work before the Home Policy Committee was also a practical appraisal of what was required if the party was to produce a major statement of policy in 1972. Accordingly, recommendations such as that the NEC and Shadow Cabinet meet early in 1972 to discuss policy, that the Policy Co-ordinating Committee representing the two bodies be reconstituted, and that the subcommittees of the Home Policy Committee be reappointed, were all agreed to by those present.[100]

The Finance and Economic Affairs Subcommittee and *Labour's Programme for Britain 1972*

The Finance and Economic Affairs Subcommittee's contribution to *Labour's Programme for Britain 1972* was restricted to two brief sections, 'Economic equality' and 'Taxation'. The NEC report to the 1972 conference described the subcommittee as having worked in particular on the costing of the public expenditure commitments in the document, and indeed the document stated how the rate of public expenditure, 'no less than private consumption, must be used to regulate the level of demand in order to ensure full employment and balance the other sectors of the economy'.[101] This summary of one aspect of the subcommittee's activity, while accurate, demonstrated how restrictive the research programme was for senior parliamentary leaders such as Jenkins and Crosland and failed to acknowledge the extent to which they worked on policy beyond the official process. Certainly neither the NEC report nor *Labour's Programme for Britain 1972* did justice to the radical social agenda being advanced by Jenkins and his colleagues who, wrote Mackintosh, had been 'rethinking socialist policy in terms of how the next Labour Government should tackle poverty, relative deprivation in the cities, the need for increased aid to the underdeveloped countries and so on'.[102] The tendency to make policy by speech-making naturally infuriated those in the party for whom the research programme was a model of how policy in the Labour Party should be made, and simply confirmed the view held by many on the left that the likes of Jenkins and Crosland were not party men.

The Finance and Economic Affairs Subcommittee met for the first time after the 1971 conference on 16 November, this meeting being restricted to those subcommittee members who were members of the NEC.[103] Before the meeting were two papers, RD.153 'Problems of Economic Growth', written by David Marquand MP and carried over from the meeting of 28 July 1971, and RD.181 'Programme of Work' (for 1972) written by the Research Department.[104] Discussion of these papers was crucial to the programme of work undertaken by the subcommittee in the second year of the research programme. Marquand's paper was in part a response to the thinking in the Industrial Policy Subcommittee paper which became *Economic Strategy, Growth and Unemployment* and which, despite being called for too late to influence that document, was nevertheless pertinent to the party's discussion of economic and industrial policy as set out in the NEC statement. Marquand (having prefaced his remarks with the warning that it was 'pointless at this stage to promulgate a complete policy for growth under the next Labour Government') opened his paper with three generalisations: first, that socialism was about redistribution, 'and the moral of the 1964–70 experience is that in a democracy redistribution is impossible without growth'; second, that there was no magic formula which would lead painlessly to a significantly better rate of growth than that of the last 20 years – 'attempts to pretend there is will destroy the credibility of the Government and lead to excessive demoralisation and disillusionment when early hopes turn sour'; and, third, saying that growth should have priority and actually giving it priority were two separate things – 'We *said* growth should have priority before 1964. We *gave* priority to the world role and the sterling parity.' The moral was (a) 'that growth is bound to conflict with other policy objectives', and (b) 'that we must anticipate such conflicts as far as possible and decide what order of priorities to adopt if they arise'.[105]

Marquand described the debate which had taken place inside the Labour Party since the general election defeat in 1970 as harmonious, to the extent that there was general agreement that the Labour government should have pursued growth more vigorously and that, in order to do better in the future, a solution to the problem of the balance of payments and cost inflation would have to be found. Beyond this there existed no consensus, but four approaches could be discerned: 'Go for growth and borrow your way out of trouble'; growth buttressed by incomes policy; growth buttressed by devaluation; and growth via devaluation. The first approach would enable the balance of payments constraint on growth to be ignored because it was in the rest of the world's interest that Britain should prosper. As a result the country could expect to be able to borrow its way out of trouble having pursued a policy of growth at the expense of the balance of payments deficit. The second approach, which insisted that the balance of payments constraint could not be ignored 'and shouldn't be avoided by parity changes which are inflationary and undesirable on social grounds', envisaged a 'social contract' between a Labour government and the trade unions 'in which rapid strides towards economic and social equality, a highly "interventionist" form of economic planning and economic growth are traded for a very stringent incomes policy'. The third approach advocated changes to the parity rate as and when necessary to deal with the impact of growth on the balance of payments. The fourth believed that the only way to secure export-led growth was to 'aim at a definite rate of increase in exports and then manipulate the exchange rate accordingly'. Marquand regarded none of these approaches alone as satisfactory and foresaw three obvious problem areas if they were taken together: the balance of payments and parity; inflation and incomes policy; investment, 'intervention' and the growth of capacity.[106] Resolving these three problems, he felt, would provide a suitable future programme of work for the subcommittee.

The programme of work the Finance and Economic Affairs Subcommittee actually undertook was the one prepared by the Research Department in 1971, the substance of which was repeated for 1972, locking Marquand and his colleagues into a study of taxation and public expenditure, which the department described the subcommittee as being 'uniquely fitted' to undertake. Seven months on from the subcommittee's first meeting this was yet to commence, as was the suggested joint study with the Industrial Policy Subcommittee on prices and incomes. In between, the subcommittee's programme of work had increased as a consequence of conference support for two resolutions notionally of interest to it: proposed public ownership of the banks, insurance companies and building societies, and nationalisation of motor insurance and a recasting of motor taxation.[107] The paper RD.181 'Programme of Work' added that the subcommittee had not so far undertaken to produce a paper of the magnitude of *Economic Strategy, Growth and Unemployment*, a comment which, if intended to spur the subcommittee to greater achievement, was somewhat ironic given that members of the subcommittee were obstructed by the research secretary, as shown above, from contributing to the 1971 NEC statement.

Jenkins and his colleagues found themselves committed to an agenda – taxation and public spending – which impeded a wider discussion of economic policy. Taxation and public expenditure were certainly extremely important subjects for Labour and it was appropriate for the Finance and Economic Affairs Subcommittee to discuss them. Between December 1971 and April 1972, by which time contributions to the NEC document were due for submission, the subcommittee considered papers on a range of related issues. These included 'The Party's Economic Policy', written by Lord Balogh, 'Negative Income Tax' by Dick Taverne, as well as office papers on 'A Public Expenditure Programme', 'Means Tests and Deductions from Earnings' and 'Demand Management',[108] which led to the inclusion in *Labour's Programme for Britain 1972* of a number of proposals designed to make the tax system fairer, 'and in particular protect those least able to bear the burdens'.[109] However, it would have made equal sense for the subcommittee to discuss in addition the three problem areas identified by Marquand, but these constituted an agenda which was too awkward for the Research Department and, more importantly, the trade unions. Certainly some of the questions Marquand posed on inflation and incomes policy highlighted the deficiencies of the Industrial Policy Subcommittee's proposals for the containment of inflation through the control of prices but not of wages (which was simply not being discussed). Union leaders had repeated their opposition to such a policy at the 1971 conference[110] and the Research Department was reluctant to encourage activity in this field, stating that the joint study with the Industrial Policy Subcommittee should proceed only 'if this is considered the right time to be looking at this operation'.[111] Marquand and Roy Jenkins obviously thought so, the former Chancellor having told conference that 'Last year may not have been the time for serious talking. This year is. We cannot be urgent about the end of the Tory Government and at the same time be leisurely about our own vital policy formation.'[112] Marquand concluded that only two types of incomes policy were likely to produce results:

> a short, sharp freeze a la 1966, which can produce impressive results in the short run, but only at the cost of building up such resentment against the inequities which will inevitably result that the policy is likely to collapse altogether once the freeze is over;
> a very mild policy, aimed at producing a slow, gradual but hopefully irreversible change in behaviour over a long period.[113]

If this was so, he argued, in demand terms incomes policy could only be effective if it was self-destructive: 'and the sort of policy which might yield dividends in the long run won't be of much help in balance of payments terms in the short'.[114]

Had the NEC statement to the 1971 conference been produced jointly by the Industrial Policy and Financial and Economic Affairs Subcommittees there would either have been no statement for want of agreement, or a much better statement than *Economic Strategy, Growth and Unemployment* turned out to be, the proposals included in the statement being improved for having been exposed to the scrutiny of Jenkins, Dell, Marquand and others. Of the two papers (the 1971 NEC statement and Marquand's 'Problems of Economic Growth') Marquand's was superior, but in 1971, in opposition, it was not the paper the Labour Party desired. Certainly the party did not want a paper which dealt with the realities of power and which required the PLP to conduct itself as a government in opposition, particularly if the government it resembled was the Labour government 1964–70. While some party members needed to experience the emotional spasm of opposition and give consideration to the formulation of new policy unhindered by the limitations of government, it was also the case that the struggle for control of the party's policy (which dated back to 1947–48 and the argument over the content of Labour's 1950 general election manifesto) was being continued by the Tribune Group of MPs, who rejected the ideas espoused by Marquand and his colleagues, because it believed they had failed the party both in opposition and in government since 1950.

Had the Finance and Economic Affairs Subcommittee incorporated a study of the balance of payments and parity, and inflation and incomes policy into its programme of work for 1972, it would have led it onto territory reserved by the Research Department for the Industrial Policy Subcommittee, as would have discussion of 'intervention', about which Marquand raised several questions in respect of regional policy, the private sector and the State Holding Company.[115] An expanded programme of work along these lines was not encouraged by the Research Department for obvious reasons. Thus, obliged by the research programme to study public expenditure and taxation, Jenkins (the leader of a parliamentary faction which included several of his colleagues from the Finance and Economic Affairs Subcommittee) pursued a wider economic and social agenda beyond the research programme in his public speeches and eventually, to great effect, in a series of six specially written speeches (for which Marquand contributed most of the writing).[116] The general theme of these was 'the stubborn persistence of avoidable deprivation and injustice, and the need for a radical and coherent strategy to combat them'. They began 'somewhat explosively'[117] with a speech on poverty at Worsley on 11 March 1972 and were subsequently collected together and published under the title *What Matters Now*.[118]

The composition of the Finance and Economic Affairs Subcommittee

Between 16 November 1971 and 27 June 1972, the date of the last subcommittee meeting prior to the publication of *Labour's Programme for Britain 1972*, the Finance and Economic Affairs Subcommittee met eight times to discuss its contribution to the NEC document.[119] These meetings were chaired by Jenkins until 13 March 1972 and subsequently by Denis Healey, when the former resigned as deputy leader and from the Shadow Cabinet in April 1972. As a consequence the Treasury portfolio, along with the chair of the Finance and Economic Affairs Subcommittee (Jenkins being no longer a member of the NEC), passed to his successor.

Given that the subcommittee was dominated by MPs who were sympathetic to Jenkins, it appears all the more extraordinary that they were diverted from following the programme of work of their choice. In the period of Jenkins's chairmanship between 16 November 1971 and 13 March 1972, during the second year of the research programme,[120] of the 29 subcommittee members who attended at least one meeting, 13 were members of the PLP, six of whom were also members of the NEC. Of these six – Tony Benn, Roy Jenkins, Ian Mikardo, Tom Bradley, Renée Short and Shirley Williams – two, Benn and Short, attended only one meeting (the meeting on 16 November for NEC members of the subcommittee only). The other PLP members were Edmund Dell, Harold Lever, David Marquand, John Roper, Joel Barnett and Dick Taverne, all of whom might be described as being sympathetic to Jenkins, and finally Michael Meacher. The only hostile PLP (and also in this case NEC) member of the subcommittee was therefore Mikardo. Jenkins was further bolstered by the presence of (Lord) Jack Diamond, Chief Secretary to the Treasury 1964–70. The trade unions were represented by Bill Simpson, the sole non-PLP NEC member, and by David Lea and Norman Willis of the TUC. Also co-opted to the subcommittee were five economists: John Hughes, Professor Kaldor, Judith Marquand, Lord Balogh and Roger Opie, one of whom, Balogh, provided the paper 'The Party's Economic Policy', discussed by the subcommittee on 13 January 1972 and again at the one-day conference on economic policy held on 25 February 1972. Up to this point there was nothing remarkable about the composition of the subcommittee. However, in addition to the above, there were *seven* members of the Research Department: Terry Pitt, Colin Moore, Andy Thomson (secretary to the subcommittee), Philip Wyatt, Alan Black, Michael Mills and Geoff Bish.[121] Of these only Moore and Thompson were ever-present,[122] but this level of representation (allied to the manipulation of the subcommittee's programme of work for 1971 and 1972) clearly demonstrates the source of the opposition at research-programme level to the pursuit by the parliamentary leadership in opposition – in this instance in the person of Jenkins – of the type of economic policies favoured by Jenkins as Chancellor of the Exchequer 1967–70.

The ability of the Research Department to dictate the substance of the subcommittee's programme of work, in spite of the fact that Jenkins and his colleagues were the single largest group within the subcommittee, demonstrates the folly of a research programme which institutionalised the influence of the Research Department over the subcommittees it serviced. It was no secret that Jenkins was disdainful of the whole research-programme process. Indeed, there is little evidence to suggest that any of the senior parliamentary leaders were particularly enamoured of the process – not Crosland and almost certainly not Wilson or Callaghan – but as a means of keeping the party occupied and united it was a necessary process. Jenkins was aware of this and, disdainful or not, the existence of Marquand's paper indicates that the former Chancellor and his parliamentary colleagues were willing to discuss economic policy within the context of the research programme.

Jenkins's departure from the subcommittee heralded the arrival of Healey, who brought with him from the PLP Douglas Houghton, John Gilbert and Robert Sheldon, each of whom was broadly sympathetic to the new chairman. This compensated for the loss of Lever and Taverne, who had resigned from the Shadow Cabinet and frontbench respectively in sympathy with Jenkins, so the balance of PLP representation on the subcommittee was undisturbed. Healey and the newly co-opted MPs were present for the final three meetings prior to publication of *Labour's Programme for Britain 1972*. The first of these was held on 24 April and continued two days later, on which occasion an office paper was submitted outlining the subcommittee's contribution to the policy statement. RD.338/April 1972 '1972 Policy Document: Financial and Economic Section'[123] demonstrated exactly whose agenda the subcommittee had been following over the course of the preceding 12 months, by including nine proposals which had appeared in the NEC statement to the 1971 conference, none of which had been discussed by the Finance and Economic Affairs Subcommittee.[124]

Healey's earliest acts as chairman involved blocking several of the proposals which appeared in the draft paper. Both the suggested surcharge above the standard rate of income tax (to start at one and a half times national average earnings) and the commitment to a wealth tax were felt to be too specific. It was also agreed that the party 'should not favour a payroll tax on top of VAT', but Healey was only tinkering at the edges. The payroll tax proposal had emerged from the Industrial Policy Subcommittee and was not to be 'dealt with in detail' by the Finance and Economic Affairs Subcommittee; likewise the section of the paper dealing with prices. These were the responsibility of the Industrial Policy Subcommittee.[125] In this decision the reason for the failure of Jenkins and his colleagues to insist on the programme of work of their choosing is revealed. As Hatfield writes of the same meeting (24 April 1972) the subcommittee 'was *told* that it could not deal with prices in detail'.[126]

The fact that the Finance and Economic Affairs Subcommittee was dominated by MPs sympathetic to the parliamentary leadership was therefore irrelevant because the Research Department, with its role at the heart of the research programme, was in a position to pull rank on the subcommittees it serviced. There was little opportunity for senior parliamentary figures such as Jenkins or Crosland (who attended only four of the 11 Industrial Policy Subcommittee meetings held between 13 July 1971 – the first meeting for which he was eligible after being co-opted to the subcommittee on 15 June 1971 – and 12 June 1972, the date of the last meeting of the subcommittee prior to publication of *Labour's Programme for Britain 1972*)[127] to defy the Research Department and remain within the official process of the research programme. Equally, there was little scope for rejecting the research programme and standing outside it while still remaining a part of the parliamentary leadership. Crosland (as discussed above) made no attempt to hide his dissatisfaction with the quality of the research programme and suggested an alternative method by which the policy might be made (much to the annoyance of Pitt and Tom McNally at the Research Department),[128] but he did so in a manner which did not undermine party unity primarily because he represented no one other than himself. Jenkins, by contrast, headed a faction within the PLP which was elitist in its approach to policy-making and which was known to desire the removal of Harold Wilson as party leader in favour of the former Chancellor, the implication of which in terms of party unity was simply too awful for many in the party to contemplate. Accordingly, Jenkins's resignation as deputy leader and his subsequent disengagement from a research programme which, no matter how flawed, by sheer force of the number of MPs and trade unionists involved was representative of both mainstream party activity and the desire for unity, was viewed as being an essentially anti-party act, and in a political party as suspicious of its leaders as the Labour Party, this could only serve to undermine party unity.

Healey inherited a situation in which the subcommittee's contribution to the NEC document was largely decided. Blocking the more contentious proposals, such as the public acquisition of overseas assets, was possible only by resorting to a vote among subcommittee members, it being the view of the majority in this instance that 'the proposed commitment to nationalise certain overseas investments should not be included. It was felt that borrowing from overseas central banks would normally be a satisfactory counter to speculation when the underlying balance of payments position was sound, and that such a proposal as contained in the draft should not be spelt out in advance.' Likewise, the subcommittee agreed that the proposals concerning the control of capital exports and parallel exchange markets at times of international exchange rate instability should also be omitted, but these were essentially negative acts.[129] There was little that was positive about the subcommittee's agenda in this period. Of the 21 main policy proposals included in the draft paper considered by the subcommittee in April 1972, nine, as stated, originated from the Industrial Policy Subcommittee and fell beyond the remit of the Finance and Economic Affairs Subcommittee, while a further four were vetoed by Healey. This left only a handful of proposals on public expenditure, taxation and the Common Market, each of which scraped in to the final document without in any way suggesting that a new approach to the economic problems which had defeated the Labour government had been discovered.

The parliamentary leadership and *Labour's Programme for Britain 1972*

Writing in *Political Quarterly* in July 1972, David Wood observed that Labour had been 'an unconscionably long time growing a new skin after quickly sloughing off the skin it wore in office'.[130] When *Labour's Programme for Britain 1972* was finally published Wood described it as being 'a substitute for a policy document' and a public relations exercise: 'After two years in Opposition, a party might have been expected to have hammered out a coherent policy that goes a little beyond commitments to repeal Conservative Acts or undo Conservative policies. Above all, the document reflects Labour's hopeless confusion on Europeanism, and preposterously develops a prices policy with no reference to wages.'[131] Elsewhere the NEC document received a cautious welcome. *Tribune*, despite a front-page headline declaring 'A few Left-wing swallows don't make a socialist summer', welcomed 'the air of self-criticism which the party leadership assumes in the document, although, of course, Labour's

National Executive Committee has for the past three or four years shown much more foresight than the parliamentary leadership'. Written by Richard Clements, the paper's editor, the article celebrated the fact that 'Many of the arguments which the Labour movement tried to put over to Labour Ministers when they were in office are now firmly entrenched in policy.'[132] Most surprising, however, was the reception given to the document by *Socialist Commentary*, which commented that in its substance 'what stamps the document most strongly is its fusion of radicalism and political relevance'.[133] It bore testimony to its imprecision that the editors of both publications were able to welcome the document. 'Nothing', wrote Wood in *The Times*, 'commits the next Labour Government yet. It points directions, but leaves the pace of advance and any possible detours to be decided later. It is at once venturesome and cautious, socialist and pragmatic, hard-shelled and soft-centred. It is a document intended to create impressions rather than to hook Labour leaders on specific commitments.'[134]

At Westminster, parliamentary leaders presented the NEC document to their colleagues in highly qualified terms. When Harold Wilson addressed the Yorkshire Group of MPs in May 1972, he warned it that the document would not give too many details as 'by "talking too much" we lost the 1959 election'.[135] Wilson's words were intended to dampen expectation and this was only one of a series of visits to meetings held by the PLP Regional Study Groups between March and May 1972, the secondary purpose of which was to shore up his position as party leader following the resignation of Roy Jenkins as deputy leader on 10 April.[136] Commenting on the Conservative Party's 'continuous attempts' to destroy him as leader of the Labour Party, he advised his fellow MPs to 'bear in mind that if a new Leader was elected they would then try to destroy him'.[137] His tour of the regional groups aside, Wilson remained detached from the research programme and the document it had produced. At the 6 July press launch of the document, it was left to Tony Benn to declare it 'the most radical and comprehensive programme ever produced by the Labour Party', Wilson choosing instead to stress the importance of the discussions taking place between the party and the trade unions in respect of the country's economic problems at the Liaison Committee.[138]

The task of presenting the NEC document to the parliamentary party fell to Callaghan, at the suggestion of Douglas Houghton, the chairman of the PLP and a confirmed ally of the former Home Secretary.[139] As chairman of the Home Policy Committee, it was only appropriate that Callaghan should play a key role in the presentation of the policy document at each stage of its development, and along with Wilson and Benn (in his capacity as chairman of the party 1971–72) he was at Transport House for the launch of the document. How it was presented to the party and to the public was important. In July 1972 none of the proposals originating from the research programme was officially party policy and the opportunity existed for the parliamentary leadership to reassure its supporters at Westminster and in the country that it was still in control of the party.

The first of two PLP meetings held to consider the document took place on 13 July and was addressed by Callaghan. The second, addressed by Benn, took place a fortnight later. This in itself was significant because Callaghan was one senior member of the parliamentary leadership (Wilson was another) for whom the research programme was not (in a positive sense at least) of paramount importance and who knew only too well that what the party said in opposition and what was possible or desirable in government were often two separate things. Benn, by contrast, was a keen supporter of the programme and, summing up the PLP's discussion of the document, told his parliamentary colleagues that policies could not be made to work 'unless they had the support of our own people, and the community as a whole'. In his opinion, the research programme had produced a document that 'was far from being too radical'.[140] For Callaghan the objective of the research programme was to forecast Britain's needs in the decade ahead, 'not to work on current problems or work out a list of priorities'. The NEC document 'would indicate to the nation and to the movement the magnitude of the problems facing Britain' and assist the party in the next stage of the policy-making process. This, he told the meeting, would require further substantial debate, but in the first 12 months of the research programme six themes had emerged:

1) There was a call to eliminate poverty and to meet the needs of the ordinary citizen.
2) There was a need to continue economic expansion on a steady basis.
3) There was a need for a more equitable distribution of wealth.
4) There was a need for increased democratic control over the nation's resources.
5) A need to tackle the problems of inflation and high prices (and here there was a need to educate the public).
6) There was a need to eliminate unemployment.[141]

No one could disagree with this, but his analysis amounted to little more than a restatement of basic Labour beliefs. In Callaghan's opinion the document was a statement of objectives. Admittedly there would be argument over how quickly these objectives could be realised, but 'there would be little argument as to the objectives themselves'. However, as a former Chancellor, he felt it necessary to warn the party that it would have to decide its priorities and stick to them, 'otherwise you could not carry out the programme without raging inflation'. Callaghan could just as easily have made this speech had there been no research programme. His sole aim was to prevent the party from splitting. Paying tribute to

Wilson, he reminded MPs how in 1964 'due to the skill of the Leader, the Party had united on a policy and been welded together as a fighting unit'.[142] This, above all else, was what was required in opposition. It did little to rescue the parliamentary leadership from the research programme, since nothing Callaghan said changed the fact that economic and industrial policy was by this time the property of the Research Department (and was about to become the property of the TUC). Giving the NEC document Green Paper status, merely postponed the moment when the parliamentary leadership would have to face up to the inevitable consequence of allowing the party to discuss policy – the actual formulation of new policy.

Labour's Programme for Britain 1972 was effectively the sum of the party's research effort since 1968, since when the party had published five major statements of policy: *Progress and Change* (1968), *Labour's Economic Strategy*, *Labour's Social Strategy* and *Agenda for a Generation* (1969), and *Economic Strategy, Growth and Unemployment* (1971), each of which had been heavily influenced by the Research Department. In office Wilson had been able to ignore both the Research Department and the party conference. In opposition this situation changed. The parliamentary leadership was faced with a situation of having to compete with the NEC and the Research Department for control of the party's policy agenda. Callaghan grafted himself onto the research programme through the Home Policy Committee, but was ultimately unable to wrest control of the process away from the Research Department. Consequently, the parliamentary leadership was not the source of new policy in opposition. Jenkins and Crosland, by attempting to influence the debate on policy from outside the official process, allowed the policy proposals of their ideological and factional opponents to go unchallenged at subcommittee level and to become party policy. As a result the parliamentary leadership became dependent upon a return to office to regain control of the party.

Notes

1 LPA, HPC, Minutes, 1970–74; LPAR, 1970–74.
2 LPA, PLP, Minutes, 13 July 1972.
3 NEC, *Economic Strategy, Growth and Unemployment*, in LPAR, 1971, pp. 371–4. A Labour government, it was suggested, might publish and publicise a list of fair prices to be policed by the housewives of Great Britain.
4 NEC, *Economic Strategy, Growth and Unemployment*, in LPAR, 1971, p. 374.
5 NEC, *Economic Strategy, Growth and Unemployment*, in LPAR, 1971, pp. 375–6.
6 NEC, *Economic Strategy, Growth and Unemployment*, in LPAR, 1971, pp. 376–7.
7 NEC, *Economic Strategy, Growth and Unemployment*, in LPAR, 1971, p. 377.
8 NEC, *Economic Strategy, Growth and Unemployment*, in LPAR, 1971, p. 377.
9 NEC, *Economic Strategy, Growth and Unemployment*, in LPAR, 1971, p. 378.
10 NEC, *Economic Strategy, Growth and Unemployment*, in LPAR, 1971, p. 378.
11 NEC, *Economic Strategy, Growth and Unemployment*, in LPAR, 1971, pp. 371–5.
12 Campbell, *Edward Heath*, p. 371.

13 Campbell, *Edward Heath*, p. 371.
14 Labour Party, *Now Britain's Strong – Let's Make It Great to Live In*, in Craig, *British General Election Manifestos*, p. 361.
15 NEC, *Economic Strategy, Growth and Unemployment*, in LPAR, 1971, pp. 376–8.
16 LPAR, 1970, p. 165.
17 NEC, *Labour's Economic Strategy* (London, 1969).
18 NEC, *Labour's Economic Strategy*, p. 56.
19 For an account of the preparation of Labour's 1970 general election manifesto, see Butler and Pinto-Duschinsky, *The British General Election of 1970*, pp. 47–61.
20 RD.111/May 1971 'Unemployment and Manpower Planning', LPA, Industrial Policy Subcommittee, Minutes and Papers, 28 April 1971–25 January 1972.
21 LPA, Industrial Policy Subcommittee, Minutes and Papers, 18 May 1971.
22 RD.129/June 1971 'Unemployment', LPA, Industrial Policy Subcommittee, Minutes and Papers, 28 April 1971–25 January 1972.
23 LPA, Industrial Policy Subcommittee, Minutes and Papers, 15 June 1971.
24 The opening paragraphs of RD.129 'Unemployment' suggested that the subcommittee might consider proposing to the Home Policy Committee 'that a paper along these lines be prepared as a basis for a statement to conference'. LPA, Industrial Policy Subcommittee, Minutes and Papers, 28 April 1971–25 January 1972.
25 LPA, Industrial Policy Subcommittee, Minutes and Papers, 15 June 1971. Hatfield describes this decision as a turning point:

> By the time of the June meeting of the Industrial Policy Committee there was pressure from the National Executive to prepare a draft document which could be presented to the annual conference. This, of course, would have to be approved by the full executive. Work began in earnest but the committee was running into difficulties. How was it possible to produce policies on the regeneration of the regions, manpower forecasting, and an approach to price controls in isolation from economic policy? The committee agreed it should recommend to the National Executive that a background paper be produced on unemployment and *economic strategy*. It was the turning point politically.
>
> A committee member said later that none of the social democrats were conscious at the time of a calculated manoeuvre by the left; indeed, there was unanimous agreement that economic strategy had to be considered by the Industrial Committee. Nevertheless they were aware that the initiative had been stolen from the right-wing oriented Jenkins (Finance and Economic Affairs) committee.

Hatfield, *The House the Left Built*, p. 61 (emphasis in original).
26 LPA, HPC, Minutes, 12 July 1971; NEC Minutes, 28 July 1971.
27 LPA, Industrial Policy Subcommittee, Minutes and Papers, 13 July 1971.
28 RD.147/July 1971 'Economic Strategy, Growth and Unemployment', LPA, Industrial Policy Subcommittee, Minutes and Papers, 28 April 1971–25 January 1972.
29 LPA, HPC Minutes, 13 September 1971; NEC Minutes, 1 October 1971. Present at this meeting were: Callaghan, Frank Allaun MP, Tom Bradley MP, Barbara Castle MP, Alex Kitson, Joan Lestor MP, Fred Mulley MP, Bill Simpson, Lady White, David Lea (TUC), Sir Harry Nicholas, Gwyn Morgan, Percy Clark and Terry Pitt. Castle, Mulley, Simpson, Lea and Pitt were members of the Industrial Policy Subcommittee.

30 LPA, Industrial Policy Subcommittee, Minutes and Papers, 21 September 1971.
31 LPA, Industrial Policy Subcommittee, Minutes and Papers, 28 April 1971–25 January 1972.
32 In addition to the seven who attended all three meetings, five subcommittee members were present at both the 13 July and 27 July meeting: Tony Benn MP; Ivor Richard MP; the economist Derek Robinson, formerly with the Organisation for Economic Co-operation and Development; Andy Thompson of the Research Department; James Tinn MP.
33 Hatfield, *The House the Left Built*, p. 52. See also M. Wickham-Jones, *Economic Strategy and the Labour Party: Politics and Policy-making, 1970–83* (London, Macmillan, 1996), pp. 121–2.
34 I. Mikardo, *Back-bencher* (London, Weidenfeld & Nicolson, 1988), p. 175.
35 Hatfield, *The House the Left Built*, p. 59.
36 Similarly in 1966 there had been 'a prolonged tussle' between the Prime Minister and the Research Department over the drafting of the manifesto. 'Under its secretary, Terry Pitt, the Department resented government pressure to tone down the socialist policies to which the party was committed.' Butler and Pinto-Duschinsky, *The British General Election of 1970*, p. 49. Also, for example, on the matter of the wealth tax proposal included in *Labour's Economic Strategy* and subsequently in *Agenda for a Generation*, this Roy Jenkins, the Chancellor, 'reluctantly said he "could live with" . . . possibly because the Prime Minister had assured him that there would still be opportunities to ditch it nearer the election'. Hatfield, *The House the Left Built*, p. 61.
37 The Study Group on Economic Strategy met five times between 27 February and 4 June 1969. The following, in addition to Pitt and Bish, were members: Tom Bradley MP (chairman), Barbara Castle MP, Bill Simpson, Sir Harry Nicholas, M. Mills (secretary), Alex Kitson and Ian Mikardo. Bradley and Mills, once again in addition to Pitt and Bish, were ever-present. See LPA, HPC, Minutes, 10 February–9 June 1969; NEC, Minutes, 26 February–25 June 1969.
38 'Jenkins, as chairman, was not keen on holding meetings, as other committee members discovered. As Shadow Chancellor of the Exchequer, he firmly believed that economic policy making should be left to him in consultation with his shadow cabinet colleagues. He had already formed his own group of financial advisers, an indication of his disdain at the quality and expertise to be found in the party organisation.' Hatfield, *The House the Left Built*, p. 57.
39 Meetings were held on 29 April, 15 June and 28 July prior to conference, also on 16 November and 14 December 1971. LPA, Finance and Economic Affairs Subcommittee, Minutes and Papers, 29 April–16 November 1971, 14 December 1971–18 November 1972.
40 There is some confusion over the date of this meeting. The minutes for the meeting held on 29 April 1971 state that the next meeting would be held on 15 May 1971. The date of the second meeting, however, is given as 15 June on the minutes. LPA, Finance and Economic Affairs Subcommittee, Minutes and Papers, 26 April–16 November 1971.
41 Present at at least one of the three meetings were: Roy Jenkins MP (29 April, 15 June, 28 July), Tom Bradley MP (29/4), Ian Mikardo (29/4, 15/6, 28/7), Shirley Williams MP (29/4, 15/6), Joel Barnett MP (29/4, 28/7), Edmund Dell MP (29/4, 15/6, 28/7), Dick Taverne MP (29/4), Andrew Thomson, secretary (29/4, 15/6, 28/7), Terry Pitt (29/4, 15/6), Geoff Bish (29/4, 15/6), John Hughes (15/6, 28/7), Douglas Houghton (15/6), Professor Nicholas Kaldor (15/6), David Lea (15/6, 28/7), David Marquand MP (15/6, 28/7), Roger Opie (15/6), John Roper MP (15/6, 28/7), Harold Lever MP (28/7). LPA, Finance

and Economic Affairs Subcommittee, Minutes and Papers, 26 April–16 November 1971.

42 The subcommittee was reconvened after the 1971 conference and met monthly under Jenkins's chairmanship from November 1971 to March 1972, his last meeting in the chair prior to his resignation as deputy leader and also from the Shadow Cabinet 10 April 1972. The Finance and Economic Affairs Subcommittee was subsequently chaired by Denis Healey, who replaced Jenkins as Shadow Chancellor, and continued to meet on a monthly basis. The pattern for meetings after the 1971 conference (under both Jenkins and Healey) refutes the notion of the Finance and Economic Affairs Subcommittee being in any way aloof from the research programme. LPA, Finance and Economic Affairs Subcommittee, Minutes and Papers, 29 April–16 November 1971, 14 December 1971–18 November 1972.

43 London, House of Commons (HC), Economic and Finance Group, Minutes, 1970–74, 27 April 1971. These minutes are incomplete, but between November 1970 and May 1971, the period in which the structure of the research programme was determined and during which the inaugural meeting of the Finance and Economic Affairs Subcommittee took place, topics discussed by the group included: Monetary Policy (November and December 1970); Inflation and Unemployment (February 1971); Incomes Policy (March 1971); Budget Prospects (March 1971); Finance Bill (April and May 1971).

44 RD.99/April 1971 'Programme of Work', LPA, Finance and Economic Affairs Subcommittee, Minutes and Papers, 29 April–16 November 1971.

45 RD.99/April 1971 'Programme of Work'.

46 RD.99/April 1971 'Programme of Work'.

47 LPA, Finance and Economic Affairs Subcommittee, Minutes and Papers, 29 April 1971.

48 These were: Re.562/January 1970 'Future Taxation Policy', by Professor Kaldor; Re.569/January 1970 'Memos from Affiliated Unions'; Re.570/January 1970 'Memos on Tax Policies'; Re.571/January 1970 'Tax Policies in the 1970s', by Douglas Jay MP; Re.586/February 1970 'Further Memos from Affiliated Unions'; Re.599/March 1970 'Preliminary Position on Taxation', proposals by Andrew Thompson. LPA, Finance and Economic Affairs Subcommittee, Minutes and Papers, 15 June 1971.

49 LPA, Finance and Economic Affairs Subcommittee, Minutes and Papers, 15 June 1971.

50 LPA, Finance and Economic Affairs Subcommittee, Minutes and Papers, 15 June 1971.

51 RD.153 'Problems of Economic Growth', by David Marquand MP, LPA, Finance and Economic Affairs Subcommittee, Minutes and Papers, 29 April 1971–16 November 1971.

52 LPA, Finance and Economic Affairs Subcommittee, Minutes and Papers, 28 July 1971.

53 LPA, Finance and Economic Affairs Subcommittee, Minutes and Papers, 16 November 1971. See also Hatfield, *The House the Left Built*, p. 57.

54 'Ian Mikardo as party chair was a member of both groups and knew that the opportunity existed for the Industrial Policy Subcommittee to dominate Labour's policy development. Having taken control of the policy process, this committee, supported by various academics and research staff, became the focus for the elaboration of the new proposals.' Wickham-Jones, *Economic Strategy and the Labour Party*, p. 122.

55 RD.94/April 1971 'Programme of Work', LPA, Industrial Policy Subcommittee, Minutes and Papers, 28 April 1971–25 January 1972.
56 Labour Party, *Now Britain's Strong – Let's Make It Great to Live In*, in Craig, *British General Election Manifestos*, p. 346.
57 RD.94/April 1971 'Programme of Work', LPA, Industrial Policy Subcommittee, Minutes and Papers, 28 April 1971–25 January 1972.
58 The disparity between the two programmes of work was evident in the NEC's report to conference in 1971. Reporting on the work of the subcommittees to date, the NEC revealed that not only had the subcommittee 'devoted several months to preparing a major document... At the time of writing it is antici-pated that this will form the basis of a National Executive Committee statement to Annual Conference', but also that they had approved 'a wide-ranging programme of work' before and were proceeding to list the range of topics which had been suggested in RD.94 'Programme of Work'. However, when it came to the activity of the Finance and Economic Affairs Subcommittee, the report read in such a manner as to suggest that the NEC had struggled to find anything to write about. Compared to the *very important work* done by the Industrial Policy Subcommittee, the Finance and Economic Affairs Subcommittee would be 'resuming work on some subjects which have been reported to Annual Conference in recent years but which have not yet reached the stage of report'. LPAR, 1971, p. 38.
59 Interview, Geoff Bish, 21 June 1997.
60 Wickham-Jones, *Economic Strategy and the Labour Party*, p. 125.
61 'Jenkins liked to work with a small team of his own advisers drafting major speeches which could then be picked up by the media.' Wickham-Jones, *Economic Strategy and the Labour Party*, p. 125.
62 LPAR, 1971, pp. 209–28.
63 LPAR, 1971, pp. 166, 226.
64 NEC, *Economic Strategy, Growth and Unemployment*, in LPAR, 1971, p. 373.
65 LPAR, 1971, p. 166.
66 LPAR, 1971, p. 165.
67 'Tony Crosland was the great inspiration before I got into Parliament and the great disappointment afterwards.' Witness Seminar (WS), 'The Campaign for Democratic Socialism', *Contemporary Record*, 7, 2 (1993), p. 371 (Lord Taverne).
68 LPA, Industrial Policy Subcommittee, Minutes and Papers, 15 June 1971 and 21 December 1971.
69 'Mr Crosland wants Labour committee to fight for power', *The Times*, 16 September 1971, p. 3.
70 'Mr Crosland wants'.
71 A. Crosland, 'Policies for the People, by the People', *Socialist Commentary* (November 1971), pp. 3–5.
72 Crosland, 'Policies for the People'.
73 LPAR, 1972, p. 39.
74 NEC, *Labour's Programme for Britain 1972* (London, 1972), pp. 5–6.
75 LPAR, 1972, pp. 39–40.
76 NEC, *Labour's Programme for Britain 1972*, pp. 32–6. On *Signposts for the Sixties* and Labour's proposals on the nationalisation of development land, see P. Williams, *Hugh Gaitskell* (London, Jonathan Cape, 1979), pp. 659–60.
77 NEC, *Labour's Programme for Britain 1972*, p. 5.
78 NEC, *Labour's Programme for Britain 1972*, p. 6.
79 LPAR, 1970, p. 184.
80 LPAR, 1971, p. 166.

81 NEC, *Labour's Programme for Britain 1972*, p. 6.
82 J. P. Mackintosh, 'Socialism or Social Democracy? The Choice for the Labour Party', *Political Quarterly*, 43, 4 (1972), pp. 479–80.
83 NEC, *Labour's Programme for Britain 1972*, pp. 13–14.
84 See LPAR, 1971, p. 226.
85 NEC, *Labour's Programme for Britain 1972*, p. 70.
86 NEC, *Labour's Programme for Britain 1972*, pp. 17–18.
87 The State Holding Company, it was imagined, would operate 'on a substantial base of majority or complete shareholdings to provide commercial and management resources and expertise; and initiating new public enterprises into the regions'. NEC, *Labour's Programme for Britain 1972*, p. 29.
88 NEC, *Labour's Programme for Britain 1972*, p. 19.
89 *HC Debs, 5th ser.*, 1971–72, vol. 829, col. 1020.
90 W. Rodgers, 'Industrial Development for the Regions', *Socialist Commentary* (March 1972), p. 10.
91 E. Dell, 'Extending Public Ownership, The British Experience', *Socialist Commentary* (December 1971), p. 13.
92 LPAR, 1972, p. 44.
93 NEC, *Labour's Programme for Britain 1972*, p. 15.
94 NEC, *Labour's Programme for Britain 1972*, p. 24.
95 See Chapter 8.
96 LPA, HPC, Minutes, 13 September 1971; NEC, Minutes, 1 October 1971.
97 RD.184/November 1971 'Programme of Work'. LPA, HPC, Minutes, 23 November 1971; NEC, Minutes, November 1971.
98 RD.184/November 1971 'Programme of Work'.
99 LPA, HPC, Minutes, 8 November 1971; NEC, Minutes, 23 November 1971.
100 It was agreed also that early discussions with the TUC on economic and industrial policy be arranged; that the study groups be reconstituted as before, and that the existing National Executive Committee members of the subcommittees be reappointed. LPA, HPC, Minutes, 8 November 1971; NEC, Minutes, 23 November 1971. The reconstituted Policy Co-ordinating Committee included the following: (for the NEC) Tony Benn, Jim Callaghan, John Chalmers, Jack Diamond, John Forrester, Joe Gormley, Bill Simpson, Sir Harry Nicholas; (for the Shadow Cabinet) Barbara Castle, Anthony Crosland, Michael Foot (from April 1972), Denis Healey, Roy Jenkins (until April 1972), Harold Lever (until April 1972), Fred Peart, William Ross (from April 1972), Ted Short, Shirley Williams. The committee met in February 1972 to discuss the Home Policy Committee document 'The Research Programme', and in April to discuss the International Committee's document 'Foreign Policy Priorities'. LPAR, 1972, p. 6. Benn, Castle, Chalmers, Callaghan, Healey, Nicholas and Short were, as from January 1972, also members of the TUC–Labour Party Liaison Committee.
101 NEC, *Labour's Programme for Britain 1972*, p. 19.
102 Mackintosh, 'Socialism or Social Democracy?', p. 480.
103 Present at this meeting were Tony Benn MP, Roy Jenkins MP, Ian Mikardo MP, Shirley Williams MP, Renée Short MP; Terry Pitt, Andy Thompson and Colin Moore from the Research Department; and Bill Simpson.
104 RD.153/July 1971 'Problems of Economic Growth' by David Marquand MP, RD.181/November 1971 'Programme of Work', LPA, Finance and Economic Affairs Subcommittee, Minutes and Papers, 29 April–16 November 1971, 14 December 1971–18 November 1972.
105 RD.153/July 1971 'Problems of Economic Growth'.

106 RD.153/July 1971 'Problems of Economic Growth'.
107 RD.181/November 1971 'Programme of Work'.
108 RD.226/January 1972 'The Party's Economic Policy' by Lord Balogh; RD.302/ March 1972 'Negative Income Tax' by Dick Taverne MP; RD.228/January 1972 'A Public Expenditure Programme'; RD.258/February 1972 'Means Tests and Deductions from Earnings' (in the Minutes for the meeting held on 10 February 1972, this paper is referred to as RD.260); RD.276/February 1972 'Demand Management'. LPA, Finance and Economic Affairs Subcommittee, Minutes and Papers, 14 December 1971–18 November 1972.
109 NEC, *Labour's Programme for Britain 1972*, p. 20.
110 For Hugh Scanlon's thoughts on the subject see LPAR, 1971, pp. 215–17.
111 RD.181/November 1971 'Programme of Work'.
112 LPAR, 1972, p. 229.
113 RD.153/July 1971 'Problems of Economic Growth'.
114 RD.153/July 1971 'Problems of Economic Growth'. Marquand added that between 1964 and 1969 'at least three quite different objectives were suggested' in respect of the Labour government's incomes policy, 'greater productivity, greater equality, greater stability', and questioned whether or not they were compatible, and if not, which took priority? He concluded that 'The premise on which the whole notion of incomes policy rests is that there exists – or could exist – a consensus as to the relative position which different groups ought to have in the incomes pecking order. Such a consensus may have existed in the past. Does it today? If not, what are the implications for policy?'.
115 Marquand asked what the purpose of regional policy was – 'to increase employment or revitalise the regions as growth centres? These may not be the same, and may be incompatible.' On the subject of a State Holding Company he asked what form it would take. 'How would you solve the problems of accountability and control?' He also asked what limits the party should place on the private sector, presuming that the party would continue to accept it, 'in terms of managerial rewards, "killing the goose that lays the golden eggs" etc.' RD.153/July 1971 'Problems of Economic Growth'.
116 Owen, *Time to Declare* p. 189.
117 Jenkins, *A Life at the Centre*, p. 353.
118 Jenkins, *What Matters Now*.
119 The first of these meetings, on 16 November 1971, was for the NEC members of the subcommittee only. Additionally, the subcommittee held a one-day conference on economic policy at the Russell Hotel in London on 25 February 1972, which was chaired by Jenkins and 'while not directly concerned with policy making,... involved a very useful exchange of views on economic policy among those present'. Each of the four sessions of the conference was devoted to discussion of a specific paper prepared by the Research Department: RD.267/February 1972 'International Monetary Policy', introduced by Harold Lever MP; RD.276/February 1972 'Demand Management', introduced by Edmund Dell MP; RD.228/January 1972 'A Public Expenditure Programme', introduced by David Marquand MP; and RD.204/December 1971 'Banking and Insurance', introduced by Ian Mikardo MP. On 29 March 1972, the subcommittee held a joint meeting with the Social Policy Subcommittee, on which occasion the paper RD.317 (Revised) 'Report of the Social Policy Subcommittee' was discussed, the minutes recording that 'although it was felt that more information was needed on the total cost of the programme there was agreement that the programme was not over-ambitious'. LPA, Finance

and Economic Affairs Subcommittee, Minutes and Papers, 29 April–16 November 1971, 14 December 1971–18 November 1972.
120 Jenkins was chairman of the subcommittee from 29 April 1971 until 13 March 1972.
121 LPA, Finance and Economic Affairs Subcommittee, Minutes and Papers, 29 April–16 November 1971, 14 December 1971–18 November 1972.
122 Pitt attended three of the five meetings held between 16 November 1971 and 13 March 1972, Wyatt one, Black, Mills and Bish two. LPA, Finance and Economic Affairs Subcommittee, Minutes and Papers, 29 April–16 November 1971, 14 December 1971–18 November 1972.
123 LPA, Finance and Economic Affairs Subcommittee, Minutes and Papers, 14 December 1971–18 November 1972.
124 These were i) Economic growth to be given priority over the balance of payments, ii) Industrial aid must be selective, iii) Gifts tax, iv) Wealth tax, v) Payroll tax, vi) Early warning system on prices, vii) Control of key prices, viii) Prices inspectorate, ix) Strengthen monopoly policy. RD.338/April 1972 '1972 Policy Statement: Financial and Economic Section', LPA, Finance and Economic Affairs Subcommittee, Minutes and Papers, 14 December 1971–18 November 1972.
125 LPA, Finance and Economic Affairs Subcommittee, Minutes and Papers, 24 April 1972.
126 Hatfield, *The House the Left Built*, p. 119, emphasis added.
127 LPA, Industrial Policy Subcommittee, Minutes and Papers, 28 April 1971–25 January 1972, 15 February 1972–28 November 1972.
128 See Hatfield, *The House the Left Built*, pp. 57–8.
129 LPA, Finance and Economic Affairs Subcommittee, Minutes and Papers, 24 and 26 April 1972. See RD.338/April 1972 '1972 Policy Document: Financial and Economic Section' for details of these proposals. LPA, Finance and Economic Affairs Subcommittee, Minutes and Papers, 14 December 1971–18 November 1972.
130 D.Wood, 'The Westminster Scene', *Political Quarterly*, 43, 2 (1972), p. 332.
131 D. Wood, 'The Westminster Scene', *Political Quarterly*, 43, 4 (1972), pp. 490–1.
132 R. Clements, 'A few Left-wing swallows don't make a socialist summer', *Tribune*, 7 July 1972, pp. 1–2.
133 Editorial, 'Knowing Where We're Going', *Socialist Commentary* (August 1972), pp. 2–3.
134 Quoted in Hatfield, *The House the Left Built*, p. 129.
135 HC, PLP Regional group minutes 1970–74, Area Groups for Study of Regional Problems, Yorkshire Group, Minutes, 8 May 1972.
136 Wilson attended the following meetings in this period: Northern Group (28 March 1972); East Midlands Group (2 May); Yorkshire Group (8 May); North West Group (10 May). HC, PLP Regional Group Minutes 1970–74, Area Groups for Study of Regional Problems, Minutes, 1972.
137 HC, PLP Regional group minutes 1970–74, Area Groups for Study of Regional Problems, Yorkshire Group, Minutes, 8 May 1972.
138 Hatfield, *The House the Left Built*, p. 128.
139 LPA, PC, Minutes, 21 June 1972.
140 LPA, PLP, Minutes, 27 July 1972.
141 LPA, PLP, Minutes, 13 July 1972.
142 LPA, PLP, Minutes, 13 July 1972.

6

THE NEC RESEARCH PROGRAMME: AUGUST 1972–JUNE 1973

During the second year of Labour's research programme in opposition, imprecision over the detail of the party's economic and industrial policy became unsustainable as a device for achieving party unity. Over the preceding 12 months party members had shared a common vocabulary in relation to the need for a more interventionist industrial policy to address the problem of rising unemployment in the regions, yet had done so without necessarily sharing a common analysis of the detail of the policy required. The collision over policy which awaited the party in the lead-up to (and beyond) the publication of a final policy document in June 1973 could be divined from the response of both *Tribune* and *Socialist Commentary* to *Labour's Programme for Britain 1972*. Of the two publications *Tribune*, which ordinarily might have been expected to have welcomed the document's publication in light of left-wing domination of the Industrial Policy Subcommittee and the generally leftward tone of the party's policy statements since the general election defeat, was distinctly cooler in its appraisal of the document than its right-wing rival. This owed more to the editor's dissatisfaction with the lack of commitment to the policies included in the document, rather than with the policies themselves. *Socialist Commentary*, by contrast, welcomed *Labour's Programme for Britain 1972*, believing that it held out the prospect for the party of a genuine debate on policy and in due course the adoption of a radical manifesto. This meant of course that the tone of the final policy document would be determined by whichever interpretation of the word 'radical' prevailed. In this respect, left and right were not speaking the same language.

The Jenkinsites in particular welcomed the prospect of a genuine debate with the left. David Marquand, for example (borrowing from Mao), had concluded his July 1971 policy paper 'Problems of Economic Growth' with the exhortation 'Let a thousand flowers bloom',[1] the significance of which lay in the willingness it implied on the part of the right to apply fresh thinking to familiar problems irrespective of the source of new thinking, be it right or left. *Socialist Commentary* responded enthusiastically to what it ultimately misinterpreted as open-mindedness on the part of the left, and to the prospect of an intellectually rigorous debate. In its August editorial greeting the publication of *Labour's Programme for Britain 1972*, it was clear that in the language of the right radicalism equated to social reformism:

> In its substance, what stamps the document most strongly is its fusion of radicalism and political relevance. This is the combination of qualities that we like to feel SOCIALIST COMMENTARY has stood for throughout its existence: neither a sectarian militancy that fails to address itself to the real problems of ordinary people nor a merely time-serving adaptation to the trends of the moment, but a principled and practical radicalism that matches widespread popular need. It is from this perspective that we applaud the Green Paper's concern with jobs, prices and housing. It is for this reason that we welcome the new and generous horizons it sets for social policy – especially its firmly drawn conclusion that social expenditure must rise faster than the general income level. We also appreciate the egalitarian spirit of its taxation proposals; including its emphasis that increased social spending cannot come from nowhere, nor just from taxes on the rich, but must imply a general contribution by the majority to help those in need and improve other public provision. And it is good to see that ideas on public ownership are not at all timid – no feeling, as in some previous Labour Party policy documents, that we are embarrassed by the subject. The suggestions here form the basis for a tough-minded and realistic policy of extending the public role in industry without dogmatism about the forms that this should take.[2]

This interpretation was not shared by the left-wing MPs, for whom it was too limited. Right and left continued to share a common vocabulary which created the impression of common ground and encouraged *Socialist Commentary* to see hope for the year ahead, but the policy objectives they pursued were quite different. The editorial was sufficiently prescient, however, to warn that 'The British Labour Party's reluctance to become enmeshed in ideological argument is long-founded and usually justified: but the whole question of industrial intervention is so central to socialism that we shall not be able for long to avoid a genuine attempt to decide what it is we are trying to achieve.'[3]

'Socialism and the Regions'[4]

The desire among Labour MPs on the right of the PLP to discuss all aspects of economic and industrial policy, publicly articulated by Edmund Dell and Bill Rodgers among others, reached its apotheosis in May 1972 when Roy Jenkins addressed the Western Area Conference of the NUM at Blackpool on the subject of 'Socialism and the Regions'. In a speech focusing on unemployment and the disparity of opportunity in the Northern regions compared to Southern England, he came out in support of an interventionist industrial strategy for the regions, arguing that government, acting through the public sector, 'can adopt a broader perspective than that of any board of directors nominally responsible to its shareholders', adding that a sympathetic and determined government would 'view an investment in a much longer time scale. It can estimate the benefit of an industrial development to the community as a whole, in terms of new jobs and better use of social capital.' Jenkins freely admitted that he had found it necessary to revise his own thinking in light of events since the general election. Such had been his faith in Keynesian techniques, he told his audience, that he had long believed public ownership would in the future 'be much less central than it had been between 1945 and 1950 or than the pioneers of the Labour Movement had imagined'. Yet by 1972, indeed well before, it had become clear that 'techniques for managing the whole economy cannot solve detailed problems – even when the problem is that of a whole region rather than a single firm'.[5] General demand management, he now believed,

> must be supplemented by more rigorous policies of direct inter-
> vention than those which we used between 1964 and 1970. We
> relied principally on a mixture of bribery and cajolery – on lavish
> grants supplemented by some Government pressure on the more
> public spirited or politically exposed businesses. These weapons
> were far better than no weapons at all and their results should not be
> underestimated, but they have not nearly solved all the problems
> which we face in this field of regional policy.[6]

Jenkins was an unlikely champion of public ownership. Praising the performance of the nationalised industries, he declared that 'For too long the question of public ownership in Britain has been dominated by dogma from both sides', a statement which, loosely translated, meant that he had previously been against it. Jenkins was not in Blackpool to recant as such, and his text contained no hint of an admission that on the issue of public ownership the Croslandites had been wrong, but in choosing to quote from the party's 1961 policy document *Signposts for the Sixties*, which had stated that 'Where national assistance is required by manufacturing industry, it should be made conditional on public participation in the enterprise',[7] he appeared to concede both that the recent Labour govern-ment, of which he had been a prominent member, had misunderstood the nature of the problems it had faced, and that state intervention was the solution.

In closing, Jenkins spoke in favour of the establishment of a State Holding Company, as 'a flexible vehicle for direct Government involvement to help achieve the broad-based mix of activities which is essential if the regions are to receive their fair share of national prosperity'. Supported by a Regional Development Bank, the State Holding Company would be 'equipped with substantial initial resources, which would make loans on specially advantageous terms'.[8] Citing the success of the Italian Industrial Reconstruction Institute (IRI) as an example of 'the practice of active state intervention in a mixed economy',[9] Jenkins argued that for a British State Holding Company to be effective 'it has to represent a broad spectrum of industry. Only in this way can it afford to adopt an unusually long time scale for some of its projects, or to take risks too large for most ordinary companies to contemplate.' The base for the 'broad spectrum of industry' regarded as necessary by Jenkins was already partially in existence, as the government already owned 49 per cent of BP, 100 per cent of Rolls-Royce, and additionally held a stake in ICL and numerous other companies. 'These', he suggested, 'supplemented by a limited amount of selective nationalisation, should provide a good base from which to diversify into the labour-using industries which the regions require.' Jenkins ended his speech on a bold note: 'We cannot allow regional disparities to continue. They will poison and embitter our whole national life. They will distort our economy and our society. There must be no timidity in our measures to eliminate them. This is a major aspect of our fight against injustice.'[10]

The establishment of a State Holding Company had first been suggested in the NEC's 1969 policy document *Labour's Economic Strategy*, the content of which was heavily influenced by Terry Pitt and Geoff Bish and which, at the time of its publication, was regarded as a hostile document by the then Chancellor (Jenkins no less) who along with Harold Wilson rejected the tenor of the proposals on certain aspects of economic policy. However, by the time the proposal resurfaced in *Economic Strategy, Growth and Unemployment*, the NEC's 1971 policy statement, the debate on regional policy in both of the major political parties had been transformed by the dramatic increase in unemployment since the general election. In this respect, Jenkins and the NEC were not far apart on the issue and there was little in his speech which did not sit easily with the view expressed in the 1971 statement that 'To obtain the right industrial and commercial base in the regions, we cannot afford to rely on the usual patchwork of response by private firms. The use of public enterprise is likely to be essential.'[11] When *Labour's Programme for Britain 1972* was published two months after Jenkins's speech, the proposed establishment of a State Holding Company 'as the instrument for integrating industries and firms into the public sector ... and initiating new public enterprise in the regions' was entirely consistent with the view expressed by the former Chancellor.[12]

How Jenkins came to be discussing the regions at this precise moment in opposition merits close examination. His speech of 5 May 1972 was the second of a series of six high-profile speeches he gave that summer, but more importantly it was the first following his resignation as deputy leader and from the Shadow Cabinet the previous month. The speech was therefore intended to demonstrate the extent of his commitment to the Labour Party, and the breadth of his interest in domestic politics at a time when he had damaged the party by resigning over the Common Market. Collectively, the six speeches were intended to hasten his rehabilitation at Westminster and at the same time to demonstrate his leadership qualities. However, in broader terms, Jenkins was giving a speech on the regions in May 1972 because regional policy was at the heart of the political debate at Westminster at the time. Six weeks earlier the Conservative government, at the instigation of the Prime Minister, had executed a fundamental U-turn in economic and industrial policy by introducing measures to dramatically expand the economy in an attempt to counter the desperately high level of unemployment.[13] On 21 March 1972, Anthony Barber, the Chancellor, had introduced a Budget which, in addition to making sweeping changes in the field of taxation (the net effect of which, writes Campbell, was an estimated extra £1 a week in the pay packets of 21 million wage earners),[14] included a range of incentives to encourage industry to invest in the regions.

Addressing the Western Area Conference of the NUM, Jenkins accused the government of stealing Labour's old clothes and wearing them with 'a mixture of brazeness and reluctance', but welcomed the 'retreat from the dogmas of 1970 and 1971'. This, he told his audience, had been forced upon the government 'by its own economic failures and the consequent fear of electoral retribution'. Yet he discerned 'no genuine intellectual or philosophical conversion. The self-confidence of Mr Heath and Mr John Davies in the days when they intrepidly hunted the lame ducks of Britain has gone. In its place is a vacuum.'[15]

On one level Jenkins's speech on the regions was simply a further contribution to a debate about industrial policy which had been taking place inside the Labour Party since April 1971. No less a person than the party leader himself had, after all, promised the creation of a State Holding Company in his speech to conference in October 1971. Yet coming from Jenkins, whose affinity with the ideas of Hugh Gaitskell marked him out as an obvious opponent of indiscriminate public ownership, and given the subtext of the event of the speech itself – Jenkins offering the party a quality of leadership Wilson was incapable of providing – it naturally received wide coverage in the press and at the same time appeared to signal a conversion of Damascene proportions. Yet it was clear he did not fully agree with the industrial policy proposals emanating from the research programme. Jenkins, as Hatfield writes, 'favoured IRC-type policies to revitalise industry and promote growth in the regions'.[16] But, obstructed from arguing his case from within the research programme, his speech of 5 May 1972 provided him with an opportunity to add his own voice to the debate on his own terms. While the details of the party's policy on the regions remained imprecise, there was little for him to take issue with. However, in the closing paragraphs of his speech, he took the precaution of stating that he remained unconvinced that public ownership contained the key to the elimination of injustice between individuals, the objective which, above all others, informed his political beliefs.[17] Certainly he was sufficiently familiar with the political objectives of his factional opponents within the party to know that when Labour's new industrial policy finally emerged it was unlikely to be entirely to his taste, and in this respect his speech (despite containing both positive and negative remarks about public ownership) set clear parameters for an interventionist industrial policy.

Jenkins's speech of 5 May 1972, as demonstrated, was motivated both by his genuine concern over the problem of unemployment in the regions and also by the need to underpin his credentials as a possible successor to Wilson. Yet this is unsatisfactory as an explanation of how what was recognisably the language of the Labour left on industrial policy (notwithstanding the words of Wilson, Dell and Rodgers on the subject) found its way into the text of his speech. When, for example, Wilson had spoken of establishing a State Holding Company on the lines of the IRC, 'but writ large this time',[18] the rhetorical element of his utterance was obvious, even if in this instance the Labour leader was sincere, albeit familiarly non-specific on the details.[19] But for Jenkins to argue the case for public ownership was a huge gamble, as his words inadvertently lent further momentum to the general leftward drift in party policy. In mitigation, he said little that had not been said by Wilson or, for that matter, Heath, both of whom were leading their parties leftwards on the economy.

Ultimately, the real significance of Jenkins's speech lay in its authorship. For the section on the State Holding Company he drew heavily on the ideas of the economist Stuart Holland of Sussex University, who between 1966 and 1968 had worked as an economic assistant to Wilson, and who in 1972 was a co-opted member of the Industrial Policy Subcommittee and the Public Sector Group. Along with Richard Pryke, Holland had co-authored the paper 'The State Holding Company'[20] in February 1972, for presentation at the two-day conference on Industrial Policy organised by the Industrial Policy Subcommittee, which took place on the 26 and 27 of February. Jenkins's references to the Italian IRI, to the desirability of hiving *on* parts of the private sector to the nationalised sector,[21] and to the existing public holdings in private industry, were taken directly from Holland and Pryke's paper. On these points he obviously concurred with Holland, who wrote the section of the paper in which the above points featured. Holland wrote that a Labour government could not afford to wait until a company ran into difficulty before stepping in to acquire a holding: 'At a very minimum it will have to approach leading private companies with an offer of investment funds in return for both a share-holding and an influence over the strategic investment decision making of the companies concerned. It will have to consider seriously whether or not compulsory powers should be made available to it to fulfil the function of securing a foothold within the main manufacturing sectors.' Such a strategy, he conceded, would be challenged by those in the party who believed that the standard techniques of Keynesian demand management and investment allowances or grants were 'sufficient not only to iron out the trade cycle but also to enable the economy to attain sustained growth at its natural rate'. One such individual was Jenkins who, even though he had found it necessary to slightly revise his position in the face of stagnant invest-ment, rising unemployment and marked inflation in both Britain and the United States, had no intention of committing political suicide by endorsing a confiscatory economic policy. This Holland recognised: 'the prospect of extending public enterprise throughout private manufacturing – even if only in one or two companies in the main manufacturing sectors – would be politically difficult if not the best gift to the Tories since the Zinoviev letter'.[22] He further accepted that finding an acceptable criterion for selecting new candidates for public ownership would be extremely difficult: 'If the biggest companies in the economy, or in each industry, were compulsorily acquired this would involve the transfer at a stroke of a major part of the economy to the public sector. As the Party is already committed to the nationalisation of insurance and shipbuilding this might not be thought politically expedient.'[23]

Equally inexpedient was Jenkins's patronage of Holland on this occasion. The Holland–Pryke paper was unmistakably ultra-interventionist in tone and it is impossible to imagine that Jenkins believed that he and Holland were singing from the same hymn sheet on the State Holding Company. Talk of intervention in the regions may have been common parlance at the time but, in allowing Holland to put words in his mouth on this occasion, Jenkins inadvertently increased the pressure upon the moderate members of the Shadow Cabinet (to which he no longer belonged) from the left wing of the party for an ideological rethink in excess of the review of policy.[24]

Stuart Holland and Labour's industrial policy

Stuart Holland was formally invited to contribute to the research programme by Judith Hart MP, the chairman of the Public Sector Group, which was set up by the Industrial Policy Subcommittee shortly after the 1971 conference and met for the first time in December that year. Holland attended his first meeting on 25 January 1972, when much of the discussion centred on the substance of the paper on the State Holding Company he had been asked to co-author. It is evident that the Public Sector Group did not share the parliamentary leadership's concept of a State Holding Company in the form of a strengthened version of the IRC,[25] from Hart's instruction to Holland and Pryke that they were to confine themselves when drafting the paper 'to indicating the problems involved in order to promote discussion rather than dissension'.[26]

Holland was further eased into the research programme process by Geoff Bish, secretary to the Industrial Policy Subcommittee, and with whom he was in regular contact in this period.[27] He was co-opted to become a member of the Industrial Policy Subcommittee as of 18 April 1972 and attended his first meeting seven days later. Further, it was agreed on 18 April that he should be invited to present a paper on planning to the subcommittee when it next met 'if time was available'.[28] Tipped off by Bish, Holland began work on the paper in advance of the invitation and was subsequently able to present a 15,000 word paper – RD.315/March 1972 'Planning and Policy Coordination'[29] – to his new colleagues when he attended his first meeting on 25 April.[30] Once co-opted, he was seldom absent when the subcommittee met. From his attendance of the meeting of 25 April 1972 until the publication of *Labour's Programme 1973* in June that year, he was present at all but two of the 12 meetings held.[31]

Once integrated into the research programme process, Holland immediately influenced the party's discussion of industrial policy. Even before the Industrial Policy Subcommittee had had the opportunity to discuss RD.315/March 1972 'Planning and Policy Coordination', one of the paper's central ideas found its way (courtesy of Bish) into the subcommittee's draft contribution to *Labour's Programme for Britain 1972*.[32] When the NEC document was subsequently published in July 1972, it revealed the party was considering the adoption of the Programme Contracts Procedure (used by the French planning system) 'in which leading companies are "invited" to submit advance programmes to the government covering key aspects of their strategic plans, including the timing and location of investment, pricing policy and so on', an option Holland outlined at length in his paper.[33]

RD.315/March 1972 'Planning and Policy Coordination' was one of a number of policy papers written by Holland in this period the impact of which, in the opinion of Mike Hartley Brewer in *The Guardian*, enabled him to 'virtually single handedly commit a great party to his particular view in the vital industrial policy field'.[34] RD.315/March 1972 'Planning and Policy Coordination', in which Holland exhaustively analysed planning as both a political and economic imperative, was one of two papers in particular that were to prove significant. The paper began by contrasting the French and British experience of planning. The first National Plan in France, he wrote, had been underpinned by a major reform of the Civil Service. Vichy collaborators were systematically removed from senior positions, thereby 'creating vacancies for new men more specifically committed to fulfilling government policy', while a new generation of 'high fliers' was sent to a newly created training school to undergo a two-year intensive course 'which included indoctrination in the rationale and methods of planning itself'. Promoted to the equivalent of British Under-Secretary while still in their early thirties, 'the result of the process was the distribution of committed advocates of planning both through the Civil Service in general and through key private enterprise companies'. By contrast, Labour's National Plan had lacked momentum. Private companies, taking note of the new government's balance of payments inheritance and the likelihood of either a deflation or devaluation plus deflation, declined to expand production in line with the Labour government's growth targets. Private enterprise was, wrote Holland, 'perfectly aware of the priority interests of both their shareholders and their own future'. Under high-growth conditions he anticipated the reverse would occur: companies would feel compelled to expand for fear of losing their share of the market vis-à-vis competing firms.[35]

Holland believed the National Plan had failed because the Labour government had 'hoped for too much through the wrong instruments' (including the IRC, which he considered 'fundamentally the wrong instrument for growth promotion').[36] A policy of indicative planning alone had been doomed from the start. It was therefore imperative, he argued, that the party commit itself to 'a major advance in intervention of the kind which would credibly change the future rather than rely on more favourable circumstances to permit loosely coordinated policies to prove more effective than last time round'.[37] The scale of Holland's ambition placed him firmly on the Tribunite left of the party. His suggestion that the Treasury be gelded and renamed the Ministry of the Budget and Economic Planning to avoid any repetition of the DEA–Treasury conflict between short and medium-term priorities, mirrored exactly the thinking of the Tribune Group of MPs at Westminster and, this being the case, Roy Jenkins could have had no clearer warning as to exactly who he was using as a speech-writer. It was equally apparent that Holland thought the events of 1964–70 had proved the likes of Jenkins wrong, and gives rise to the question, who was using whom? Holland wrote that 'The old assumptions that Keynesian macro policies plus progressive taxation will result in social justice have been eroded by the recent revelations on the persistent inequality of the sixties';[38] whereas Jenkins conceded only that 'General demand management must be supplemented by more rigorous policies of direct intervention than those which we used between 1964 and 1970.'[39]

Holland defined planning as 'the matter of establishing priorities between different types of activity, rather than allowing the overall distribution of activity between sectors to be determined solely by the market', and set out the case for the introduction of programme contracts (referred to above) to be applied to the private sector, for which purpose he once again drew on the experience of the French. He believed the Programme Contracts Procedure was one way of overcoming industry's scepticism over government growth targets which over the years had been repeatedly undermined by stop–go economics, a policy which itself derived from reliance on Keynesian demand management policies.[40] While such a system alone could not rectify this problem,

> it would prove a considerable advance on an exclusively macro economic policy if pursued through leading companies on a widespread and continuing basis. The psychological impact of knowing that the government is acting at the level of firms themselves would be likely to have a considerable effect on companies' own participation in the policy. They want to sustain their previous rate of growth and if possible extend it – at a minimum for market share and profits alone. If the government dealt with them alone on an ad hoc basis, or through a para-governmental loans agency such as IRC, which was only tenuously related with the sectoral policy of the National Plan, they would have strong grounds for scepticism. But if it can deal both with them and with other companies in other sectors to whom they sell and from whom they buy, as well as with the level of aggregate consumer demand, they risk being left out in the cold by not cooperating.[41]

He added that there was a strong case for making such contracts compulsory, 'requiring the leading firms by law to submit a true report of their medium term projects, prices, imports, exports, finance, employment, innovation, product substitution and location. Where firms had no such projects – or claimed they had not – the law would require them to elaborate them.' As for the criteria by which these leading firms might be selected, he was happy again to look across the Channel, where planners had sought through industrial restructuring and mergers to establish a ratio 'whereby 20 per cent of the total number of national firms would constitute 80 per cent of total market share', and whom the government would subsequently deal with directly. A further incentive to British companies to comply with government growth targets would be provided by the prospect of the State Holding Company purchasing shares in those companies where expansion of production was not forthcoming.[42]

Whether the introduction of programme contracts alone (even if compulsory) would be sufficient to ensure higher growth would depend on the state of the economy when Labour took office, and Holland pointed out that the 'recovery of growth may well lie outside private enterprise itself, and in public enterprise'. Yet the existing public industries – coal, steel, power and transport – were unsuitable instruments of growth promotion as they were 'essentially "growth dependent" sectors, dependent for their growth on demand for their output from manufacturing industry'. This in turn led Holland to argue that a future Labour government must acquire through the State Holding Company 'the real commanding heights of industry – the manufacturing sectors which through their own orders can command increases in investment, output and employment in other industrial sectors and services'. For this reason the State Holding Company must not resemble the IRC, belatedly injecting funds into lame-duck companies 'whose sectoral distribution would be accidental, and whose very problems would constitute an obstacle to rapid investment expansion'.[43] The State Holding Company would succeed as a growth promotion instrument only if it took shares in leading companies capable of driving the economy. Conversely, if programme contracts proved successful, he argued, this would not be necessary. Either way the obstacles to growth and consequently to a redistributive social policy would be greatly reduced, the prospect of which, he believed, should appeal to both left and right in the party: 'the case for the extension of public ownership through leading companies in the commanding heights of manufacturing should hardly deter either those committed to extensive public ownership for its own sake, or those prepared to accept the extension of public ownership to do the jobs which private enterprise and Keynesian policies alone cannot do'.[44]

Holland submitted the second of the two papers, RD.442/October 1972 'Planning Strategy, Tactics and Techniques',[45] to the Industrial Policy Subcommittee on 31 October 1972. Just as RD.315/March 1972 'Planning and Policy Coordination' was the source of the proposal on programme contracts, the second paper was the source of what became known as the 'twenty-five companies' proposal. Both were to prove highly controversial when they were included in *Labour's Programme 1973*. Holland used this paper to argue the need for government to counter the top 100 manufacturing companies' increasing net share of manufacturing output. Between 1925 and 1950, this share had remained static at roughly 20 per cent of net output,[46] but between 1950 and 1970 it had increased to more than 50 per cent. By 1980 it was anticipated this would have increased to nearly two-thirds. This trend, wrote Holland, 'strongly corroborates the case already made for supplementing macro policies and indicative planning with more direct and more imperative micro policies through both the State Holding Company and the Programme Contracts system'.[47]

The threat to Labour's regional strategy posed by the top 100 companies' domination of manufacturing output was, Holland felt, clear: 'there is increasing evidence that multinational companies prefer to go multi-national rather than multi-regional. i.e. they secure greater wage cost, pricing, profit and blackmail gains by going to other countries rather than the less developed regions of the home country. And since the top hundred British manufacturers either already are multinational or are capable of going multinational on an increasing scale, this has major implications for regional development.'[48] One way a Labour government might counter this threat was by harnessing the market power of leading companies through the State Holding Company. State acquisition of the market leaders throughout the main manufacturing sectors would, he believed, compel other large private companies 'to break from their defensive investment positions (otherwise justified for themselves by twenty-five years of low stop–go growth). If they do not increase the scale of investment and their rate of application of available technical progress in new products and production techniques they will lose market share within their sector to the newly expanding State leader.'[49]

Holland believed that the rate at which a relatively small number of firms was becoming dominant in particular industries 'gives the Party the strongest possible case for claiming that modern British capitalism has developed a private enterprise heart-land which must be brought within public accountability and control', adding that if handled correctly – by drawing on the success of Renault and Alfa-Romeo as both good products and equally good regional employment promoters – 'we can give a new political glamour to the case for both State leadership and the Programme Contracts system'. Such was the degree of concentration within the top 100 manufacturing companies, that control might be secured by nationalising as few as 20 companies plus a leading bank and two or three insurance companies ('if banking and insurance are not to be nationalised outright'). The remaining leading companies, he predicted, would be pulled along by the newly acquired 20 leading state companies and would locate and expand production accordingly. Alternatively, all 100 companies could be controlled through the Programme Contracts System, which might be made compulsory.[50]

Holland was not so naive as to imagine that the proposed nationalisation of two dozen leading private companies would pass unremarked upon by Labour's political opponents. He suggested that, when the general election came, the party should state simply that 'we wish to bring our instruments of economic management more into line with the continental economies by securing an initial public holding package of not more than two dozen firms'.[51] While accepting that Labour would be politically vulnerable over this proposal irrespective of whatever wording was employed to make it sound less menacing, Holland chose to stress the advantages of the policy:

> ...twenty firms brought into public ownership from the top seventy manufacturers, plus the three main manufacturing companies in which the government already has a substantial stake, could give us direct control of 48 per cent of the employment, 38 per cent of the net profit and 33 per cent of the turnover of the top hundred manufacturers.

As already stressed, the impact effect of such shares would be greater than nationalising smaller firms precisely because the firms concerned are actual or potential leaders. But putting the proportions against total manufacturing means that the proportions would give us a total manufacturing share today of half the quoted figures, and more by 1980 (like the proportions themselves) as the leaders further increase their share of British manufacturing.[52]

Holland offered the Labour Party a blueprint for socialising the market. This, after all, was an objective which had been set out by the NEC in both *Economic Strategy, Growth and Unemployment* and *Labour's Programme for Britain 1972*.[53] Both the programme contracts and 'twenty-five companies' proposals were entirely in keeping with this objective and it was therefore unsurprising that both were included in *Labour's Programme 1973*. Moreover, their inclusion demonstrates the extent to which individuals such as Judith Hart and Geoff Bish supervised the discussion of policy in circumstances in which the outcome was predetermined by their own political objectives. Holland's policy work in this period has of course been thoroughly analysed elsewhere,[54] yet the question remains as to how one individual could become – quite briefly – so influential so easily. In part, Holland's impact upon the research programme owed much to the the structure of the programme itself. As a member of both the Public Sector Group and the Economic Planning Group, both of which came under the umbrella of the Industrial Policy Subcommittee, of which he was also a member, Holland was effectively hidden from the parliamentary leadership and Callaghan in particular at the Home Policy Committee. The Public Sector Group, for example, where Holland did his most productive work in respect of the State Holding Company, was virtually hermetically sealed by Hart and of all of the policy committees and groups this was identifiably the domain of the left. From 25 January 1972 (the date on which Holland attended his first meeting) until the publication of *Labour's Programme 1973* in June 1973, membership of this particular group at no time exceeded 12,[55] from among whom there emerged a core group of six. In addition to Hart and Holland, this included Pryke and Lord Balogh (under whom both Holland and Pryke had worked in the Cabinet Office in 1966), Margaret Jackson from the Research Department and secretary to the group, and finally Ian Mikardo.[56] This was friendly territory and it is essentially because he promoted his ideas in non-critical forums so much of the time that he was so influential. Hartley Brewer, writing in 1975, found it astonishing that

> throughout this whole period no other member of the industrial policy subcommittee or its working groups submitted a single paper offering support, opposition, or alternative to Holland's view, in spite of frequent appeals from Geoff Bish of the research

department. As any experienced committee member knows, whoever commits proposals to paper is likely to prevail.

It seems extraordinary that not even Tony Crosland, who spoke up against Holland's plans and had frequently underlined the need for well worked out policies to be formulated in opposition, never put pen to paper.[57]

Crosland did speak up at Industrial Policy Subcommittee meetings against Holland,[58] but his attendance record was poor and he was present at only four of the eight meetings held between August 1972 and June 1973.[59] Equally critical and with a better record of attendance was Edmund Dell, often in a minority of one in Crosland's absence. Yet the minutes confirm Hartley Brewer's assertion: neither he nor Crosland committed their own proposals to paper for discussion by the subcommittee.[60] Crosland's explanation for the paucity of his written contribution to Labour's policy debate in opposition was characteristically curt: 'a decade is my time-span, not eternity'.[61] That he felt either unable or disinclined to match the left and Holland in particular, paper for paper at research-programme level, is apparent. Yet the responsibility to do so was by no means his alone. Senior figures in the PLP, including the leader of the party himself,[62] did not take the research programme seriously and in due course the party paid a heavy price for their failure to do so.

Chickens home to roost: *Labour's Programme 1973*

Three years after the party's general election defeat in June 1970, Labour's NEC finally published the document from which the policies to be included in the party's next election manifesto would be drawn. *Labour's Programme 1973* was published on 7 June 1973. Recipients of a draft of the document prior to publication found attached a note explaining that the party at least now had 'one document covering several hundred points in place of several hundred documents covering one point'.[63] In his foreword to the document Ron Hayward, Labour's general secretary, stated quite clearly that it was not a manifesto, and to underline this point Clause V of the party's constitution was reproduced in full and in bold type, leaving little room for misunderstanding as to its status:

(1) The Party Conference shall decide from time to time what specific proposals of legislative, financial or administrative reform shall be included in the Party Programme.

(2) The National Executive Committee and the Parliamentary Committee of the Labour Party shall decide which items from the Party Programme shall be included in the Manifesto

which shall be issued by the National Executive Committee prior to every General Election.[64]

But, whatever the constitution said, it was difficult for Labour to dispel the impression given by the document that the proposals contained in it *were* the policies of the party. The tone of the document was uncompromising. The inclusion of objectives described as socialist goals, for example 'To bring about a fundamental and irreversible shift in the balance of power and wealth in favour of working people and their families',[65] when set alongside the party's industrial policy proposals, sounded menacing and, to some members of the Shadow Cabinet, undemocratic.[66] However, such was the extent to which the research programme had self-generated momentum, and equally such was the impact of Heath's U-turn on industrial policy on Labour's left wing, that moderate opinion in the PLP had simply been drowned out in the period of the document's gestation. Consequently, the language of *Labour's Programme 1973* was uninhibited:

> It is not for those who want to change society to defend themselves in the face of today's evidence. That onus is upon those who want to stay as we are. Last year saw Slater-Walker take over, in *one* year, no fewer than 29 companies – yet there is always a horrified reaction if a democratic Labour Party proposes to obtain a mandate from the electorate to do less than that in *five years*. When we took over the steel industry in 1967 only 14 companies were involved! The central question, therefore, is, who wields economic power in Britain. Shall an elected government take powers for the community, or shall we for ever try to run a system where Savundra, John Bloom and Bernie Cornfeld are regarded as wizards until their empires collapse – leaving the public to pick up pieces?[67]

In this one paragraph the twin impact of Heath and Holland was discernible, and also the reason why, in June 1973, Labour had the industrial policy it had, as set out in the pages which followed. It was presented as part of an overall strategy – no doubt envisaged by the authors of the policy as being palatable to all members of the Labour Party – of loading the scales in favour of equality: 'Social equality is not about higher private consumption; it is about extending opportunities to those who are currently denied them.' It was, needless to say, about both. But in 1973 party members – and the Croslandites/revisionists in particular – were unable to agree on how inflation fuelled by working-class private consumption could be contained without resorting to institutionalised inequality through deflation and wage control (incomes policy). With the publication of *Labour's Programme 1973*, it was clear that the party as a whole was unwilling to accept that increased working-class private consumption was itself evidence of greater social equality. This could not easily be admitted, as it implied the Conservative Party understood Labour's traditional base of support better than some sections of the Labour Party, but for anyone willing to consider this proposition it must have been apparent that the concept of the social wage as a counter-inflationary tool was flawed.[68]

The NEC document listed 11 areas a Labour government would need to tackle if Britain's problems were to be solved,[69] an increase on the seven areas listed in *Labour's Programme for Britain 1972*.[70] The additional areas listed on this occasion were Pensions; Industrial Relations and Industrial Democracy; Citizens Rights; and the Common Market. The commitment to increase pensions, to £16 a week for married couples and £10 for a single person, and to link pension rates to average industrial earnings, and the commitment to repeal the Industrial Relations Act and to introduce legislation to extend industrial democracy, reflected the 'progress' being made between the Labour Party and the TUC at meetings of the TUC–Labour Party Liaison Committee, which continued to take place throughout the summer of 1973.[71] The inclusion of Citizens Rights and the Common Market, involving the restoration and furtherance of democracy at central and local government level, and the renegotiation of the Treaty of Accession to the European Communities respectively, signalled Labour's intention to undo much of Heath's flagship legislation, namely Peter Walker's reorganisation of local government and British membership of the Common Market on the terms agreed to by Heath.[72] For the rest, the listed points restated those set out previously in *Economic Strategy, Growth and Unemployment* in 1971, and in *Labour's Programme for Britain 1972*. A future Labour government would extend price controls to take in prices at *retail* level; repeal the Industrial Relations Act and the Housing Finance Act; introduce disability benefits; seek to achieve and maintain full employment; introduce a wealth tax; and so on.[73] Only when the 11 major areas of policy had been successfully tackled, would a Labour government 'bring in our other urgent plans for further progress'.[74]

The opening section of the policy document, setting out the party's objectives in both high-minded and largely non-specific terms, would in all probability have sufficed in the eyes of the parliamentary leadership. Certainly the leader of the party was never happier than on those occasions when rhetoric took precedence over detail. The stated intention of bringing in 'our other urgent plans for further progress', but only *after* the 11 listed points had been tackled (several of which were plainly unattainable, not least full employment) appeared an obvious tactic to enable a future Labour government to distance itself from the party and its policies. When the PLP met to discuss the NEC document on 11 July 1973, Stan Orme raised the by then familiar concern that 'there was a feeling at grass roots level that the PLP was not firmly committed to the programme'.[75] Twelve months earlier, in the course of the PLP's discussion of *Labour's Programme for Britain 1972*, it had been the turn of Orme's Tribunite colleague Frank Allaun to voice the concern that 'the PLP was in danger of being left behind the Movement as a whole; it seemed as if the Green Paper were too radical for some Members'.[76]

Orme and Allaun had every reason to be concerned. Set out immediately below the pledge on the 11 listed points was a section on the costing of the party's proposals, which stressed 'that not everything can be done at once'.[77] Revealing that the commitment to increase pensions would cost £1,400 million a year alone, and that a significant proportion of the funding required to finance other proposals in the document was dependent upon reducing unemployment and a faster rate of growth than had been achieved by the previous Labour government, *Labour's Programme 1973* failed to guarantee that the necessary levels of public expenditure would be forthcoming and was, therefore, little more than a wish list. Wilson, of course, described it as 'a fearless, forthright programme', which the party 'had every right to be proud of'. This alone should have been sufficient to set alarm bells ringing for those in the party who held bitter memories of 1966–70. On the listed 11 points he was undoubtedly willing to be held to account, and once returned to Downing Street he was conscientious in his observance of the policies on which Labour had been elected. 'My job', he told a meeting of the NEC two days after becoming Prime Minister once more, 'is to be the custodian of the Manifesto.'[78] The soaring phrases he employed in praise of the document at the PLP meeting in July 1973, of which 'a restatement of our Socialist principles' and 'a forward-looking and specific policy statement for a generation' are just two examples,[79] might wisely have been seen for what they undoubtedly were: rhetoric. For, conspicuous by their absence from the party's February 1974 general election manifesto, were several of the industrial policy proposals included in *Labour's Programme 1973*.[80]

When it came to the detail of what *Labour's Programme 1973* actually had to say about the party's 'New Economic Strategy', the language was that of Holland and an increasingly evangelistic Benn. Radical socialist policies, the document explained, drawing heavily on Holland's paper RD.442/October 1972 'Planning Strategy, Tactics and Techniques', were the only possible response to the transformation which had taken place in the economy over the past 50 years. Holland's statistics on the growth of private industry's increasing net share of manufacturing output were repeated once more to justify the party's intention to act directly at the level of the giant firm for the reason that 'The interests of . . . huge private companies cannot be expected to coincide with the interests of the national economy.' A State Holding Company (renamed the National Enterprise Board) would accordingly be set up 'to provide an instrument for exercising control in the area of profitable manufacturing industry'. Programme contracts, which Holland had written about at length in RD.315/March 1972 'Planning and Policy Coordination', reappeared as planning agreements, to be applied to at least the largest 100 manufacturing firms, in addition to all of the major public enterprises.[81] These proposals were to be underpinned by the introduction of a new Industry Act, much of the legislative detail of which had been prepared by Benn at the Industrial Policy Subcommittee.[82] To ensure compliance with the Planning Agreement system, the new Act would empower the relevant minister to:

> *obtain any information* deemed necessary from individual companies;
> *provide any support* that may be needed, in the national interest, to individual companies, in return for a public shareholding;
> *seek agreement* with companies on a wide range of industrial matters, including prices, profits, investment programmes and industrial relations policies and to issue, if necessary in the national interest, *directives* on these matters;
> *invest* in individual companies, or to *purchase* them outright, preferably by agreement with the company concerned, or, if necessary in the national interest, by Statutory Instrument, approved by Parliament;
> provide clear statutory *authority* to prevent the take-over of British firms by foreign interests, if necessary by the acquisition of the company or the companies concerned;
> provide, if this is necessary in the national interest, for *reserve powers* to remove directors from firms with which the Government has a planning agreement;
> provide the means by which *company law* can be revised in the light of the changing needs of shareholders, consumers, workers and the community as a whole;
> put in an 'Official Trustee' to assume temporary control of any company which fails to meet its responsibilities to its workers, to its customers, or to the community as a whole;
> provide for the application of these powers to large *multi-national companies*.

To these proposals was added the rider: 'The exercise of these powers will often involve Statutory Instruments being laid before Parliament. In view of the importance of these Statutory Instruments, we are considering changes in the procedures of Parliament to provide for additional democratic safeguards.'[83]

Benn's thinking on industrial policy had been influenced, along with others on Labour's left wing (the direction in which he was gravitating at this time), by Heath's dramatic U-turn on economic and industrial policy in March 1972. He had read the government's 1972 Industry Act with a careful eye and had quickly absorbed its implications for Labour's own consideration of what type of industrial policy was henceforth possible and acceptable. Writing in the *Sunday Times* in March 1973, the first anniversary of John Davies's announcement of a new Bill for industry, he welcomed the 'very important historical role' performed by Heath 'in *preparing for* the fundamental and irreversible transfer in the balance of power and wealth which has to take place, even if only to allow inflation to be tackled'. The article appeared under the heading 'Heath's spadework for socialism' and listed 17 new areas of government control.[84] Benn wrote that 'The whole nature of the mixed economy operating on market forces has been transformed by this quiet revolution in a way that is not yet fully appreciated.' Heath's government had not, he argued, adopted socialist policies, but significantly it had created instruments that Labour could make use of in office, 'for objectives that would be markedly different'. However, Heath's most important contribution by far was that by 'burying the argument about intervention, accepting a role for public ownership and plumping for a managed economy the Government has made it possible for the debate to concentrate on the question "In whose interest is the economy to be managed?"' Justifying Labour's interventionist plans, Benn concluded: 'What we are witnessing is the breakdown of the wartime and post-war consensus which survived for nearly a generation. We must move towards a new consensus, markedly more favourable to Labour, markedly more equal and markedly more democratic. This new consensus, once we have identified it, could last another generation and form the basis for national partnership that would command confidence and release the energies of the people.'[85] When the PLP met to discuss *Labour's Programme 1973* in July 1973, Wilson pointed to the the proposed new Industry Act as evidence of the party's determination to make structural change in the economy,[86] yet, as already stated, much of the above detail was unsurprisingly absent from the party's manifesto in February 1974.[87]

The other significant point of interest in the document was the party's attempt to agree a policy on incomes. After three years in opposition, parliamentary leaders were pinning their hopes on holding down the cost of living, in return for which it was hoped that workers might voluntarily 'moderate their expectations on money wages'. The idea that government provision of a social wage – in lieu of an increase in the value of the money wage – might persuade trade unionists to moderate their pay claims was not only desperately optimistic (and did not work)[88] but also threatened to bankrupt the country. However, the party's discussions with the trade unions at the TUC–Labour Party Liaison Committee had established that anything other than a voluntary policy on incomes – that is, a 'free-for-all'[89] – was unacceptable to union leaders. As with so many of the party's objectives, the containment of incomes was dependent upon higher growth. The document's authors spoke unconvincingly of their confidence that action on prices and an understanding with the TUC would create 'the right economic climate for money incomes to grow in line with production', and were forced to concede that 'a policy of price restraint cannot succeed for very long if wages and salaries are moving out of line with the growth of productivity'.[90]

In truth it hardly mattered what type of policy on incomes the party came up with, as the likelihood of a future Labour government securing the level of increase in production necessary to avoid a balance of payments crisis (and the subsequent introduction of deflationary economic measures to reduce private consumption) was remote. Parliamentary leaders were negotiating with trade unions leaders – in parallel with the party's ambitious discussion of policy through the research programme (and the document listed several areas of policy where agreement had already been reached)[91] – a licence to muddle through. Nothing in *Labour's Programme 1973* suggested otherwise.

The National Enterprise Board

No aspect of *Labour's Programme 1973* demonstrated the extent to which the party had diverged from the parliamentary leadership as the research programme had progressed, more than the Public Sector Group's proposals for the creation of a State Holding Company. The National Enterprise Board (NEB), the name given to the State Holding Company by the group, the policy document stated, would provide for the party for the first time 'an instrument for exercising control in the area of profitable manufacturing industry'. Among the tasks it was envisaged the NEB might carry out, 'if sufficiently large and ... given sufficient scope', were job creation; investment promotion; technological development; growth of exports; promotion of government price policies; tackling the spread of multinational companies; the spread of industrial democracy; and import substitution. This new tool would be required if the party was to match 'the rapidly changing structure of modern capitalism with new means of intervention'. Without the NEB, the document warned, the next Labour government would preside over an economy 'where the power of decision rests with leading private companies, with long-term implications for the credibility of Labour economic management, and indeed the survival of Britain as an economic force'.[92]

However, it was the inclusion of one specifically worded sentence which proved most contentious when *Labour's Programme 1973* was published: 'For the range of tasks suggested, some twenty-five of our largest manufacturers (Category 1 firms)[93] would be required, very early on in the life of the Board.'[94] This particular proposal was first revealed when the Public Sector Group's Green Paper on the National Enterprise Board was published in April 1973, in which it was stated that to achieve a controlling interest over a large slice of the economy, 'About one-third of the turnover of the top hundred manufacturers, two-fifths of their profits and about half their employment should be vested in NEB. Dependent on their size, the takeover of some twenty to twenty-five companies would yield control of an area of the economy of this degree.'[95] This was a defining moment for the the party. It was the point at which it became clear that, despite sharing a common vocabulary in respect of greater state intervention in industry, left and right were in fact irreconcilable on this issue.

At various times in opposition both Wilson and Jenkins had publicly advocated the creation of a State Holding Company. Neither had demurred when it became party policy in 1971.[96] But Wilson had at all times spoken of the State Holding Company performing the tasks of the abolished IRC, and he was therefore strongly placed to oppose the proposals which eventually emerged from the Public Sector Group. Jenkins, having drawn heavily on Holland and Pryke's 1972 paper on the State Holding Company, was in a weaker position, being to some extent compromised by his past association with Holland. For, where the Public Sector Group's Green Paper stated that 'To be effective NEB must... acquire a substantial base in the private sector among Category 1 firms in manufacturing industry', Holland and Pryke's earlier paper had equally clearly stated that a State Holding Company was viable 'only if it represented the broad spectrum of manufacturing industry' and, further, that for it to be effective, 'it is vital that it should from an early date possess a large industrial base in the form of factories operating in a wide range of industries and most parts of the country'.[97] Jenkins himself had stated that the State Holding Company would need to represent 'a broad spectrum of industry'. It was ironic that he subsequently dismissed the 25 companies proposal as 'dogmatic' and not 'remotely sensible',[98] particularly so given his propensity for making a virtue of his own consistency in matters of policy. It can be argued that the 'twenty-five companies' proposal of 1973 was discernible both in Holland's and Pryke's paper of 1972 and, indeed, in Jenkins's own words.

Why then did the parliamentary leadership not dispose of Holland's proposals for the State Holding Company in 1972? Given that the substance of the proposals which proved unacceptable to Wilson and a majority of his Shadow Cabinet colleagues in 1973 were to be found in Holland's and Pryke's earlier paper, why did the parliamentary leadership allow these ideas to become so firmly established at research programme level? First and most obviously, the research programme was the property of the NEC, over which body the Shadow Cabinet had no authority and was therefore unable to directly influence the discussion of policy. Senior Shadow Cabinet members were involved in the research programme through their membership of the NEC, or as co-opted members of a subcommittee or study group, and Callaghan particularly, as chairman of the Home Policy Committee, worked hard to ensure that the programme structure took into account the legitimate interests of the PLP. But perhaps most significantly, it made no sense politically for parliamentary leaders to become embroiled prematurely in a debate with the party on this issue. For, despite the fact that the proposals for a State Holding Company in *Labour's Programme for Britain 1972* bore Holland's imprint, the document itself was presented to the party only as the 'basis for discussion throughout the country'.[99] It was therefore still conceivable, however unlikely, that Wilson's version of a State Holding Company modelled on the IRC might prevail, and that when the NEC published its final policy document in 1973 Holland's proposals would be excised from the text. This did not happen. Holland's contribution to the policy debate was organic; well before the publication of the Public Sector Group's Green Paper, he had become part of the fabric of Labour's discussion of economic and industrial policy.

Where Jenkins's fleeting patronage of Holland is difficult to explain and can perhaps only be understood in terms of the former's aborted leadership challenge to Wilson, or simply as an error of judgement, Wilson's response to the impact of Holland upon the party's thinking on economic and industrial policy was astute. The 'twenty-five companies' proposal had the effect of at last securing the party leader's involvement in the research programme. Until this time he had remained detached from the process, an arrangement which appears to have suited both Wilson and the party. But, when the time came to distinguish between self-indulgence and preparing for power, he exploited both his position as leader of the party *and* the party's desire for unity to secure the revision of the Public Sector Group's proposals in accordance with his own view of what the party's policy should be. Having bided his time throughout the period of the research programme, he was able to reject the 'twenty-five companies' proposal in his own time and in the name of unity at the party conference in October, contriving even to elicit the applause of delegates in the process:

> My own view on the 25 companies proposal has been stated. I am against it. The Parliamentary Committee is against it. I will leave it with these words, that the Parliamentary Committee charged by the Constitution with the duty of sitting down with the Executive to select, from the programme adopted by the Conference the items for including in the election manifesto, entirely reserves its full constitutional rights on this matter, and there could be nothing more comradely than that.[100]

James Callaghan was subsequently to state the same point privately in terms somewhat less comradely: 'You can't write a Manifesto for the Party in opposition and expect it to have any relationship to what the Party does in Government.'[101]

The parliamentary leadership and *Labour's Programme 1973*

With the exception of the 'twenty-five companies' proposal, Wilson described the NEC policy document as the 'best the National Executive has brought forward';[102] a view shared by Crosland, who thought the document excellent, 'the best one the Party has produced'.[103] That senior parliamentary leaders felt able to respond so generously to a document which was the product of a research programme by which they been ill-served, owed much to the existence – since February 1972 – of a parallel programme of policy formulation, the TUC–Labour Party Liaison Committee, through which sufficient commitments had been agreed by party leaders to render much of the NEC policy document redundant in its own right. When final agreement between party leaders and the TUC on a future Labour government's economic and industrial policy and legislative timetable was eventually reached, it transpired that there existed between the two policy processes a degree of overlap. However, in May 1973, for the parliamentary leadership meeting with the NEC to discuss the policy document, it was unmistakably a case of unions first, party second.

When the meeting between the Shadow Cabinet and the NEC and other frontbench spokesmen took place on 16 May 1973, much of the opening part of the discussion centred on the exact status of *Labour's Programme 1973*, despite the inclusion at the front of the document of the disclaimer that it was not a manifesto. Responding to Barbara Castle's observation that the policy document certainly had some manifesto touches to it, such as the commitment to increase pensions, Harold Wilson pointed out that agreements reached with the TUC, for instance the repeal of the Industrial Relations Act and Housing Finance Act, as well as an increase in pensions, could not be broken. On pensions specifically, he admitted that the commitment was 'costly', but it had appeared in the joint statement issued with the TUC earlier in the year,[104] and 'Anything we have said with the TUC has already taken on to itself a manifesto mantle.'[105] The party had no choice but to repeat these commitments in the NEC document even if their inclusion created confusion in the minds of the public as to the difference between the party programme and the manifesto.

The potential for confusion arose because *Labour's Programme 1973* contained commitments which originated from beyond the research programme and were plainly intended for inclusion in the manifesto, instead of containing only those proposals which were the product of the research programme itself and which were intended for inclusion in the party programme, but not necessarily the manifesto. The party was presenting to the country a document which relied upon the casual reader having the wit to discriminate between the commitment on pensions, which would be included in the manifesto because it emerged from the Liaison Committee, and the 'twenty-five companies' proposal, which had emerged from the research programme and was not intended for the manifesto because the party leader was against it. The situation could have been avoided had Labour published a separate document for each of the two policy processes simultaneously, rather than five months apart.[106] However, to have done so would have revealed the parliamentary leadership's preoccupation with the Liaison Committee, which was only too evident in Wilson's insistence that the party could not go back on any agreements reached with the TUC, and which therefore begged the question: exactly which commitments would a future Labour government be willing to go back on? The answer to this question party activists knew only too well. Generally speaking, the response of senior parliamentary leaders on this occasion can be summarised thus: the policy document contained many good things, most of which unfortunately would be unaffordable given the prevailing economic climate and the predetermined allocation of resources to underpin *equally* unaffordable, but politically necessary, agreements reached with the TUC at the Liaison Committee.

The parliamentary leadership was untroubled by *Labour's Programme 1973* because the real deal over policy was being struck elsewhere. Strengthened in its relationship with the party by its agreement with the trade unions at the Liaison Committee, the parliamentary leadership set about lowering expectations raised by the publication of the NEC policy document. *Labour's Programme 1973* held out the prospect of major structural changes in the way society was organised but, at the insistence of senior parliamentary leaders and in common with *Labour's Programme for Britain 1972*, the document stated clearly that when Labour came to power it would have 'a very long list of commitments – many requiring lengthy legislation, and many requiring substantial money and resources', which would oblige a Labour government to decide on its priorities in consultation with the party.[107] At the 16 May meeting, Crosland was swift to point out that the prospects for public expenditure in the first year of the Labour government if the party won the general election were not good, and that ministers would in fact be faced with the prospect of having to reduce expenditure.[108] This warning, while true, was laughable. Crosland, like Wilson, was fully aware that the party was making policy commitments at the Liaison Committee that the country could not afford. It was not just the policy proposals which had emerged from the research programme to be included in *Labour's Programme 1973* that were unrealistic, but the whole of Labour's public expenditure programme. It would take more than the cancellation of Maplin Airport to pay for the commitments arising out of both the Liaison Committee and the research programme.[109]

In this respect it was Denis Healey, up until this point a relatively muted voice since his appointment as Shadow Chancellor, who sought to place the party's policy objectives in context by calling for the incorporation into the policy document of a section on the likely inheritance from the Conservative government. 'A section on what we inherit is something the movement will understand very well because they saw it last time.'[110] This assertion was open to dispute but, even if it were so, it did not free the parliamentary leadership from its obligations to the TUC. Healey informed his colleagues that the annual cost of the commitments in the policy document amounted to upwards of three times the amount a Labour government would receive in tax revenue if taxes remained as they were, a remark which illustrated the spuriousness of the party's argument over growth since the 1950s.[111] In terms of paying for its programme, the only tool at the disposal of the party was taxation and this, Healey told the meeting, would force the party to define its priorities:

> ...the scope for increasing tax revenue by soaking the rich or even those one and a half times above average income, is very limited. Only one-quarter of the population has over average income. Only about ten per cent of the population has over one and a half times the average income. That is why the average income discussion is misleading and offensive to the majority of workers in the country. If you increase the tax on one and a half times average earnings, about £3,000 a year...If you try to increase tax at higher levels, the yield is much smaller.[112]

A Labour government, he concluded, would have no option other than to 'increase the tax on people certainly from a little under average'.[113]

His analysis was both candid and brave, yet Healey was unwilling to pursue it to its logical conclusion. He did not accept that the agreement with the TUC was unaffordable and regarded it as having a vital place in a future Labour government's fight against inflation.[114] He did accept that allocating a high proportion of the resources at the disposal of a future Labour government to honour commitments such as the increase in pensions, would inevitably result in other aspects of the party's programme remaining unrealised for at least the duration of the first Parliament. Thus was the parliamentary leadership saved from the party in opposition.

Notes

1 D. Marquand, RD.153/July 1971 'Problems of Economic Growth'.
2 Editorial, 'Knowing Where We're Going', *Socialist Commentary* (August 1972), pp. 2–3.
3 Ibid.
4 The title of a speech given by Roy Jenkins on 5 May 1972 and included in the book of his speeches published that year under the title *What Matters Now*.
5 Jenkins, *What Matters Now*, pp. 30–1.
6 Jenkins, *What Matters Now*, p. 31.
7 Quoted in Jenkins, *What Matters Now*, pp. 31–2.
8 Jenkins, *What Matters Now*, p. 34.
9 In an earlier passage of his speech, Jenkins had stated how since 1968 'the Italian Government has decreed that all new projects undertaken by the State Holding Companies should be in the Italian Development Area, the South. 60 per cent of gross investment undertaken by the Holding Companies has to be located there.' Jenkins, *What Matters Now*, p. 34.
10 Jenkins, *What Matters Now*, pp. 35–7.
11 NEC, *Economic Strategy, Growth and Unemployment*, in LPAR, 1971, p. 377.
12 NEC, *Labour's Programme for Britain 1972*, p. 29.
13 The number of people officially registered as unemployed reached 1,000,000 in January 1972. 'From 1972 onwards', writes Campbell, 'the Government's whole economic policy...was a rerun of Maudling's dash for sustainable growth in 1963–4.' Campbell, *Edward Heath*, p. 444.
14 Campbell, *Edward Heath*, p. 445. 'Barber', writes Campbell, 'took £1 billion off income tax by increasing allowances; he made cuts in purchase tax worth another £1,380 million and increased pensions and social security benefits.' Ibid.
15 Jenkins, *What Matters Now*, pp. 26–7.
16 Hatfield, *The House the Left Built*, p. 92.
17 Jenkins, *What Matters Now*, p. 36.
18 LPAR, 1971, p. 166.
19 Wilson repeated this pledge in the House of Commons during the debate on unemployment on 24 January 1972, which took place at Labour's request and censured 'Her Majesty's Government for the fact that their doctrinaire and irresponsible policies have forced the total registered unemployed in the United Kingdom to 1,023,583 persons.' *HC Debs, 5th ser.*, 1971–72, vol. 829, col. 997.
20 RD.271/February 1972 'The State Holding Company' by S. Holland and R. Pryke, LPA, Industrial Policy Subcommittee, Minutes and Papers, 15 February–28 November 1972.
21 'Because our nationalised industries have been managing their affairs rather well over the last ten or fifteen years, they have built up a pool of able managers. In view of this record, it is both foolish and discreditable that the present Government should seek to hive off parts of the nationalised industries and return them to the private sector. We should move firmly in the other direction. We should seek to hive on parts of the private sector to the nationalised sector to diversify wherever it sees a good opportunity.' Jenkins, *What Matters Now*, p. 32.
22 RD.271/February 1972 'The State Holding Company' by Holland and Pryke, LPA, Industrial Policy Subcommittee, Minutes and Papers, 15 February–28 November 1972, p. 9. For a history of the Zinoviev letter, see D. Marquand, *Ramsey MacDonald* (London, Jonathan Cape, 1977), pp. 381–8.

23 RD.271/February 1972 'The State Holding Company' by Holland and Pryke, LPA, Industrial Policy Subcommittee, Minutes and Papers, 15 February–28 November 1972, p. 22.

24 When the Tribune Group met on 25 June 1973 to discuss how it might preserve the gains it had made on economic and industrial policy, Eric Heffer told the group that 'it would be a good idea to use Jenkins's speech on [the] State Holding Company in our arguments with the right-wing'. LPA, Jo Richardson Papers (JRP), Tribune Group Minutes (TGM), 25 June 1973.

25 The previous day Wilson, speaking in the House of Commons, had called upon the government to re-establish a strengthened IRC to forge a new partnership between government and industry. *HC Debs, 5th ser.*, 1971–72, vol. 829, col. 1019.

26 LPA, Public Sector Group, Minutes and Papers, 25 January 1972.

27 Hatfield, *The House the Left Built*, p. 121.

28 LPA, Public Sector Group, Minutes and Papers, 18 April 1972.

29 LPA, Industrial Policy Subcommittee, Minutes and Papers, 15 February–28 November 1972.

30 Hatfield, *The House the Left Built*, p. 121. Holland's paper was RD.315/March 1972, 'Planning and Policy Coordination'. LPA, Industrial Policy Subcommittee, Minutes and Papers, 15 February–28 November 1972.

31 LPA, Industrial Policy Subcommittee, Minutes and Papers, 15 February–28 November 1972; NEC, Minutes, 24 January–23 May 1973.

32 LPA, Industrial Policy Subcommittee, Minutes and Papers, 25th April 1972.

33 NEC, *Labour's Programme for Britain 1972*, p. 17.

34 Hartley Brewer, 'Scaled-down version'.

35 RD.315/March 1972 'Planning and Policy Coordination', pp. 2–6. LPA, Industrial Policy Subcommittee, Minutes and Papers, 15 February 1972–28 November 1972.

36 It might be argued that on the strength of these words alone Jenkins should have distanced himself from Holland, as it was plain the latter was not intending a State Holding Company on the lines of the IRC, unlike both Jenkins and Wilson. The IRC, Holland further explained, 'was inadequate to assure a major effect on the promotion of national economic growth both because it was too small and because it lent funds to firms which were already prepared to employ them, rather than persuaded firms to undertake investment and location projects which they otherwise would not . . . this does not mean to say that there would be no role for a para-governmental State loans agency of the IRC type'. RD.315/March 1972 'Planning and Policy Coordination', p. 24. LPA, Industrial Policy Subcommittee, Minutes and Papers, 15 February 1972–28 November 1972.

37 RD.315/March 1972 'Planning and Policy Coordination', p. 7.

38 RD.315/March 1972 'Planning and Policy Coordination', pp. 9–10.

39 Jenkins, *What Matters Now*, p. 31.

40 RD.315/March 1972 'Planning and Policy Coordination', pp. 11–14.

41 RD.315/March 1972 'Planning and Policy Coordination', p. 15.

42 RD.315/March 1972 'Planning and Policy Coordination', pp. 15–17.

43 RD.315/March 1972 'Planning and Policy Coordination', pp. 18–19.

44 RD.315/March 1972 'Planning and Policy Coordination', p. 20.

45 RD.442/October 1972 'Planning Strategy, Tactics and Techniques', by Stuart Holland, LPA, Industrial Policy Subcommittee, Minutes and Papers, 15 February–28 November 1972.

46 Due to 'the slow inter-war recovery and depression, plus the quota system during shortages which favoured small and medium firms'. RD.442/October 1972, 'Planning Strategy, Tactics and Techniques', p. 4.

47 RD.442/October 1972 'Planning Strategy, Tactics and Techniques', p. 4.

48 A process described by Holland as the State as entrepreneur.

49 RD.442/October 1972 'Planning Strategy, Tactics and Techniques', p. 7.

50 RD.442/October 1972 'Planning Strategy, Tactics and Techniques', pp. 8–11.

51 RD.442/October 1972 'Planning Strategy, Tactics and Techniques', p. 28.

52 RD.442/October 1972 'Planning Strategy, Tactics and Techniques', pp. 31–2.

53 *Economic Strategy, Growth and Unemployment* stated that the NEC desired 'an economic order in which industrial and financial decisions are dictated by the needs of the whole community' (*Economic Strategy, Growth and Unemployment*, in LPAR, 1971, p. 371); *Labour's Programme for Britain 1972* that 'We put the principles of democracy and socialism above considerations of class and market economics. We aim to bring about a society based on co-operation instead of competition; where production is for people's needs not for private profit.' NEC, *Labour's Programme for Britain 1972*, p. 5.

54 See in particular Hatfield, *The House the Left Built* and Wickham-Jones, *Economic Strategy and the Labour Party*.

55 Between 25 January 1972 and the publication of *Labour's Programme 1973*, the following attended at least one meeting of the Public Sector Group: Judith Hart MP, Richard Pryke, Lord Delacourt-Smith, Margaret Jackson (secretary), Stuart Holland, David Gee, Ian Mikardo MP, Lord Balogh, Jim Mortimer, Tony Banks, Derek Robinson, Tony Benn MP. LPA, Public Sector Group, Minutes and Papers, 25 January 1972–27 November 1973.

56 There existed even among these six a core within a core: Pryke and Jackson, for example, attended all 13 of the meetings held prior to the publication of the group's Green Paper on the National Enterprise Board, published in April 1973, and along with Hart (11) and, initially, Charles Delacourt-Smith (who died during the course of the study) formed the nucleus of the group. Holland attended nine meetings in this period, Mikardo eight, and Balogh six. LPA, Public Sector Group, Minutes and Papers, 25 January 1972–27 November 1973.

57 Hartley Brewer, 'Scaled-down version'.

58 See, for example, Industrial Policy Subcommittee, Minutes and Papers, 28 November 1972, 5 and 30 April 1973.

59 The Industrial Policy Subcommittee in fact met ten times in this period, but the minutes of the two meetings which took place between 27 February and 5 April 1973 were unavailable at the time of writing.

60 Crosland, as stated, attended four out of eight meetings held for which the minutes were available at the time of writing – 28 November 1972, 27 February, 5 and 30 April 1973; Dell also attended four meetings – 23 January and 30 April 1973 – but of the two had a far better record of attendance from the date of Crosland's co-option as a member of the subcommittee as of 13 July 1971. Of the 20 meetings held between that date and 30 April 1973, for which the minutes were available at the time of writing, Dell attended 14 meetings to Crosland's eight. LPA Industrial Policy Subcommittee, Minutes and Papers, 28 April 1971–28 November 1972; NEC Minutes, 24 January–23 May 1973.

61 Crosland, *Socialism Now*, p. 17.

62 Wilson subsequently observed how the research programme, to his obvious distaste, had produced 'grandiose proposals for nationalising anything and pretty nearly everything'. H. Wilson, *Final Term: The Labour Government 1974–76* (London, Weidenfeld & Nicolson, 1979), p. 28.

63 Hatfield, *The House the Left Built*, p. 171.
64 NEC, *Labour's Programme 1973*, p. 6.
65 NEC, *Labour's Programme 1973*, p. 7. Tony Benn worked patiently for the inclusion of this phrase in the document, as can be seen from his diary entries for 17 March and 7 and 14 May 1973. T. Benn, *Against the Tide: Diaries 1973–76* (London, Hutchinson, 1989), pp. 11, 26 and 32. It also featured prominently in his speech to conference in October 1973, on which occasion he told delegates that the document's proposals on industrial policy 'occupies a central place in meeting our central objective of bringing about the fundamental and irreversible shift in the balance of wealth and power in favour of working people and their families'. LPAR, 1973, p. 185.
66 'Shirley Williams attacked the Industrial Powers Bill as being undemocratic. Harold Lever said he was reminded of a corporate state.' Lever was in favour of deleting the phrase 'irreversible transfer of wealth and power'. Benn, *Against the Tide*, 14 May 1973, pp. 32–3.
67 NEC, *Labour's Programme 1973*, p. 8. Emil Savundra, Bloom and Cornfeld were each caught up in private-sector financial scandals in the late 1960s and early 1970s.
68 The Croslandites/revisionists continued to wrestle with this problem in opposition. In his Fabian pamphlet of January 1971, Crosland argued that working-class people desired such things as washing-machines, cars and package holidays 'because the things are desirable in themselves'. Crosland, 'A Social-Democratic Britain', in Crosland, *Socialism Now*, p. 79. Peter Stephenson argued that greater equality would not bring affluence.

> I believe that at present, and for some considerable time to come, the easiest way for a manual worker to feel he has individual human dignity is to have money in his pocket over whose spending he has discretion free from any pressures of necessity.
>
> In my working-class childhood in Yorkshire, there was no doubt about what created social distinctions: it was money. And that was far less corrosive of the dignity of the working man than the subtle snobberies of the South. In so far as we now have a more generally materialistic society where the worker, when he has got money to spend, can come nearer to enjoying an equal role with people from other social classes than ever before. Social provision does not have the same impact. Inevitably, it comes from the hands of those who run society, even though they may have impeccable socialist motives. It is necessary for the attainment of socialism that an increasing proportion of national income should go through social hands; we all accept this. But when faced with the average man's desire to keep money to spend for himself, to buy attention for himself, we should try to show compassion, not impatience.

P. Stephenson, 'Money to Spend on Himself', *Socialist Commentary* (September 1970), pp. 8–9.
69 See NEC, *Labour's Programme 1973*, pp. 11–12. Hatfield also reproduces this section of the NEC document in *The House the Left Built*, pp. 172–4.
70 These were: Full Employment; Prices; Housing; Equality; Welfare; Education; Economic Development.
71 NEC, *Labour's Programme 1973*, p. 11.

72 Walker's Bill received the royal assent in October 1972 and came into effect in April 1974. The number of counties was reduced from 58 to 54, and the number of lesser units from 1,300 to 400. Campbell, *Edward Heath*, p. 380.

73 For a comparison see *Labour's Programme 1973*, p. 11, and *Labour's Programme for Britain 1972*, p. 7.

74 NEC, *Labour's Programme 1973*, p. 12.

75 LPA, PLP, Minutes, 11 July 1973.

76 LPA, PLP, Minutes, 27 July 1972.

77 NEC, *Labour's Programme 1973*, p. 12.

78 Castle, *The Castle Diaries*, 6 March 1974, p. 429.

79 LPA, PLP, Minutes, 11 July 1973.

80 For a comparison of the two documents see NEC, *Labour's Programme 1973*, pp. 13–39, and Labour Party, *Let Us Work Together – Labour's Way out of the Crisis*, February 1974, in Craig, *British General Election Manifestos*, pp. 398–406.

81 NEC, *Labour's Programme 1973*, pp. 13–33.

82 See Benn's policy paper presented at the Industrial Policy Subcommittee meeting of 27 March 1973. RD./March 1973 'Industrial Power and Industrial Policy'. The minutes of this meeting were unavailable at the time of writing.

83 NEC, *Labour's Programme 1973*, pp. 18–19.

84 Benn, 'Heath's spadework for socialism'. The 17 new areas of control Benn referred to derived from a number of legislative measures, for example: 'Power to nationalise' (Rolls-Royce (Purchase) Act 1971), which he described as 'A stark method of acquisition very different from the elaborate and detailed nationalisation Acts of the past without generous compensation for shareholders, workers or subcontractors', and 'Power to appoint a Commissioner', for which provision had been made in the Housing Finance Act for the Secretary of State to appoint a Housing Commissioner if an authority failed to comply with the duties set out by government order. Benn regarded the latter as 'an entirely new power which could have implications for industry'. Ultimately, several of the new powers were included in Labour's new Industry Act as proposed in *Labour's Programme 1973*.

85 Benn, 'Heath's spadework for socialism'.

86 LPA, PLP, Minutes, 11 July 1973.

87 Specifically, the manifesto failed to give any details as to the content of the planned Industry Bill, or about planning agreements.

88 Denis Healey, who as Chancellor of the Exchequer 1974–79 was responsible for implementing the economic aspects of the party's agreement with the TUC on the social wage, writes:

> When I introduced my third budget in April 1975, I pointed out that the Government had carried out its side of the Social Contract by repealing Heath's anti-union legislation, by starting on the redistribution of wealth and income through its tax changes, and by increasing old age pensions and other benefits. In fact the value of the services provided by the Government, which we tried to get people to see as their 'social wage' amounted to about £1,000 a year for every member of the working population. But the unions defaulted on their part of the contract. Len Murray, the General Secretary of the TUC, had warned me in February that the going rate for wage increases was already thirty per cent, although inflation was still only twenty per cent. Because earnings were rising so much faster than prices, at a time when the increased price of oil and other commodities had cut

our real national income by about four per cent, our balance of payments deficit had swollen to 33.8 billion, some five per cent of GDP. By June inflation had risen to twenty-six per cent and basic hourly wage rates were up thirty-two per cent on the year. A more effective policy for controlling wage increases was now an absolute precondition for saving the economy as a whole.

Healey, *The Time of My Life*, p. 394.
89 Both Callaghan and Jenkins used this expression in opposition when advocating the adoption of an incomes policy of some description other than voluntary. See LPAR, 1970, pp. 164, 226.
90 NEC, *Labour's Programme 1973*, p. 24.
91 Agreements reached between the Labour Party and the TUC listed in the NEC document included: price controls, particularly on food and with subsidies where necessary; a large and immediate increase in pensions; the abolition of prescription charges; an increase in housebuilding; public ownership of land; subsidised fares on public transport; a massive expansion in industrial training; repeal of the Industrial Relations and Housing Finance Acts and so on. See NEC, *Labour's Programme 1973*, p. 14 for a full list. These were commitments the parliamentary leadership would have no option but to keep. None of the above would go the way of planning agreements, for example.
92 NEC, *Labour's Programme 1973*, pp. 33–4.
93 'Category 1 firms are defined in the White Paper on Phase Two of the Freeze (Cmnd 5267) as those enterprises in manufacturing, mining, public utilities, transport, postal services and telecommunications, whose sales in the domestic market have a value of more than £50m per year.' Labour Party, *The National Enterprise Board – Labour's State Holding Company: Report of a Labour Party Study Group* (London, 1973), p. 21, n. 1.
94 NEC, *Labour's Programme 1973*, p. 34.
95 Labour Party, *The National Enterprise Board – Labour's State Holding Company: Report of a Labour Party Study Group*, p. 21.
96 When conference endorsed *Economic Strategy, Growth and Unemployment*, the creation of a State Holding Company became party policy.
97 RD.271/February 1972 'The State Holding Company', by Holland and Pryke, pp. 11 and 17, LPA, Industrial Policy Subcommittee, Minutes and Papers, 15 February–28 November 1972.
98 Hatfield, *The House the Left Built*, p. 111.
99 NEC, *Labour's Programme for Britain 1972*, p. 5.
100 LPAR, 1973, p. 167. For an account of the 'twenty-five' companies episode, see Hatfield, *The House the Left Built*, pp. 171–90.
101 'We're now entirely free to do what we like', he added. Benn, *Against the Tide*, 9 July 1974, p. 194. Interviewed on BBC Radio 4 in January 1973, Callaghan stated that he had never 'taken the view that what Conference says must always be holy writ. If you're elected by Conference you're elected to give them advice too, and you may have to go back to Conference and say, look, we've tried our best to meet what you want done, but we're sorry, it can't be done and we must advise you accordingly. Leadership isn't just a question of taking what the Conference tells you to do and doing it, it also means you've got to give your best and honest advice to the Conference.' Tape transcript, 'Talking Politics', BBC Radio 4, 6 January 1973. LPA, TPP, D/PITT/C44.

102 Hatfield, *The House the Left Built*, p. 201.
103 'Report of joint meeting of the National Executive Committee and the Parliamentary Committee and other Parliamentary Spokesmen, held on Wednesday, 16 May 1973', p. 6, LPA.
104 In January 1973 the TUC–Labour Party Liaison Committee issued a joint statement, *Economic Policy and the Cost of Living*, which committed a future Labour government to increase pensions to £10 per week for a single person, and £16 per week for a married couple. See TUC–Labour Party Liaison Committee, *Economic Policy and the Cost of Living*, in TUC Report, 1973, pp. 313–14.
105 'Report of joint meeting of the National Executive Committee and the Parliamentary Committee and other Parliamentary Spokesmen, held on Wednesday, 16 May 1973', p. 5, LPA.
106 *Economic Policy and the Cost of Living* was published in January 1973. The NEC policy document was published on 7 June 1973.
107 NEC, *Labour's Programme 1973*, p. 10.
108 'Report of joint meeting of the National Executive Committee and the Parliamentary Committee and other Parliamentary Spokesmen, held on Wednesday, 16 May 1973', p. 6, LPA.
109 *Labour's Programme 1973* estimated that up to £4,000 million might be raised by cancelling capital projects such as Maplin Airport and London motorways. NEC, *Labour's Programme 1973*, p. 12.
110 'Report of joint meeting of the National Executive Committee and the Parliamentary Committee and other Parliamentary Spokesmen, held on Wednesday, 16 May 1973', p. 9, LPA. This was exactly the thinking Stuart Holland had sought to dispose of in his 1972 policy paper 'Planning and Policy Coordination', in which he wrote that the positive support of the movement 'only seems probable if the Party is seen to be committed to a major advance in intervention of the kind which could credibly change the future rather than rely on more favourable circumstances to permit loosely coordinated policies to prove more effective than the last time round'. RD.315/March 1972, 'Planning and Policy Coordination', by Stuart Holland. LPA, Industrial Policy Subcommittee, Minutes and Papers, 15 February–28 November 1972. Healey was apparently willing to allow a Labour government once more to be governed by the circumstances of the day.
111 The revisionists hoped to finance Labour's social expenditure from higher growth, which proved unattainable, at least consistently so. Yet despite this they continued to deny that the realisation of their social policies rested on revenue raised from taxation, most famously so during the 1959 general election campaign when Gaitskell claimed that Labour's programme could be paid for without requiring an increase in taxation. See D. Butler and R. Rose, *The British General Election of 1959* (London, Macmillan, 1960), pp. 59–63. For an analysis of Labour's tax policies 1964–70, see E. Shaw, *The Labour Party since 1945* (Oxford, Blackwell, 1996), pp. 70–93.
112 'Report of joint meeting of the National Executive Committee and the Parliamentary Committee and other Parliamentary Spokesmen, held on Wednesday, 16 May 1973', p. 9, LPA.
113 Ibid.
114 Ibid.

7

PARLIAMENTARY
FACTIONALISM 1970–74:
THE JENKINSITES

The NEC research programme was dominated by the NEC and the Research Department, yet the parliamentary faction that looked upon Roy Jenkins as its natural leader did not respond organisationally to this development. The Jenkinsites included among their number several of the key organisers of the Campaign for Democratic Socialism (CDS), the organisation formed in 1960 to reverse the vote at conference that year in support of a unilateralist defence policy. The reason these individuals did not organise in opposition along similar lines, to meet the intellectual challenge provided by left-wing proposals on economic and industrial policy matters, is explained within the context of their primary objective of securing British membership of the Common Market. They achieved this in defiance of official party policy, a course of action which resulted in their marginalisation within the PLP and Jenkins's resignation as deputy leader.

Pre-history: the Campaign for Democratic Socialism[1]

In February 1960 Bill Rodgers and Dick Taverne, parliamentary candidates for Labour in 1957 and 1959 respectively[2] organised a letter of support for Hugh Gaitskell in the aftermath of the Labour leader's failed attempt the previous year to revise Clause IV of the party's constitution.[3] Signatories to this letter were a group of young parliamentary candidates who were determined, in the wake of eight wasted years in opposition and the general election defeat of 1959, to make one last effort to change the Labour Party, and who believed they had been 'rather badly let down by some senior members of the Party particularly in Parliament who ought to have been very actively supporting Gaitskell'. Rodgers had observed how during the campaign on Clause IV, 'speeches had been made by leading members of the Party . . . which had no relation to what Hugh Gaitskell was saying, although they were meant to be supportive'.[4]

Between February and October 1960 Rodgers and Taverne, together with Michael Shanks of the *Financial Times* and Ivan Yates of *Reynolds*

News, were in contact with Gaitskell's closest supporters at Westminster – Tony Crosland, Douglas Jay, Roy Jenkins and Patrick Gordon Walker – and a second group of like-minded Gaitskell supporters in Oxford – Philip Williams of Nuffield College, Frank Pickstock, a local Oxford councillor, Ron Owen of Oxford City Council and Brian Walden, former chairman of the National Association of Labour Student Organisations.[5] 'Essentially the cause lay in our wish to provide a rallying point for revisionists or Croslandites, the younger generation who had been very much inspired by Crosland's *The Future of Socialism*.'[6]

Two weeks after Gaitskell was defeated on defence at conference in October 1960,[7] Rodgers, Pickstock and Denis Howell[8] published a manifesto appealing for grass-roots organisation to resist the leftward trend in the party.[9] 'All of us working in constituencies were conscious that the voices raised were not rank and file at all', Rodgers told journalists present at the launch. 'They were the voices of a loud, persistent and organised minority.'[10] On 24 November, the Campaign for Democratic Socialism was officially launched with Rodgers as its chairman. CDS, writes Stephen Haseler, 'saw that there was a real need for an alternative pressure group to Victory for Socialism, *Tribune*, and the Campaign for Nuclear Disarmament. It was a deeply held view that one of the reasons for the unilateralist victory at Scarborough was that these pressure groups had, up until 1960, been subjected to no organised opposition at grass-roots level.'[11]

Rodgers and his colleagues were not natural apparatchiks, 'although that is what Tony Crosland made us for a short while'.[12] CDS did what its factional opponents on the left had always done, but did it better and with greater sophistication.[13] Witnessing the success of the *Tribune* Brains Trusts[14] and the impact of *Tribune*, which appeared in the constituencies each week telling activists 'what the issues were to be',[15] Rodgers's response was to challenge Crosland: 'Why aren't we like that?' Consequently, CDS briefed heavily and produced its own broadsheet, *Campaign*, for distribution among its supporters. Speeches were written 'to be delivered at meetings and for Trade Unions'.[16] The defeat on defence was accordingly reversed at conference in 1961. Gaitskell had been saved, *The Spectator* concluded,

> by a combination of his own courage, the astonishing discovery of an enormous reservoir of fiercely loyal support... and above all, by the Campaign for Democratic Socialism who have gone out into the field and organised and drilled and persuaded and canvassed and generally put their backs into it.[17]

In this way the myth was born. The reversal of the 1960 vote supporting unilateralism had ceased to be in doubt from the moment the unions began to swing behind the party leader, 'so that by July it was clear that the

1961 Blackpool conference was going to be as triumphant a victory for Gaitskell as the 1960 Scarborough one had been a triumphant defeat'.[18] Significantly, CDS was perceived to have influenced the outcome.

After Blackpool the twin aims of CDS continued to be the modernisation of the Labour Party and the adoption of CDS-friendly parliamentary candidates.[19] In respect of the latter, the targeting of regional organisers paid off handsomely. Of the 29 Labour MPs returned in by-elections in the 1959–64 Parliament, 14 were closely associated with CDS and a further nine were firmly on the right and 'loyalist'.[20] Taverne was one such candidate. His Lincoln seat fell within 'the great barony of Jim Cattermole', the East Midlands regional organiser.[21] Taverne's selection 'was just one example of the attempts by CDS to manipulate the candidate selection process to its advantage. In its national campaign it had the support of the majority of the Labour Party's regional organisers (seven of the 12 were sympathetic to CDS in 1961), persons with a key role in the candidate selection process.'[22]

CDS was diverted by the defence issue from its original objective and was largely unsuccessful in its attempts to modernise the Labour Party.[23] Clause IV was retained unaltered, and 'the commitment to change the composition of the NEC, to get Mikardo and Driberg off the NEC, failed'.[24] An opportunity was missed. After the 1959 general election defeat Gaitskell, in whom the revisionists invested so much hope for the future of the party, had 'had enough personal standing and enough assent from his colleagues to seek structural changes strengthening him for future battles: an appointed parliamentary committee certainly, perhaps even a reconstituted NEC representing directly both the Party in the country and that at Westminster. Instead he chose to assault a cherished myth. "We were wrong (*all* of us)," wrote Crosland, "to go for *doctrine*; we should have gone for *power*." '[25]

Organising for opposition: the deputy leadership

On 25 June 1970, one week after Labour's general election defeat, a meeting was held at Dick Taverne's London flat to discuss whether or not Roy Jenkins should contest the deputy leadership (George Brown having lost his seat) and the Labour Party's likely attitude to the Common Market in opposition. In addition to Taverne, those present included Jenkins, George Thomson, Bill Rodgers, David Marquand and David Owen, among others.[26] Out of this meeting, writes Jenkins,

> there emerged the nucleus of a campaign organisation and indeed of the continuing focus of the committed pro-Europeans in the parliamentary Labour Party. This group became the 'Walston group', so called because of occasional meetings in the

Albany apartment of Lord Walston, which continued at least until the leadership election of March 1976, and even a few times thereafter.[27]

Less than a fortnight after this meeting Jenkins was elected deputy leader of the Labour Party. Prominent among those MPs openly committed to the former Chancellor succeeding Harold Wilson as leader were Rodgers and Taverne, whose CDS past appeared to perpetually unnerve the party leader: 'I don't know why I go on,' Wilson is reported to have remarked in July 1971 at the height of his troubles over the Common Market, 'but I'll smash CDS before I go.'[28] Wilson's words demonstrated the negative impact of his deputy's spectacular rise in the PLP (for which Wilson, ironically, was responsible)[29] and his ability to inspire loyalty in Labour's most able (and notorious) organisers and likely future ministers. Confirmed Jenkins supporters in the PLP included, in addition to Rodgers and Taverne, David Marquand, David Owen,[30] George Thomson, Tom Bradley, Robert Maclennan, Dickson Mabon, Roy Hattersley and, after his election to Parliament in 1973, Giles Radice.[31] This support was supplemented – unusually so for a British politician[32] – by an extra-parliamentary entourage. This was, write Crewe and King,

> a loose and disparate grouping, and its membership altered gradually over the years. Different people were associated with it to different degrees. At any one time it might include John Harris (Lord Harris of Greenwich), Jenkins' former press adviser who had served under him as a minister at the Home Office: Anthony Lester, one of Britain's leading civil-rights lawyers: and a number of younger Labour activists, such as Clive Lindley, Colin Phipps, Jim Daly, Michael Barnes and Matthew Oakeshott.[33]

As Jenkins's vote in the ballot for the deputy leadership revealed, in a run-off against a left-wing candidate he could command the support of a majority of the PLP. But it is impossible to calculate exactly how many of the 133 MPs who voted for him on 8 July 1970 were 100 per cent for him in all circumstances. Crucially, on this occasion, the PLP was voting for a new deputy rather than a new leader. The level of support he received as the sole candidate of the centre-right no doubt exaggerated his true strength.[34]

In opposition two groups facilitated activity in support of Jenkins. The first, the 1963 Club, was a dining club established by Rodgers and Denis Howell in memory of Hugh Gaitskell, which met once a month for informal discussions when the House of Commons was sitting. Among those who attended were Jenkins, Tony Crosland, Douglas Jay, Patrick Gordon Walker, Taverne, Bradley, Dickson Mabon, Marquand, Owen, Maclennan,

Charlie Pannell and Jack Diamond, not all of whom had metamorphosised into fully fledged devotees of the former Chancellor.[35] Less overt than the meetings of the 1963 Club were the activities of a shifting group of ten or so MPs who met regularly at each other's homes over lunch in this period. These lunches were an extension of those occasionally held at the home of Lord Walston, and were attended by Rodgers, Marquand, Owen, Maclennan and Mabon certainly, by Taverne initially, and also by several MPs who were not among the 69 pro-Market rebels in the 28 October 1971 vote,[36] but who had 'previously made clear their pro-Market views on many occasions'.[37]

Jenkins's supporters, therefore, can be characterised by the informality of their networking at Westminster. Primarily they were friends who spoke constantly and confided in one another. A formal structure, be it the taking of either minutes or formal decisions, was not necessary. Given the personnel, this naturally gave rise to suspicions within the Labour Party of secret campaigns and a hidden agenda, even though the individuals concerned could not have been more open in their twin desires to see Jenkins succeed Wilson, and Britain join the Common Market.

The Common Market and high politics

Certain parallels between CDS and pro-Jenkins activity in opposition can be drawn. Just as CDS was diverted from modernising the Labour Party by the debate on defence, so were the former Chancellor's supporters diverted from their objective of a Jenkins-led party (and all that might have entailed for Labour's ideology) by the debate on the Common Market. The more they pursued their European ideal at the expense of party unity, the more remote Jenkins's chances of succeeding or replacing Wilson became. Jenkins, in his own view, 'held the lead position on the inside track for the succession to Wilson' from 1968 until his resignation from the Shadow Cabinet and as deputy leader in April 1972,[38] a point on which not all of his contemporaries agree,[39] but, as it transpired, his personal ambition proved irreconcilable with his sense of the national interest. At a meeting of the PLP on 19 July 1971, he demonstrated his leadership qualities to brilliant effect but for a cause increasingly perceived as being closer to his heart than the Labour Party – Europe. The impact of his exhortation to his parliamentary colleagues at this meeting to 'face the problem realistically and look beyond the narrow political considerations of the moment',[40] in Benn's estimation, 'changed the political situation in the Party at one stroke'. Jenkins, he surmised (accurately as it turned out), would not succeed Wilson because 'by splitting the Party in the way he has done, I think he will find that people won't forgive him; certainly the Left will never forgive him'.[41]

Benn's dire prognosis was initially refuted by the results of the November 1971 ballots for the deputy leadership and the chair of the PLP, and by the

December ballot for the Shadow Cabinet. In November, Jenkins again defeated Foot to retain his position as deputy leader, and Douglas Houghton rebuffed Norman Pentland's challenge for the chair of the PLP. The following month Shirley Williams, Harold Lever and George Thomson, all prominent pro-Marketeers, were re-elected to the Shadow Cabinet, increasing their poll of the previous year by 15, 14 and 19 votes, to secure third, seventh and ninth place respectively.[42] These results demolished Callaghan's opportunistic argument that a pro-Market stance in defiance of conference 'would immolate the Party and thoroughly upset the constituencies which would have consequences for the Shadow Cabinet elections'.[43] The Shadow Cabinet ballot bluntly underlined the strength of Jenkins's argument that if the PLP held firm on Europe there was little the NEC, conference or the unions could do about it. Jenkins, being Jenkins, phrased it high-mindedly in terms of character and integrity. 'It is now obvious', noted Tony Benn, 'that the Common Marketeers have been able to defy the PLP and get re-elected and there is something very interesting in that. It means Bill Rodgers's CDS group have got a majority in the PLP and that is something one will have to accept.'[44]

On the issue of British membership of the Common Market, a majority of the centre of the PLP were loyal to the party leader and tacitly endorsed his deliberately vague leadership, but support for the pro-Marketeers was otherwise natural. The pro-Market The Economist interpreted the results of the parliamentary ballots as an acknowledgement that from amid the ranks of the pro-Marketeers would be drawn 'the ministerial backbone of a future Labour government'.[45] This Jenkins's supporters themselves believed. A general election victory would carry them into their 'rightful heritage once more', the administrative talents among their number enabling them to work their way back into the key positions of power.[46] Benn understandably found this faith in high politics 'very interesting', for it ran counter to his own message since June 1970 'that power must be passed to the people'.[47] In a climate in which Tribune was instructing its readership how constituency parties could rid themselves of their pro-Market MPs when it came to readoption,[48] the parliamentary secret ballots enabled the centre of the PLP to realign with the right without fear of retribution from the constituencies and without risk of splitting the party and isolating the party leader, as would almost certainly have been the case had the centre-right alliance held over the Common Market.

The marginalisation of Jenkins and his supporters in the PLP

The pro-Market rebellion of 28 October 1971 marginalised Jenkins and his supporters. None of them remained any less committed to the Labour Party, but each had openly identified themselves with a cause which their factional opponents were able to argue had first call on their loyalty. The pro-Marketeers in fact committed no greater sacrilege than to refuse to respect a fake PLP majority against entry. They believed that, in addition to the 69 who voted for entry and the 20 who abstained, at least another 40 or 50 favoured entry and that these MPs knew the PLP decision to vote against entry was nonsense.[49]

On the eve of the 28 October 1971 vote, Wilson had called for unity, rejecting any suggestion of reprisals and recriminations, expressing his belief in a 'united Party which evaluates and evokes the talents of each member, on the basis of the part he can play in the future of this Socialist Movement of ours'.[50] An obvious candidate for reprisal was Rodgers, lauded in *The Times* as the 'Supreme Marketeer' and 'plus Royalist que le Roi'.[51] Rodgers received Wilson's personal assurance that his pro-Market views provided no impediment to his remaining on Labour's front bench,[52] yet on 19 January 1972, along with several pro-Market colleagues, he was sacked.[53] This, writes David Owen,

> was a direct challenge to Roy Jenkins for Bill had acted as chief of staff of the pro-market campaign and was known to be very close to Roy. But, cleverly, Wilson did reappoint Dick Taverne. It was a neatly judged knifing of Roy Jenkins, diminishing him without provoking him. Other people who had voted for the European Community, including Cledwyn Hughes, a former Cabinet Minister, and four other junior spokesmen, one of them David Marquand, were not reappointed. Wilson's action showed how impotent Roy had become as Deputy Leader. People tempted to support him began to wonder who he could shelter if he had not got the authority to protect even Bill Rodgers.[54]

Wilson may have been settling old scores and nothing more, particularly so in the case of Rodgers who, in the course of the previous year, had appeared impervious to the authority of the elected leader of the parliamentary party, but the cull not only met with the approval of a significant section of the PLP, but also appeared to signal that open season on Jenkins and his supporters had begun. The redistribution of power in the PLP which resulted from the centre-left alliance on the Common Market thus facilitated the marginalisation of this faction.

Despite Jenkins's successes in the deputy leadership ballots of 1970 and 1971, and the attendant successes of Houghton, Williams, Lever and Thomson, he and his supporters had begun to lose ground within the party almost immediately after the general election defeat in 1970. At *New Statesman*, Richard Crossman lost no time in bringing the paper out against membership of the Common Market, a largely insignificant gesture in itself, but one which set the tone for the months to follow.

In September 1970 the parliamentary leadership and the NEC managed to stave off a hostile TGWU resolution at Blackpool opposing membership by only 95,000 votes.[55] Six weeks later Tony Benn published an open letter to his Bristol South-East constituents arguing the case for a referendum to determine the issue of British membership.[56] The difficulty facing the pro-Marketeers in holding the party to the existing policy was summed up by Alan Lee Williams, the former MP for Hornchurch,[57] in an article reporting from the Scottish TUC for *Europe Left* the journal of the Labour Committee for Europe (LCE):[58] 'The debate was characterised by lies, half truths, prejudices, selected facts and CP [Communist Party] jargon (exploitation of the Third World, inherent contradictions in the capitalist system of the Common Market, a threat to world peace, Common Market a capitalist group stemming the tide of socialism etc.). These speeches were warmly received by a majority of the delegates.'[59]

Socialist Commentary accused the left of using the Common Market as 'a peg and a pretext for an attempt to make life in the Party as difficult as possible for men who are an important part of the coalition of views that the Party must contain'.[60] Jenkins and his supporters found it increasingly difficult to maintain their position in the party. Throughout opposition they were hounded by a new generation of left-wing MPs 'who had won or held their seats despite, rather than because of, the record of the Labour Government'.[61] This 'Polytechnic Brigade' (as they were dubbed by Rodgers) were both articulate and highly motivated, and receptive to the uncompromising rhetoric of Jack Jones and Hugh Scanlon.[62] This difficulty was compounded by a lack of support for entry from any of the party's official institutions. The Shadow Cabinet, the PLP, conference and the NEC all officially opposed membership on the Heath terms, as did the TUC. In the constituencies, opposition to the Common Market owed much to worries about higher food prices, a traditional Labour concern.[63] Typically, many CLPs in best Bevanite tradition took their lead on the issue 'from who said what, not necessarily what was said'.[64]

Jenkins and his supporters were the victims of their own consistency. In opposition they continued to argue the case for British membership just as they had done in government, but in doing so they echoed the words of 'intensely unpopular' Conservative ministers.[65] Worse still, many of Heath's policies were an extension of those of the Labour government in which the same individuals had featured prominently. Higher rents, the withdrawal of school milk, the reform of industrial relations, prescription charges, rising prices and an unacceptably high level of unemployment all smacked in one form or another of the Labour government's betrayal of its manifesto promises.[66] 'Once the lid was taken off,... where the Labour pro-Europeans were putting forward arguments which were mainly seen as Tory arguments, then the passions were able to grow and manifest themselves.'[67] It did not help that Jenkins and his colleagues received plaudits from the pro-Market establishment press, or that the Labour Committee for Europe, of which Jenkins was joint president along with George Brown and Michael Stewart, had access to substantial funds, the source of which was not the Labour Party.[68] Jenkins may well have been, in Benn's words, 'the hero of every drawing room',[69] but his problem was that of Gaitskell in 1962 in reverse; all the wrong people were cheering.[70]

Equally damaging to the pro-Jenkins camp at times was a tendency to inadvertently undermine its own position. Initially in opposition Jenkins found the position on the NEC 'just tolerable'[71] and along with Wilson sought to resist the gradual build-up of anti-Market sentiment within the party. To this end the International Subcommittee of the NEC was persuaded (with some difficulty) on 10 November 1970 to renew Labour's affiliation to the Monnet Committee for the United States of Europe.[72] But by the time the NEC discussed whether or not to hold a special conference on the Common Market on 23 June 1971, Jenkins's resistance to the proposal, along with that of Wilson, was defeated by the actions of a confirmed pro-Market ally. It was Shirley Williams, writes Jenkins, 'who gave us a special conference ... she was absolutely sound on the merits of the issue, but she decided on democratic rights that we have a special conference. So she suddenly defected and by a majority of one we had a special conference.'[73]

The consequence of Williams's action was not the special conference itself, which Jenkins concedes 'did not in fact do much harm', but that the occasion of the conference required a speech from Wilson 'which while pedestrian, took him quietly almost out of intellectual hailing distance with us'. Prior to the special conference, at a private meeting on 9 June 1971, Jenkins had appealed to Wilson to 'do a Gaitskell' and take 'the hard, difficult, consistent, unpopular line' by sticking to the pro-Market policy of the Labour government.[74] Wilson certainly knew the value of the pro-Marketeers, for as *The Economist* spelt out, they numbered 'far, far more of the men and women who would be vital to a future Labour Government' than did the anti-Marketeers, adding that 'age and parliamentary clout are on the side of the pro-Marketeers'.[75] Had he responded positively to Jenkins's appeal he would undoubtedly have carried a majority of the PLP with him, as the scale of the 28 October 1971 rebellion indicated, but in so doing he would have finally cut his links with the left and rendered himself vulnerable to the putsch his deputy was so keen to assure him would not follow from the demonstration of leadership he advocated.[76]

Intellectually Wilson sided with the wrong faction over the Common Market and no doubt knew it. *The Economist* informed its readers that 'he could have achieved greater unity by sticking to his Common Market convictions'.[77] Realistically Wilson had little choice. The TUC had voted against entry, and he was not, writes Pimlott, 'so naive as to imagine that he could purchase his own survival by taking the very risky step of backing the pro-European cause'.[78] Wilson shadowed Callaghan on the Common Market issue, and where Callaghan went 'so would much Centrist, non-intellectual, and trade union opinion'.[79] And without the support of the party leader, the fate of Jenkins and his supporters was sealed.

The road to resignation[80]

However much people wrote or spoke of Jenkins as the next Labour leader, Wilson remained the elected incumbent. Many of the party's ablest young MPs were dedicated to the former Chancellor and he remained, as his re-election as deputy leader in November 1971 demonstrated, immensely powerful in the PLP. But among those who did not follow him into the 'aye' lobby on the night of 28 October 1971 were Callaghan, Healey and Crosland,[81] the latter two having been among the 100 Labour signatories of a letter in support of British membership published in *The Guardian* on 11 May 1971, before Wilson's decision to oppose entry had become known.[82] Had Callaghan, Healey and Crosland voted with Jenkins, Wilson's position would have been untenable. But they did not and Jenkins was sunk.

Once Wilson adopted an anti-Market position (which extended to an acceptance of Benn's referendum proposal) pressure on Jenkins both on the NEC and the Shadow Cabinet increased. On 29 March 1972 the NEC met to appoint a successor to Sir Harry Nicholas, the party's general secretary, the expectation being that Gwyn Morgan, Nicholas's deputy and the candidate of moderate opinion in the PLP, would succeed him. Wilson's decision to oppose the pro-Market Morgan's candidature signalled for the first time that being pro-Market was a bar to preferment at party official level (as was also, on this occasion, a candidate's close association with both Jenkins and Callaghan). The post went instead to Ron Hayward, who was 'not so much left-wing as without intellectual ballast and incapable of seeing beyond the narrowest confines of party politics',[83] and whose credentials were decisively championed by Benn in his capacity as chairman of the party that year.[84] Having been, in Jenkins's words, 'sand-bagged in the morning [the pro-Europeans] then proceeded to be garotted in the afternoon'.[85] At a meeting of the Shadow Cabinet held later the same day, Benn's proposal for a referendum on Britain's membership of the Common Market was approved by eight votes to six,[86] overturning a vote of eight to four against taken only a fortnight earlier on 15 March 1972.[87] In between, Benn's proposal had remained on the table on the initiative of the party leader, who had originally opposed it.[88] By his actions Wilson joined the ranks of Jenkins's tormentors. As Jenkins has written:

> I had decided – we all agreed that this meant the hard-line antis
> on the Shadow Cabinet were determined to use their majority,

199

which they now had – particularly now Wilson had swung in favour – to do everything in their power, they were not doing it with any restraint from the party position, to erect a series of hoops which we would have to spend the summer jumping through. If we let that go on, it would have been a complete erosion of one's position in the country.[89]

Neither Jenkins nor his allies in the Shadow Cabinet wanted to resign. They wanted 'as far as we possibly could to maintain our position on the Shadow Cabinet, to maintain the balance of power within the Labour Party', to get Britain into the Common Market and then defeat the Conservative government. Resignation was a tactical error, but Jenkins was damned out of his own mouth.[90] Asked by Bruce Millan at a meeting of the PLP on 4 November 1971 (prior to the deputy leadership ballot) what his future voting intentions on the Common Market were likely to be, he volunteered that he could not 'go against majority decisions and remain' in his post.[91] He did not support the Shadow Cabinet decision of 29 March 1972, and accordingly resigned as deputy leader, and from the Shadow Cabinet along with George Thomson and Harold Lever, on 10 April 1972.

The marginalisation of Jenkins and his supporters in the PLP: after Gaitskell

How was it that such a powerful section of right-wing opinion in the PLP was first marginalised and then excluded from the centre of power in the party? Jenkins after all was a central figure in the Gaitskellite faction which had dominated the party since 1955 and which, in alliance with the centre of the PLP, continued after Labour's defeat in 1970 to hold virtually every significant position in the upper echelons of the Labour Party with the exception of the office of the leader itself. Jenkins was the overwhelming choice of the PLP to succeed George Brown as deputy leader, and in the ballot for the Shadow Cabinet the first three places were filled by Callaghan, Healey and Crosland. All four men were proteges of Hugh Dalton.[92] The prominence of this centre-right group of senior MPs in 1970, and the likelihood of one of their number emerging to eventually succeed Wilson, in part compensated for the fact that the party leader had not been their first choice to replace Gaitskell in 1963. However, none of them had so objected to Wilson that he had felt compelled to decline Wilson's offer of a seat in his Cabinet.

The demise of Labour's right wing was determined by the double rupture of the alliance which brought Gaitskell the leadership. First, the Gaitskellite faction lost the support of the TGWU after 1956, which under the leadership of Frank Cousins transferred its allegiance to the left.[93] Second, after 1970, the pro-Market right lost the support of the centre of the PLP over the issue of the Common Market. In between, it lost the leader, Gaitskell. The loss of the TGWU was a blow to the right and to Gaitskell personally. Many of the problems he faced as leader after 1959 derived from the fact that his attempt to revise Clause IV had displeased Cousins. The latter was initially appeased by the election of Wilson as leader, and it was not until 1966 and the seamen's strike that the parliamentary leadership was once again troubled by the unions.[94] The split between the right and centre of the PLP was more serious. This had first threatened in 1962, when Gaitskell's decision to oppose British entry cost him the support of nearly all of his most dedicated supporters on the right,[95] but significantly not that of the centre of the PLP. On that occasion the British application was rejected, and by January 1963 Gaitskell was dead. The issue receded in importance, but the fault lines of a future split – with the right in a minority – had been identified.

When the Common Market once more became the dominant political issue of the day after 1970 Wilson, ironically, given Jenkins's appeal to him to do a Gaitskell over Europe,[96] did precisely that but to the latter's horror chose the 1962 anti-Common Market model, rather than the 1960 anti-left model his deputy had had in mind. Wilson's decision to oppose entry transformed the balance of power in the PLP. The centre-left majority against entry headed by the party leader and bolstered by Callaghan, although temporary, made a minority of the right wing which, in alliance with the centre, could otherwise have expected to be in a majority on virtually all other policy issues. What was in theory still a position of strength, proved insufficient in the face of a determined campaign by the left to wrest control of policy in the PLP from the revisionists. Writing in *Political Quarterly*, John Mackintosh observed that, after the vote of 28 October 1971,

> the further struggle had little to do with the Common Market. It had become a struggle for power and place within the Party; a kind of pure 'politics' divorced almost totally from any issues of principle. Many on the Left admitted that they would not have accepted conference decisions and three-line whips to vote in favour of entry. They were using the arguments of party unity, the supremacy of conference decisions and attacks on elitists, academics and intellectuals in the Party, to try and tilt the balance of power in favour of the Left.[97]

Despite the fact that conference and the NEC had been in conflict with the Labour government on several occasions after 1966, centre-right dominance of the PLP had provided Wilson and his colleagues with a legitimate base of support within the party. When the centre-right split over the Common Market the future of the Labour Party was changed. Jenkins and his supporters were so preoccupied with the Common Market that they did not see the left coming up.[98]

At the heart of the centre-right alliance were Jenkins and Callaghan. The former was representative of the revisionist tendency which had flourished under Gaitskell, the latter was the 'articulate voice of homespun Labourism'.[99] On a personal level the two were not naturally compatible, a problem exacerbated by the fact that they were rivals for the succession. Neither would challenge Wilson for fear of letting the other in.[100] This balance was disrupted by Wilson's indecision over Europe which allowed Callaghan sufficient opportunity to lure him into an anti-Market stance and away from Jenkins. 'I have no doubt', writes Owen, 'that if Jim Callaghan had supported entry in 1971, as he had as Chancellor when it was debated in 1967 and as Home Secretary when Labour formally applied in 1970, then Harold Wilson would not have come out against the terms of the negotiations.'[101]

If it is true that Wilson found it necessary to follow Callaghan on the Common Market to preserve his position as leader, it is equally true that it came naturally to him to do so. Jenkins's line on the Common Market demanded a style of leadership which Wilson, having witnessed Gaitskell's folly over Clause IV and defence, had concluded could never unify the party. He had long believed 'that it was impossible to lead the Labour Party, particularly in opposition, by laying all one's cards on the table. Many issues had to be fudged as a matter of sound leadership tactics.' Once Wilson decided to oppose the Heath terms a majority of the MPs in the centre of the PLP – for whom politics, parochially, meant British politics – were happy to support him, preferring, in Mackintosh's words, 'ambivalence to a clear lead based on definite principles'.[102]

In the opinion of Jenkins's supporters it was Callaghan rather than the party leader who was 'the real villain of the piece over Europe. He was the first of the top leaders to take an anti line.'[103] But, even if Callaghan had not adopted the pose of the anti-Marketeer, there is good reason to believe that Wilson would have found it difficult to hold the party to a pro-Market line. Eighteen months into opposition the Labour leadership had still not repaired the damage caused to the party–trade union relationship by *In Place of Strife*. It was not until February 1972, and the inaugural meeting of the TUC–Labour Party Liaison Committee, that relations were formally returned to normal, and it is questionable whether or not Wilson could have risked further alienating the industrial wing of the labour movement by ignoring the opposition of the NEC, conference and the TUC to entry, without undermining Labour's prospects in the general election.

A once-and-for-all campaign: the non-revival of CDS

Given the extent to which Jenkins's position was systematically eroded by the left, why was there no revival of CDS? Between 1964 and 1977, when the Campaign for Labour Victory (CLV) was launched with Rodgers in the chair at the first meeting,[104] 'there was no organisational expression of social democratic ideology fighting in the constituencies and motivating the rank and file'.[105] There is no single explanation. Rodgers has stated that as early as 1961 it was felt that CDS 'had achieved our great object not only by winning at Scarborough but by raising morale, and so we believed the Left was in retreat'.[106] By 1970 this was palpably not the case. More realistically, CDS was strictly of its time. The combination of factors which had originally brought it into existence had ceased to exist well before the party returned to opposition in 1970. Crucially, and obviously, the right no longer had the leader. Those who had played key roles in setting up CDS and who were by this time in Parliament, were natural loyalists, rather than natural dissenters. CDS had worked in support of Gaitskell (but without his endorsement) and was therefore immune to accusations of disloyalty, and of being a party within a party. Had CDS continued after 1964, known to be hostile to Wilson, its position, as Rodgers has admitted, would have been indefensible: 'It was very difficult to find a visible position in the political spectrum which was loyalist but which was positive and radical enough to be distinguishable as our own end to raise the resources to maintain it.'[107]

As it was, CDS was wound up because its founders were of the opinion at the time that things were reasonably under control and not going too badly.[108] Even when it became apparent that things were no longer under control, the feeling among CDS veterans that it had been a once-and-for-all campaign ensured that there would be no revival, even though the need to counter the left was becoming more urgent.[109]

Just as Rodgers and Taverne had published their letter of support for Gaitskell in 1960 entirely on their own initiative,[110] so it was for a new generation to lead the way in opposition. By 1970 the founders of CDS were in Parliament and ten years further on in their political careers; several had served as junior ministers in the Labour government.[111] One of the strengths of CDS had been its non-PLP status, so it was simply not possible for the right to think in terms of reviving something which actually no longer existed. There were many in the Labour Party who were convinced CDS had never gone away,[112] but those in the know knew it was never coming back.

An article of faith: the Common Market and the Labour Committee for Europe[113]

In 1960 CDS had sought to modernise the party. Ten years on many of the same people looked to the Common Market (as they had done in 1962) to transform Britain's economic prospects and those of a future Labour government. Clause IV and the Common Market were interchangeable as issues of fundamental disagreement between the pro-Market right and the left. The real division was the incompatibility of two conflicting socialist blueprints. For the pro-Marketeers, Labour's future was inextricably linked to membership of the Common Market:

> ... having tried all sorts of ways of going for growth, one of the few remaining methods of stimulating investment and thus improving Britain's competitive capacity seemed to be to join the EEC, because of the investment boom in all those countries which originally formed the Common Market. In short, in the eyes of the pro-Marketeers, failure to join this time would not only leave Britain with its present diminishing influence in world affairs, but would also mean that any future labour Government would end up with the same disappointing record as the 1964–70 administrations. Viewed in this light, the accusation by anti-Marketeers that Heath's Conservative administration had been eased round a difficult corner by the votes of the pro-European Labour MPs is of trivial importance, compared with the value of securing the pre-requisite conditions for successful Labour governments, for national prosperity and confidence for the foreseeable future.[114]

The left countered with the argument that because the community of the six was essentially a capitalist community, it would be impossible for a future Labour government to introduce a socialist planned economy.[115] Given the number of resolutions at conference in favour of this brand of socialism,[116] the left was on popular ground. The efficacy of the pro-Market argument was further undermined by the fact that its proponents were the same people whom the party held responsible for the failure of the Labour government's economic policies. Neither Jenkins, Rodgers nor Taverne 'had satisfactorily explained why the whole DEA–National Plan–growth concept did not come off'.[117] In the eyes of the activist left they stood before the party as political mountebanks peddling yet another bogus prescription for the party's (and the nation's) ailments.

Jenkins and his supporters were dedicated to securing British entry to the Common Market, and to resisting any commitment to withdraw once in, which threatened in the guise of Benn's referendum proposal. The chief vehicle for this activity was the Labour Committee for Europe (LCE), run by Jim Cattermole. Formed as the Labour Common Market Committee in January 1962, with the support of 21 MPs and five peers,[118] it had by 1971 attracted the support of over 90 MPs and 19 peers.[119] Such were the resources at Cattermole's disposal, that between 3 and 28 September 1971, in the lead-up to the 28 October vote, LCE was able to hold

11 highly publicised meetings across the country, addressed by Labour's leading pro-Marketeers.[120] Cattermole ran LCE from offices in Buckingham Gate in south-west London on a budget which gave it a huge advantage over its opponents. Thousands of pounds were available for propaganda.[121] This included holding educational conferences for Labour Party members on the most contentious aspects of membership, particularly Industrial, Regional and Social Policy, and the Common Agricultural Policy.[122] By 1973 LCE had approximately 660 members. In his efforts to expand the organisation in the constituencies, Cattermole sought to place two or three members in every constituency to argue the pro-Market case at CLP meetings: 'we cannot engage in a wide publicity campaign for members... we must rely on our present membership giving us the names of possible new names which we can follow up'.[123]

Although LCE activity was supremely well organised and in some respects replicated the tactics of CDS (members attended union conferences where the Common Market was being debated, and it had its own journal – *Europe Left* – just as CDS had had *Campaign*), it was not directed towards structural change in the Labour Party. Its twin aims were fulfilled, Britain joined the Common Market and did not subsequently withdraw, but by the time these aims had been achieved the Labour Party had ceased to be a party in which the pro-Marketeers felt comfortable.[124] LCE therefore made little difference to the leftward drift of the Labour Party, as the contrasting fortunes of Jenkins and Michael Foot in the 1976 ballot for the leadership of the party in 1976 demonstrated.[125] It was not until CLV was launched in 1977 that the centre-right, once more united under Callaghan and acting with his approval,[126] actively sought to reverse the gains made by the left since 1970 by attempting to secure the selection of parliamentary candidates who could be expected to join their ranks if elected.[127]

Writing in 1972, Rodgers concluded that every party moves away from the centre when it falls from office. 'In any political party there will be tensions between its component parts. Interests, ideology and personalities tend to pull apart.'[128] This analysis, while correct, neglected to acknowledge the painful legacy of the Labour government. Rodgers had been at the DEA and at the Foreign Office when the hopes of the party's activists, as Wayland Kennet wrote, had been dashed: 'Many socialists feel that the last Government betrayed their ideals and that its dismissal was therefore justified, and that a section of the Parliamentary Labour Party is perfectly prepared to betray them again, and indeed has probably already done so by voting "for the Government" on the European Communities Bill.'[129]

It was the whiff of betrayal hanging over Jenkins and his supporters which ultimately tainted their legitimate desire to see Britain join the Common Market. Rodgers's analysis underestimated the seriousness of intent of those on the left forcing the division in the PLP to breaking point. The rebellion of 28 October 1971 was all too easily presented by left-wingers as the first step towards breaking with the party. When Dick Taverne resigned his seat in October 1972, having been deselected by his general management committee (GMC), and abandoned by the NEC,[130] it confirmed the worst prejudices of those who saw in his decision to contest the seat, under the banner of Democratic Labour, what they imagined to be the secret wish of his fellow pro-Marketeers.[131] 'I say nothing of our departed colleague', said Benn announcing news of Taverne's resignation from the chair at conference. 'I say nothing because other men have done it before and they have never been able to do any damage to us.'[132] Benn concluded that Britain was witnessing the birth of a new political party invented by the press. Such an analysis might have been designed to discomfort Jenkins, who received nothing but praise in the establishment press for his stand on the Common Market.

What Matters Now: Jenkins outside the Shadow Cabinet[133]

Twenty-four hours after voting in favour of British membership of the Common Market in defiance of Labour Party policy and a three-line whip, Jenkins appealed for unity:

> I want to see a coherent opposition, fighting and destroying the Tory Government on the issues – unemployment, prices, regional policy, callous unfairness on social services and taxation – where they are most vulnerable and we are wholly united. I believe the great majority of the party want to heal the breach. I do certainly. But it is a matter of plain commonsense and this cannot be done by trying to concentrate our main political effort for the next year or more upon the one issue on which we cannot agree.[134]

Within six months of these events he had resigned from the Shadow Cabinet and sacrificed his seat on the NEC, and his place in the research programme, in the process. The man who would be Gaitskell's heir had contrived not only to remove himself from the centre of power in the party, but also several of his key supporters. What the Labour left had desired for 17 years since Gaitskell's election as party leader in 1955 – the exclusion of the revisionists from the parliamentary leadership – Jenkins freely conceded in April 1972.

Resignation made sense only if it held out the prospect for Jenkins and his supporters of gaining both the leadership and control of the party's policy agenda. This initially appeared to be the motive. On 11 March 1972, four weeks prior to his resignation, Jenkins had given the first of a series of six specifically prepared speeches, the purpose behind which, writes Owen, was 'straightforward and political. It was to be the "Unauthorized Programme".'[135] Owen, one of a number of people (including both David and Judith Marquand)[136] who contributed to the speeches, believed that Jenkins had 'accepted that we were embarking on an outright challenge to Wilson and all that his style of leadership implied'.[137] However, interviewed on BBC Radio's 'The World This Weekend' on 12 March, Jenkins dismissed the idea of a leadership challenge, telling Gordon Clough that he resented the way the press had reacted to the speech and blaming it for creating 'a great leadership crisis which does not exist'.[138] This, writes Owen, gave rise to 'deep anxiety about whether Roy, despite his ambition, had the stomach for an open fight to achieve it, or whether he would always prefer the indirect, less overt feline approach'.[139] Owen had good reason to be concerned as Jenkins, upon learning of the Sunday papers' treatment of the speech, which they had interpreted as an attack on Wilson,[140] took fright and hastily arranged to rerecord the BBC interview 'so as to make it more emollient'.[141]

The moment Jenkins dismissed talk of a challenge to Wilson he left himself with nowhere to go in the Labour Party. The subsequent grand sweep of the 'Unauthorized Programme' (the subject of the six speeches being: 'The New Challenge of Injustice'; 'Socialism and the Regions'; 'The Challenge of World Poverty'; 'Inequality and Work'; 'Socialism and the Cities'; and 'Poverty is Preventable') merely begged the question 'When is a leadership challenge not a leadership challenge?' The answer obviously was 'When Roy Jenkins is the challenger'. And yet the 'Unauthorized Programme' offered the Labour Party a genuinely radical and coherent alternative to the dogmatic policies emerging from the research programme.[142] *Socialist Commentary* obviously thought so and carried the texts of the speeches verbatim.[143] Mackintosh, writing in *Political Quarterly*, welcomed the thought behind the speeches and the acceptance that 'in a highly complex society, government intervention to diminish class barriers in education or to end homelessness has to be carefully thought out if the desired results are to be obtained'.[144] What is more, Jenkins was a credible alternative to Wilson, with a clear idea of what he wanted to achieve for the Labour Party and for Britain. 'The challenge of injustice', he wrote in 1972,

> though centuries old in substance, has now taken on a new and more subtle form. To meet that new challenge we need a new kind of politics. Three centuries ago, the poet Andrew Marvell wrote of Cromwell
>
> > *... Casting the Kingdoms old*
> > *Into another mould.*
>
> That is our task too. We have to break the mould of custom, selfishness and apathy which condemns so many of our fellow countrymen to avoidable indignity and deprivation. In place of

the politics of envy, we must put the politics of compassion; in place of the politics of cupidity, the politics of injustice; in place of the politics of opportunism, the politics of principle. Only so can we hope to succeed. Only so will success be worth having.[145]

Yet, if Jenkins was not offering himself as the person to carry this programme out either as leader of the Labour Party or as a senior member of a future Labour government, the 'Unauthorized Programme' had no point. Outside the Shadow Cabinet and no longer chairman of the NEC Finance and Economic Affairs Subcommittee, eloquence was no substitute for influence.

Jenkins was not Gaitskell and never sought to be compared to his hero, but 1972 was the year when the dissimilarities between the two cost the Labour Party dearly. Jenkins's reluctance to compete with his factional opponents from within the Shadow Cabinet and the research programme further cemented the gains made by the left in respect of the party's economic and industrial policy and attitude towards the Common Market. His withdrawal from the parliamentary leadership was deeply resented by those who remained. Crosland, who along with Edmund Dell was isolated on the Industrial Policy Subcommittee,[146] was, his wife writes, attending up to nine committee meetings each week 'to fight against the Left getting its way, while Roy stood on the sidelines...berating Labour's collective leadership for giving way to the Left...and wrote elegant biographical pieces for *The Times* for a fat fee'.[147] Plainly, Jenkins's desire was to be Prime Minister rather than party leader.[148] He was not the man to lead the fight to save the Labour Party, yet neither was he beyond blocking the advancement of Crosland who had responded, albeit belatedly, to the intellectual challenge provided by left-wing domination of the research programme.

Despite the sweep of the 'Unauthorized Programme', Jenkins's behaviour after his resignation from the Shadow Cabinet was negative. His return to the Shadow Cabinet in October 1973 notwithstanding,[149] he neither wanted the Labour Party to win the general election when it came, nor believed it deserved to.[150] On this point he was at odds with his younger supporters in the PLP who, while sharing his opinion that the party was undeserving of power, nevertheless desired a Labour victory because they believed in government.[151]

Neither Jenkins nor his supporters willed their fate in opposition. They could not resist the process of marginalisation because collectively they were resolved upon a course of action which carried them beyond the politics of the Labour Party, and which therefore advanced the process. Jenkins sacrificed the deputy leadership; Taverne, George Thomson and Ray Gunter, their seats.[152] Wilson made no effort to save them because he could afford not to. 'It is always easier for a Labour leader to fall out with his right wing than with his left', *The Economist* observed, 'for the right can be relied upon to be as moderate in its bitterness as in its policies.'[153] In opposition Jenkins and his supporters were perhaps the only faction in a position to split the party and undermine Labour's chances of winning a general election. By the same measure, they became the main impediment to unity and it was for this reason, ultimately, that they lost their place in the Labour Party.

Notes

1 For an account of the Campaign for Democratic Socialism, see B. Brivati, 'The Campaign for Democratic Socialism 1960–1964', PhD thesis, Queen Mary and Westfield College, London, 1992.

2 Rodgers was elected MP for Stockton-on-Tees in April 1962; Taverne as MP for Lincoln in March the same year.

3 No one suggested it would be a good idea, but Rodgers felt that someone from Gaitskell down ought to have suggested it. Interview, Lord Rodgers of Quarry Bank, 25 June 1996.

4 WS, 'Campaign for Democratic Socialism', pp. 366–7 (Lord Rodgers).

5 S. Haseler, *The Gaitskellites* (London, Macmillan, 1969), p. 210, n. 1.

6 WS, 'Campaign for Democratic Socialism', p. 366 (Lord Rodgers).

7 Conference voted in favour of the unilateralist motion moved by the Amalgamated Engineering Union by a margin of 407,000 votes. For an account of the party's debate on defence, see Williams, *Hugh Gaitskell*, pp. 574–653.

8 'Roy Jenkins then said: "Denis Howell, a member of Parliament who has just lost his seat, he knows the Trade Unions. Why don't we bring him along?"' WS, 'Campaign for Democratic Socialism', p. 367 (Lord Rodgers).

9 See Haseler, *The Gaitskellites*, p. 210.

10 *The Times*, 19 October 1960, p. 12. Quoted in Haseler, *The Gaitskellites*, p. 211, n. 2.

11 Haseler, *The Gaitskellites*, p. 211. 'Mikardo attempted in 1960 to launch a national organisation through Victory for Socialism but he maintain[ed] that it failed because he just did not have the resources to run a national organisation.' WS, 'Campaign for Democratic Socialism', p. 364 (Brian Brivati). 'In 1958 a few of us took over a small and moribund society called Victory for Socialism and set about building it into a nationwide organisation. It was a mistake, and after a year or two we cut out of it because many of the branches had been taken over by the trotskyists, and we had no means of stopping them.' Mikardo, *Back-bencher*, p. 109.

12 WS, 'Campaign for Democratic Socialism', p. 384 (Lord Rodgers).

13 Interview, Lord Rodgers.

14 See Mikardo, *Back-bencher*, pp. 123–5.

15 WS, 'Campaign for Democratic Socialism', p. 371 (Brian Magee).

16 WS, 'Campaign for Democratic Socialism', pp. 367, 373 (Lord Rodgers).

17 *The Spectator*, 12 May 1961, p. 670. Quoted in Haseler, *The Gaitskellites*, p. 225, n. 2.

18 Jenkins, *A Life at the Centre*, p. 145.

19 WS, 'Campaign for Democratic Socialism', p. 377 (Dick Taverne).

20 Haseler, *The Gaitskellites*, p. 218, n. 2.

21 WS, 'Campaign for Democratic Socialism', p. 378 (David Marquand).

22 P. Seyd, 'The Tavernite', *Political Quarterly*, 45, 2 (1974), pp. 244–5.

23 On the question of CDS and the modernisation of the Labour Party, see WS, 'Campaign for Democratic Socialism', pp. 379–80.

24 WS, 'Campaign for Democratic Socialism', p. 374 (Patrick Seyd).

25 Williams, *Hugh Gaitskell*, pp. 618–19.

26 Jenkins puts the number in attendance at about 12. For accounts of this meeting, see D. Taverne, *The Future of the Left* (London, Jonathan Cape, 1974), p. 102; Jenkins, *A Life at the Centre*, p. 310; and Owen, *Time to Declare*, p. 167.

27 Jenkins, *A Life at the Centre*, p. 310. Lord Owen writes that the Walston group 'was never referred to by that name, it probably developed into a Jenkinsite grouping but I do not think it was specifically a pro-Jenkins movement'. Lord Owen, letter to the author, 26 November 1996.

28 Benn, *Office Without Power*, 20 July 1971, p. 359.

29 See Jenkins, *A Life at the Centre*, pp. 125–98.

30 Owen was not a natural Jenkinsite: '... my political heart belonged to Tony Crosland. I did not make a wholehearted commitment to Roy as the future leader of the Labour Party until the summer of 1971, when it became clear to me that Tony Crosland was not prepared to recognize that Britain's entry into the European Community was a major issue.' Owen, *Time to Declare*, p. 167. Lord Owen writes: 'I suppose one could say that for a short period from 1972–74 I was giving a primacy to Roy Jenkins vis à vis my friendship with Tony Crosland but I think my philosophical identification with Tony Crosland remained'. Lord Owen, letter to the author.

31 David Marquand, letter to the author, 15 November 1996.

32 I. Crewe and A. King, *SDP: The Birth, Life and Death of the Social Democratic Party* (Oxford, Oxford University Press, 1994), p. 55.

33 Crewe and King, *SDP*, p. 55–6.

34 David Marquand writes: 'It would be perfectly rationable to support Jenkins in one election, but not to support him in a subsequent election – not because one's opinion of his merits had changed, but simply because one's view of the possibility of his winning had changed. Against that background, my own view would be that the vote he received in the Deputy Leadership election in 1970 exaggerated his strength.' Marquand, letter to the author, 22 November 1996.

35 Lord Rodgers, letter to the author, 24 July 1996. See also Crosland, *Tony Crosland*, pp. 250–2.

36 Lord Rodgers, letter to the author.

37 Interview, Lord Rodgers.

38 Jenkins, *A Life at the Centre*, p. 350.

39 Lord Callaghan writes: 'Despite Roy Jenkins' great abilities, I did not think at any time in the 1960s or 70s that he would become leader of the Labour Party.' Lord Callaghan, letter to the author, 19 November 1996.

40 LPA, PLP, Minutes, 19 July 1971.

41 Benn, *Office Without Power*, 19 July 1971, p. 358.

42 Voting in the first ballot for the deputy leadership on 10 November 1971 was as follows: Jenkins 140, Foot 96, Benn 46. In the second ballot on 18 November: Jenkins 140, Foot 126. For the chair of the PLP (10 Nov.): Houghton 139, Pentland 132. For the Shadow Cabinet (2 Dec.): Williams 137, Lever 129, Thomson 126. LPA, PLP, Minutes, 10 November–2 December 1971, Session 1971–72.

43 Benn, *Office Without Power*, 13 October 1971, p. 379.

44 Benn, *Office Without Power*, 10 November 1971, p. 384

45 *The Economist*, 'Letter for Harold', 27 February 1971, pp. 29–30.

46 Taverne, *The Future of the Left*, p. 54.

47 Wood, 'The Westminster Scene', *Political Quarterly*, 43, 4 (1972), pp. 486–8.
48 W. Rodgers, 'Personal Column', *Socialist Commentary* (November 1971), p. 12.
49 Interview, Lord Rodgers.
50 LPAR, 1971, p. 162.
51 Times Diary, 'Bill Rodgers: Supreme Marketeer', *The Times*, 6 October 1971, p. 14.
52 Ziegler, *Wilson*, p. 384.
53 Rodgers's General Management Committee voted against entry by ten votes to 9, but subsequently recorded a 34:0 vote of confidence in their MP. Rodgers, 'Personal Column', *Socialist Commentary* (December 1971), p. 7.
54 Owen, *Time to Declare*, p. 187.
55 Conference voted as follows on the TGWU's Composite Resolution 15, opposing British entry: for 2,954,000, against 3,049,000. LPAR, 1970, p. 200.
56 A. W. Benn, 'The Common Market – Towards a Decision', LPA, PC Minutes, 11 November 1970.
57 Alan Lee Williams sat as Labour MP for Hornchurch 1966–70.
58 Formed in 1962 as the Labour Common Market Committee.
59 *Europe Left*, 2, 3 (May 1971), p. 2. LPA, Labour Committee for Europe (LCE), Minutes and Papers, 1964–80.
60 Editorial, 'What Kind of Party?' *Socialist Commentary* (October 1971), p. 1.
61 J. P. Mackintosh, 'The Problems of the Labour Party', *Political Quarterly*, 43, 1 (1972), p. 6.
62 Interview, Lord Rodgers.
63 In opinion polls taken in March, May and June 1971, 66 per cent (NOP), 65 per cent (Opinion Research Centre) and 58 per cent (Gallup) respectively were against British membership of the Common Market. *The Economist*, 'If it's participation you're after . . .', 3 July 1971, pp. 25–6.
64 WS, 'Committee for Europe', p. 405 (Jim Cattermole).
65 WS, 'Committee for Europe', p. 402 (Peter Stephenson).
66 Wood, 'The Westminster Scene', *Political Quarterly*, 43, 2 (1972), p. 219.
67 WS, 'Committee for Europe', p. 402 (Peter Stephenson).
68 Lord Thomson writes: 'The Labour Committee for Europe was part of the general European Movement, and was financed from European Movement resources.' Lord Thomson, letter to the author, 16 November 1996. This is confirmed by Lord Jenkins: 'I think the bulk of the money (which was small) came from the all party umbrella organisation, the European Movement.' Lord Jenkins, letter to the author, 20 November 1996. The proposed budget for LCE for 1 April 1973–31 March 1974 was £32,500. The sum of £2,500 was allocated for propaganda and advertising, and a similar sum for the activities of regional groups. Research Institute costs were £10,900. LPA, LCE, Minutes and Papers, 1964–80.
69 'Roy, of course, is the hero of every drawing room but whether he speaks for the British people or not, I don't know.' Benn, *Office Without Power*, 25 September 1972, p. 449.
70 When Gaitskell rejected British entry at conference in 1962, his wife, Dora, found the response to his speech perplexing. 'Standing ovations at Labour Conferences were not yet merely ritual, and the Scarborough roles were now reversed as the cheers were led by those NEC members on the platform who had then been so reticent, while George Brown and Sam Watson now hardly pretended to applaud. Roy Jenkins prudently stood up, but other Marketeers – Jack Diamond, Bill Rodgers, Ray Gunter – would not do so. A trade union loyalist, very close to the Gaitskells, found Hugh "radiant . . . with the flowing tide"

but Dora worried: "Charlie, all the wrong people are cheering." ' Williams, *Hugh Gaitskell*, p. 736.

71 WS, 'Committee for Europe', p. 412 (Lord Jenkins).

72 The NEC then voted against payment of subscription fees. 'It required the combined efforts of Wilson, Callaghan, Healey and me to secure a wafer thin majority for affiliation.' Jenkins, *A Life at the Centre*, pp. 315–16. Affiliation was first discussed by the NEC on 28 October 1970, and was referred to the International Subcommittee for discussion. Affiliation was finally approved on 10 November 1970. LPA, International Subcommittee Minutes, 10 November 1970; NEC, Minutes, 25 November 1970.

73 WS, 'Committee for Europe', p. 412 (Lord Jenkins).

74 Jenkins, *A Life at the Centre*, pp. 86, 320.

75 *The Economist*, 'When the roundabout stops', 20 February 1971, pp. 12–13.

76 Jenkins, *A Life at the Centre*, p. 320.

77 *The Economist*, 'The ides of July', 24 July 1971, pp. 13–16.

78 Pimlott, *Harold Wilson*, p. 582.

79 Pimlott, *Harold Wilson*, p. 581.

80 Jenkins uses this heading for the chapter covering these events in his memoirs. See Jenkins, *A Life at the Centre*, pp. 327–49.

81 Callaghan and Healey voted against entry; Crosland abstained.

82 On 11 May 1971, the Labour pro-Marketeers published an advertisement in *The Guardian* supporting British membership of the Common Market. It was signed by 100 MPs, including several leading members of the Shadow Cabinet including both Healey and Crosland. For an account of the attempt to secure Callaghan's signature, see Owen, *Time to Declare*, p. 175.

83 Jenkins, *A Life at the Centre*, p. 341.

84 WS, 'Committee for Europe', p. 413 (Lord Jenkins). See also Benn, *Office Without Power*, 4 March 1972, p. 411.

85 Jenkins, *A Life at the Centre*, p. 341.

86 Shore, Foot, Peart, Wilson, Benn, Callaghan, Short and Mellish voted for the referendum; Jenkins, Williams, Lever, Crosland, Houghton and Thomson against. For accounts of these events see Benn, *Office Without Power*, 29 March 1972, pp. 418–21 and Jenkins, *A Life at the Centre*, pp. 341–4.

87 On 22 March 1972, the NEC voted (in the absence of Wilson, Callaghan and Healey) by 13 to 11 in favour of a referendum. It was for this reason that the Shadow Cabinet reconsidered Benn's proposal. Benn, *Office Without Power*, 22 March 1972, pp. 416–17.

88 LPA, PC, Minutes, 15 March 1972.

89 WS, 'Committee for Europe', p. 414 (Lord Jenkins).

90 WS, 'Committee for Europe', pp. 415–16 (Lord Jenkins).

91 LPA, PLP, Minutes, 4 November 1971.

92 Chancellor of the Exchequer 1945–47 and talent spotter for the Labour centre-right.

93 'The defection of the TGWU from the right-wing camp after Cousins's surprise election as General Secretary in the spring of 1956, following the sudden deaths of first Deakin and then his moderate successor Jock Tiffin, brought a greater degree of uncertainty to the balance of political power inside the Labour Movement.' Taylor, *The Trade Union Question*, p. 132.

94 The 1966 seamen's strike was particularly damaging to the Labour government, triggering yet another sterling crisis. See Wilson, *The Labour Government 1964–1970*, ch. 14, and Pimlott, *Harold Wilson*, pp. 405–69. Government–trade union relations never properly recovered from this episode.

95 CDS anti-Marketeers in 1962 included Douglas Jay, Tam Dalyell, Guy Barnett and William Blyton. Haseler, *The Gaitskellites*, p. 229.
96 Jenkins, *A Life at the Centre*, pp. 319–20.
97 Mackintosh, 'The Problems', p. 15.
98 Interview, Lord Rodgers.
99 Taylor, *The Trade Union Question*, p. 349.
100 See Pimlott, *Harold Wilson*, pp. 543–50.
101 Owen, *Time to Declare*, p. 177.
102 Mackintosh, 'The Problems', pp. 9–13.
103 Pimlott, *Harold Wilson*, p. 581.
104 The Campaign for Labour Victory was launched in February 1977. Its secretary was Alec McGivan. See G. Daly, 'The Campaign for Labour Victory and the Origins of the SDP', *Contemporary Record*, 7, 2 (Autumn 1993), pp. 282–305.
105 B. Brivati and D. Wincott, 'The Evolution of Social Democracy in Britain', *Contemporary Record*, 7, 2 (Autumn 1993), p. 362.
106 WS, 'Campaign for Democratic Socialism', p. 380 (Lord Rodgers).
107 WS, 'Campaign for Democratic Socialism', p. 384 (Lord Rodgers).
108 Interview, Lord Rodgers.
109 'I remember once going to see Frank Pickstock and asking his advice. He said, "No, don't revive CDS. Circumstances are different, it was a once-and-for-all." ' WS, 'Campaign for Democratic Socialism', p. 384 (Lord Rodgers).
110 Interview, Lord Rodgers.
111 Rodgers, Taverne and Howell, for example, served at the Board of Trade (Rodgers), the Treasury (Rodgers and Taverne) and Housing and Local Government (Howell).
112 LPA, JRP, TGM, 4 February 1974.
113 'When I heard Charlie Pannell say that for him Europe was an article of faith, he put it above the Labour Party and the Labour Movement, I was finally convinced that this was a deep split.' Benn, *Office Without Power*, 19 October 1971, p. 381.
114 Mackintosh, 'The Problems', pp. 12–13.
115 WS, 'Committee for Europe', p. 401 (Peter Stephenson).
116 In 1971 the Conference Arrangements Committee received 49 resolutions on public ownership. LPA, NEC, Minutes, 1 October 1971.
117 Mackintosh, 'The Problems', p. 5.
118 WS, 'Committee for Europe', p. 386 (Roger Broad).
119 LPA, LCE, Minutes and Papers, 1964–80.
120 *Europe Left*, 2, 6 (1971), p. 7. LPA, LCE, Minutes and Papers, 1964–80.
121 For details of LCE funding see footnote 68 above.
122 'Committee Seminar', Oxford, 27–28 April 1973. LPA, LCE, Minutes and Papers, 1964–80, p. 845.
123 J. Cattermole, 'Report for Officers Meeting', LPA, LCE, Minutes and Papers 1964–80, pp. 807–8.
124 See Jenkins, *A Life at the Centre*, pp. 424–45.
125 In the first ballot Callaghan polled 84, Foot 90 and Jenkins 56. Benn got 37 votes, Healey 30 and Crosland 17. In the final ballot Callaghan polled 176, Foot 137. However, Jenkins's vote was by no means a true representation of his support in the PLP. Unlike in the deputy leadership ballots of 1970 and 1971, on this occasion he was not the sole candidate of the centre-right. David Marquand writes: 'Quite a few people thought that, in an ideal world he would be the best party leader, but did not vote for him, either because they thought he could not win or because they thought that, if he did win, the

party would be bitterly split.' David Marquand, letter to the author, 22 November 1996.

126 Interview, Lord Rodgers.

127 'Sally Malnick was active in the offices of CLV. Her first task was going through *The Times Guide to the House of Commons* to see which Labour MP was likely to retire or die and to ensure that the local CLV had a moderate candidate to succeed. Daly, 'The Campaign for Labour Victory', p. 285.

128 Rodgers, 'Personal Column', *Socialist Commentary* (December 1972), pp. 3–4.

129 Lord (Wayland) Kennet, 'The Policies of the Party', *Political Quarterly*, 43, 4 (1972), p. 390.

130 The NEC Organisation Subcommittee ruled that there had been a breach in natural justice in Lincoln and that Taverne's appeal against his deselection be upheld. This ruling was overturned by the NEC the following day, 26 July 1972, by 12 votes to eight. LPA, Organisation Subcommittee Minutes, 25 July 1972; NEC, Minutes, 26 July 1972.

131 On 1 March 1973, Taverne, the Democratic Labour candidate, polled 21,967 votes, 13,191 more that the Labour Party candidate. LPAR, 1973, p. 26.

132 LPAR, 1972, p. 348.

133 *What Matters Now* was the title under which Jenkins collected for publication the series of speeches he made in 1972.

134 'Speech to Heywood & Royston Constituency Labour Party, 29 October 1971', LPA, TPP (Labour Party), D/PITT/C44.

135 Owen, *Time to Declare*, p. 189. In 1885, Joseph Chamberlain MP made a series of speeches in which he advocated, among other things, the introduction of democratic councils with powers of compulsory purchase for the transfer of land to tenants and labourers; free education; and National Councils for Ireland, Scotland and Wales. Chamberlain's policy proposals, stated without Gladstone's approval, were referred to as the 'Unauthorised Programme'. See R. Jay, *Joseph Chamberlain: A Political Study* (Oxford, Oxford University Press, 1981), pp. 96–148.

136 In the foreword to *What Matters Now*, Jenkins gives credit to Judith Marquand in particular, and also to Matthew Oakeshott and Nicholas Bosanquet.

137 Owen, *Time to Declare*, p. 190. Others saw it differently. Jenkins wrote in his memoirs that 'The intention was to set out an across-the-board range of policies which would strike a more serious and more principled note than the short-term party manoeuvring which, in contrast with his performance in 1963–4, had by this time become the stock-in-trade of Harold Wilson's leadership. They would show that I had not become obsessed with Europe to the exclusion of all else.' Jenkins, *A Life at the Centre*, p. 339. Bill Rodgers regarded the speeches as being necessary to preserve the pro-Marketeers' position in the party after the 28 October 1971 vote: 'We arranged for Roy to make a series of speeches called What Matters Now? – he was helped in writing them by David Marquand in particular and others – to keep Roy's flame burning and to emphasise that although we had voted against the party on the Market, we had wider interests. That was always my view, my consistent view, although I was a good European, I never thought we could rally the Party on the basis of Europe.' Lord Rodgers, interview with the author.

138 Owen, *Time to Declare*, p. 190. Jenkins later reflected that 'In 1972–3 it might have been better for the future health of the Labour Party had I challenged, but had I done so I might well have achieved just about the outcome that Michael Heseltine did in 1990. I half regret I did not do that, but not on ground of ambition.' See Jenkins, *A Life at the Centre*, p. 621.

139 Owen, *Time to Declare*, p. 190.
140 'Mr Roy Jenkins, deputy leader, yesterday began what must be regarded as a campaign to wrest the party leadership of the Labour Party from Mr Harold Wilson. He did not mention Mr Wilson by name, nor even the leadership in the abstract. But most people will see a reference to Mr Wilson's leadership, and Mr Foot's exhuberant oratory, in these words: "When the next election comes, we shall not be judged by the vehemence of our perorations, still less by the dexterity with which we follow the transient twists and turns of public opinion. We shall be judged by the quality of the programme we put before our fellow citizens and by the consistency and courage with which we advocate it."' J. Margach, 'Jenkins opens his bid for Labour leadership', *The Sunday Times*, 12 March 1972, p. 1.
141 Jenkins, *A Life at the Centre*, p. 340. See, for example, *The Times*, 'Mr Jenkins denies campaigning for Labour Party leadership', 13 March 1972, p. 1.
142 For a comparison of Jenkins's speeches with *Labour's Programme for Britain 1972*, see R. Marris, 'The unauthorised programme', *New Statesman*, 8 September 1972, pp. 10–11. For *Tribune*'s view of *What Matters Now*, see R. Clements, 'Roy Jenkins: the politics of nostalgia', *Tribune*, 29 September 1972, p. 5.
143 See *Socialist Commentary*, April–July, September–October 1972.
144 Mackintosh, 'Socialism or Social Democracy?', p. 480.
145 Jenkins, *What Matters Now*, p. 22. The eloquence of Jenkins's speeches owed much to those around him. In his memoirs Jenkins writes 'Thanks to the hand of David Marquand the peroration also contained a quotation from Andrew Marvell, "Casting the kingdoms old into another mould", which foreshadowed part of the message of the SDP.' Jenkins, *A Life at the Centre*, p. 339.
146 See Wickham-Jones, *Economic Strategy and the Labour Party*, p. 126.
147 Crosland, *Tony Crosland*, p. 252. In July 1970 Jenkins was commissioned by William Rees-Mogg to write a series of biographical essays for *The Times*. See Jenkins, *A Life at the Centre*, p. 308. Crosland was particularly offended by a speech Jenkins had given in Oxford on 9 March 1973, in which he set out

> three rules which the Labour Party ought to apply in its policy-making and presentation. First, is the measure proposed necessary and desirable to create a better society and to serve the interests of the broad range of people we represent? Second, if included in the programme, is there a good chance that it can be carried out and made to work effectively, bearing in mind both our practical experience in the past as well as our aspirations for the future? Third, is what we are proposing likely to win, rather than alienate support for the Labour Party, and thus give us the opportunity to do anything at all, as opposed to expatiating in impotence?

The Times, 'Mr Jenkins on the Labour Party's malaise', 10 March 1973, p. 4.
148 See Jenkins, *A Life at the Centre*, p. 621.
149 Jenkins received 144 votes, coming fifth in the ballot behind Crosland (145 votes), Prentice (146), Foot (147) and Callaghan (150). LPA, PLP, Minutes, 1 November 1973.
150 See Jenkins, *A Life at the Centre*, p. 364.
151 Interview, Lord Rodgers.

152 Taverne was deselected because of pro-Market views among other things; Thomson resigned his seat to escape anti-Market pressure from his CLP; Gunter resigned because he did not accept the decision to oppose membership.
153 *The Economist*, 'Doubting Harold', 10 July 1971, pp. 15–17.

8

THE TUC–LABOUR PARTY LIAISON COMMITTEE 1972–74: HOW THE PARLIAMENTARY LEADERSHIP WAS SAVED FROM THE LABOUR PARTY

At the Labour Party Conference in Blackpool in 1970, Jack Jones and Hugh Scanlon very publicly committed the 1,931,000 votes[1] at their disposal in support of Composite Resolution 16, which called upon the parliamentary leadership to 'reflect the views and aspirations of the Labour and Trade Union Movement, by framing their policies on Annual Conference decisions'.[2] By September 1972, Jones and Scanlon were sitting across the table from Edward Heath in 10 Downing Street, exploring the possibility of a voluntary agreement on wages. Conference did not cease to be important to Jones and Scanlon after 1970, but the sovereignty of conference decisions was not a priority for the two union leaders thereafter. Similarly, by the time the Labour Party published its general election manifesto in February 1974, the differences of opinion that had been so vividly apparent at Blackpool in 1970 (when Jones, from the conference floor, had shouted his objections to James Callaghan's reference to incomes policy 'rather vociferously')[3] had been finessed by a series of monthly meetings between the TUC, PLP and NEC, out of which a joint statement on economic policy emerged.[4] As a result of the improvement in relations between the PLP and the TUC, the parliamentary leadership was empowered in its relationship with the party and in this respect the situation in January 1974, as the general election approached, was the very reverse of Blackpool in 1970.

By 1972 the Conservative government and Labour's parliamentary leadership had farcically cast themselves in the roles of rival suitors for the hand of the TUC. The previous Labour government's unsuccessful attempt to reform industrial relations in 1969, if not forgotten by the TUC, had been forgiven; and, while the Conservative government's Industrial Relations Act remained the single most contentious issue affecting government–trade union relations, union leaders accepted Heath's invitation to discuss a deal on the economy. In this way the leaders of the two main political parties contrived to diminish the authority of the executive in British domestic politics. As Edmund Dell writes of the Social Contract between the Labour Party and the TUC: 'Here was a party which felt compelled to enter into a contract . . . with a powerful sectional interest. This could only mean that it should be a major purpose, if that party entered government, to remove the privileges on which that sectional power was founded. Labour had no such intention. Its radicalism on relations with the trade unions had been exhausted by the battle over Barbara Castle's *In Place of Strife*.'[5] So, if Jack Jones had no need to shout his objections from the conference floor in 1972, it was because he had been invited to submit his demands from a distance of no more than the width of a table in Downing Street or Chequers, the House of Commons, Transport House or Congress House.[6]

Healing the breach: the Labour Party and the trade unions, 1970–72

It was Heath, writes Barbara Castle, who did most to heal the breach between the Labour Party and the trade unions in opposition.[7] However, the significance of the Conservatives' economic and industrial polices in this period lies not in the failed attempted reform of the trade unions, the pursuit of which indeed prompted a reconciliation between the two wings of the labour movement, but in the fact that Heath's subsequent offer to employers and unions, 'to share fully with the Government the benefits and obligations involved in running the national economy',[8] conferred on the trade unions the status of social partner. As Campbell writes of Heath's attitude towards the trade unions in this period, 'Having experienced the ruin they could make of his hopes by their hostility, he set himself to treat them, over long sessions at Downing Street and Chequers, with almost exaggerated deference and consideration.'[9] With the Labour Party by 1972 having abandoned the pretence that it was capable of governing without the consent of the unions, the tripartite talks Heath proposed were immensely significant. For, if the alternative to a government willing to deal with a major sectional interest was an opposition also willing to deal, trade union leaders were provided with no incentive to compromise in pursuit of their demands. Accordingly, what Heath and TUC representatives were unable to agree in talks held between September and November 1972, the Labour Party and the TUC were able to agree by January 1973.[10]

The path to better relations between the parliamentary leadership and trade union leaders began to emerge at Blackpool in 1970. When Jack Jones was not shouting down his fellow comrades, he was launching his campaign for a better deal for the nation's pensioners. Speaking in the debate on social security, he called upon the NEC to organise a major national campaign to secure an increase in pensions that year,[11] and phrased it in such a way as to suggest what the parliamentary leadership might do to begin to restore the confidence of the general secretary of the TGWU at least. 'Winning a better deal for the aged', he told conference, 'must have high priority in Labour's activities both inside and outside Parliament.'[12] Speaking from the rostrum for the third time in four days, Jones uttered no obviously conciliatory words and indeed used the occasion to attack once more the intellectuals whose lack of understanding of the trade union movement he believed had produced both the Labour government's statutory incomes policy and *In Place of Strife*. If the workers had to pay more in national insurance to finance the increase in pensions, he asserted, they would do so 'because we are not grab-alls, we do stand for social justice', adding that he hoped the *Manchester Guardian*, 'or whatever they call it', would take note of that.[13]

In moving the TGWU's emergency resolution on pensions, Jones called for an early meeting of the National Council of Labour (NCL), 'an almost moribund outfit, consisting of leaders of the Labour Party, TUC and the Co-operative movement',[14] to develop the envisaged national campaign.[15] Reviving the NCL advanced the prospect of a reconciliation between party and trade union leaders, if only because it brought them together in the same room to discuss an issue it was difficult to imagine them failing to agree upon. On 2 March 1971 representatives of the three bodies duly came together for the first time since August 1969 at the House of Commons. As a dry-run for the TUC–Labour Party Liaison Committee, the meeting was a disaster. 'What should have been a meeting of common minds', writes Jones, 'turned into a sparring match between Roy Jenkins, then deputy leader of the Labour Party, and myself. In answer to the constant question "Where is the money to come from?" I mentioned, in passing, the case for levying a wealth tax. Quoting from a ministerial reply in the House of Commons, I claimed that a five per cent tax on those with a total income of £50,000 a year or more would raise as much as £600 million. Jenkins immediately retorted that the suggestion was "irresponsible"; he later withdrew the word when I protested but said, nevertheless, in his opinion it was ill-considered.'[16] The minutes record only that Jenkins, along with Callaghan, drew attention to the Labour government's record on pensions, 'and stressed the need to press for substantial increases in pensions before the Budget'. Whatever the precise details of the disagreement between Jenkins and Jones, a joint declaration calling for a 'substantial and immediate pensions increase' was agreed, as was the establishment of a joint working party to plan a campaign on behalf of the elderly, for which Terry Pitt was to act as secretary.[17]

Jones writes that the difficulty he experienced at this meeting 'convinced me that some other body was needed to bring the unions and Labour more closely together'. With the politicians, he found, 'it was for the most part a contest with intellectual snobbery or languid indifference. Idealism, hope and courage always had a greater hold on trade unionists: to right a wrong, to live and breathe brotherhood, to hold out a helping hand to the worker in difficulty.'[18] In practical terms this resulted in the establishment of the TUC–Labour Party Liaison Committee in January 1972, where the ability of parliamentary leaders to resist trade union demands was substantially diminished. Unsurprisingly, the subsequent agreement on economic and industrial policy, announced by party and trade union leaders in February 1973, was reached in the absence of Jenkins. By resigning the deputy leadership in April 1972, he forfeited both his seat on the NEC and the opportunity to challenge trade union leaders on matters of policy from within the Liaison Committee, one example being the increase in pensions (which by 1973, it was anticipated, would cost a future Labour government approximately £1,400 million to implement). However, his presence at the table was not missed. His absence was in fact conducive to agreement between party and trade union leaders, and indeed enhanced the prospect of an agreement. Certainly whether or not an increase in pensions was affordable ceased to be an issue.[19]

The trade unions' terms for a reconciliation emerged from this and a second NCL meeting which took place three months later on 14 June. By September 1971 the TUC was committed to an increase in pensions, the repeal of the Industrial Relations Act, and to opposing British membership of the Common Market on the terms on offer. These were the issues upon which the breach between the Labour Party and the TUC was to be healed. The first meeting of the NCL, called to consider how a campaign in support of higher pensions should be organised, went beyond this issue to express its outright opposition to the Industrial Relations Bill. When the NCL met again in June 1971, pensions continued to be a priority issue (and a statement was agreed calling upon the government to double the one pound increase in the weekly pension due in September), but also considered on this occasion was a paper on the subject of unemployment, submitted by Sir Harry Nicholas.[20] This widening of the NCL's agenda occurred because no other formal joint body existed to facilitate a dialogue between party and trade union leaders, and it was this Jones sought to rectify when he addressed the 1971 Labour Party Conference at Brighton. 'There is no reason', he told conference, 'why a joint policy cannot be worked out. But let us have the closest possible liaison. This is not just a matter for brainstorming in the back rooms of Congress or Transport House just before the next election. In the past we have not had the dialogue necessary.'[21] Jones made his appeal against the backdrop of an increasingly bitter rearguard action by the trade unions against the Industrial Relations Act. The basis of any agreement between the TUC and the Labour Party would therefore be the repeal of the government's legislation. What Jones offered the parliamentary leadership, under the guise of joint policy, was unity on the unions' terms.

By 1971 the anxiety of the TUC to heal the breach over *In Place of Strife* was due entirely to the government's industrial relations legislation.[22] At Brighton, Jones called upon the parliamentary leadership to pledge to repeal the Act in the first session of the next Labour government, so as to 'restore the advances that the unions had made in the last 100 years'.[23] Having listened to what he had to say, Wilson and his senior colleagues can have been under no illusion that the context of any policy discussions between themselves and the TUC would be trade unionism itself. In this respect the establishment of the TUC–Labour Party Liaison Committee was a retrograde step, a victory for labourism over revisionism, which casts doubt on the wisdom of Roy Jenkins's self-imposed exile from the heart of the parliamentary leadership for nearly the whole of the period the Liaison Committee met to discuss the economic and industrial policies of the next Labour government.

Establishing the TUC–Labour Party Liaison Committee

Prior to the government's introduction of its industrial relations legislation, Jones and Scanlon had been determined to shun the parliamentary leadership for as long as the phrase 'statutory incomes policy' remained a part of the latter's vocabulary. Only when the Industrial Relations Bill became law and it became apparent that the Act would not be repealed without the aid of the PLP, did Jones make his conciliatory speech at the Brighton conference. Both Jones's speech, and the fact that the trade unions were already working closely with the Labour Party at Westminster on the Industrial Relations Bill Working Party chaired by Barbara Castle,[24] pointed towards some form of co-operation between the political and industrial wings of the labour movement along the lines of the Liaison Committee. Within a month of the speech, the Home Policy Committee resolved that 'early discussions with the TUC be arranged',[25] a decision endorsed by the NEC on 23 November 1971. On 30 November, Sir Harry Nicholas wrote to Vic Feather, the general secretary of the TUC, formally proposing a series of meetings between the party and the TUC to discuss economic and industrial policy.[26] Feather's reply to this letter, welcoming the proposal, was considered by the NEC on 22 December 1971, when it was decided that the NEC's representatives on the Liaison Committee would be Tony Benn MP, Ian Mikardo MP, John Chalmers, Alex Kitson, Sir Harry Nicholas and Barbara Castle MP.

In terms of the distribution of power within the Labour Party, the establishment of the Liaison Committee was highly significant. Where the NEC research programme was intended to reduce the influence of the parliamentary leadership on the party's consideration of policy in opposition (and here Ken Lomas's resolution satisfied the mood of disaffected constituency activists) the Liaison Committee had the opposite effect and returned Wilson and his colleagues to the heart of the policymaking process.[27] The prospect of this clearly appalled the more pluralist minded members of the NEC; Jones has written that 'it took a devil of a lot of pressure to overcome the objections of the NEC to the Parliamentary Labour Party having direct representatives on the Committee'. If this is so, disagreement between Jones and the NEC over the composition of the Liaison Committee can be seen in terms of the activist left's struggle to enlist the support of the the trade unions against the parliamentary leadership at conference. For those members of the NEC for whom the sovereignty of conference decisions was of paramount importance, the trade unions were the only possible counterweight to a recalcitrant parliamentary leadership. However, for Jones at least, conference resolutions which did not receive the endorsement of the parliamentary leadership were of little value.[28] Likewise a Liaison Committee which did not include prospective Labour ministers: 'To most of us at the TUC it would have been a waste of time if they had not been there. We wanted commitments, especially on the repeal of the Industrial Relations Act, and only the leaders of the Party could deliver these.'[29] Obviously for Jones the issue of conference sovereignty took second place to the interests of his own members. The casualties in this process were those left-wing members of the NEC who, having failed to keep the most powerful trade union leaders and the parliamentary leadership apart, ensured that the NEC's was the weakest voice in Labour's own tripartite discussions.[30]

A semantic difference: the first meeting of the TUC–Labour Party Liaison Committee, February 1972

The TUC–Labour Party Liaison Committee met for the first time on 21 February 1972, at the House of Commons. Its membership comprised six representatives each from the PLP, NEC and TUC.[31] Support was provided by office staff from both Transport House and Congress House.[32] For those meetings held at the House of Commons the chair was taken by the PLP; at Congress House by the TUC; and at Transport House by the NEC.[33] Whatever significance the NEC attached to Labour's ten-month-old research programme, it had clearly been superseded by a process which brought together the labour movement's political and industrial elites.

By bringing together Vic Feather, Jack Jones and Hugh Scanlon for the TUC, with Harold Wilson for the Labour Party, the Liaison Committee unavoidably recalled the crisis meetings that had taken place between the TUC and Wilson as Prime Minister in June 1969, following the publication of *In Place of Strife*. Obliged by the Conservative government to revisit this territory in February 1972, the first meeting of the Liaison Committee was a predictably tense affair, undermined by both the recent history of party–trade union relations, and the latent suspicion of some TUC representatives that the legislative measures introduced by the Conservative government in the field of industrial relations were privately supported by some senior parliamentary leaders. TUC suspicions were not calmed when Douglas Houghton, the chairman of the PLP, drew attention to the statement on the Industrial Relations Bill issued by the PLP in December 1970, which required that a new Bill be prepared before the existing legislation was repealed.[34] Houghton's 'immensely provocative' comment, supported by Roy Jenkins, was taken by Hugh Scanlon as evidence of an equivocatory attitude towards repeal. Houghton's words, he insisted, 'did not constitute a *pledge* to repeal'.[35] Scanlon's objection was the signal for the TUC to circle the wagons. Jack Jones promptly read out the TGWU resolution calling upon the PLP to pledge to repeal the Industrial Relations Act (carried without dissent by conference at Brighton in 1971); he was followed by his 'terrible twin' (Scanlon)[36] who announced that the TUC would not talk 'with the sword of Damocles hanging over their heads'. Jones and Scanlon particularly (Vic Feather was a far more conciliatory figure) appeared determined to discern in the PLP's position on industrial relations an ambiguity that did not exist, but which Houghton's and Jenkins's words on the subject unfortunately implied. Certainly Jenkins's assertion that the difference between the PLP and the TUC was semantic,[37] made little impression on either Jones or Scanlon, for whom his contribution demonstrated the negative impact of the intellectuals in Labour's ranks upon party–trade union relations.[38]

That Jenkins would prove a source of friction between party and trade union leaders was perhaps inevitable (there being that about his manner which his critics on the left of the party found insufficiently plebeian).[39] Because it was known that he favoured an incomes policy, and because it was also known that he was not entirely unsympathetic to the objectives which lay behind the government's industrial relations legislation (and unlike Wilson he was not compelled to perform a U-turn on the subject of trade union reform), and finally, most significantly, because he might so easily succeed Wilson as leader of the Labour Party, those TUC and party representatives on the committee intent on reaching an agreement at any price were necessarily discomfited by his prescence. The fact that Wilson also was known to favour an incomes policy, and that *In Place of Strife* had been as much his White Paper as it had been Barbara Castle's, and that such a man *was* leader of the Labour Party, appeared not to count against him in the way it did against his deputy. The difference, of course, was that of those senior members of the parliamentary leadership sitting around the table at the Liaison Committee, only Jenkins had demonstrated a willingness to rank the interests of the Labour Party below that of his own commitment to British membership of the Common Market. However, the willingness of the assembled trade union representatives to rank the interests of their members above those of the Labour Party passed unremarked upon.

The meeting was rescued by Wilson, who intervened to reassure the TUC that the PLP was committed to the repeal of the Act 'and we hope to work out a replacement. We would want to have the repeal in the first session'. This, according to Tony Benn's diary account of the meeting, was the beginning of the accord Jack Jones was seeking. The defensiveness of the TUC attested to the unease felt by trade union leaders when forced to discuss trade unionism in a legislative context. Wilson did his best to overcome this: 'Let's get an agreed document between us.'[40]

Once the TUC had been persuaded that there was 'general agreement that all wings of the Party were firmly committed to repeal, and that was quite clear', the meeting proceeded in a more comradely fashion. For the TUC, the purpose of talking to the parliamentary leadership was to ensure the removal of the existing restriction on trade union activity and to ensure that such activity would remain free from restriction in the future.[41] Subsequent to this the TUC held out the prospect of a number of points which might be considered *voluntarily*, such as the setting up of an independent conciliation and arbitration service and the reform of the Wages Council system.[42] As for the content of the repeal legislation, the TUC pointed out that 'such a document would need to stress that many positive developments – for example on the question of status quo – were essentially matters for collective bargaining rather than legislation', adding that 'The state's role had to be seen more as a supporting one, and the development of conciliation and arbitration services was a good example of this.'[43] From this it was agreed that Congress House would prepare a document setting out the TUC's voluntary approach to industrial relations for circulation prior to the next meeting. This first meeting of the Liaison Committee demonstrated the likely extent of any concession from the TUC in respect of industrial relations. Clearly, the key word in the TUC's vocabulary in February 1972 was 'voluntary'.

The TUC's approach to industrial relations established the context in which all policy issues were to be discussed by the Liaison Committee. Just as *In Place of Strife* and the Industrial Relations Act had proved unacceptable to the TUC, so did any suggestion of a statutory incomes policy. Accordingly, the basis for the discussion of economic policy was to be the TUC's *Economic Review 1972* and the NEC's 1971 statement *Economic Strategy, Growth and Unemployment*, neither of which advocated a statutory policy. Opening the discussion on economic policy, the TUC pointed out that there existed 'a very close cooperation between

Congress House and Transport House on economic issues and this was considerably reflected in the two statements'.[44] This process of co-operation was further advanced by the decision to circulate the TUC document to those Labour Party representatives attending the two conferences on policy organised by the Finance and Economic Affairs Subcommittee and the Industrial Policy Subcommittee, scheduled to take place between 25 and 27 February.

The TUC and the NEC had, in the form of their respective policy statements, clear policy agendas which they sought to pursue through the Liaison Committee. The PLP, officially tied to *Economic Strategy, Growth and Unemployment*, alone of the three bodies which made up the Liaison Committee, was effectively prevented from raising any issue which fell beyond the contents of the NEC statement (a document that was very much the property of the Industrial Policy Subcommittee, and by extension the Research Department) on the grounds that what was not in the NEC document could not be party policy. Clearly the NEC had hopes that the research programme would provide the basis of a common economic and industrial policy for both the Labour Party and the trade unions. However, one consequence of the Conservative government's attempted reform of industrial relations was a heightening of sectional consciousness among trade unionists. The TUC did not see its role at the Liaison Committee as being primarily to create an imbalance in PLP–NEC relations. The TUC was concerned about the fundamentals of trade unionism itself, rather than with the NEC research programme, of which the limitations in February 1972 (given the parliamentary leadership's lack of enthusiasm for the process) were all too obvious.

The TUC's motivation for taking part in the Liaison Committee, measured in terms of what might be conceded to the PLP, was essentially negative. Jones and Scanlon, for example, were there to prevent legislation on trade unions and incomes policy, just as they had at Blackpool in 1970. The PLP, by comparison, was taking part because of an urgent need to resolve the problem of wage inflation, as in light of the trade unions' rejection of incomes policy the Labour Party had no credible economic policy. When Harold Lever (another of the intellectuals on Jones's list) spoke of the threat to Labour's electoral prospects if the party failed to produce specific ideas to counteract rising inflation, he met with a hardened response from the TUC, and found himself on the receiving end of a lecture on the uniqueness of the situation in Britain. It was not a matter of wage rates, the TUC explained, so much as output rates. Instead of harking back to incomes policy, he was told, he and his colleagues would do well to emphasise 'the waste of output caused by unemployment and the attendant adverse effects on unit costs'.[45] And so the first meeting of the TUC–Labour Party Liaison Committee ended as it began.

Repealing the Industrial Relations Act: the TUC–Labour Party Liaison Committee, February–July 1972

Between February and July 1972, Liaison Committee meetings were dominated by the issue of industrial relations. In March the TUC submitted the paper 'Industrial Relations and the Law',[46] stating once more that 'the development of good industrial relations should not be looked at primarily in the context of the law';[47] in April, the NEC and the PLP responded by submitting their own paper, 'Legislation and Industrial Relations'.[48] Both papers were scrutinised paragraph by paragraph and formed the basis of the committee's discussion of the issue at these meetings.[49] All subsequent meetings in this period proceeded in this fashion.

Predictably, and for obvious reasons, the TUC dominated the Liaison Committee's discussion of industrial relations. As Jones writes, 'right, left and centre of the TUC General Council... were agreed that the unions were in real danger'.[50] Accordingly, the purpose of the TUC paper submitted to the March meeting was 'to explore in particular the interaction between trade union function and legislation'. The paper provided clear examples of the areas in which the TUC believed the state had a role to play, such as in the development of conciliation and arbitration services, which was specifically proposed in this paper.[51] The TUC was under no illusion that the monthly meetings of the Liaison Committee alone would be sufficient to guarantee the inclusion of its key policy proposals in any future agreement. Certainly the PLP kept up the pretence that it would not be bounced into an agreement with the TUC and at times insisted on considering even the most non-contentious of proposals at meetings of the NEC–PLP side of the Liaison Committee before 'adopting any firm position'.[52] The TUC's proposal for an independent conciliation and arbitration service was entirely acceptable to the Labour Party,[53] yet the PLP and the NEC still went through the motions of discussing the party's response to the proposal away from the Liaison Committee. The party, after all, was *supposed to be* negotiating with the TUC.

However, of primary concern to Jack Jones (the source of the TUC proposal) was ensuring that the Labour leadership actually absorbed the proposals the TUC placed before it at the Liaison Committee. To this end, in an attempt to have the PLP and the NEC agree to the development of an independent conciliation and arbitration service, Jones set out his thoughts on this subject and on methods of making progress on low pay and industrial democracy in an article for *New Statesman*.[54] This appeared three days prior to the first meeting of the Liaison Committee in February 1972. His decision to use the article to duplicate the contents of the TUC paper, 'Industrial Relations and the Law', demonstrated the depth of his understanding of the people he was dealing with at the Liaison

Committee. Placing the article in *New Statesman* was, he felt, the only way he could be sure the parliamentary leadership would take notice of the proposal:

> I wanted the article to be published in the *New Statesman* because I knew that it was more likely to be read by Labour's leaders than any 'paper' submitted through the TUC or Labour Party research departments. I also hoped that my friends in those research departments would read the article, because I wanted them to know that it was the blueprint I would be sticking to in policy discussions within the Liaison Committee. All too often, in the TUC and Labour Party discussions, academic researchers prepared papers on policy and committee members gave their instant reactions. I thought this was a hit and miss approach to policy-making. I was determined to fight my corner and the *New Statesman* piece was part of that. In fact the eventual setting up of ACAS [the Advisory Conciliation and Arbitration Service] and certain aspects of the Employment Protection legislation of the 1974 Labour Government were initiated in that article.[55]

Jones proposed that, in countering the Conservative government's legislation, the Labour Party should place 'special emphasis' on the development (at both regional and national level) of a voluntary conciliation and arbitration service:

> This would replace the legal rigmarole of the Industrial Relations Act, particularly the NIRC and the CIR, with a simple, clearly understood (and much less costly) means of providing workpeople and their unions with an optional alternative to the use of the strike weapon. This approach would have the double advantage of removing legal restraints on the right to strike and the free functioning of the trade union movement and at the same time help to avoid strike explosions by offering reasonable means to secure a measure of industrial justice when the normal negotiating methods have broken down.[56]

The Labour Party got the message about a voluntary conciliation and arbitration service. On 13 April the NEC and the PLP agreed the proposal was acceptable.[57] There were some misgivings, such as that the TUC proposal did not include the provision for an 'outside body' to encourage the reform of industrial relations, 'even if the suggested CAS, through a separate division, was the body responsible for this',[58] but, most significantly, agreement on the main proposal was forthcoming. The Labour Party's acceptance of the TUC proposal vindicated Jones's faith in the Liaison

Committee as the best way of securing the parliamentary leadership's agreement on those policies of vital importance to the trade unions. This, neither conference nor the NEC research programme could guarantee. The Liaison Committee was a vehicle for the trade unions in this respect. Concessions on policy were one-sided and the committee must therefore be considered hostile territory for the PLP because of the absence of an obvious 'get-out'. Whereas conference resolutions and the policies produced by the NEC research programme could be ignored or stifled, the agreements on policy reached between the party and the TUC at the Liaison Committee could not be broken without threatening the continuance of a future Labour government. The PLP's problem was therefore one of resentment stemming from the knowledge that the party was making an agreement with the TUC which was basically the wrong agreement for both the Labour Party and the country. PLP representatives found it difficult to contain their frustration. Douglas Houghton, noted Benn, continued to be 'provocative'; Barbara Castle 'just can't help annoying people'; while Harold Lever kept 'touching on sensitive spots'. 'In fairness', Benn concluded, 'we have to sort this out because it is an important series of discussions that we are now having, and there is no point in concealing the fact.'[59]

The Liaison Committee ushered in an approach to party–trade union relations which Michael Foot was to subsequently pursue with vigour as Secretary of State for Employment 1974–76. Foot's 'only policy', Conrad Heron, the second permanent secretary at the Department of Employment, told Barbara Castle in July 1974, 'is to find out what the unions want'.[60] In April 1972, the PLP told the TUC that the main provisions of a future Labour government's repeal legislation 'would clearly need to begin with a TUC document for the Liaison Committee'.[61] This was duly produced and discussed when the Liaison Committee met in June 1972. The TUC paper, 'Industrial Relations – The Scope of Future Legislation', included a synopsis of the points the TUC wished to see covered in the repeal legislation.[62] While by this time 'the general lines on the CAS and the repeal legislation were becoming clear', the Liaison Committee's discussion of the paper demonstrated the extent to which the TUC saw the repeal legislation as an opportunity to strengthen trade unionism itself. Perhaps unavoidably, this created scope for misunderstanding and highlighted the fragility of the enterprise. When, for example, the PLP questioned the TUC as to whether the envisaged conciliation and arbitration service would provide 'a means for resolving disputes about the closed shop, so that an alternative would be available to recourse to strike action', the TUC responded that the services of the CAS 'would be available but not mandatory',[63] yet the significance of the question was that the PLP was flirting with the ghost of *In Place of Strife*. The TUC would not countenance a dimension to the repeal legislation which made provision for mandatory arbitration for any type of dispute, or which bore even the slightest resemblance to the 'conciliation pause' proposal in Castle's contentious White Paper.[64] Had the PLP pushed the TUC too hard on this or any other policy issue – such as inflation or the cost of an increase in pensions – the Liaison Committee might have easily folded.[65]

As it was, on 24 July 1972, the Liaison Committee was able to publish a statement announcing that broad agreement had been reached on the nature of the legislation a future Labour government would introduce to replace the Industrial Relations Act:

> The TUC and the Labour Party have broadly agreed the outline of legislation to replace the Industrial Relations Act, although the details remain to be finalised. The proposed legislation would repeal the whole Act. The other main sections of the proposed legislation would provide that workers would have the right to belong to a trade union, would be protected against unfair dismissals, enjoy shorter qualifying periods for minimum notice and longer periods of notice from employers.
>
> Trade unions would be able to take employers who refused recognition or information for collective bargaining purposes before arbitration committees; trade union members would have a legal right to meet with trade union officials at their workplace, and their representatives would have statutory rights on safety matters. Where redundancies are planned, employers would be required to give a minimum period of notice to the union concerned to give time for genuine consultations to take place. Collective agreements would not be regarded as legally binding unless both parties expressly so agreed. The new law on trade disputes would give full protection for trade unionists. Other matters are still under discussion.[66]

Agreement on the repeal legislation represented only the beginning of the Liaison Committee's work. The TUC, having persuaded the Labour Party to agree to repeal the Act, exploited the opportunity provided by the existence of the Liaison Committee to discuss with the PLP the economic policies of the next Labour government. The Liaison Committee's decision to discuss economic policy had in fact been taken at the first meeting in February 1972, but in the July statement it was duly announced that the committee would be discussing 'the wider economic and industrial policies of the next Labour Government',[67] and that the basis of these discussions would be the TUC's *Economic Review* (as was the case in February), and the NEC document *Labour's Programme for Britain 1972*, published two weeks earlier and which had superseded *Economic Strategy, Growth and Unemployment* as Labour's most up-to-date policy document.

The TUC and Heath: the Chequers and Downing Street talks

On 3 July 1972, three weeks prior to the publication by the Liaison Committee of the statement announcing that agreement on repeal of the Industrial Relations Act had been reached, Edward Heath announced to the House of Commons that he had invited the TUC and the CBI to take part in joint discussions with a view to securing an agreement on economic co-operation. Relations between the government and the TUC had taken a more positive turn in December 1971, when Heath had invited the TUC General Council to Downing Street and had gone 'out of his way to emphasise that he wanted to do business with the TUC'.[68] The government's need for a deal with the trade unions had increased amid the calamity of the seven-week miners' strike, which had resulted in a pay award averaging 27 per cent, and which did grievous damage to the government's attempts to control wage inflation.[69] By February 1972 (coincidentally the month in which the TUC–Labour Party Liaison Committee began to meet), it was apparent that the government, no less than the Labour Party, could see no way forward on economic policy without the consent of organised labour. As Douglas Hurd (a witness to the events at the time) writes, 'The facts of power in Britain were against the Government. They were also against any realistic economic policy.'[70]

In a political broadcast to the nation ten days after the end of the miners' strike, Heath sent out a positive signal to the TUC, stating that 'We must find a more sensible way to settle our differences . . . After all, it is the Government's job to see that the interests of all sections of the community are properly looked after.'[71] Heath's broadcast was music to the ears of Vic Feather who, in Jack Jones's words, 'seemed to fancy himself as unofficial ambassador for the TUC and special adviser to Ted Heath'.[72] Whatever Feather's exact status other than as general secretary of the TUC, he was to play a crucial role in bringing the government and the TUC together. In a series of secret meetings with Heath and Sir William Armstrong, the head of the Home Civil Service, he attempted 'to guide the Prime Minister's hand to what would be acceptable. Heath asked questions, Feather offered answers . . . Feather came away satisfied that Heath wanted to reach an agreement.'[73] 'Heath for his part', writes John Campbell, 'was persuaded that Feather could deliver one.'[74] Feather, however, 'delivered' the unions only inasmuch as the TUC General Council rejected a motion objecting to the talks by 21 votes to nine.[75]

When TUC representatives[76] eventually sat down with Heath, they did so as members of the National Economic Development Council (NEDC),[77] which served as a convenient fig-leaf for those union leaders who were opposed to talking to the government while the Industrial Relations Act remained on the statute book, but who nonetheless thought it wise to keep a watchful eye on their more enthusiastic colleagues.[78] Although Feather could command a majority on the General Council in favour of the talks (and opposed to confrontation with the government),[79] a TUC delegation that did not include Jones and Scanlon (both of whom were highly sceptical about the process) would have lacked credibility. Jones particularly, while obviously desiring the repeal of the Industrial Relations Act, was clearly of the view that an agreement on repeal was more likely to be reached by talking to the Labour Party than by talking to the government. He believed the premise of the talks with the government to be flawed, given that repeal of the Act was not on the agenda. Further, Heath believed that an agreement on wages and prices was possible in isolation from the wider issues of concern to the TUC, a misreading of the situation for which Jones believed Feather to be responsible.[80] Certainly Feather, Alf Allen, Lord Cooper and Sir Sidney Greene were willing to make such an agreement; Jones and Scanlon, to Heath's amazement and Feather's disappointment, were not.[81] However, to be either amazed or disappointed was to underestimate the determination of Jones and Scanlon to keep their eyes on the main prize, the repeal of the legislative measure which in their estimation threatened the existence of free trade unionism in Britain.

Feather, ever in search of a deal, sought to convince Jones of the wisdom of talking to Heath on the grounds that the Prime Minister was 'coming our way', to which Jones responded with brutal clarity: 'Tell them that we'll get nowhere without getting rid of the Industrial Relations Act.' While Jones gradually came to accept that talks about rising unemployment and inflation were in the best interests of his members, and an opportunity to express the concern of the TUC over low-paid workers and the pensioners,[82] he proved a shrewder judge of Heath's character than Feather, rightly perceiving that the Prime Minister would ultimately refuse to give way on the Act, a reality he feared Feather and the more emollient TUC representatives had closed their eyes to, but of which they would be painfully reminded.

In fairness, Feather desired the repeal of the Industrial Relations Act and the introduction of a conciliation and arbitration service 'as an *alternative* to the Act' no less than Jones.[83] However, to satisfy his more sceptical colleagues (and to the detriment of the talks process) he was obliged to take a harder line towards the government than he might otherwise have done.[84] Heath's new-found courtesy towards the trade unions notwithstanding, the 'terrible twins' were 'unwilling to be swallowed up'.[85] The talks proceeded on the understanding that 'there should be no question of statutory wage control'.[86]

Substantive talks between the government, the TUC and (on the periphery) the CBI began at Chequers on 26 September 1972. At two meetings of the NEDC held prior to this date, Heath had given his blessing to the conciliation and arbitration service being planned by the TUC and the CBI, and had also agreed to effectively place the Industrial Relations Act 'on ice',[87] two gestures which ensured that the talks began in an atmosphere of goodwill. It had also been agreed that an NEDC working group would examine two issues prior to substantive talks taking place: 1) a definition of the lower paid and an assessment of the ways and means of implementing a programme for improving their position; 2) prices and what action could be taken to reduce the rate of price increases during the coming year.[88] The NEDC met to discuss the findings of the working group at Chequers on 14 September.

At the 26 September meeting Heath put forward a number of proposals intended to serve as the basis for discussion, including a commitment to achieve a 5 per cent rate of growth to cover the next two years, while at the same time aiming to keep growth of retail prices resulting from cost increases within a limit of 5 per cent; manufactured goods to be kept within a price limit of 4 per cent; government action to limit price increases where it had the ability to influence them; pay increases of up to £2 a week; a new body to be set up to help the traditionally low-paid industries to achieve greater efficiency as a basis for higher wages; the introduction of threshold agreements with a flat-rate amount of 20p for each increase of 1 per cent above a threshold of 6 per cent to deal with once-and-for-all factors which in 1973 could cause prices to rise by more than 5 per cent; a reduction by one hour in the working week, roughly equivalent to a pay rise of about 2.5 per cent; and measures to ensure that pensioners enjoyed the benefit of the nation's increasing prosperity.[89]

The TUC presented its counter-proposals on 16 October, calling for VAT to be introduced at a lower rate of 7.5 per cent (as opposed to 10 per cent); the Housing Finance Act rent increases to be abandoned; measures to be introduced to check the growth of house prices and halt land speculation; the renegotiation of the Common Agricultural Policy; a weekly pay increase of up to £3.40; and thresholds to be introduced at 5 per cent (as opposed to 6 per cent). Additionally, the TUC argued for a wealth tax and a surcharge on capital gains; limitation of dividend payments; the prevention of betterment profits accruing to private property developers; the reversal of the 1972 Budget concessions on investment and high earned income and estate duty; higher pensions; and a move away from means-tested benefits in favour of substantial increases in family allowances. Finally, the TUC requested that an assurance be given that the non-operation of the Industrial Relations Act would continue.[90]

What followed has been set down in greater detail elsewhere.[91] Further meetings took place at Downing Street in an effort to reach an agreement and in the cause of which, writes Hurd, 'the Prime Minister wore himself and others to the point of exhaustion'.[92] Heath outlined a number of further possibilities, including a 50 p increase in the needs allowance for the calculation of rent rebates; an extension of the award period for family incomes supplements; free school meals and welfare milk from six months to one year so that entitlement to these would not change because of changed circumstances; a lump sum payment to those receiving national insurance retirement and supplementary pensions; and government consultation with local authorities on moderating the growth of local rates.[93] However, when Jones persisted in raising the issue of the Industrial Relations Act (and in addition pensions, VAT and rents), Heath announced that these were matters for Parliament, not the TUC.[94] The goodwill that had been so much in evidence in July evaporated. The TUC, mournfully in Feather's case, told the Prime Minister that it would be unable to make a positive recommendation to the General Council on the possibilities he had outlined, and withdrew.[95] Four days later Heath announced to the House of Commons that his government would be introducing measures (with immediate effect) for an interim 90-day standstill on increases in wages, prices, rents and dividends. To the satisfaction of no one, the tripartite talks had produced a return to a prices and incomes policy.

Economic Policy and the Cost of Living

What the TUC could not agree with the government, it could agree with the Labour Party. The Liaison Committee had continued to meet throughout the period of the tripartite talks. On the eve of the NEDC meeting of 26 September, the Liaison Committee had met to discuss economic policy, the agreed basis of the discussion being the NEC document *Labour's Programme for Britain 1972* and the TUC's *Economic Review*. Labour leaders clearly hoped that the NEC document would 'create a climate within which there could be active trade union co-operation with a Labour Government'. The TUC, for its part, welcomed the approach to industrial, regional and taxation policy set out in the NEC document, but added that it should be borne in mind that 'collective bargaining realities could not be ignored and it was therefore important that the Labour Party should not have too simple an approach to the area of wage negotiations'.[96]

The PLP in fact took it for granted that the TUC would want more than was set out in *Labour's Programme for Britain 1972*. Politically, the PLP needed the TUC to be more precise about wage negotions, thus enabling the party to dispel the impression that it had 'nothing useful to say about the problem of inflation which was uppermost in the public mind'. To this the TUC (ever on the defensive when the subject of wages arose in any discussion with either of the main political parties) unhelpfully responded that 'it was difficult to assess how far it would be possible to go in defining concrete problems and solutions in the field of wage negotiations'.[97] This response was in keeping with the TUC's approach to discussing a deal on wages. Only when the PLP had agreed to act on prices would the TUC consider becoming less reticent about wages.

By November 1972 the Liaison Committee was cautiously feeling its way towards an understanding on prices that would form the basis of a joint document which would also cover housing and land, poverty and pensions, industry and investment. Predictably, the issue of wages, prices and the national income was to be the subject of *further* work. How these inter-linked issues would be dealt with by the TUC and a future Labour government was, the committee acknowledged, of vital importance and would 'depend to some extent on the specific circumstances of the economy at the time'. Fine words, yet within a matter of months it was to become clear that the PLP had committed a future Labour government to the introduction of a number of specific measures demanded by the TUC, irrespective of the economic circumstances of the day. Certainly little attention appears to have been paid to the comment in the course of the meeting that 'an open-ended subsidy to keep food prices within the given figure – even if this did not fall foul of Common Market considerations – might lead to a very high Exchequer expenditure commitment, to be financed by taxation'.[98]

By the end of January 1973, a joint statement encompassing the above had been agreed by the Liaison Committee and was subsequently published by the Labour Party in pamphlet form on 28 February. *Economic Policy and the Cost of Living* was the document which at least some of the TUC representatives on the NEDC had hoped would emerge from the unsuccessful tripartite talks. It emerged instead from the Liaison Committee because six months earlier the PLP had conceded what Heath would not: the repeal of the Industrial Relations Act. Further, when the TUC had submitted its counter-proposals to the government's own proposals on 16 October 1972, one priority had been the abandonment of the Housing Finance Act rent increases. *Economic Policy and the Cost of Living* confirmed that a Labour government would repeal the Act in its entirety.[99] On this and on a host of other policy issues the Labour Party satisfied the TUC's demands. Under the heading 'An Alternative Strategy', the Liaison Committee joint statement suggested that 'The key to any alternative strategy to fight inflation is direct statutory action on prices – and, above all, direct action on the prices of those items that loom largest in the budgets of workpeople.'[100] Accordingly, food prices would be controlled, subsidies provided and special measures taken to deal with increases in the prices of basic foods such as milk, bread, sugar, meat and potatoes. Indeed, price controls would be further extended to prevent the erosion of real wages, a move which, it was confidently stated, would 'influence the whole climate of collective bargaining'. Council tenants would be given a better deal, both on rents and on security; subsidies to public sector housing would be increased to match the £300 million plus a year given in tax relief to the owner occupier. Additionally, a Labour government 'would aim for a large-scale *redistribution of income and wealth*'.[101]

The content of *Economic Policy and the Cost of Living* reflected Labour's dual representation on the Liaison Committee. The commitments on economic policy included under the heading 'An Alternative Economic Strategy' were the result of a TUC–PLP dialogue which guaranteed their implementation. By contrast, the industrial policy commitments included under the heading 'Investment, Employment and Economic Growth' bore the stamp of the NEC and resembled the content of *Labour's Programme for Britain 1972*. The ideas on public enterprise contained in *Economic Policy and the Cost of Living* drew on the ideas of Stuart Holland, the source of much of the Industrial Policy Subcommittee's contribution to the NEC policy document.[102] For this reason alone it was unlikely that the commitments on industrial policy would be honoured.

Together with the July 1972 statement pledging the repeal of the Industrial Relations Act, the Liaison Committee hoped that the approach set out in *Economic Policy and the Cost of Living* would 'further engender the strong feeling of mutual confidence which alone will make it possible to reach the wide-ranging agreement which is necessary to control inflation and achieve sustained growth in the standard of living'. The conclusion stated that the first task of a newly elected Labour government, 'having due regard to the circumstances at that time', would be to conclude with the TUC, 'on the basis of the understandings being reached on the Liaison Committee, a wide-ranging agreement on the policies to be pursued in all these aspects of our economic life and to discuss with them the order of priorities of their fulfilment'.[103]

The Times responded to publication of *Economic Policy and the Cost of Living* with an editorial proclaiming that the Liaison Committee had produced 'A policy which could not work', and which spelt out what Labour's parliamentary leadership knew to be true, but had no wish to be reminded of:

> The essential issue remains that of inflation; the main cause of inflation has been the consistent tendency to award ourselves wage and salary increases going beyond what the increase in productivity would pay for. Profits as a share of the Gross National Product have until recently been falling. No prices and incomes policy which fails to grasp this issue is of any use at all. The Government, belatedly and under the grave handicap of a sharp rise in world food prices, is trying to deal with the essential problem. The joint Labour Party and TUC document runs away from it. Most people in the Parliamentary Labour Party know perfectly well that a one-sided policy is quite useless; Mr Wilson has been through all this before; it adds nothing to the credit of British politics that the alternative Government should come out with a policy which could do nothing to defeat inflation, and something to stoke it up.[104]

There was of course a limit to the number of times the parliamentary leadership desired to be reminded – by *The Times* or by anyone else – of the deficiencies of the joint statement or, for that matter, of any of the party's policy statements in opposition. *Economic Policy and the Cost of Living* was not the policy document the PLP would have preferred, but the Liaison Committee at least provided Wilson and his senior colleagues with a structure through which the more exotic NEC research programme proposals could be filtered, forgotten or ameliorated. When, for example, the Liaison Committee joint statement spoke of it being the *aim* (my italics) of a future Labour government to tax wealth (as did *Labour's Programme for Britain 1972*) it could be taken as read that this would not be a top priority for Labour's Shadow Chancellor, Denis Healey,[105] given that in this period he was publicly talking in terms of the need for the party to decide upon its priorities so that a Labour government might keep its promises.[106] The Labour Party after all (with one or two notable exceptions)[107] did actually want to win the general election when it came and the Social Contract with the trade unions which emerged from the Liaison Committee was ultimately the least worst cost of trying to do so. And, as Jones has written, 'On the whole I guess that Harold Wilson, Jim Callaghan and the rest preferred to deal with the Liaison Committee rather than the NEC.'[108]

In place of an agreement on wages

In his speech to conference in 1972, Denis Healey observed that the TUC's preconditions for an incomes policy had been met by the Labour Party. Four weeks earlier Jack Jones had moved a successful TGWU motion at the TUC meeting in Brighton, which declared that 'no consideration can be given to any policy on incomes unless it is an integral part of an economic strategy which includes control of rents, profits, dividends and prices and is designed to secure a redistribution of income and wealth nationally and globally. Congress therefore calls for new constructive policies to include effective price and import controls, in particular of food prices, the withdrawal of the Housing Finance Act and control over property and land speculation.'[109] *Labour's Programme for Britain 1972*, Healey told conference, offered the labour movement just such a strategy.[110] Having restated in *Economic Policy and the Cost of Living* the pledges included in *Labour's Programme for Britain 1972* on prices, the Industrial Relations Act and the Housing Finance Act, the parliamentary leadership's chief concern in April 1973 was that it was 'putting a great many goodies on the table for the trade unions and it is becoming urgent that we should see what is coming from the other side' (as Crosland was to phrase it a year later when the party was once again in government).[111] Labour's problem was that it had made its concessions to the TUC too early.

Progress at the Liaison Committee on an incomes policy of any description was painfully slow and only heightened the fears of Wilson and his colleagues that when the election came the party would be all too easily portrayed by both the Conservatives and Liberals as the party with an inflationary programme.[112] In truth the TUC was unsympathetic to the idea of wage restraint under any circumstances. At the TUC meeting Jones had revealingly quoted Ernest Bevin: 'You cannot place a ceiling on wages while one man works for another man's profit.' This rather undermined Healey's words on the subject a month later.[113] At the Liaison Committee, Labour Party representatives expressed their concern that *Economic Policy and the Cost of Living* was not reaching as many trade unionists as they would like. Widespread distribution of the joint statement among trade unionists was a vital aspect of the parliamentary leadership's attempt to demonstrate how the Labour Party had committed itself to an economic policy which made an agreement on wages both natural, sensible and in the national interest. However, given that the TUC believed it to be 'largely for the Labour Party to take this a stage further with Labour Party affiliated unions', Wilson and his colleagues had little reason to be confident about the sincerity of the unions in respect of an agreement on wages.[114]

On the eve of the February 1974 general election, the Labour Party found itself with a campaign document based on *Economic Policy and the Cost of Living*, against which every item in the document had been checked.[115] However, by February 1974, the relevance of an agreement with the trade unions was in question due to the party's inability to win any of the recently held by-elections. On 8 November 1973, Labour had failed to win any of the four by-elections held that day.[116] Worse, the party's own investigation of the local campaigns had found little to suggest that even on an organisational level the party was ready for a general election. In Glasgow Govan, the party had performed so poorly that the seat had fallen to the Scottish Nationalists, a defeat attributed to the fact that: 1) 'The candidate was, on balance, a factor against Labour'; 2) 'It was not a happy campaign'; 3) 'The organisation was inept in the extreme'; 4) 'The literature was diabolical'.[117]

But it was the absence of an agreement on wages with the TUC that continued to dominate the party's discussion of policy in the months leading up to the general election, as Labour leaders became increasingly desperate for the TUC to make a public declaration in support of a voluntary incomes policy. Only if such a declaration was forthcoming could the party claim to have a policy on inflation.[118] In these circumstances, the final Liaison Committee meeting prior to the general election was potentially the most important of the 19 held since February 1972. Crucially, both Jones and Scanlon were absent when the Liaison Committee met on 4 January 1974 at Congress House. Despite the location of the meeting, the TUC was under-represented. Only Sir Sidney Greene, George Smith and Len Murray (plus his officials) were present and between them they lacked the authority to commit the trade unions to a deal on wages even had they been inclined to do so, which they were not. This did not deter James Callaghan from pointing out to the TUC that the Labour Party had a campaign document with an obvious weakness, the lack of a reference to incomes, and without such a reference the party would lack credibility with the electorate. 'Could the TUC help on this?', he asked. Harold Wilson pointed out that he had already had this point 'thrown at him by Robin Day and others on TV yesterday'. Seeking to appeal to reason, Denis Healey suggested that what was required 'was a statement of *intention* by the TUC – something going beyond what you think might happen'. Healey was followed by Reg Prentice, who suggested that the Liaison Committee should 'say we *believe* in an incomes policy, even though we recognise it would have to be voluntary'. 'Lucky for him Jack Jones wasn't there – I can imagine the explosion at this point', Castle concluded in her diary.[119]

In the end, the absence of Jones and Scanlon from the meeting made little difference. The TUC, said Len Murray, 'was not going to give an absolute firm pledge on wages'.[120] Indeed, the TUC hoped the phrase 'incomes policy' would be forgotten. *Economic Policy and the Cost of Living*, he continued, provided the scope for a broad understanding between the TUC and the Labour Party. It was therefore 'reasonable for the Labour Party to put to the TUC that if they made significant moves on the agreed objectives then they would expect all parties to conform to these objectives. The TUC would examine the Labour Party document and would certainly respond.'

Two weeks prior to this meeting Wilson had given a speech in Leeds, in the course of which the full extent of the party's concession to the trade unions on both economic and industrial policy was laid bare: pensions would be increased to £10 and £16 per week for the single person and married couple respectively, 'and thereafter linked to national average earnings'; strict price controls on essential foods and other goods and services 'which are important in their effect on the cost of living of the ordinary family' would be introduced; all building land required for development, redevelopment and improvement would be taken into public ownership and an Act introduced 'to ensure there is sufficient money at reasonable rates for the building of local authority houses to rent'; the Housing Finance Act would be repealed; tax reform to redistribute both income and wealth, including an annual wealth tax, would be introduced; the Industrial Relations Act would be repealed 'as a matter of extreme urgency', followed by the introduction of an Employment Protection Act and then by an Industrial Democracy Act; private companies would be controlled through an Industry Act; a National Enterprise Board would be created and a number of industries (including shipbuilding, the ports and aircraft) taken into public ownership; North Sea oil and gas would be brought under government control; post-school-leaving education would be reformed and a national scheme of nursery schools introduced. 'The Labour Party', Wilson stated, 'has an urgent duty today to put before the nation its realistic, relevant, up-to-date policies for dealing with the desperately urgent economic and social problems facing the nation'.[121] Two weeks later the TUC stated categorically that no pledge on wages would be given.

Postscript: the Social Contract

Edmund Dell, having described the Social Contract at the time as 'codswallop', found it necessary, in retrospect, to revise his opinion. The Social Contract was in fact 'worse than codswallop', he wrote in 1991:[122]

> Those within the Labour Party who could not see the concessions as good in themselves had to be reconciled to them by the thought of the contract against inflation. But if there was to be a contract, there would also have to be regard to the ability of the trade unions to deliver their part of the bargain. Either pay restraint was in the interests of trade union members or it was not. If it was, and was seen to be, there seemed little reason to pay for it by way of political concessions. If it was not, or was not seen to be, it seemed unlikely that consent could be bought by a contract of this kind. Satisfying the ambitions of trade union leaders for political influence has low priority among trade union members.[123]

Three years and eight months in opposition gave the Labour Party a programme that could not work. Conversely, three years and eight months of Conservative government bequeathed to the British people a Labour government they neither particularly wanted nor could afford. Wilson and his colleagues took office in March 1974 without a majority and without a programme they would willingly have described as their own.[124] The Liaison Committee had saved them from the party and the NEC research programme inasmuch as it facilitated a return to high politics after the skirmish with the party at Blackpool in 1970. Other than that it produced little more than a bad agreement for the party and a programme which ensured the ineffectualness of the Labour government 1974–79.

Notes

1 Minkin, *The Labour Party Conference*, pp. 93–7.
2 LPAR, 1970, p. 180.
3 J. Jones, *Union Man* (London, Collins, 1986), p. 226.

4 Labour Party, *Economic Policy and the Cost of Living* (London, 1973).
5 E. Dell, *A Hard Pounding* (Oxford, Oxford University Press, 1991), pp. 15–16.
6 Between July and October 1972, Heath met TUC and CBI representatives at both Downing Street and Chequers. Meetings of the TUC–Labour Party Liaison Committee took place on a rotating basis at the House of Commons, Transport House and Congress House.
7 Castle, *The Castle Diaries 1974–76* (London, Weidenfeld & Nicolson, 1980), p. 3.
8 Campbell, *Edward Heath*, pp. 473–4.
9 Campbell, *Edward Heath*, p. 474.
10 What became known as the 'Tripartite Talks' are dealt with at greater length and in greater detail below.
11 In some respects Jones was pushing at an open door. The Conservative Party's general election manifesto in 1970 had promised that a Conservative government would take urgent action 'to give some pension as of right to the over-eighties who now get no retirement pension at all'. Conservative Party, *A Better Tomorrow* (1970), in Craig, *British General Election Manifestos*, p. 337. This Keith Joseph (as Secretary of State for Health and Social Security) duly delivered in the government's first year in office. Additionally, pensions were provided for younger widows aged between 40 and 50. Campbell, *Edward Heath*, p. 383. A one pound increase in the weekly pension was also promised in the autumn of 1971. Jones, *Union Man*, p. 235. As Butler and Kavanagh write, by February 1974 the parties were falling over themselves in their attempt to secure the pensioners' vote: 'The one area in which the parties' statements resembled an auction was pensions. This was an issue on which Conservatives had overtaken Labour popular ratings as "the party best able to handle" the issue. In large part this was a consequence of Sir Keith Joseph's 55 per cent increase in the basic pension since 1970 and his £10 Christmas bonus for pensioners.' Butler and Kavanagh, *The British General Election of February 1974*, p. 56.
12 LPAR, 1970, p. 240.
13 LPAR, 1970, p. 240.
14 Jones, *Union Man*, p. 235.
15 LPAR, 1970, p. 240.
16 Jones, *Union Man*, p. 235.
17 LPA, National Council of Labour, Minutes, 2 March 1971.
18 Jones, *Union Man*, pp. 235–6.
19 This was also the case when the Liaison Committee began to consider the content of the legislation to repeal the Industrial Relations Act: 'Now that Messrs Jenkins and Lever have departed to the back benches', wrote John Torode in *New Statesman* following Jenkins's resignation as deputy leader, 'there is less opposition to a proposal to divorce government from industrial disputes.' J. Torode, 'In place of strikes?', *New Statesman*, 21 April 1972, p. 3.
20 LPA, RD.128/June 1971 'Unemployment', National Council of Labour, Minutes, 14 June 1971.
21 LPAR, 1971, p. 169.
22 The unveiling of the government's intended industrial relations legislation at the Conservative Party Conference in October 1970 paved the way for a reconciliation between the TUC and the parliamentary leadership. At Westminster, Harold Wilson's was the first name on an amendment tabled by the party when the House of Commons debated Robert Carr's consultative document in November 1970. Signed by Roy Jenkins, Barbara Castle, Eric Heffer, Paul Rose and Harold Walker in addition to Wilson, the amendment condemned the document as being 'motivated by hostility to the trade union movement', and

placed on record the party's determination to reject any legislation based upon it. LPA, Parliamentary Committee, Minutes, 26 November 1970. Further, an Industrial Relations Bill Working Party, chaired by Barbara Castle, was set up to fight the Bill on the floor of the House of Commons. Support for the trade unions among the party's trade union-sponsored MPs had of course remained strong throughout the period of the Labour government, and was a factor in the decision taken by the Cabinet in 1969 not to persist with *In Place of Strife*. In the period following the publication of Carr's document, the Tribune Group of MPs at Westminster were particularly active in opposing the legislation which followed, and even went as far as to disrupt the business of the House.

23 LPAR, 1971, pp. 168–9.

24 LPAR, 1971, p. 89.

25 LPA, HPC, Minutes, 8 November 1971; NEC, Minutes, 23 November 1971.

26 LPA, RD.199/November 1971 'Discussions with the TUC', HPC, Minutes, 6 December 1971; NEC, Minutes, 22 December 1971.

27 Wilson, it should be remembered, had no formal role in the NEC's formulation of a new party programme.

28 For example, the *Report of the National Executive Committee 1971–72*, freely distributed at the 1971 conference, included the commitment to repeal in its entirety the Industrial Relations Act. This was not enough for Jones, who in moving the TGWU's Composite Resolution during the debate on industrial relations called upon the PLP to 'give a specific declaration that when Labour is returned to office the legislation formulated in the present Government's Industrial Relations Act would be completely repealed in the first session of a new Labour Government'. LPAR, 1971, pp. 46, 168. This said, the NEC's statement on the issue was an important step towards reconciliation between party and trade union leaders. As Robert Taylor writes, 'Callaghan's firm public declaration in April 1971 that the Labour party would repeal the hated measure if it was returned to office at the next general election did much to reconcile differences of view that had festered inside the unions after their unhappy experience with the Wilson government.' Taylor, *The Trade Union Question*, p. 224.

29 Jones, *Union Man*, p. 237.

30 NEC and Transport House officials suspected that Wilson would use the Liaison Committee 'to bypass the executive because the former Committee tended to produce documents which were more amenable to Labour's parliamentary leadership and because Wilson could very rarely command a majority on the latter'. W. Stallard, 'Policy-making in the Labour Party: The Liaison Committee in Opposition and in Government 1970–1979', *Teaching Politics*, 16, 1 (1987), pp. 42–55.

31 Between 21 February 1972 and 4 January 1974, during which period the Liaison Committee met 19 times prior to the general election, the PLP was at various times represented by the following: Harold Wilson, Roy Jenkins, Douglas Houghton, Bob Mellish, Harold Lever, James Callaghan, Reg Prentice, Denis Healey, Edward Short, Sir Elwyn Jones and Shirley Williams, each of whom was either a member of the Shadow Cabinet or an officer of the party. Representing the NEC: Tony Benn MP, Barbara Castle MP, John Chalmers, Ian Mikardo MP, Alex Kitson, Bill Simpson, Sir Harry Nicholas, Ron Hayward. From party headquarters for the NEC: Gwyn Morgan, Terry Pitt, Geoff Bish, Margaret Jackson and Andy Thompson. Representing the TUC: Jack Jones (TGWU), Hugh Scanlon (AUEW), Lord Cooper (NUGMW), Sir Sidney Greene (National Union of Railwaymen, NUR), George Smith (UCATT), Alf Allen (USDAW), David Basnett (NUGMW), Vic Feather, Len Murray and Norman Willis. From

Congress House for the TUC: Ken Graham, David Lea, C.H. Hartwell, and B. Callaghan. LPA, TUC–Labour Party Liaison Committee, Minutes and Papers, 21 February 1972–26 July 1976.

32 A report of each meeting was compiled by Terry Pitt for the Labour Party, and by David Lea for the TUC.

33 Present on the occasion of the first meeting of the TUC–Labour Party Liaison Committee were Harold Wilson, Roy Jenkins, Douglas Houghton, Bob Mellish and Harold Lever for the PLP; Tony Benn MP, Barbara Castle MP, John Chalmers, Ian Mikardo MP, Sir Harry Nicholas, Gwyn Morgan and Terry Pitt for the NEC; Jack Jones, Hugh Scanlon, Vic Feather, Len Murray, Ken Graham and David Lea for the TUC. LPA, TUC–Labour Party Liaison Committee, Minutes and Papers, 21 February 1972–26 July 1976.

34 The statement issued by the PLP was as follows:

> Having studied the Conservative Government's Industrial Relations Bill the Parliamentary Labour Party is even more strengthened and united in its condemnation of the underlying purpose of the Bill to undermine and weaken the traditional rights of organised labour; the Party resolves to oppose the Bill with all its Parliamentary force and resources; and calls upon the NEC in conjunction with the PLP and TUC to develop our constructive alternative to the Tory Bill which will ensure that a workable accord between a future Labour Government and the unions and their members can be put to the electorate as a firm basis for the repeal of the Industrial Relations Bill now before Parliament.

LPA, PLP, Minutes, 3 December 1970.

35 Benn, *Office Without Power*, 21 February 1972, p. 407.

36 Jones's and Scanlon's activities in the late 1960s and early 1970s earned them the sobriquet the 'terrible twins'.

37 Benn, *Office Without Power*, 21 February 1972, p. 407.

38 See, for example, Jones's speech to the 1970 Labour Party Conference. LPAR, p. 113.

39 Jenkins was an easy target for his detractors. Drucker writes that 'Jenkins was always held in suspicion by large groups in the party because he combined right-wing policies with an inability to pronounce the letter "r".' H. M. Drucker, *Doctrine and Ethos in the Labour Party* (London, Allen & Unwin, 1979), p. 14. Similarly, Benn in a diary entry for December 1957 describes the young Jenkins as 'a caricature of an up-and-coming young politician in a Victorian novel'. T. Benn, *Years of Hope: Diaries, Papers and Letters, 1940–1962* (London, Hutchinson, 1994), p. 256.

40 Benn, *Office Without Power*, 21 February 1972, p. 407.

41 'At the outset', writes Stallard, the Liaison Committee 'was not a policy-making exercise as such but simply a political mechanism to oppose the 1971 Industrial Relations Act.' Stallard, 'Policy-making in the Labour Party', p. 44.

42 LPA, TUC–Labour Party Liaison Committee, Minutes and Papers, 21 February 1972.

43 LPA, TUC–Labour Party Liaison Committee, Minutes and Papers, 21 February 1972.

44 LPA, TUC–Labour Party Liaison Committee, Minutes and Papers, 21 February 1972.

45 LPA, TUC–Labour Party Liaison Committee, Minutes and Papers, 21 February 1972.

46 Liaison Committee 2/1, 'Industrial Relations and the Law', LPA, TUC–Labour Party Liaison Committee, Minutes and Papers, 21 February 1972–26 July 1976.
47 LPA, TUC–Labour Party Liaison Committee, Minutes and Papers, 20 March 1972.
48 RD.339, 'Legislation and Industrial Relations', LPA, TUC–Labour Party Liaison Committee, Minutes and Papers, 21 February 1972–26 July 1976.
49 When, for example, the Liaison Committee considered a TUC paper on a conciliation and arbitration service (Liaison Committee 4/1) in May 1972, the whole of the meeting was given over to scrutiny of the paper paragraph by paragraph. In this respect the Liaison Committee proved equally as thorough a method of formulating policy as the NEC research programme.
50 Jones, *Union Man*, p. 227.
51 LPA, TUC–Labour Party Liaison Committee, Minutes and Papers, 20 March 1972.
52 LPA, TUC–Labour Party Liaison Committee, Minutes and Papers, 20 March 1972.
53 LPA, NEC–PLP side of the TUC–Labour Liaison Committee, Minutes, 13 April 1972.
54 J. Jones, 'How to rebuild industrial relations', *New Statesman*, 18 February 1972, pp. 10–12.
55 Jones, *Union Man*, p. 245.
56 Jones, 'How to rebuild', pp. 10–12.
57 On 3 August 1972, the TUC and the CBI voluntarily agreed to establish the Advisory Conciliation and Arbitration Service (ACAS), to begin its work as of 1 September 1972.
58 LPA, NEC–PLP side of the Liaison Committee Minutes, 13 April 1972.
59 Benn, *Office Without Power*, 20 March 1972, p. 415.
60 Castle, *The Castle Diaries 1964–1976*, 30 July 1974, p. 491.
61 LPA, TUC–Labour Party Liaison Committee, Minutes and Papers, 24 April 1972.
62 TUC, 'Industrial Relations – The Scope of Future Legislation' (Liaison Cttee 4/2). LPA, TUC–Labour Party Liaison Committee, Minutes and Papers, 21 February 1972–26 July 1976.
63 LPA, TUC–Labour Party Liaison Committee, Minutes and Papers, 19 June 1972.
64 The clauses included in *In Place of Strife* which provoked the greatest hostility from the trade unions were those which conferred on the Secretary of State the power to order a 28-day 'conciliation pause' before a strike could take place, to impose a financial penalty for any contravention of such an order, and to insist on a secret ballot of those involved in a dispute before official strike action could take place.
65 The TUC was absolutely determined to repel legislative interference. Legislation could be used to improve poor working conditions, but as a rule the TUC believed that 'Once you've embraced the law it can be used against you.' Interview, Lord Murray of Epping Forest, 18 December 1996.
66 TUC Report, 1972, p. 107.
67 TUC Report, 1972, p. 107.
68 E. Silver, *Victor Feather TUC* (London, Gollancz, 1973), p. 207.
69 The miners' strike began on 9 January 1972 and ended, in triumph for the NUM, in February 1972.
70 D. Hurd, *An End to Promises* (London, Collins, 1979), p. 103.
71 Campbell, *Edward Heath*, pp. 420–1.
72 Jones, *Union Man*, p. 255.

73 Silver, *Victor Feather TUC*, p. 210. See also Campbell, *Edward Heath*, pp. 471–2.
74 Campbell, *Edward Heath*, p. 472.
75 Jones, *Union Man*, p. 255.
76 The TUC representatives were Feather, Jones, Scanlon and, to quote Campbell, 'three generally acquiescent moderates', Lord Cooper (GMWU), Sir Sidney Greene (NUR) and Alf Allen (USDAW). Campbell, *Edward Heath*, p. 474. Cooper and Greene, Jones appears to have regarded with suspicion: 'For the most part the TUC team were united, but at times Alf Allen and Jack Cooper were at pains to emphasize their differences from the "terrible twins"' Jones, *Union Man*, p. 256.
77 The tripartite National Economic Development Council (NEDC), a voluntary body made up of six representatives each from the government, TUC and CBI, was formed in 1960.
78 Jones joined the discussions to stiffen the resolve of those colleagues whom he feared might be seduced by the setting and the courtesy shown to them by the Prime Minister, thus bringing to mind the words of Ramsey MacDonald from his diary of 12 May 1924, in reply to one of the 'Left incorruptibles' when asked why he had been at the Palace: 'Because its allurements are so great that I cannot trust you to go.' Marquand, *Ramsey MacDonald*, p. 314.
79 Jones, *Union Man*, p. 255.
80 Jones, *Union Man*, p. 258. John Campbell writes: 'The warm *rapport* between Heath and Feather...probably led both men to misinterpret the other's position. Heath looked to Feather to bring his side along with him in the same way that he could speak for the Government. But Feather could not in the last resort speak for Jones and Scanlon. Fot his part Feather was probably misled by Heath's anxiety to get an agreement into believing that he had no sticking point. Heath was ready to go a long way – too far, some of his colleagues and officials sometimes felt – to win the TUC's co-operation. But in the end he insisted that he was discussing with the unions, not negotiating.' Campbell, *Edward Heath*, p. 475.
81 Campbell, *Edward Heath*, p. 477. See also Jones, *Union Man*, pp. 257–8.
82 Jones, *Union Man*, p. 255.
83 Jones, *Union Man*, p. 255.
84 See Taylor, *The Trade Union Question*, p. 203.
85 Jones was not easily taken in: 'Heath was at his most courteous with the TUC representatives. This led me to reflect on those lines from *Alice In Wonderland*: "How carefully he seems to grin,/ How neatly spreads his claws,/ And welcomes little fishes in/With gently smiling jaws."' Jones, *Union Man*, p. 256.
86 Campbell, *Edward Heath*, p. 470.
87 Campbell, *Edward Heath*, p. 463.
88 TUC Report, 1972, p. 274.
89 TUC Report, 1972, pp. 274–5.
90 TUC Report, 1972, p. 275.
91 See, for example, Campbell, *Edward Heath*, pp. 468–83; Taylor, *The Trade Union Question*, pp. 202–4.
92 Hurd, *An End to Promises*, p. 104.
93 TUC Report, 1972, p. 276.
94 Campbell, *Edward Heath*, p. 476.
95 TUC Report, 1972, p. 276.
96 LPA, TUC–Labour Party Liaison Committee, Minutes and Papers, 25 September 1972.
97 LPA, TUC–Labour Party Liaison Committee, Minutes and Papers, 25 September 1972.

98 LPA, TUC–Labour Party Liaison Committee, Minutes and Papers, 20 November 1972.
99 Specifically, *Economic Policy and the Cost of Living*, in addition to addressing the issue of rent increases, met the TUC demands of 16 October in respect of price surveillance; house prices and land speculation; holding down food prices; a wealth tax and capital gains.
100 Labour Party, *Economic Policy and the Cost of Living*, in TUC Report, 1973, p. 313.
101 Labour Party, *Economic Policy and the Cost of Living*, in TUC Report, 1973, p. 313.
102 For example:

> Fundamental to the British economic problem, therefore, is the problem of *investment* and, more generally, the problem of control and the disposition of capital. The expansion of investment and the control of capital will thus be one of the central tasks of the next Labour Goverment. And this will mean the development of new public enterprise and effective public supervision of the investment policy of large private corporations. For it is these big firms which now dominate the growth the growth sectors of the economy – to the extent, indeed, that no less than half of the nation's manufacturing output is already accounted for by the leading 100 companies, with this degree of concentration growing year by year.

Labour Party, *Economic Policy and the Cost of Living*, in TUC Report, 1973, p. 314.
103 Labour Party, *Economic Policy and the Cost of Living*, in TUC Report, 1973, p. 315.
104 Editorial, 'A policy which could not work', *The Times*, 1 March 1973, p. 17.
105 '"Oh, yes, there will be a wealth tax", Denis Healey assured me in the early months when he was wooing the trade unions, but it never came.' Jones, *Union Man*, p. 285.
106 At Blackpool in 1972, Healey warned conference:

> ...if we were to get into office and produce even a mild disappointment in our performance compared with our election programme we could do damage to the whole structure of our Party democracy which some people would be only too glad and able to exploit. So we must be certain this time that we do not promise more than we can perform, and let us if necessary err on the side of caution rather than over-ambition.

LPAR, 1972, pp. 290–1. For Healey's speech in full, see LPAR, 1972, pp. 288–94.
107 'In 1970 I wanted Labour to win and thought it deserved to do so. In 1974 I took a different view on both points.' Jenkins, *A Life at the Centre*, p. 364.
108 Jones, *Union Man*, p. 282.
109 TUC Report, 1972, p. 479.
110 LPAR, 1972, p. 292.
111 Dell, *A Hard Pounding*, p. 45.
112 During the general election campaign in February 1974, write Butler and Kavanagh, Wilson spoke of the need for a 'social contract' between government, industry and the trade unions,

> with each party willing to make sacrifices to reach agreement on a strategy to curb rising prices. He added: 'We have agreed such a new contract with the TUC'. The next night Mr Scanlon revealed the

incomplete state of the agreement in a television interview with Robin Day ('We are not agreed on any specific policy as of now'). Mr Heath and other Conservatives poured scorn on Labour's 'non-existent' agreement with the unions and renewed their central charge against Labour; namely, that it had no policy for dealing with wages and incomes. In fact, Mr Wilson was referring, perhaps too grandly, to the long policy document drawn up by the Labour Party and the TUC in February 1973. This assumed that the unions would voluntarily exercise restraint on wage demands in return for such measures as repeal of the Housing Finance Act, restoring free collective bargaining, increased pensions and strict price controls on key services and commodities. It was premature of Mr Wilson to produce this as a 'contract', as Labour leaders were hoping to agree on the details later in the year.

Butler and Kavanagh, *The British General Election of February 1974*, p. 98.

113 TUC Report, 1972, p. 479. By quoting Bevin, Jones inadvertently exposed the hollowness of Hugh Scanlon's words on the subject of incomes policy in his speech to the Labour Party Conference at Blackpool in 1970, when he said the unions would talk about an incomes policy 'when we own the means of production, distribution and exchange'. LPAR, 1970, p. 121. Jones's use of the Bevin quote suggested that even in these circumstances the unions would still be fundamentally opposed to a deal on incomes.

114 LPA, TUC–Labour Party Liaison Committee, Minutes and Papers, 16 April 1973.

115 LPA, TUC–Labour Party Liaison Committee, Minutes and Papers, 4 January 1974.

116 Hove, Berwick on Tweed, Edinburgh North, Glasgow Govan. LPAR, 1974, p. 51.

117 'Report of Scottish Labour Group on Govan By-election', LPA, PC, Minutes, Session 1973–74.

118 See Healey's comments at the PLP meeting of 18 December 1973. LPA, PLP, Minutes, 18 December 1973.

119 Castle, *The Castle Diaries 1974–76*, 4 January 1974, p. 19.

120 LPA, TUC–Labour Party Liaison Committee, Minutes and Papers, 4 January 1974, and Castle, *The Castle Diaries, 1974–76*, 4 January 1974, p. 20.

121 'News Release', 21 December 1973, LPA, PLP, Minutes, Session 1973–74.

122 A direct consequence was that the Labour Party committed itself to accepting the threshold system which the Heath Government had negotiated. With the oil price explosion many triggerings of the threshold became inevitable unless the threshold system was renegotiated. The Heath Government had not felt able to renegotiate; how much less a Labour Party committed to the Social Contract. Probably Labour's relationship with the trade unions would have left it little choice even without the Social Contract. The contract put the matter beyond peradventure and hence committed the new Government to an inflationary future.

Dell, *A Hard Pounding*, p. 15. For Wilson's account of the Labour government's retention of the threshold agreement, see Wilson, *Final Term*, pp. 42–3.

123 Dell, *A Hard Pounding*, p. 15.

124 In the February 1974 general election the Labour Party won 301 seats, the Conservatives 297 and the Liberals 14. Labour polled 37.1 per cent of the vote, the Conservatives 37.8 per cent and the Liberals 19.3 per cent. For full details of the result and the performance of the minor parties, see Butler and Kavanagh, *The British General Election of February 1974*, pp. 275–6.

CONCLUSION

Harold Wilson returned to Downing Street on 4 March 1974 to lead a minority Labour government, and a sort of normality returned to British politics.[1] The miners returned to work (handsomely rewarded) and the state of emergency and the three-day working week that had provided the backdrop to the February general election came to an end. It was universally accepted that a second general election would be necessary before long, but Wilson and his colleagues lost little time in addressing the most contentious legislative measures of the Heath government: the Industrial Relations Act, the Housing Finance Act and the Common Market. For the TUC, everything (including the Social Contract) took second place to the repeal of the Industrial Relations Act. Len Murray, installed as general secretary of the TUC in succession to Victor Feather, left ministers in no doubt that the Act had to go 'before taking any further chances with the voters'. By July 1974 he had his wish. The Trade Union and Labour Relations Act 1974 repealed the Industrial Relations Act and abolished the NIRC. Ministers acted with no less urgency over housing. Within four days of taking office, the Labour government announced a rent freeze 'and took steps towards the dismantling of the Housing Finance Act'. The sale of council houses was actively discouraged by Anthony Crosland, newly appointed as Secretary of State for the Environment. As for the Common Market, responsibility for the renegotiation of the terms of British membership lay with James Callaghan at the Foreign Office, who announced, in all seriousness, that he intended to follow the manifesto on the issue, in a speech that just happened to be given on April Fool's Day.

Political debts were promptly settled. In his March Budget, Denis Healey announced that the pensions and benefits increases agreed by the TUC–Labour Party Liaison Committee would take effect from July. A Prices Act legislating for food subsidies to the value of £500 million followed. Free collective bargaining was restored. Reg Prentice, at Education, threw a bone to the party conference and announced his intention 'to accelerate the shift to comprehensive education'. White Papers on industrial policy, pensions, land and devolution were published. A second general election, to be held in October, was called on 18 September. As Butler and Kavanagh write:

> ...there was little inclination to doubt that Labour would win an early election. An indication of the Conservatives' problems was given in an ORC Survey published in *The Times* on August 5. When asked to recall things the government had done, 43 per cent of those questioned mentioned increased pensions, 26 per cent getting the miners back to work, 19 per cent 'trying to keep food prices down' and 13 per cent freezing rents. A mere 16 per cent were unable to think of anything the Labour Party had done since the election (70 per cent were unable to think of anything the Conservatives had done). Labour therefore had compiled a useful record in the eyes of the voters.[2]

Labour was re-elected in October 1974 with an overall majority of three. The minority Labour government had, in the six months it lasted, in Healey's words, 'carried out its side of the Social Contract. In fact the value of the services provided by the Government, which we tried to get people to see as their "social wage" amounted to about £1,000 a year for every member of the working population.' The problem for the new government, and for Healey in particular, as the member of the government charged with the responsibility for steering the economy for the next five years, was that, despite the minority government's fidelity to the trade unions and its considerable largesse, wages between March and September 1974 had increased at twice the rate of prices. The trade unions, forebodingly, had 'defaulted on their part of the contract'.[3]

*   *   *

There was a leadership job to be done in the Labour Party in opposition 1970–74 and the most important people in this respect were Callaghan and Roy Jenkins (and, to a much lesser extent, Crosland) to whom it fell to attempt to bridge the gap between social democracy and Thatcherism. They did not succeed because, whereas Callaghan might possibly have carried the party with him, his primary concern was party unity. Jenkins had made the leap to economic conservatism in advance of Callaghan, but lacked an institutional base of support in the party and therefore could only have led it to another 1931. It was Callaghan who proved the more influential and who subsequently became Prime Minister. He was not the man to produce a new set of ideas for the party, but his roots in the labour movement ran deep and he was equipped to bind together the party's disparate component parts. As a member of the NEC he was able to pacify the trade unions by signalling the parliamentary leadership's determination to repeal the Industrial Relations Act, thereby removing the threat after 1970 of further demonstrations of the negative power of the trade union block vote at conference. Equally importantly, at the Home Policy Committee he was able to influence the party's organisational activity in opposition by exploiting his authority as chairman, to insist that the structure of the NEC research programme included a prominent role for the PLP. This reduced the scope for disagreement between the parliamentary leadership and the party. Callaghan's great skill was to be able to do this without damaging party unity. With the exception of his reference to incomes policy at Blackpool in 1970, he neither said nor did anything to vex the party in respect of the NEC research programme. Yet throughout, his chairmanship of the Home Policy Committee was of an overtly pro-PLP nature. Unsurprisingly, when Anthony Howard profiled Callaghan for *New Statesman* in July 1971, he entitled his piece 'The Professional'. But there were limits to Callaghan's ability to act as a counterweight to the NEC research programme itself, which provided the party with a process for adopting the policies Harold Wilson had excluded from the general election manifesto in 1970.

Initially, the parliamentary leadership's problem in opposition was how to stifle the party's desire for new policies. With the advent of the research programme, it became one of how to dilute or dispose of the new policies that emerged. This was made more difficult by the behaviour of Jenkins. The former Chancellor lacked the institutional base of support enjoyed by Callaghan, whom he perceived as his main rival for the leadership in succession to Wilson. So he sought to enhance his standing in the party by building his reputation as a public figure. However, whereas Callaghan could wear the party hat of his choice (PLP, NEC, party treasurer, trade unionist) to advance his long-term prospects, Jenkins, once he resigned the deputy leadership, had no platform inside the Labour Party from which to state his position on the policy issues of the day. Forced by his own actions to address the party through a series of public speeches in 1972, he was more specific on industrial policy than was helpful for the parliamentary leadership. By inviting Stuart Holland to put words in his mouth, Jenkins inadvertently gave encouragement to the Industrial Policy Subcommittee's efforts to radically rewrite the party's economic and industrial policies.

Unlike his hero, Hugh Gaitskell, who secured the leadership of the party in 1955 with the support of the trade unions, Jenkins had only his supporters in the PLP and in the anti-Labour press, which meant his leadership ambitions were unrealistic as well as destructive. And yet he had an important role to play in opposition. Crosland, much the least effective of the three, was too ambivalent about public ownership to be the voice of Labour's centre-right in the party's consideration of policy. Jenkins (and others such as Harold Lever, who understood the importance of private capital in the economy) was the man to ask the awkward questions when the parliamentary leadership sat down with the trade unions. For Jenkins to be of service to the Labour Party required a willingness to remain part of the parliamentary leadership and argue for the realistic policies on wage inflation and trade union reform that the party desperately required. His decision to resign the deputy leadership was therefore an appalling miscalculation which, because of his lack of an institutional base, cost him his place in the party's hierarchy. When the crucial decisions on the content of Labour's 1974 general election manifesto were taken at the Liaison Committee, he was not present. His absence was a great disservice to the party. Of those parliamentary leaders who were present when, for example, the repeal of the Industrial Relations Act and the hugely expensive increase in pensions were conceded, none was capable of challenging the trade unions as effectively as Jenkins. In this respect, just as Callaghan was important in opposition because of what he did, Jenkins was important because of what he failed to do.

Jenkins was dependent upon Edward Heath to provide an external stimulus for change in the Labour Party by taking on the trade unions and reforming them, and by making British membership of the Common Market work. Crosland, a phantom intellectual presence in opposition, could not provide an internal stimulus because he actually believed in socialism. (Jenkins, to his credit, realised that for the Labour Party to prosper socialism would have to go.) Crosland was still trying to make socialism work, but after 1970 he was no nearer to doing so than he had been in 1956. Callaghan, both in opposition and subsequently as Prime Minister, moved only as fast in trying to change the party as he could carry the party and the trade unions (Jack Jones especially) with him. As Prime Minister in 1976, he inherited an economy in crisis and a government lacking a parliamentary majority. By this time he had reached the conclusion that time was up for the social democratic consensus[4] and made no attempt to disguise the fact in his speech to the 1976 Labour Party Conference.[5] Hereafter his aim was to save the Labour Party by making a Labour government saddled with unaffordable policies and overbearing trade union partners work as effectively as he could in an effort to cushion the blow the electorate was lining up to deliver. 'You know there are times, perhaps once every thirty years, when there is a sea-change in British politics', Callaghan told Bernard Donoughue, the head of the Policy Unit. 'It then does not matter what you say or what you do. There is a shift in what the public wants and what it approves of. I suspect there is now such a sea-change – and it is for Mrs Thatcher.'[6] To his credit, he nearly succeeded. Inflation and wages were brought under control (unemployment, critically, was not) and he remained personally more popular than Thatcher to the end. Paradoxically, the Callaghan government was simultaneously the swan-song of Old Labour *and* the beginning of New Labour. The seed of Labour's recovery (financial rectitude) was planted by Callaghan, but the party failed to notice. There has always been a deep strand of prudence in the Labour Party: Gordon Brown would have been a good man for the International Monetary Fund

(IMF) crisis. In 1976, Callaghan's achievement as Prime Minister was to save the Labour Party from another 1931 when the IMF crisis was at its most intense.[7]

In office 1964–70, the parliamentary leadership had felt able to disregard the party conference on a range of policy issues. In opposition, Wilson and his colleagues had to be saved from the party and the NEC research programme by the TUC–Labour Party Liaison Committee, which they used to establish the notion of priority in matters of policy. The establishment of the TUC–Labour Party Liaison Committee in opposition was highly significant. The Labour Party had had over 50 years to clarify precisely where the division between itself and the trade unions lay, yet in February 1972, the machinery necessary to enable a dialogue on policy between the PLP and the TUC had to be created ad hoc. The Liaison Committee was created to do something, both organisationally and constitutionally, that the Labour Party, astonishingly, had not previously thought about. Much of the content of *Labour's Programme 1973* was excluded from Labour's February 1974 general election manifesto because of the priority given to policies agreed at the Liaison Committee. However, where a Labour government might break its promises to the party with relative impunity, it could not break its promises to the TUC. Rather than being the answer to the parliamentary leadership's problems, the Social Contract with the TUC was part of the problem for the Labour government 1974–79. It was also a disaster for the country. Yet at the time, it was generally believed that whichever party reached an agreement with the trade unions would be rewarded by the electorate when the general election came. The actual impact of the agreement can be measured in terms of Labour's share of the vote in February 1974. The Labour Party secured only 37.1 per cent of the vote in the February 1974 general election, 5.9 per cent down on 1970, and the first time since 1935 that it had secured less than 40 per cent of the vote. Had the Conservative Party not performed so poorly, securing only 37.8 per cent of the vote, Labour would have been consigned to the further period in opposition it deserved and required.[8] Wilson and his colleagues were fully aware of the flaws in the party's agreement with the TUC, hence their attempts to refashion it when better placed to do so, as ministers once again after 1974. But it was not until the Labour government had faced the IMF in 1976 that a more realistic approach to economic and industrial policy was implemented. This was where the Labour Party had needed to be in 1972, which was never likely. Its chances of recasting relations with the TUC had not been improved by Jenkins's self-imposed exile from the parliamentary leadership.

Rather than accept the Labour government's reduction in public expenditure (regarded as the work of the Conservative Party) some on the left wing of the party preferred to see the Labour government fall. Labour had established the social democratic consensus model for government

1945–51 and many in the party were uncomfortable with the idea of reforming it. To have undertaken the task would have betrayed where the party came from, most recently 1931, when Labour had survived as a party rather than as a party of government. Consequently, compared to the task undertaken by the Conservative Party under Margaret Thatcher after 1979, Labour's policy activity in opposition 1970–74 was parochial.

Whatever the Labour Party did in opposition, once the revision of the social democratic consensus had been attempted by Heath and it became clear that Britain needed to move right rather than left, Labour was inexorably bound on a course leading to the disaster of the 1983 general election.[9] The parliamentary leadership could not move the party rightwards after the failure of Crosland's redistribution-from-growth strategy between 1964 and 1970, so the party's sole source of ideas was its left wing. Just as the Labour government 1964–70 led to *Labour's Programme 1973* and *Economic Policy and the Cost of Living*, these policy documents in turn (combined with Heath's conversion to an interventionist industrial strategy) led the British electorate to Thatcher, and the Labour Party to 1983. Labour could do nothing but go in the wrong direction after 1970. For the second time since 1951 an extended period in opposition was wasted, despite Callaghan's best efforts to persuade the party to rethink its economic ideology after he became Prime Minister in 1976. In this respect, it was perhaps inevitable that the Labour Party chose Michael Foot rather than Healey to replace Callaghan when he stepped down as leader in 1980. Yet, if Callaghan had remained as leader, he was too close to the trade unions (as the 'winter of discontent' of 1978–79 demonstrated) to even attempt to revise the social democratic consensus. And by 1980 the Campaign for Labour Party Democracy, championed by Tony Benn, had made sufficient inroads in Labour's organisational structure to resist the party leader at every turn whoever he was.

Ultimately, it was in Labour's long-term interest to remain in opposition after 1979 for as long as it took to come to terms with the revision of the social democratic consensus, finally carried out by Thatcher. The road from 1970 to 1994 and Tony Blair was lengthy and painful, but necessary. The party could not have made the journey any shorter or any less painfully, with Jenkins or with anyone else, because only the Conservative Party was capable of performing the task which enabled the Labour Party to become relevant again. Labour needed Thatcher. Nothing the party did in opposition between 1970 and 1974 changed that. The shock the Labour Party needed to absorb was of a scale that required four successive general election defeats before it was able to embrace the rhetoric of the market and private capital. Prior to this, Labour lacked the capacity for this view. Attempts by Crosland and Jenkins to find a position for the party that allowed for intervention in the economy but stopped short of damaging capitalism were inadequate.

Thatcher reconnected the Labour Party with the electorate and made economic conservatives of socialists. Labour's problem in office 1964–70 and in opposition 1970–74, was that it was trying to make an ideology (socialism) and a model for government (the social democratic consensus) work long beyond the point when it had become obvious that they had failed economically. Returning to government before the model had been success-fully reformed could only harm the Labour Party as a political force and electoral machine. This is why, in the first instance, Heath was so important to Labour and why he proved so damaging. Labour needed Heath to com-plete the unfinished work of the Wilson government which, among other things, included reforming industrial relations. Equally, Labour needed Heath to succeed because it would have enabled the party to return to office in due course in a more prosperous and stable political environment, which in turn would have seen the party changed through the process of governing to become a natural party of government. It would also have freed up Labour to govern on its own agenda. Essentially, Labour needed the Conservative Party to secure the economic environment for the party to succeed in government. This was the case in 1997. The Conservatives' sound management of the economy after exiting the Exchange Rate Mechanism in September 1992 enabled the Blair government to focus upon progressive and recognisably Labour issues such as the minimum wage, New Deal and House of Lords reform. However, in 1974, Heath's failure in government catapulted Labour back into office prematurely, in a hostile economic climate that could only exacerbate ideological tensions (with enormous implications for party coherence and electoral effectiveness) and with a set of policies enthusiastically welcomed by the TUC but few others.

A successful Heath government 1970–74, having established the super-iority of capitalism over socialism, may well have made it easier for Labour to return to office after a gap of less than 18 years and thus have spared the party from the trauma of 1983. Thatcher, however, succeeded where Heath failed and changed the Labour Party in the process. The process took 18 years because of Labour's fling with the trade unions as a partner in government 1974–79, a relationship that delivered unsustainable financial commitments in the form of subsidies and increased pensions, and failed to deliver a wages policy or trade union reform. A further five years of Labour government convinced voters that they needed Thatcher to cleanse the country of Labour's socialism. They did not necessarily desire all the measures subsequently introduced by Thatcher, but they desired Labour even less. Thatcher saved the Labour Party, and her successors – John Major and his Chancellor, Kenneth Clarke, among them – made it possible for Blair to govern on his own agenda because the economic and trade union problems had been corrected. Previously, Labour governments had been damaged by the economy they inherited from the Conservatives and by trade unions whose centrality to British economic performance had been cemented by the social democratic consensus. In 1997, thanks to Thatcher and Major, Labour took office in favourable conditions.

Labour needed 18 years in opposition because it took that long (or at least until Blair's election as leader in 1994 and the revision of Clause IV in 1995) for the party to realise that the electorate, including a significant section of its own traditional support, had become economically conservative. Thatcher's service to Labour was to demolish socialism and in so doing free the party from its incubus and allow it to govern. It took four successive election defeats but Labour eventually got the message. The significance of Labour's period in opposition 1970–74 is that it unleashed a policy process whose radical outcome forced the parliamentary leadership into the arms of the TUC, guaranteeing the failure of the Labour government 1974–79 and making the journey back to office that much harder and that much longer.

Notes

1 The first two paragraphs of this conclusion draw on Butler and Kavanagh, *The British General Election of October 1974* (London, Macmillan, 1975), pp. 18–53.
2 Butler and Kavanagh, *The British General Election of October 1974*, p. 52.
3 Healey, *The Time of My Life*, p. 394.
4 Keynesian demand management and full employment.
5   For too long, perhaps ever since the war, we postponed facing up to fundamental choices and fundamental changes in our society and in our economy. That is what I mean when I say that we have been living on borrowed time. For too long this country – all of us, yes this Conference too – has been ready to settle for borrowing money abroad to maintain our standards of life, instead of grappling with the fundamental problem of British industry.
      We used to think that you could spend your way out of a recession and increase employment by cutting taxes and boosting Government spending. I tell you in all candour that that option no longer exists, and that insofar as it ever did exist, it only worked on each occasion since the war by injecting a bigger dose of inflation into the economy, followed by a higher level of unemployment as the next step. Higher inflation followed by higher unemployment. We have just escaped from the highest rate of inflation this country has known; we have not yet escaped from the consequences: high unemployment. That is the history of the last twenty years. Each time we did this, the twin evils of unemployment and inflation have hit hardest those least able to stand them. Not those with the strongest bargaining power, no, it has not hit those. It has hit the poor, the old and the sick. We have struggled, as a Party, to try to maintain their standards, and indeed to improve them, against the strength of free collective bargaining power that we have seen exerted as some people have tried to maintain their standards against this economic policy.
      Now we must get back to fundamentals. First, overcoming unemployment now unambiguously depends on our labour costs being at least comparable with those of our major competitors. Second, we can only become competitive by having the right kind of investment at the right kind of level, and by significantly improving the productivity of labour and capital. Third, we will fail – and I say this to those who have been pressing about public expenditure, to which I will come back – if we

think we can buy our way out by printing what Denis Healey calls 'confetti money' to pay ourselves more than we produce.

LPAR, 1976, p. 188.

6 B. Donoughue, *Prime Minister: The Conduct of Policy under Harold Wilson and James Callaghan* (London, Jonathan Cape, 1987), p. 191.

7 For accounts of Callaghan's handling of the 1976 IMF crisis, see Morgan, *Callaghan: A Life*, pp. 523–54; E. Pearce, *Denis Healey: A Life in Our Times* (London, Little, Brown, 2002), pp. 474–501; Benn, *Against the Tide*, November 1976, pp. 635–60.

8 The Conservative Party's share of the vote fell by 8.6 per cent in February 1974, down from 46.4 per cent in June 1970. For a statistical analysis of the February 1974 general election, see M. Steed, 'The Results Analysed', in Butler and Kavanagh, *The British General Election of February 1974*, pp. 313–39.

9 In the 1983 general election Labour's share of the vote sank to 27.6 per cent, its lowest since 1918.

BIBLIOGRAPHY

Primary Sources

Archives

London, British Library of Political and Economic Science (BLPES)

Anthony Crosland Papers (ACP), Part II, Member of Parliament, c.1950–77, 4/13.

London, House of Commons (HC)

Parliamentary Labour Party Subject Group Minutes 1970–74:
    Economic and Finance Group.
    Health and Social Security Group.
    Northern Ireland Group.
    Parliamentary Affairs Group.
    Power and Steel Group.
    Social Security Group.
    Trade and Industry Group.
Parliamentary Labour Party Regional Group Minutes 1970–74:
    East Midlands.
    Greater London Group.
    Northern Group.
    North West Group.
    Yorkshire Group.

Manchester, Labour Party Archive (LPA), National Museum of Labour History

Banking and Insurance Study Group, Minutes and Papers, 1972–73.
Capital Shares Study Group, Minutes and Papers, 1971–72.
Capital Taxation Working Party, Minutes and Papers, 1973.
Conference Arrangements Committee, Minutes, 1970–74.
Energy Subcommittee, Minutes and Papers, 1973–75.
Finance and Economic Affairs Subcommittee, Minutes and Papers, 1971–73.

Finance and General Purposes Committee, Minutes, 1970–74.
Michael Foot Collection (MFC), Cabinet Papers (CP), C1.
Home Policy Committee (HPC), Minutes, 1970–74.
Housing Finance Working Group, Minutes and Papers, 1971–74.
Industrial Policy Subcommittee, Minutes and Papers, 1971–73.
Joint Working Party on Tax Credits, Minutes and Papers, 1972–73.
Labour Committee for Europe, Minutes and Papers, 1964–80.
Local Government Finance Working Party, Minutes and Papers, 1972–73.
Mergers and Monopolies Working Group, Minutes and Papers, 1973.
Ian Mikardo Papers (IMP).
National Council of Labour, Minutes and Papers, 1960–73.
National Executive Committee (NEC), Minutes, 1964–74.
NEC–Parliamentary Committee, Minutes, 1972–73.
Parliamentary Committee (PC), Minutes, 1970–74.
Parliamentary Labour Party (PLP), Minutes, 1970–74.
Terry Pitt Papers (TPP).
Public Sector Group, Minutes and Papers, 1972–73.
Regional and Local Government Subcommittee, Minutes and Papers, 1971–73.
Jo Richardson Papers (JRP) (including Tribune Group Minutes, TGM) 1965–75.
Social Policy Subcommittee, Minutes and Papers, 1971–72.
Study Group on Land Policy, Minutes and Papers, 1972–73.
TUC–Labour Party Liaison Committee, Minutes and Papers, 1972–76.
Working Group on Inflation, Papers, 1973.

Warwick, Modern Records Centre

R. H. S. Crossman Papers, MSS 154.
East Midlands Labour Party, Regional Organiser's Papers, MSS 009.
Transport and General Workers' Union (Jack Jones), MSS 126.

Printed Primary Sources

Hansard, *House of Commons Debates, 5th series.*
HC, 1970–71, Standing Committees, vols VI and VII.
Labour Party, *Economic Policy and the Cost of Living* (London, 1973).
——, *The National Enterprise Board – Labour's State Holding Company: Report of a Labour Party Study Group* (London, 1973).
Labour Party, General Election Manifestos:
   Time for Decision (London, 1966).
   Now Britain's Strong – Let's Make It Great to Live In (London, 1970).
   Let Us Work Together – Labour's Way out of the Crisis (London, 1974).
   Britain Will Win With Labour (London, 1974).
Labour Party, Labour Party Annual Reports (LPAR), 1968–74 (London).
Labour Party National Executive Committee:
   Progress and Change (London, 1968).
   Agenda for a Generation (London, 1969).
   Labour's Economic Strategy (London, 1969).

Building a Socialist Britain (London, 1970).
Economic Strategy, Growth and Unemployment (London, 1971).
Labour's Programme for Britain 1972 (London, 1972).
Labour's Programme 1973 (London, 1973).
TUC Reports, 1965–74 (London).

NEWSPAPERS 1965–75
The Daily Telegraph.
The Guardian.
The Sunday Times.
The Times.

JOURNALS 1965–93
British Journal of Political Science.
Contemporary Record.
Encounter.
Political Quarterly.
Socialist Commentary.

PERIODICALS 1955–75
The Economist.
Europe Left.
Labour Weekly.
The Listener.
New Statesman.
The Spectator.
Tribune.

Interviews

Geoff Bish, 21 June 1997.
Michael Foot, 27 June 1996.
Lord Murray of Epping Forest, 18 December 1996.
Lord Orme, 24 June 1996.
Lord Rodgers of Quarry Bank, 25 June 1996.
Dennis Skinner MP, 25 June 1996.
Lord Taverne, 4 April 1997.

Correspondence

Frank Allaun, 26 May 1996.
Lord Callaghan of Cardiff, 19 November 1996.
Richard Clements, 8 July 1996.
Lord Jenkins of Hillhead, 20 November 1996.
Professor David Marquand, 15 and 22 November 1996.

Lord Orme, 12 November 1996.
Lord Owen, 26 November 1996.
Lord Rodgers of Quarry Bank, 24 July 1996.
Lord Taverne, 13 June 1996.
Lord Thomson of Monifieth, 16 November 1996.

Secondary Sources

Autobiography, Biography, Diaries, Letters, Memoirs

T. Benn, *Office Without Power: Diaries 1968–72* (London, Hutchinson, 1988).
——, *Against the Tide: Diaries 1973–76* (London, Hutchinson, 1989).
——, *Years of Hope: Diaries, Papers and Letters, 1940–1962* (London, Hutchinson, 1994).
B. Brivati, *Hugh Gaitskell* (London, Richard Cohen Books, 1996).
G. Brown, *In My Way* (London, Gollancz, 1971).
J. Callaghan, *Time and Chance* (London, Collins, 1987).
J. Campbell, *Edward Heath* (London, Jonathan Cape, 1993).
B. Castle, *The Castle Diaries 1964–1976* (London, Papermac, 1990).
——, *Fighting All the Way* (London, Macmillan, 1994).
——, *The Castle Diaries 1974–76* (London, Weidenfeld & Nicolson, 1980).
A. Crosland, *Socialism Now* (London, Jonathan Cape, 1974).
C. A. R. Crosland, *The Future of Socialism* (London, Jonathan Cape, 1956).
S. Crosland, *Tony Crosland* (London, Jonathan Cape, 1982).
E. Dell, *A Hard Pounding* (Oxford, Oxford University Press, 1991).
B. Donoughue, *Prime Minister: The Conduct of Policy under Harold Wilson and James Callaghan* (London, Jonathan Cape, 1987).
B. Donoughue and G. W. Jones, *Herbert Morrison: Portrait of a Politician* (London, Weidenfeld & Nicolson, 1973).
M. Foot, *Aneurin Bevan 1945–1960* (London, Davis-Poynter, 1973).
K. Harris, *Attlee* (London, Weidenfeld & Nicolson, 1982).
R. Hattersley, *Who Goes Home? Scenes from a Political Life* (London, Little, Brown, 1996).
D. Healey, *The Time of My Life* (London, Michael Joseph, 1989).
E. Heath, *The Course of My Life* (London, Hodder & Stoughton, 1998).
A. Howard (ed.), *The Crossman Diaries* (London, Methuen, 1979).
D. Hurd, *An End to Promises* (London, Collins, 1979).
R. Jay, *Joseph Chamberlain: A Political Study* (Oxford, Oxford University Press, 1981).
K. Jefferys, *Anthony Crosland* (London, Richard Cohen Books, 1999).
R. Jenkins, *A Life at the Centre* (London, Macmillan, 1991).
——, *What Matters Now* (London, Fontana, 1972).
J. Jones, *Union Man* (London, Collins, 1986).
M. Jones, *Michael Foot* (London, Gollancz, 1994).
P. Kellner and C. Hitchens, *Callaghan: The Road to Number Ten* (London, Cassell, 1976).
D. Marquand, *Ramsey MacDonald* (London, Jonathan Cape, 1977).
I. Mikardo, *Back-bencher* (London, Weidenfeld & Nicolson, 1988).
J. Morgan (ed.), *The Backbench Diaries of Richard Crossman* (London, Hamish Hamilton and Jonathan Cape, 1981).

K. O. Morgan, *Callaghan: A Life* (Oxford, Oxford University Press, 1997).

D. Owen, *Time to Declare*, revised edn (London, Penguin, 1992).

P. Paterson, *Tired and Emotional: The Life of Lord George Brown* (London, Chatto & Windus, 1993).

E. Pearce, *Denis Healey: A Life in Our Times* (London, Little, Brown, 2002).

B. Pimlott, *Harold Wilson* (London, HarperCollins, 1992).

——, *Hugh Dalton* (London, Jonathan Cape, 1985).

G. Radice, *Friends and Rivals* (London, Little, Brown, 2002).

W. T. Rodgers, *Fourth Among Equals* (London, Politico's, 2000).

E. Silver, *Victor Feather, TUC* (London, Gollancz, 1973).

D. Taverne, *The Future of the Left* (London, Jonathan Cape, 1974).

P. M. Williams, *Hugh Gaitskell* (London, Jonathan Cape, 1979).

H. Wilson, *The Labour Government 1964–1970: A Personal Record* (London, Weidenfeld & Nicolson, 1971).

——, *Final Term: The Labour Government 1974–1976* (London, Weidenfeld & Nicolson, 1979).

P. Ziegler, *Wilson: The Authorised Life* (London, Weidenfeld & Nicolson, 1993).

Other works

S. Ball and A. Seldon (eds), *The Heath Government: A Reappraisal* (London, Longman, 1996).

W. Beckerman (ed.), *The Labour Government's Economic Record 1964–1970* (London, Duckworth, 1972).

S. Beer, *Britain Against Itself* (London, Faber & Faber, 1982).

S. Brittan, *Steering the Economy: The Role of the Treasury* (London, Secker & Warburg, 1969).

K. Burk and A. Cairncross, '*Goodbye, Great Britain*': *The 1976 IMF Crisis* (London, Yale University Press, 1992).

D. Butler and R. Rose, *The British General Election of 1959* (London, Macmillan, 1960).

D. Butler and A. King, *The British General Election of 1966* (London, Macmillan, 1966).

D. Butler and M. Pinto-Duschinsky, *The British General Election of 1970* (London, Macmillan, 1971).

D. Butler and D. Kavanagh, *The British General Election of February 1974* (London, Macmillan, 1974).

——, *The British General Election of October 1974* (London, Macmillan, 1975).

A. Cairncross, *The British Economy since 1945* (Oxford, Blackwell, 1992).

H. Clegg, *How to Run an Incomes Policy: And Why We Made Such a Mess of the Last One* (London, Heinemann, 1971).

J. Cole, *As It Seemed to Me: Political Memoirs* (London, Weidenfeld & Nicolson, 1995).

P. Cosgrave, *The Strange Death of Socialist Britain* (London, Constable, 1992).

F. W. S. Craig (ed.), *British General Election Manifestos 1900–1974* (London, Macmillan, 1975).

I. Crewe and A. King, *SDP: The Birth, Life and Death of the Social Democratic Party* (Oxford, Oxford University Press, 1994).

R. Currie, *Industrial Politics* (Oxford, Clarendon Press, 1979).

E. Dell, *A Strange Eventful History: Democratic Socialism in Britain* (London, Harper Collins, 1999).

E. Dell, *The Chancellors: A History of the Chancellors of the Exchequer, 1945–90* (London, Harper Collins, 1996).

G. Dorfman, *Government versus Trade Unionism in Britain since 1968* (London, Macmillan, 1979).

H. M. Drucker, *Doctrine and Ethos in the Labour Party* (London, Allen & Unwin, 1979).

S. E. Finer, *The Changing British Party System 1945–79* (Washington, DC, American Enterprise Institute for Public Policy Research, 1980).

G. Foote, *The Labour Party's Political Thought*, 2nd edn (London, Croom Helm, 1986).

G. H. Gallup, *The Gallup International Public Opinion Polls: Great Britain 1937–1975, vol. II* (London/New York, Random House, 1976).

I. Gilmour and M. Garnett, *Whatever Happened to the Tories: The Conservative Party since 1945* (London, Fourth Estate, 1997).

S. Haseler, *The Gaitskellites: Revisionism in the British Labour Party 1951–64* (London, Macmillan, 1969).

——, *The Tragedy of Labour* (Oxford, Blackwell, 1980).

M. Hatfield, *The House the Left Built: Inside Labour Policy-making 1970–75* (London, Gollancz, 1978).

R. Hattersley, *Who Goes Home?: Scenes from a Political Life* (London, Little, Brown, 1995).

D. Hill, *Tribune 40* (London, Quartet, 1977).

M. Holmes, *The Failure of the Heath Government* (London, Macmillan, 1997).

M. Holmes, *The Labour Government 1974–1979: Political Aims and Economic Reality* (Basingstoke, Macmillan, 1985).

P. Jenkins, *The Battle of Downing Street* (London, Knight, 1970).

A. King (ed.), *Why is Britain Becoming Harder to Govern?* (London, BBC, 1976).

C. King, *The Cecil King Diary 1965–1970* (London, Jonathan Cape, 1972).

U. Kitzinger, *Diplomacy and Persuasion: How Britain Joined the Common Market* (London, Thames & Hudson, 1973).

J. Margach, *The Anatomy of Power* (London, W. H. Allen, 1979).

T. C. May, *Trade Unions and Pressure Group Politics* (London, Saxon House, 1975).

R. McKenzie, *British Political Parties*, 2nd revised edn (London, Mercury Books, 1963).

K. Middlemas, *Power, Competition and the State, vol. II: Threats to the Postwar Settlement: Britain 1961–74* (London, Macmillan, 1990).

L. Minkin, *The Labour Party Conference* (Manchester, Manchester University Press, 1980).

K. O. Morgan, *Labour in Power* (Oxford, Oxford University Press, 1985).

K. O. Morgan, 'The High and Low Politics of Labour: Keir Hardie to Michael Foot', in M. Bentley and J. Stevenson (eds), *High and Low Politics in Modern Britain* (Oxford, Clarendon Press, 1983), pp. 285–312.

L. Panitch, *Social Democracy and Industrial Militancy* (Cambridge, Cambridge University Press, 1976).

B. Pimlott, *Labour and the Left in the 1930s* (Cambridge, Cambridge University Press, 1977).

B. Pimlott and C. Cook, *Trade Unions in British Politics*, 2nd edn (London, Longman, 1991).

R. Rhodes James, *Ambitions and Realities, 1964–70* (London, Weidenfeld & Nicolson, 1972).

P. Seyd, *The Rise and Fall of the Labour Left* (London, Macmillan, 1987).

P. Seyd and P. Whiteley, *Labour's Grass Roots* (Oxford, Clarendon Press, 1992).

E. Shaw, *The Labour Party since 1945* (Oxford, Blackwell, 1996).

P. Shore, *Leading the Left* (London, Weidenfeld & Nicolson, 1993).

W. Stallard, *The Labour Party in Opposition and Government 1970–1979* (University of Keele PhD thesis, 1985).

R. Taylor, *The Trade Union Question in British Politics* (Oxford, Blackwell, 1993).

Times Newspapers Limited, *The Times Guide to the House of Commons 1966* (London, 1966).

——, *The Times Guide to the House of Commons 1970* (London, 1970).

J. Tomlinson, 'The Labour Government and the Trade Unions 1945–51', in N. Tiratsoo (ed.), *The Attlee Years* (London, Pinter, 1991), pp. 90–105.

D. Walker, 'The First Wilson Governments, 1964–1970', in P. Hennessy and A. Seldon, *Ruling Performance* (Oxford, Blackwell, 1987), pp. 186–215.

P. Walker, *Staying Power* (London, Bloomsbury, 1991).

P. Whitehead, *The Writing on the Wall* (London, Michael Joseph, 1985).

M. Wickham-Jones, *Economic Strategy and the Labour Party: Politics and Policy-making, 1970–83* (London, Macmillan, 1996).

P. M. Williams, 'Changing Styles of Labour Leadership', in D. Kavanagh, *The Politics of the Labour Party* (London, Allen & Unwin, 1982), pp. 50–68.

Journal Articles

S. Brittan, 'The Economic Contradictions of Democracy', *British Journal of Political Science*, 5, 2 (1975), pp. 129–59.

B. Brivati and D. Wincott, 'The Evolution of Social Democracy in Britain', *Contemporary Record*, 7, 2 (Autumn 1993), pp. 360–2.

D. Eden, 'Colin Welch's Crosland', *Encounter*, 52, 6 (June 1979), pp. 91–3.

G. Daly, 'The Campaign for Labour Victory and the Origins of the SDP', *Contemporary Record*, 7, 2 (1993), pp. 282–305.

E. Heffer, 'Labour's Future', *Political Quarterly*, 43, 4 (1972), pp. 380–8.

M. Holmes and N. J. Horsewood, 'Controversy, the Post War Consensus', *Contemporary Record*, 2, 2 (1988), pp. 24–7.

M. Holmes and M. A. Young, 'Heath's Government Reassessed', *Contemporary Record*, 3, 2 (1989), pp. 24–7.

W. Kennet, 'The Policies of the Party', *Political Quarterly*, 43, 4 (1972), pp. 389–402.

J. P. Mackintosh, 'The Problems of the Labour Party', *Political Quarterly*, 43, 1 (1972), pp. 2–18.

J. P. Mackintosh, 'Socialism or Social Democracy? The Choice for the Labour Party', *Political Quarterly*, 43, 4 (1972), pp. 470–84.

K. Middlemas, 'Corporatism, Its Rise and Fall', *Contemporary Record*, 2, 1 (1988), pp. 8–9.

A. Mitchell, 'Clay Cross', *Political Quarterly*, 45, 2 (1974), pp. 165–78.

P. Seyd, 'The Tavernite', Political Quarterly, 45, 2 (1974), pp. 243–6.

W. Stallard, 'Policy-making in the Labour Party: The Liaison Committee in Opposition and in Government 1970–1979', *Teaching Politics*, 16, 1 (1987), pp. 42–55.

Symposium, 'The Trade Unions and the Fall of Heath', *Contemporary Record*, 2, 1 (1988), pp. 36–46.

Symposium, 'Conservative Party Policy Making 1965–70', *Contemporary Record*, 3, 3 and 4 (1990), pp. 36–8 and pp. 34–6.

Witness Seminar (WS), 'The Campaign for Democratic Socialism 1960–64', *Contemporary Record*, 7, 2 (1993), pp. 363–85.

Witness Seminar (WS), 'The Labour Committee for Europe', *Contemporary Record*, 7, 2 (1993), pp. 386–416.

Witness Seminar (WS), 'The Launch of the SDP 1979–81', *Contemporary Record*, 7, 2 (1993), pp. 417–64.

D. Wood, 'The Westminster Scene', *Political Quarterly*, 43, 2 (1972), pp. 212–22.

D. Wood, 'The Westminster Scene', *Political Quarterly*, 43, 3 (1972), pp. 328–39.

D. Wood, 'The Westminster Scene', *Political Quarterly*, 43, 4 (1972), pp. 485–98.

INDEX

SHORT LOAN COLLECTION

WITHDRAWN

eBooks – at www.eBookstore.tandf.co.uk

A library at your fingertips!

eBooks are electronic versions of printed books. You can store them on your PC/laptop or browse them online.

They have advantages for anyone needing rapid access to a wide variety of published, copyright information.

eBooks can help your research by enabling you to bookmark chapters, annotate text and use instant searches to find specific words or phrases. Several eBook files would fit on even a small laptop or PDA.

NEW: Save money by eSubscribing: cheap, online access to any eBook for as long as you need it.

Annual subscription packages

We now offer special low-cost bulk subscriptions to packages of eBooks in certain subject areas. These are available to libraries or to individuals.

For more information please contact webmaster.ebooks@tandf.co.uk

We're continually developing the eBook concept, so keep up to date by visiting the website.

www.eBookstore.tandf.co.uk